GOOD PICTURES

G

O

P

I

U

R

STANFORD
UNIVERSITY
PRESS

O D

C T

E S

STANFORD UNIVERSITY PRESS
Stanford, California

Publication of this book has been aided by a grant from the Wyeth Foundation for American Art Publication Fund of CAA.

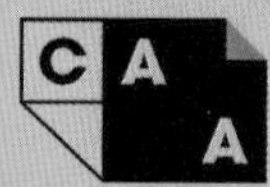

Printed in the United States of America on acid-free, archival-quality paper

Library of Congress Cataloging-in-Publication Data
Names: Beil, Kim, author.
Title: Good pictures : a history of popular photography / Kim Beil.
Description: Stanford, California : Stanford University Press, 2020. | Includes bibliographical
    references and index.
Identifiers: LCCN 2019051251 (print) | LCCN 2019051252 (ebook) |
    ISBN 9781503608665 (paperback) | ISBN 9781503612327 (ebook)
Subjects: LCSH: Photography—Philosophy. | Photography—Social aspects—History. | Aesthetics.
Classification: LCC TR183 .B39 2020 (print) | LCC TR183 (ebook) | DDC 770.1—dc23
LC record available at https://lccn.loc.gov/2019051251
LC ebook record available at https://lccn.loc.gov/2019051252

Frontispiece: *How to Make Good Pictures* (Rochester, NY: Eastman Kodak Co., 1933). Cover. Source: Author's collection. Courtesy: Eastman Kodak Co.

Designed by Kevin Barrett Kane

Typeset at Stanford University Press in 11/15 Crimson with Fira Sans display

HOW TO MAKE GOOD PICTURES

A Book for the Amateur Photographer

EASTMAN KODAK COMPANY
ROCHESTER, N.Y.~THE KODAK CITY

CONTENTS

How To: An Introduction to Good Photography 1

HOW TO

AN INTRODUCTION TO GOOD PHOTOGRAPHY

FOR NEARLY A CENTURY, Kodak published a series of instructional guidebooks, *How to Make Good Pictures*, that were updated regularly from 1912 until 1995.[1] Like thousands of other amateur photographers, I learned from these books. Paging through them now, I find that their sample pictures bear a strong relationship to photos in my own family albums. Pictures of people posed in soft window light or gazing at dramatic landscapes look uncannily familiar, despite the fact that the Kodak subjects are strangers to me. As a child learning how to take pictures, I followed Kodak's advice and directed my friends and family: "Don't look at the camera! Act natural!" Some rules like these are still in circulation, but the soft-focus, backlit portraits from the Kodak handbooks of my childhood are as outdated as the models' feathered hairstyles. These pictures just aren't fashionable anymore. They're no longer considered "good pictures." This book is about those stylistic rules and how they change.

The look of old pictures has become a style in itself in recent years. Digital filters can easily simulate the effects of time on color prints or the lens aberrations associated with nineteenth-century photographs. Initially, critics accused social media photographers of nostalgia or a "fetishization of the past."[2] Quickly, though, criticism dissipated as these pictures became the new "good pictures." Aesthetic trends saturate social media rapidly; users are inundated with popular styles and quickly learn to emulate them.

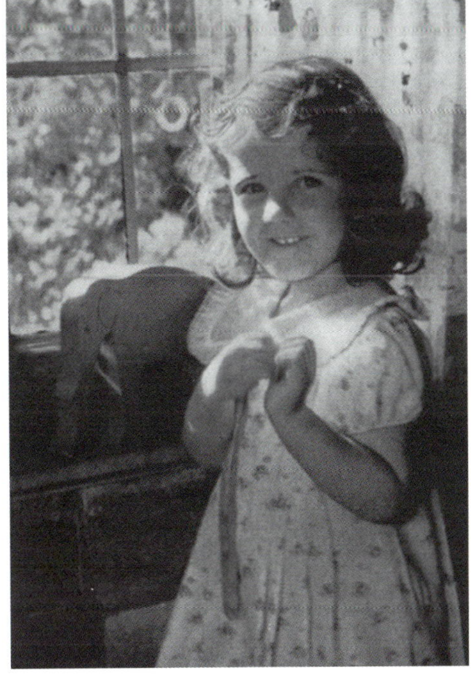

FIGURE 1. Photographer unknown, "Window Light," in *How to Make Good Pictures* (Rochester, NY: Eastman Kodak, 1936), 98.
Source: Author's collection.

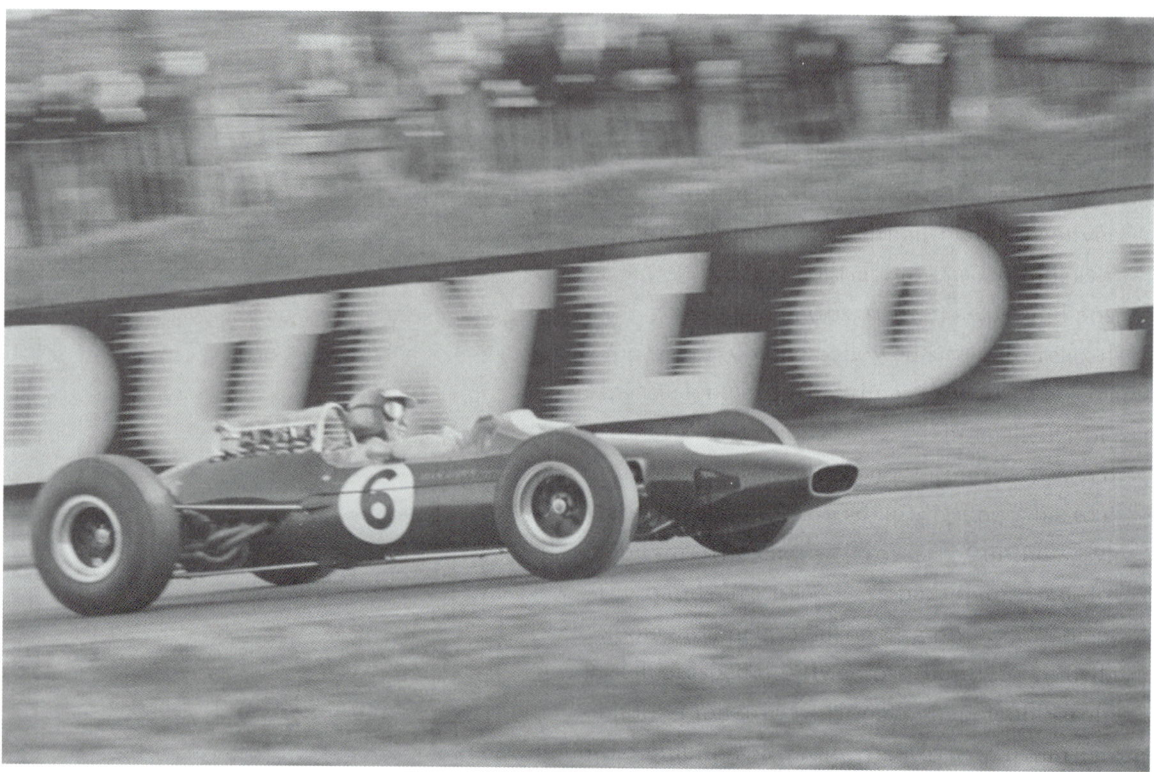

FIGURE 2. Max LeGrand, "Race of Champions, Brands Hatch," 1965. Black-and-white negative.

Source: Courtesy of the Miles Collier Collections, Max LeGrand Photograph Collection.

The life cycle of these trends may be shorter than in the era of analog photography, but the pattern of attention they receive—from initial interest, to widespread adoption, then critical backlash—is no different today than it was in the nineteenth century.

The Kodak how-to guides issued dozens of updates not only because the technology of their cameras and film changed, but because styles changed too. New styles often deliberately rejected former rules, as in the fad for intentionally blurred pictures or the use of grainy film in the 1960s. Sometimes trends developed in total ignorance of any preceding prohibition, such as the preference for high-angle selfies that emerged in the early 2000s, thoroughly overturning earlier portrait conventions that favored a low angle of view. Tracking changing rules like these across multiple editions denaturalizes the dogma of the "good picture."

The handbooks also elucidate why some styles were preferred over others. Despite their clichéd association with words, pictures don't always speak for themselves. Critics and photographers write about them, naming trends and justifying or disparaging new styles. To return to the selfie example, for a photographer raised on the norms of social media, the low-angle portraits of the interwar years look positively bad, and their makers appear ignorant of what now seems to be a universal rule. In contrast, the conventions of nineteenth-century portraiture can seem so unfamiliar to contemporary viewers that this entire class of pictures is treated as a singular genre. In many encyclopedic histories of photography, nineteenth-century portraits are discussed only in terms of the differences between their photographic processes. In fact, this period experienced dozens of passing trends. Stylistic changes in pose, as well as lighting, scale, and focus, were communicated through privately shared pictures or displays in studio windows. For a contemporary viewer, however, many of these stylistic differences go unnoticed when one is distracted by the unfamiliar medium of a daguerreotype or a tintype.

Studying instructional literature makes it easier to recognize the changing historical criteria for good pictures. Books and articles enumerated the steps necessary to achieve the popular looks and later denounced the styles that had become too commonplace. Learning to appreciate the changeable nature of these proscriptions also affords us the critical distance necessary to reflect on the assumed superiority of contemporary techniques.

Trends are especially evident when they have recently passed out of favor. In many cases, styles were only formally named when critics began to dismiss them as overused or too "trendy," when previously, they were thought of simply as good pictures. Still, these outmoded styles don't stay dead for long. They provide a rich source for later generations' aesthetic experimentation. The curator Clément Chéroux

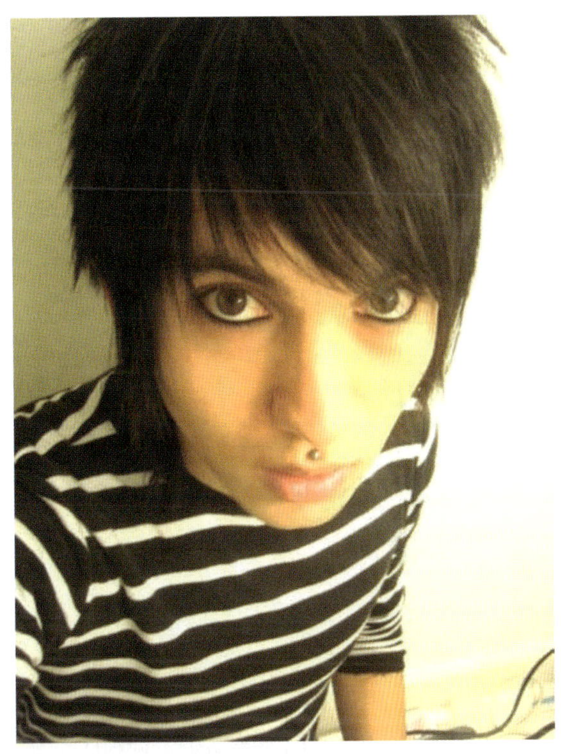

FIGURE 3. Ryan Tacata, "Untitled (Self-Portrait)," ca. 2005. Digital photograph.

Source: Courtesy of the artist.

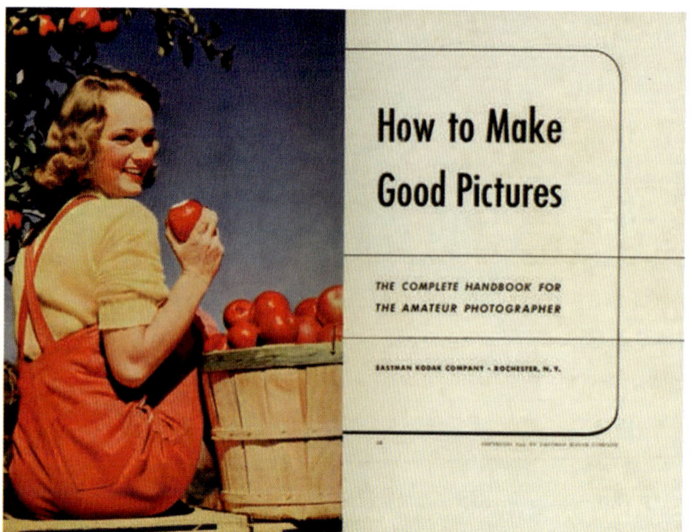

FIGURE 4. *How to Make Good Pictures* (Rochester, NY: Eastman Kodak Co., 1943).

Source: Collection of the Prelinger Library.

has revealed a notable example of this lineage: photographic tricks popular at the turn of the century that were rediscovered by subsequent art photographers, including May Ray and André Kertész. Once-familiar photographic effects became avant-garde a generation or two later.[3] Historical styles sometimes return to mainstream photography as well. Beyond the generative relationship between advanced art and amateurism, pillaging the scrapheap of history is characteristic of photographic practice as a whole. Some critics, including Walter Benjamin, condemned the appropriation of avant-garde principles by commercial photographers in the 1930s. In their secondary uses, the unusual angles and close-ups originally intended to disrupt conventional perspective by photographers such as Aleksandr Rodchenko and László Moholy-Nagy were emptied of political intent and instead became a style, deployed for aesthetic appeal without revolutionary meaning.[4]

I take a more optimistic view. Even derivative styles have historical value. All pictures do cultural work and can allow insight into the concerns of their makers and viewers. Through their makers' aesthetic choices, photographs indicate not only that they are "good pictures" but that they are good pictures *according to the rules of a specific time and place.* Photographs reveal their allegiance to particular social groups through the formal decisions they exhibit, not only through their choice of subject matter. Subverting or rejecting dominant stylistic rules is a critical practice in conversation with the aesthetic mores of one's time, as well as with the longer historical practice of photography. But upholding the prevailing rules also indicates a choice and a mode of communication. I am interested in how photographs of many genres use style to summon an audience and how one style may resonate differently as it passes in and out of favor among different groups of viewers.

POPULAR PICTURES

In this book, I identify styles and techniques that would have been either widely seen or imitated by large numbers of photographers in the United States. These kinds of photographs have often been defined as "vernacular."[5] That term is usually taken to account for everything from amateur snapshots to pictures made by professionals for small audiences, such as wedding photos and school portraits, as well as work that is much more public, including pictures produced by photojournalists and scientific or commercial photographers. It is so capacious that the category of the vernacular is defined mostly by what it excludes: fine art.[6] Longtime Museum of Modern Art curator John Szarkowski famously included many types of photographs in the exhibitions he staged at the museum from the 1960s through the 1980s. However, these diverse photographs were meant to illustrate Szarkowski's belief in the fundamental creativity of the medium, not necessarily the creative vision of the individual photographers. Scientific studies, snapshots, and other pictures whose makers' names have been lost to history revealed these medium-specific traits all the more authentically for Szarkowski because they were taken by untrained practitioners.[7]

The art/not art dialectic is still broadly enforced in photo criticism.[8] In a recent exhibition review, a writer for the *Boston Globe* claimed, "With an art photograph, form trumps content, ever and always. With vernacular photography—snapshots and candids and commercial portraits and the like—content is king. It's who and what, when and where that count, not how."[9] This pernicious assumption has been long-standing. Many twentieth-century scholars in the newly professionalized field of photographic history suggested that only pictures made under the banner of fine art were made with intention and regard for aesthetic impact. The historian Helmut Gernsheim's description of the field was typical. Prefacing his century-long study of "aesthetic trends," Gernsheim explained, "In considering the artistic aspect of photography we are not concerned with photographs intended to serve scientific or technical purposes, although some of them do have great aesthetic appeal, which is of course incidental. We can also ignore the billions of snapshots taken every year by the estimated hundred million camera users all over the world for no other purpose than to serve as mementoes of family events and holidays. . . . [They] bear the same relationship to composed creative pictures, as noise does to music."[10] I reject the claim that these types of photographs—from technical photos to snapshots and more—are made without consideration for aesthetic appeal. These photographs are made with intention, even if artistic originality is not their goal. Sometimes these intentions are subconscious. In many genres, photographers are motivated by the achievement of similarity, since it is their adherence to the rules that makes such pictures legible to their intended viewers.

Handbooks, instructional articles, and how-to manuals aren't alone responsible for this great uniformity. Although their recommendations for how and when to take pictures may have opened up possibilities for new camera users, seeing other peoples' pictures—in both casual, familial contexts and nationally distributed magazines and books—likely had the greatest effect on photographic output. In a study of photographic practice among the French working and middle classes in the 1960s, Pierre Bourdieu noted that "everything seems to obey implicit canons which are very generally imposed and which informed amateurs or aesthetes notice as such, but only to denounce them as examples of poor taste or technical clumsiness."[11] The rules are not only communicated through instructional articles; they are intuited when people compare their own pictures with those made by others. Even unstated rules are reinforced by positive comments, as well as by the technological possibilities of the film, camera, and accessories.

The categories of amateur and aesthete have changed dramatically since the rise of social media. Standards of taste are now applied across much larger groups, fortified by users' "likes" but also by the platforms' algorithms and human curators who privilege some styles and types of content over others. This uniformity is not new, although the similarities among pictures are now visible on a much larger scale.[12] In 1974, long before the advent of Instagram, Susan Sontag declared that the popular subjects of color snapshots were encroaching on the experience of the real world: "The image-surfeited are likely to find sunsets corny; they now look, alas, too much like photographs."[13] Although both Sontag and

Bourdieu suggested that certain classes of photographers rejected popular tropes, even that dismissal is a kind of uniformity. Whether making pictures in accordance with or in defiance of the rules, photographers' formal choices signal their participation in a particular visual culture, whether high-brow or mainstream.

As the instructional literature reveals, stylistic changes have an impact on many genres of photographic practice. Photographers of all kinds are eager to keep up with these changes or forge new ones, whether they learn from other pictures or from instructional books and articles. While one might suspect that some genres are insulated from stylistic considerations, such as family photography, I would counter that the similarity of subject matter over time (posing tableside at a holiday dinner or before the front door on the first day of school) makes it harder to see the differences among such pictures. Although these variations are sometimes the result of technological changes, they also reflect deliberate choices made by amateur photographers who had to consider which type of camera or film to use. Technological differences also mark pictures as exemplary of particular locations, eras, and, sometimes, distinct socioeconomic groups.

The give-and-take between popular use and commercial interests is characteristic of "popular culture," according to Raymond Williams, who wrote, "There is a kind of culture that has been developed by a people or by the majority of a people to express their own meanings and values, over a range from customs to works."[14] At first glance, it would appear that amateur photographs fit this bill: authentic expressions made without consideration of external pressures from either high art or commercial imagery. This is certainly what Gernsheim and Szarkowski believed. But as Williams clarified, "There is also a different kind of culture that has been developed for a people by an internal or external social group, and embedded in them by a range of processes from repressive imposition to commercial saturation." Kodak's guides, to take but one example, were not simply altruistic. Teaching consumers how to make "good pictures," was meant to encourage people to make *more* pictures. Williams concluded that "influential interaction constantly occurs" between two originating sites, the commercial and the folk cultures.[15] Similarly, photography handbooks borrowed from trends born of amateur practice even as they set themselves up as the arbiters of that practice, for reasons that may have been both artistically and commercially motivated.

Studying the changes in instructional literature over time reveals that even the most entrenched rules are anything but universal or natural. A style may be taken up again by a later group to signify something vastly different from its original instantiation. In fact, much of the history of photographic practice through the second half of the twentieth century consists of dismissing the stringent advice of earlier handbooks and sometimes even rejecting the affordances of new technologies. When these new visual codes are recognized, shared, and reproduced—in other words, when they become identifiable styles or trends—they represent a distinctive form of visual communication.

WHO MAKES GOOD PICTURES?

Instructional literature in photography, from the nineteenth century to the present, has fashioned itself as a conversation between a more knowledgeable practitioner and a less experienced one. Although the contemporary terms *amateur* and *professional* are difficult to map onto nineteenth-century photographic practice, which was overwhelmingly a commercial activity before the invention of the Kodak camera in 1888, the distinction between established photographers and rookies remains salient.

American how-to guides begin by speaking directly to readers, validating their purchase of the book at hand and offering varied paths through its narrative, attempting to account for everyone from complete novices to experienced photographers. A *Popular Mechanics* handbook announced in 1948, "This is a book for the amateur photographer who is growing. It is a guide book that will help him advance from the push-button stage to that of the artist and craftsman."[16] In contrast, Andreas Feininger pitched his tome *On Photography* to both amateurs and professionals, noting that his readers might "find it even easier to digest than other much simpler-looking books—and less insulting to your intelligence."[17] Some authors made a point of self-identifying as amateurs, or one-time amateurs, addressing the handbook to a version of their former selves. Henry G. Abbott introduced his 1899 guide with the following proviso: "This work is based on the experiences of the writer who is an amateur, not a professional. He has not graduated and probably never will, and is constantly running up against troublesome problems. He well remembers all the perplexities he had to contend with and hopes and believes that this volume will save the amateur much worry and needless expense."[18]

Although many books in the genre begin with similar promises of technical inclusivity, rhetorical and visual examples quickly narrow such broadly defined notions of their readership. Wherever possible, I call attention to the gendered and racialized assumptions of the literature and attempt to understand how these expectations might have affected the many people involved in photography even when they were not hailed by its rhetorical address. Instructional authors, like many of the spokespeople for public culture in the United States during the nineteenth and twentieth centuries, were overwhelmingly white men of the middle or upper classes. It cannot be assumed, however, that the only people who read these publications were those readers imagined by this homogeneous group of authors. Historical evidence in the form of photographs made by women and people of color proves that many people made pictures, not just those to whom the guides spoke directly.

It is difficult to know how these photographers would have responded to the rhetorical gaps that sometimes loomed between themselves and the books' intended audience. These readers might have recognized themselves as part of the large public of photographers to whom a book was directed. At the same time, they may have bristled at the gender, race, and class assumptions of the text, as I certainly did when reading them during my own photographic education.[19] Lacking the institutional support to publish alternative how-to guides, minority contributions to critical discourse were predominantly visual in nature during the nineteenth and twentieth centuries in the United States. Photographers created their own visual cultures, whether by disregarding hegemonic rules or simply by making pictures of people who were

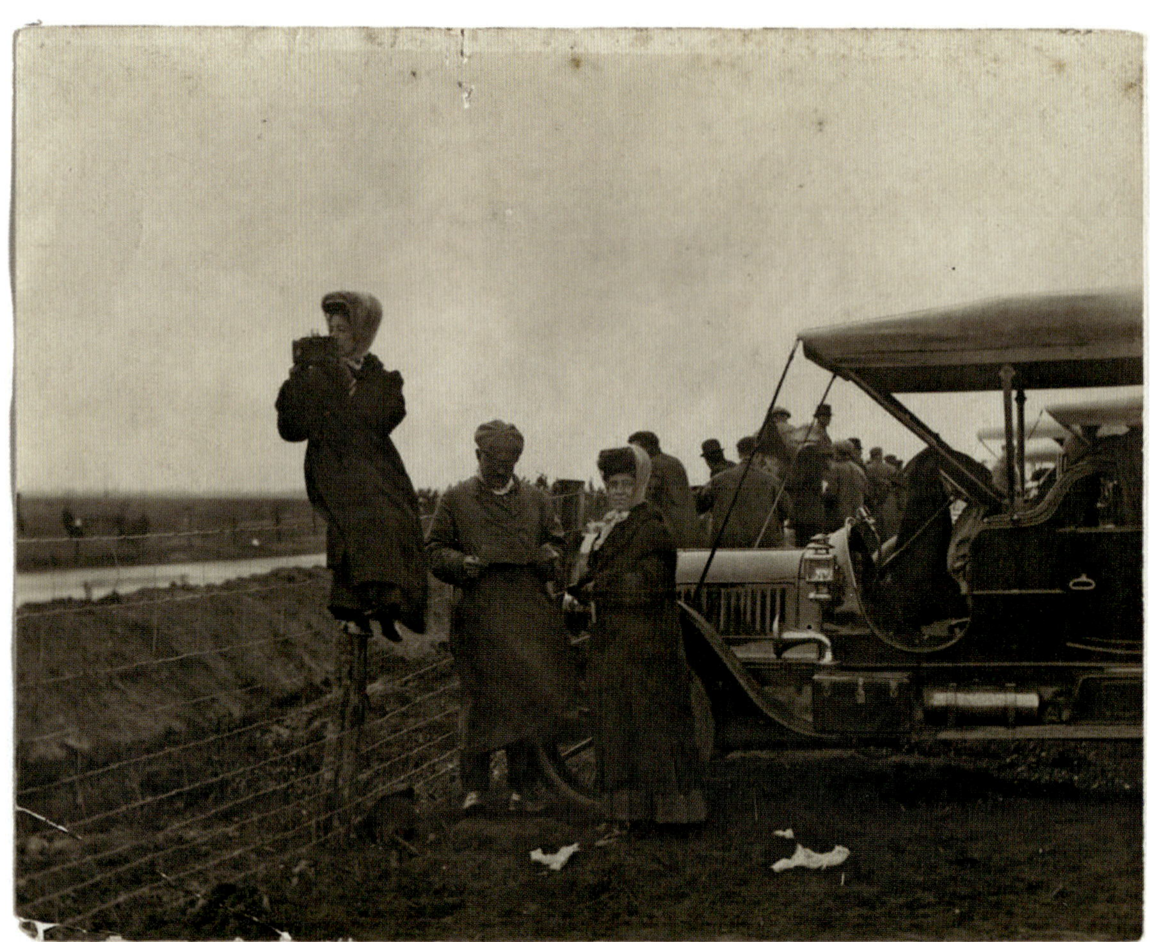

absent from mainstream discourse. Throughout this book, I point to the absences and unspoken assumptions of the instructional literature in hopes of indicating where photographers might have read guidebooks against the grain.

In nineteenth-century American literature, anecdotal asides almost unanimously describe photographers as men, while women are merely ingenuous or fussy portrait subjects. Nineteenth-century women readers of the photographic press had to navigate these limitations, just as they did when they encountered generic masculine pronouns in other literature of the time. In fact, photography was considered a suitable artistic pursuit for women of the nineteenth century, and women's work was included in amateur exhibitions, though it was sometimes relegated to a "ladies" category.[20] The photographer Catherine Weed Barnes took exception to this designation, arguing that "if the work of men and women is admitted to the same exhibition it should be on equal terms. Do not admit a woman's pictures because they are made by a woman, but because they are made well."[21] In reading the instructional literature, women photographers may have identified with the public summoned by the call to "photographers" even if they were excluded by the gendered pronouns.

While the nineteenth-century photographic press envisioned a uniformly male, middle- or upper-class readership, sometimes these assumptions were the product of linguistic convention, but they were also aspirational. Early photographers were not only gentlemen, but also scientists, inventors, and striving entrepreneurs. In short, they were not all the elite men assumed by the photographic literature of the day. Although the first decade of photography attracted experimenters with the means to practice without the guarantee of profit, many abandoned the process after

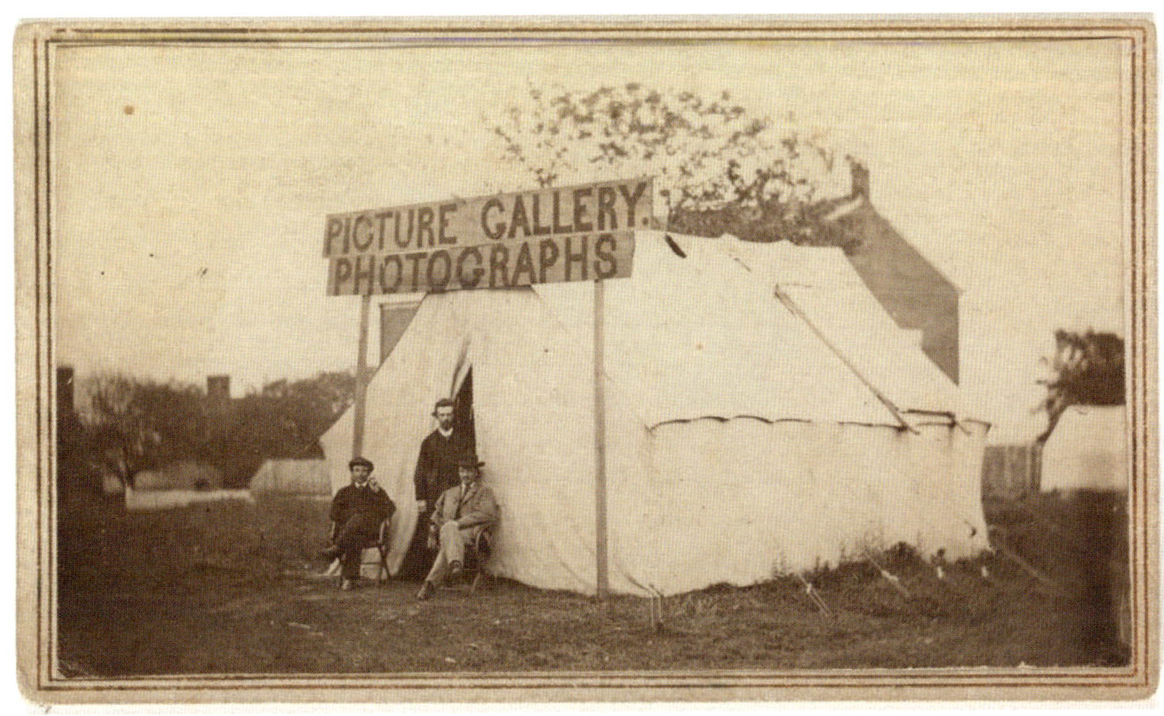

FIGURE 6. Photographer unknown, "[Picture Gallery Photographs]," 1860s. Albumen silver print. 2 3/16" × 3 11/16" (mount).

Source: Metropolitan Museum of Art, Purchase, Alfred Stieglitz Society Gifts, 2013

the simple success of recording a picture, any picture.[22] Others picked up photography when it became clear that portraiture could attract a large clientele. The free black man Augustus Washington, for example, turned to photography in the 1840s to pay off debts he had accrued as a student at Dartmouth College.[23] Some photographers established itinerant practices, traveling the countryside with horse-drawn darkrooms to serve rural communities or towns without local photographers.

By the 1880s, many of the debates over photographic quality were also veiled arguments about social class, as photographers began to professionalize.[24] The photographic press was rife with criticisms of the "dollar a dozen" men at this time. These photographers who promised inexpensive portraits were thought to be dragging down the profession with their poor-quality pictures, and although this was largely unstated, critics were also dismissive of the lower class of sitters such studios served.[25] Itinerant photography declined after the advent of the inexpensive Kodak Brownie camera in 1900, when individuals could finally afford to purchase their own cameras, almost regardless of social class.

Kodak, seeking to expand its market and emphasize the ease and fun of amateur photography, developed a trademark image: the "Kodak Girl." For more than sixty years, the young woman appeared in illustrations wearing a striped dress and toting a Kodak camera.[26] By the middle of the twentieth century, though, photography was being repositioned as a technical and masculine hobby. The Kodak Girl, and women in general, were increasingly sidelined from serious practice. The major photographic magazines founded during the interwar period, *Popular Photography* (1937) and *U.S. Camera* (1938), upheld these gender roles for decades. With their detailed instructions and casual rhetorical style, the magazines demystified photography's aesthetic tenets, even as they highlighted its technical demands. While simple box cameras were still popular, the instructional literature focused on the growing numbers of cameras with interchangeable lenses, electronic flashes, and built-in light metering systems. Product guides compared the merits of new accoutrements for the amateur photographer's kit, while do-it-yourself instructions rewarded the photographer possessed of mechanical ingenuity.

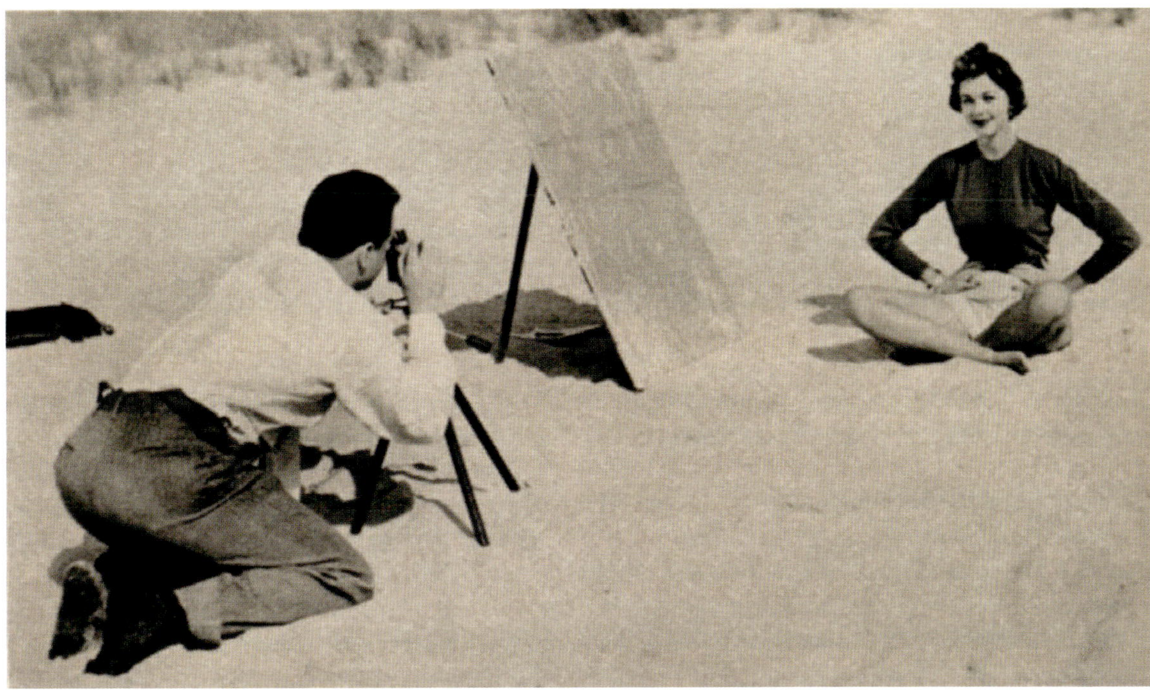

At the end of World War II, with traditional notions of masculinity under threat from women's entrance into the workforce and the rise of white-collar work, do-it-yourself projects promised men an arena in which to reassert their technical and manual dominance.[27] To re-establish male authority, women were cast in the role of the Luddite or naïf. Women, especially the wives or girlfriends of photographers, became the foil for the newly capable, technologically savvy male pho-tographer.[28] Against women's apparently hapless, bumbling confusion at f-stops and shutter speeds, the male photographer's mastery over the medium was intended to stand out in sharp relief. Although women appeared frequently in the pages of how-to manuals and instructional articles during this era, they were usually relegated to the role of model or long-suffering assistant.

Photography of women was considered its own genre at midcen-tury, with books dedicated to the techniques of picturing women in poses that emphasized their vulnerability and availability to the desir-ous gaze. Popular stories about famous fashion photographers, such

FIGURE 7. Photographer unknown, "Use a Reflector for Fill-In Lighting," ca. 1957. *How to Take Better Pictures* (New York: Maco Magazine Corp., 1957), 70.

as Bert Stern, emphasized their outsized sexual appetites and the (ostensible) receptivity of models to their advances.[29] Peter Gowland, one of the era's foremost glamour photographers, issued a warning to the readers of *How to Photograph Women,* his handbook: "Whether you're a professional or an amateur, keep your photography on an impersonal basis. Don't be a wise guy. Keep your hands on your camera. When you pose her, direct her, don't push. Never use your photography as a means of making dates or getting a girl out in the woods."[30] Gowland was a frequent contributor to the popular photography periodicals, and his guidebook went into five editions after its first publication in 1953. His description acknowledges the mythology of the relationship between photographers and their subjects, but even as it cautions against abuses of this power, it also draws attention to them, transporting the fantasies depicted in his pictures into the realm of possibility.

Photographic literature also made broad assumptions about the race of its readership. For example, while dozens of articles described the difficulties of accurately reproducing skin tones with the monochrome processes of the nineteenth century, no mention was made of complexions other than pale pink or ruddy. Even the exceptionally detailed hand-painting manuals of the nineteenth century failed to imagine sitters with darker features. Many guides, such as Marcus Aurelius Root's 1864 *The Camera and the Pencil,* went to great lengths to describe the appropriate mixture of colors for tinting backdrops, furniture, and clothing from silks and furs to cotton fabrics. But "Naples yellow with madder pink" was the lone formula for skin, despite the fact that people of many skin tones were eager patrons of photographic portraiture.[31]

Even in the late 1840s, less than a decade after photography's unveiling and well before the art was made widely accessible by the invention of the less expensive formats, photographers offered their services to readers of the abolitionist press, including *National Era, Frederick Douglass' Paper,* and the Canadian publication, *Provincial Freeman.* In these pages, locally owned studios competed with franchises, such as John Plumbe's National Daguerrean Gallery, for the patronage of readers of all races. Plumbe, a white photographer whose first gallery was in Washington, DC, also offered "instruction and apparatus furnished on reasonable terms," as early as 1847.[32] While photographers of color had unequal access to the formal schools of photography that emerged at the end of the nineteenth century, through lessons and apprenticeships, this earlier generation of photographers learned the craft directly from other practitioners, both black and white.

Jules Lion, a French-born free man of color living in New Orleans, is credited as one of the earliest daguerreotypists in the United States, producing work of exceptional quality just months after Daguerre's announcement in Paris.[33] Although Lion returned to his work as a lithographer shortly after his experiments in photography, many other black photographers set up studios or worked as itinerant practitioners and photographers' assistants in the United States during the nineteenth century. One of the most celebrated of these was James Presley Ball who, after having learned the craft from another black photographer, John B. Bailey of Boston, went on to operate a successful studio in Cincinnati in the 1850s. Ball's studio welcomed customers of all races and was profiled in the nationally circulating magazine *Gleason's Pictorial and Drawing Room Companion*, which hailed his daguerreotypes as having "an accuracy and softness of expression unsurpassed by any establishment in the Union."[34] Setting aside the boosterish tone that was common among popular writers of the time, this statement reveals that the rules for "good pictures" applied even to photographers who were not included in the audience imagined by the instructional literature.

In contrast to the handbooks' presumptions, photography was practiced by and for Americans of all races and genders since its very earliest days on the continent. Even though photographers like Ball or Catherine Weed Barnes do not often appear in the period literature, they also learned from these books and periodicals. The pictorial record shows that, by and large, they produced work in harmony with the dominant aesthetic concerns of their times. Indeed, Barnes's desire was precisely that her work be judged according to the same standards as photographs made by men. In an attempt to rectify the historical bias of the literature, I acknowledge their presence here and throughout the rest of this book, I aim to imagine how diverse photographers might have read the handbooks (or talked back to them) during the medium's long history.

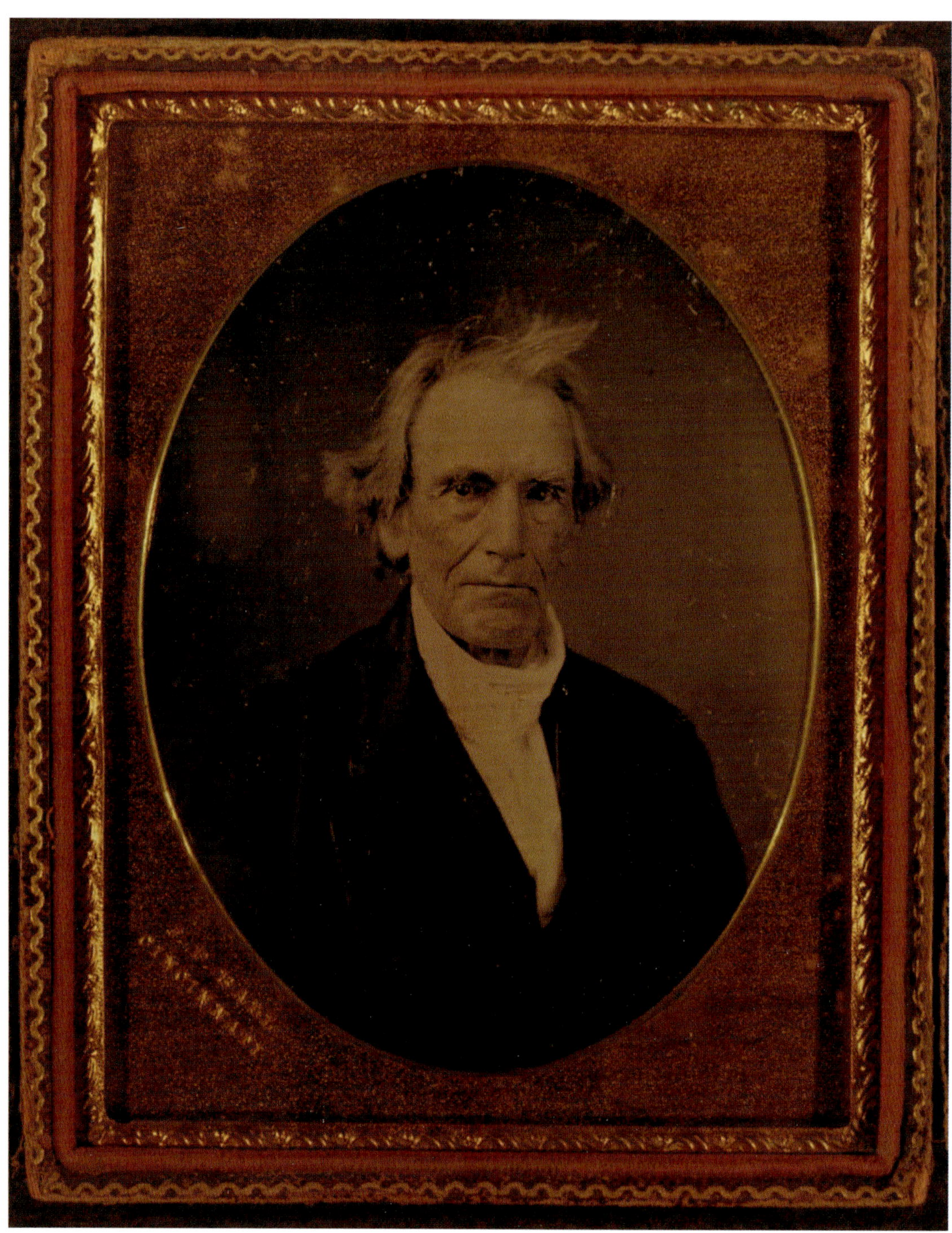

DEFINING AND REDEFINING GOOD PHOTOGRAPHY

Over the course of photography's history, it has often been alleged that aesthetic trends are either handed down from other artistic traditions or are the inevitable result of photographic technology. In truth, photographic aesthetics, forged by amateurs and professionals of all kinds, cannot be explained by any one of these factors alone. Despite the how-to authors' exhortations, not everyone followed their advice. Photographers persisted in making pictures with subjects centered in the frame, with distracting backgrounds, or with tilted horizons. Sometimes they broke these rules intentionally; sometimes accidents inspired their own trends. Many one-time technical failures, such as soft focus, visible film grain, overexposure, or blur, also became markers of a photographer's creative use of the medium. Although the instructional literature gave every indication of authority, it also adapted to and eventually incorporated prevailing aesthetic trends.

Read across many generations of photographic practice, the guidebooks reveal that the statement "how to make good pictures" is actually a question, one that has no fixed answer. As much as instructional literature claimed to define photography, it has also been defined *by* photography. A good photograph may be best described as one that provokes recognition and inspires imitation. It is then included in the next generation of how-to books, adapted, discarded, and sometimes picked up again by later photographers. *Good Pictures* follows the life and afterlife of fifty of these styles and the stories they told on their way to becoming the history of photography in the United States.

< FIGURE 8. James Presley Ball, "Unidentified Man, Hand-and-Shoulders Portrait," ca. 1847—1860. Daguerreotype.

Source: Library of Congress Prints and Photographs Division.

PART I

1839–1860

THE FIRST METHOD for recording an image from nature was announced in January 1839, by Louis-Jacques-Mandé Daguerre, a French artist and entrepreneur. By the end of the year, his discovery was rivaled by another technique for preserving images of the world, this one invented by an Englishman, William Henry Fox Talbot. News of these two processes traveled quickly; one of the first American reports of the French process was published by Samuel F. B. Morse, inventor of the telegraph, in spring 1839. Morse established a studio in New York later that year, where he made daguerreotypes and provided instruction to other aspiring photographers in the United States.

During the medium's earliest years, the instructional literature focused on the chemical formulas and procedures necessary to record an image successfully. The first practitioners of photography included many scientists; they were more likely to be pharmacists or opticians than artists. By the mid-1840s, the field had expanded to include entrepreneurs eager to capitalize on a medium that promised to replace the market for traditional painted portraits.

Eventually the instructional literature began to include essays on aesthetics, which often recommended that photographers improve their work by studying the compositional elements of famous paintings.

Medium-specific stylistic elements also arose, often in relation to the unique technical properties of photography, such as the extraordinary detail of the finely polished daguerreotype plate. In addition to monographic books, two periodicals published in the United States, *The Daguerreian Journal* and *Humphrey's Journal of the Daguerreotype and Photographic Arts*, were crucial to establishing, consolidating, and disseminating the medium's techniques and emerging aesthetic conventions.

1

THE AMERICAN PROCESS

LONDON'S CRYSTAL PALACE exhibition of 1851 offered the first major opportunity to compare the photographic output of one country against another. The Americans' daguerreotypes, photographic images made on silver-plated copper sheets and displayed behind glass, were routinely praised by judges and the press for their great clarity and sharpness. American photographers took home three of the five medals awarded to daguerreotypes at the exhibition.[1]

Even before this first international competition, the *Daguerreian Journal* proudly declared, "It is generally acknowledged that the Daguerreian Art is more successfully practiced in America than in any other country. Most of the artists pursuing this art in France, England, and Germany, consider it to their advantage in advertising to say, 'Daguerreotypes by the American Process.' This alone is sufficient proof of the high estimation in which the people of those countries hold our productions."[2] Daguerre himself, the inventor of the process, especially admired the work of the American photographer Edward Anthony in 1847. Daguerre wrote to Anthony, in a letter that was frequently cited by the American photographic press, "It is with great satisfaction that I express all the pleasure that your daguerreotype portraits have given me. I certify that these pictures, in execution, are among the most perfect I have ever seen."[3]

The superiority of American daguerreotypes was cemented by counterexample. British daguerreotypes were roundly criticized through the 1840s and 1850s; members of the press and the photographic industry often attributed the dark and ill-defined English daguerreotypes to

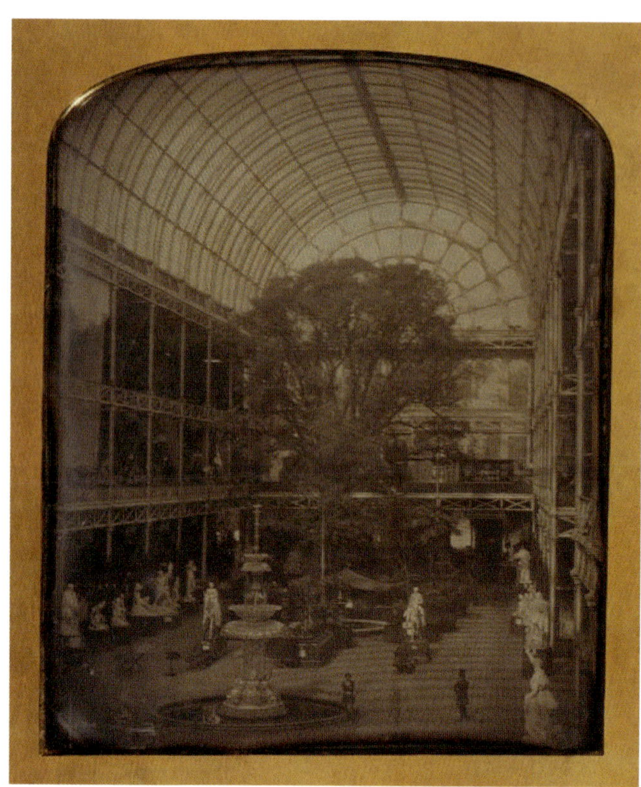

 John Jabez Edwin Mayall, "The Crystal Palace at Hyde Park, London," 1851. Daguerreotype, 12″ × 9 ¹¹⁄₁₆″.

Source: J. Paul Getty Museum, Los Angeles. Digital image courtesy of the Getty's Open Content Program.

the poor quality of London's smoggy air. One journalist wrote, "The excellence of American pictures is evident, which is to be accounted for by several reasons. In the first place, American skies are freer from fog and clouds—from bituminous coal not being much used, the atmosphere of our cities is free from smoke, at least upon the Atlantic coasts."[4] The smog hypothesis persisted, despite having been disproven by the establishment of Mayall's American Daguerreotype Institution in London in 1846.

Closing the successful Philadelphia studio that he founded in the early 1840s, John Jabez Edwin Mayall relocated to London. His technical and artistic mastery of large-scale pictures made him popular among upper-class patrons. A review of photographic studios in London maintained, "Mayall is known as the 'American Daguerreotypist,' and is considered about the best in London. His specimens are certainly proof that the fogs of London are not the cause of Daguerreotypists failing in procuring clear pictures; for many of his are equal to the best ever taken."[5] Mayall's pictures were admired for their "breadth of effect, masses of light and shade—the latter without blackness—so beautifully reflected into, that every gradation may be traced in uninterrupted continuity."[6] Sharp focus combined with a wide tonal range and clarity in the shadows was prized in early daguerreotypes, which were often either faint or exceptionally dark, as in the 1847 example made by an unnamed photographer (Figure 11).

In practice, the qualities of American daguerreotypes were achieved through a number of technical and chemical inventions. Their sharp and clear aesthetic was neither simply a result of air quality nor a national proclivity for ingenuity, though at least one American writer suggested that: "Our people are readier in picking up processes and acquiring the mastery of the art than our trans-Atlantic rivals."[7] American photographic products had been sold in Europe since the early 1840s. Such merchandise often used its national origin metonymically, as a guarantor of technical prowess. Wolcott's American Mixture, named after Alexander S. Wolcott, was an accelerator that improved the sensitivity of the plates used in the daguerreotype process with a concoction

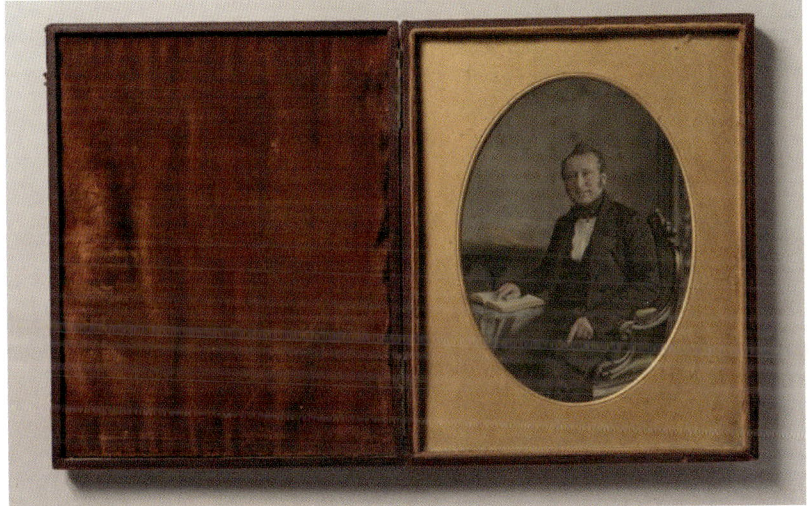

FIGURE 10. John Jabez Edwin Mayall, "Seated Man Pointing to a Passage in an Open Book," ca. 1850. Daguerreotype with applied color, 6″ × 4¼″.

Source: Metropolitan Museum of Art, Bequest of Herbert Mitchell, 2008.

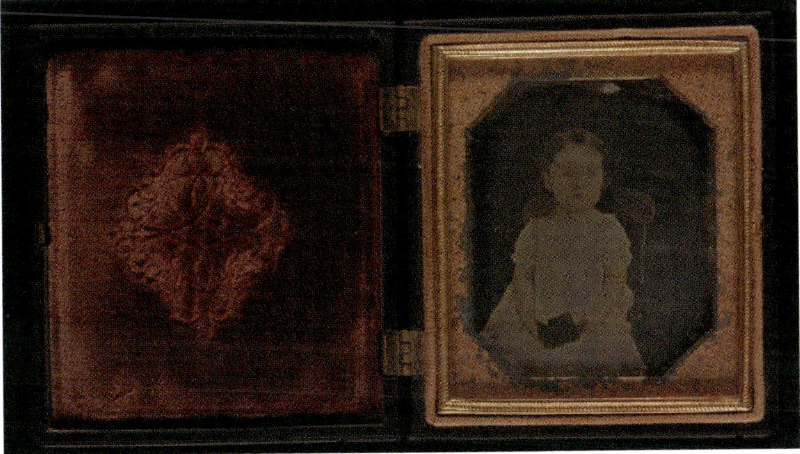

FIGURE 11. Photographer unknown, "Unidentified Girl, Three-Quarter Length Portrait, Holding a Daguerreotype Case," 1847. Daguerreotype.

Source: Library of Congress Prints and Photographs Division.

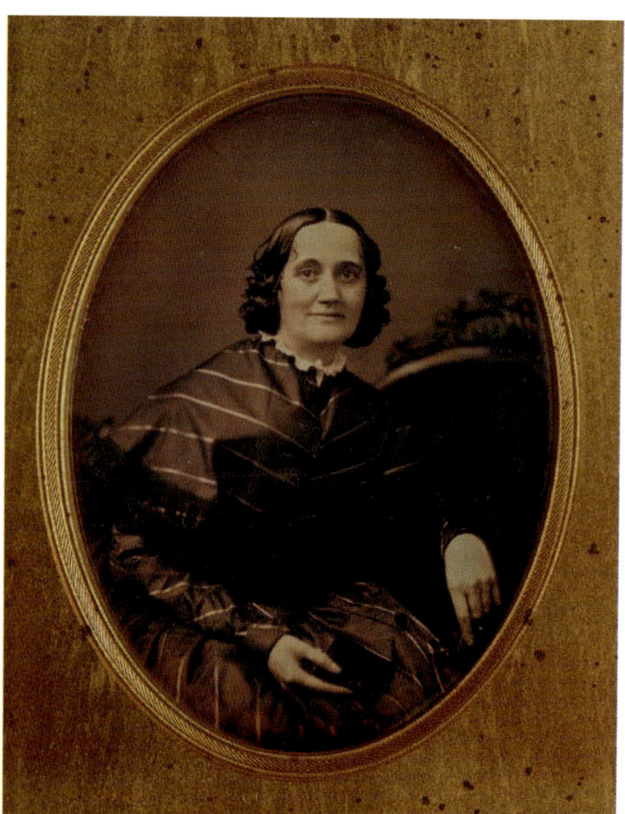

of bromine, iodine, and chlorine. Photographers using the American Mixture could make pictures more rapidly in less light, which improved sharpness and definition.[8] The practice of electroplating, adding additional layers of silver to the polished copper plate through galvanizing, also contributed to the brilliance of American daguerreotypes and was described in France as the "American process."[9] The smooth surface and bright sheen of silver heightened detail in shadow areas. Mechanical changes too contributed to the clarity of American daguerreotypes: lateral polishing rather than circular buffing improved the visibility of the image on the reflective surface of the daguerreotype.[10] The photographer John Adams Whipple used steam-driven machines to ensure a uniform polish (steam power also ran a fan to cool his clients under the hot skylights of his studio). Finally, gilding the daguerreotype after exposure and development stabilized the image and imparted it with a richness and depth of tonality, a practice frequently used by the Boston studio of Southworth and Hawes.[11]

This early preference for sharp and clear daguerreotype images represents one of the first widespread aesthetic trends within photography. Although it was often difficult for critics to understand the methods by which these stylistic attributes were obtained, photographic journals worked to illuminate the "American process" for their readers and make "American daguerreotypes" the paradigm for photographic production during the Daguerreian period.

2

PORTRAIT PROPS AND POSES

DURING THE 1850S, as the increased light sensitivity of photographic emulsions made the medium more suitable for portraiture, supporters sang the praises of the exact likeness, whether made with the new collodion on glass plate technique or the older daguerreotype method.[1] As one advertisement enthused, "The best index of the mind is a daguerreotype of the face."[2]

However, not all portraits succeeded in representing their subjects' characters, despite the exhaustive cataloging of facial features. A popular French treatise, excerpted in American journals, accused these portraits of "having *too strong* a resemblance; they are a sort of permanent mirror, where self love does not always find its expectation [emphasis added]."[3] Overly objective images revealed too much, especially those "defects" of complexion that portrait painters had long artfully improved.[4] One journal explained, "Photographers generally, with educated eyes, demand much sharper pictures than their customers, while it is known that the best portrait painters constantly censure photographers for producing *too much sharpness*, and that some of the first photographers practiced throwing the picture just a little out [of focus]."[5] The sharply focused pictures by photographers eager to display their technical skill were at cross-purposes with the grace and dignity expected from portraits. The American photographer Levi Hill complained, "We daily see likenesses which, though marked by every peculiarity of feature in the person represented, are yet entirely devoid of that essence, or predominant trait of character."[6] These highly detailed pictures failed to capture the sitter's true character, that ideal emanation of spirit to which Victorians aspired.

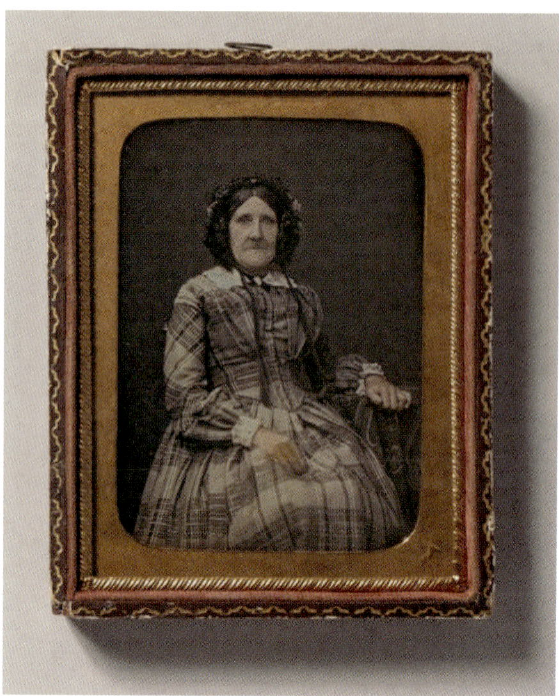

The most talented photographers were capable of "calling up" the best aspects of the sitter's personality, so that the expression on her face might match the character she sought to exude.[7] This theoretical advice translated into practical recommendations that included conversational topics appropriate for the studio, as well as high-backed chairs, sturdy props, and posing apparatuses, which allowed sitters to relax during the long exposure times. Awkward poses and strained expressions betrayed the challenge of sitting still for several seconds or more, as was common through the 1860s. "It is not possible to give a picture the character of easy calmness, while the hands are firmly clasped or pressed down upon the knee, or if resting on a stand or pedestal, grasped tightly across the edge," chided the photographer E. K. Hough.[8] Napoleon Sarony, a New York–based photographer known for his celebrity portraits, even patented a moveable rest that supported sitters in several pre-set poses. [See also Chapter 46, "Selfie."]

The British photographer Henry Peach Robinson was an early critic of such stock poses. In an article for the *London Photographic Times*, reprinted in the United States in 1858, Robinson wrote, "A person unacquainted with photography . . . on looking over the specimens of many portrait photographers, would suppose there was only one position in which a sitter could be placed, namely, the one elbow on a little round table, with the hand twisted as near the body as possible, the other hand placed on the knee, with the elbow stuck stiffly out at an angle, the legs crossed and turned flat to the camera to satisfy the exigencies of focus."[9] The need for absolute stillness, coupled with the distorting effects of short lenses (preferred because they required less light), resulted in homogeneous poses that presented the body frozen in one focal plane.

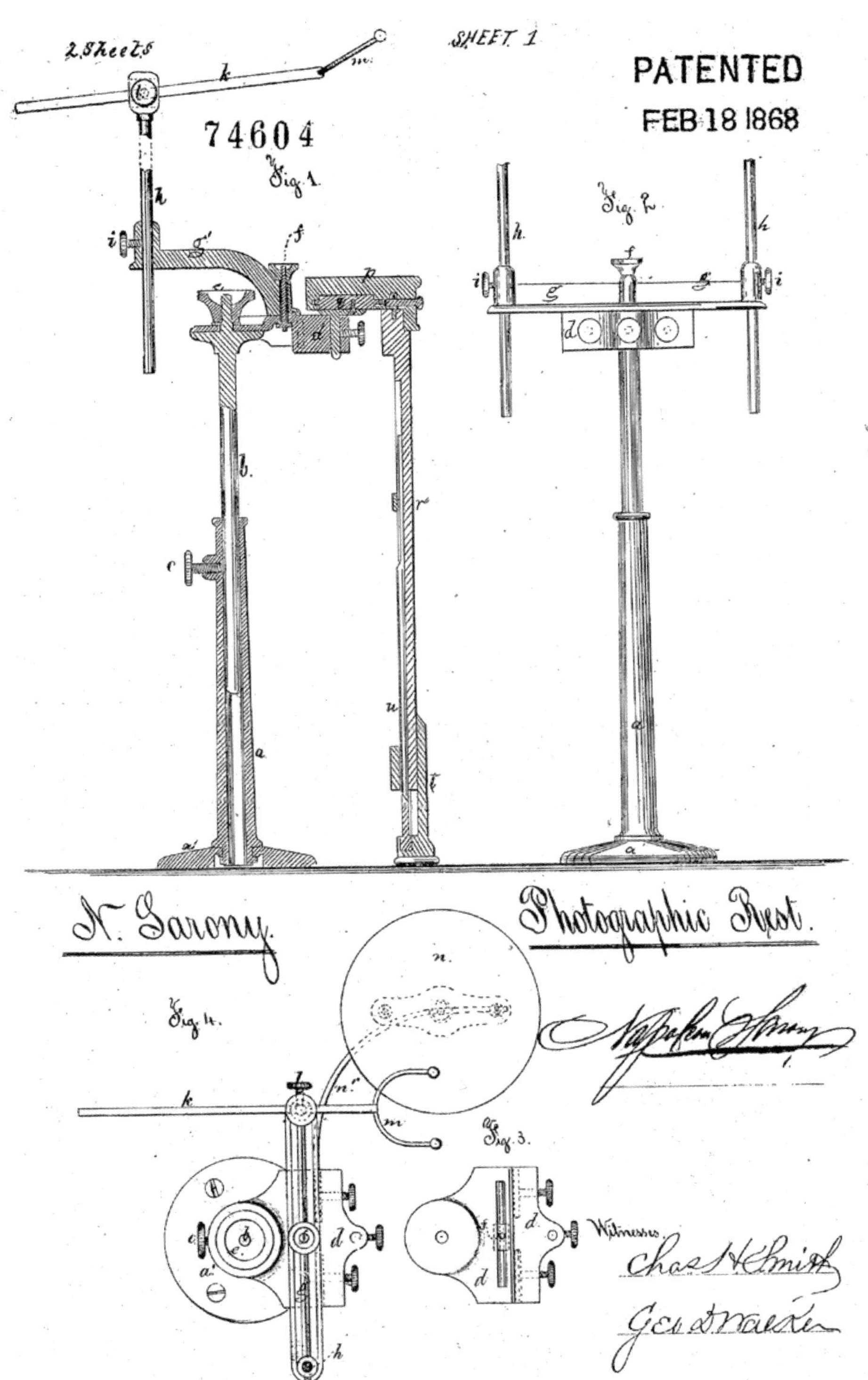
2 Sheets
SHEET 1
PATENTED
FEB 18 1868
74604
Fig. 1.
Fig. 2.
Fig. 4.
Fig. 3.
N. Sarony.
Photographic Rest.
Witnesses.
Chas H Smith
Geo D Walker

Advent of the carte-de-visite by André-Adolphe-Eugène Disdéri in 1854, and its global popularization by the close of the decade, changed portrait standards radically. The carte-de-visite format consisted of a small albumen paper print affixed to heavy cardstock. A four-lens camera on sliding rails allowed photographers to make as many as eight different exposures on a single negative plate; the resulting images were cut apart and mounted separately after development and printing. Although the process streamlined the darkroom work, it introduced new challenges in the studio. Photographers needed to move their sitters quickly from one pose to the next because the collodion negative plate had to be exposed while the chemicals were still wet. The aspect ratio of the 2¼″ × 3 ½″carte-de-visite image, mounted on a 2½″ × 4″ paper card also invited full-length poses, which photographers claimed were even more lifelike because they captured the whole body's posture. The new lenses required to adequately expose the tall, narrow plates were typically longer in focal length than those used by daguerreotype studios earlier in the century.

FIGURE 15. Photographer unknown (American), "Untitled [Boy Holding Cap, Resting Arm on a Column]," ca. 1840s. Daguerreotype.

Source: Metropolitan Museum of Art.

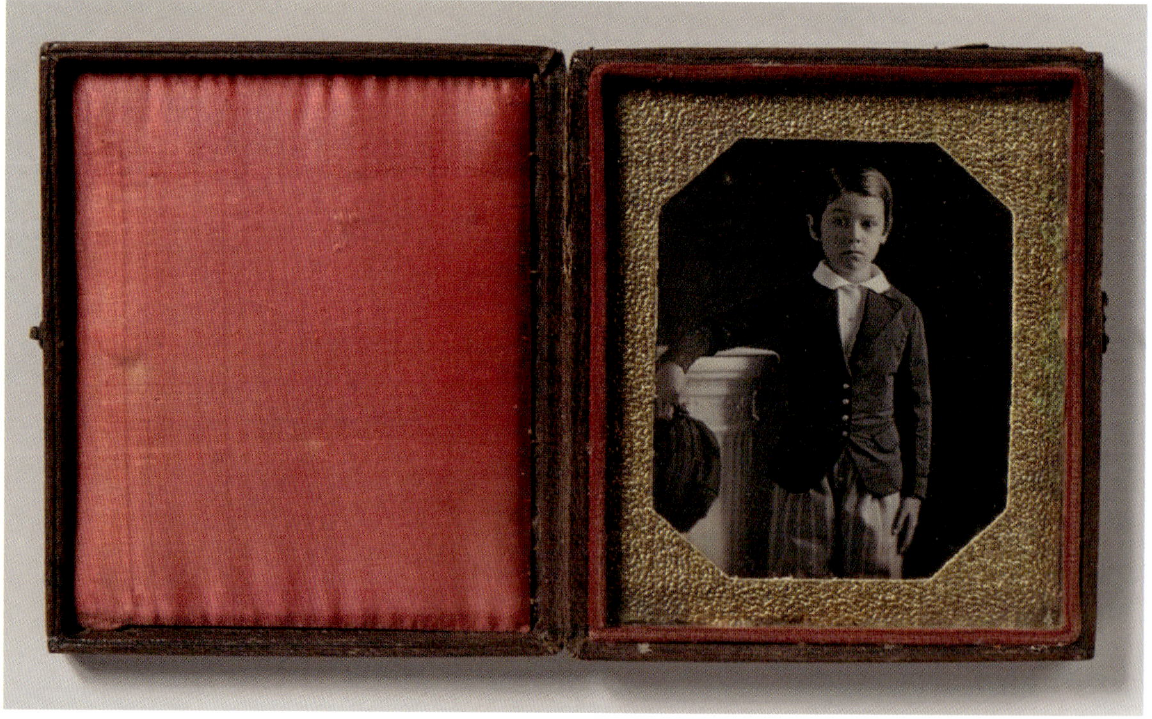

The eventual adoption of these longer lenses for all portrait work was an unintended and beneficial consequence of *cartomania*, as the fad for cartes-de-visite was dubbed by the press.[10] In comparison to the faster, shorter lenses used previously, the carte-de-visite lens created less distortion, making portraits appear increasingly true to life. [See also Chapter 12, "Retouching Cabinet Cards."]

With the standardization of this size also came redundancy. Even the new poses and accessories quickly became clichéd, especially as their visibility increased in the larger 4½″ × 6″ cards that were introduced in the late 1860s. In his well-known guide, the American photographer Marcus Aurelius Root wished the many "fancy backgrounds, curtain, &c. be rigorously banished."[11] Another photographer mocked still more typical elements: "The pose, invariably stereotyped; here the inevitable little table, the irrepressible columns, chairs, hanging curtains."[12] Robinson, the English photographer, also found these images overcrowded with accessories. He counseled, "Vases of flowers, elaborate patterns on table covers, books, and the great variety of trifles sometimes seen, are all very well when surprise is intended to be given by the minute detail afforded by the lens; but the time for all this has passed . . . we now look rather for fine expression and a good pose."[13] The strategies originally established to highlight technical accuracy gradually retreated during the 1870s, as photographic portraits were increasingly judged for their ability to suggest character, rather than their representation of the highly detailed, observable features of the face.

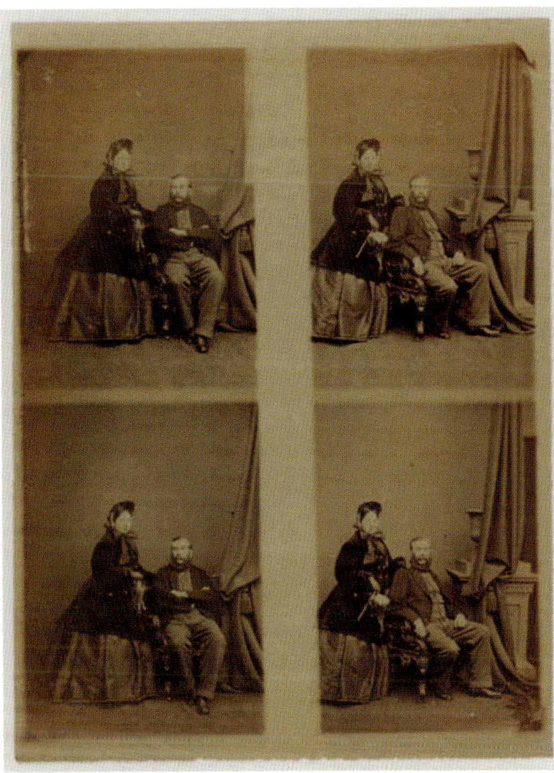

FIGURE 16. Photographer unknown, "Untitled [Mr. and Mrs. E. Walker, March 6, 1863]," 1863. Albumen silver print, 8 13/16″ × 6 7/16″.

Source: J. Paul Getty Museum, Los Angeles, Digital image courtesy of the Getty's Open Content Program.

3

HAND PAINTING

EBULLIENT ANNOUNCEMENTS of photography's invention were tempered by one shortcoming: the medium's lack of color. Samuel F. B. Morse likened Daguerre's work to the chiaroscuro of mezzotint prints.[1] Another observer noted, "in the absence of color they [Daguerre's images] are as perfect images of the objects they represent, as are those which are seen by reflection from a highly polished surface."[2] Of the first five patents issued in the United States related to photography, three concerned the medium's colorlessness.[3] These improvements described modes of adding color to the surface of the daguerreotype by hand painting with pigments or through a galvanizing process.[4] The recording of natural color was the desideratum of early photography, although it remained largely unattainable until the twentieth century.

Nearly every book-length manual published in the nineteenth century included a chapter on coloring or painting photographs. How-to articles on adding color also proliferated in the photographic press. One writer reasoned, "The want of color is chiefly felt in portraits; this deficiency imparts a cold and almost cadaverous air; it renders the likeness less perfect, and often gives an appearance of greater age."[5] This author and many others detailed methods for preparing the surface of the image, recommending types of brushes and the precise pigments to use on each area of the picture. These lists reveal the dominant racial assumptions of the time, providing a single formula for "flesh tints," while offering extensive and varied advice on how to color studio elements, from backdrops and drapery to silks, feathers and furs.[6]

[See also Chapter 40, "Golden Hour."]

> FIGURE 17. Augustus Washington, "Urias A. McGill," 1854–1860. Daguerreotype with applied color.

Source: Library of Congress, Prints and Photographs Division.

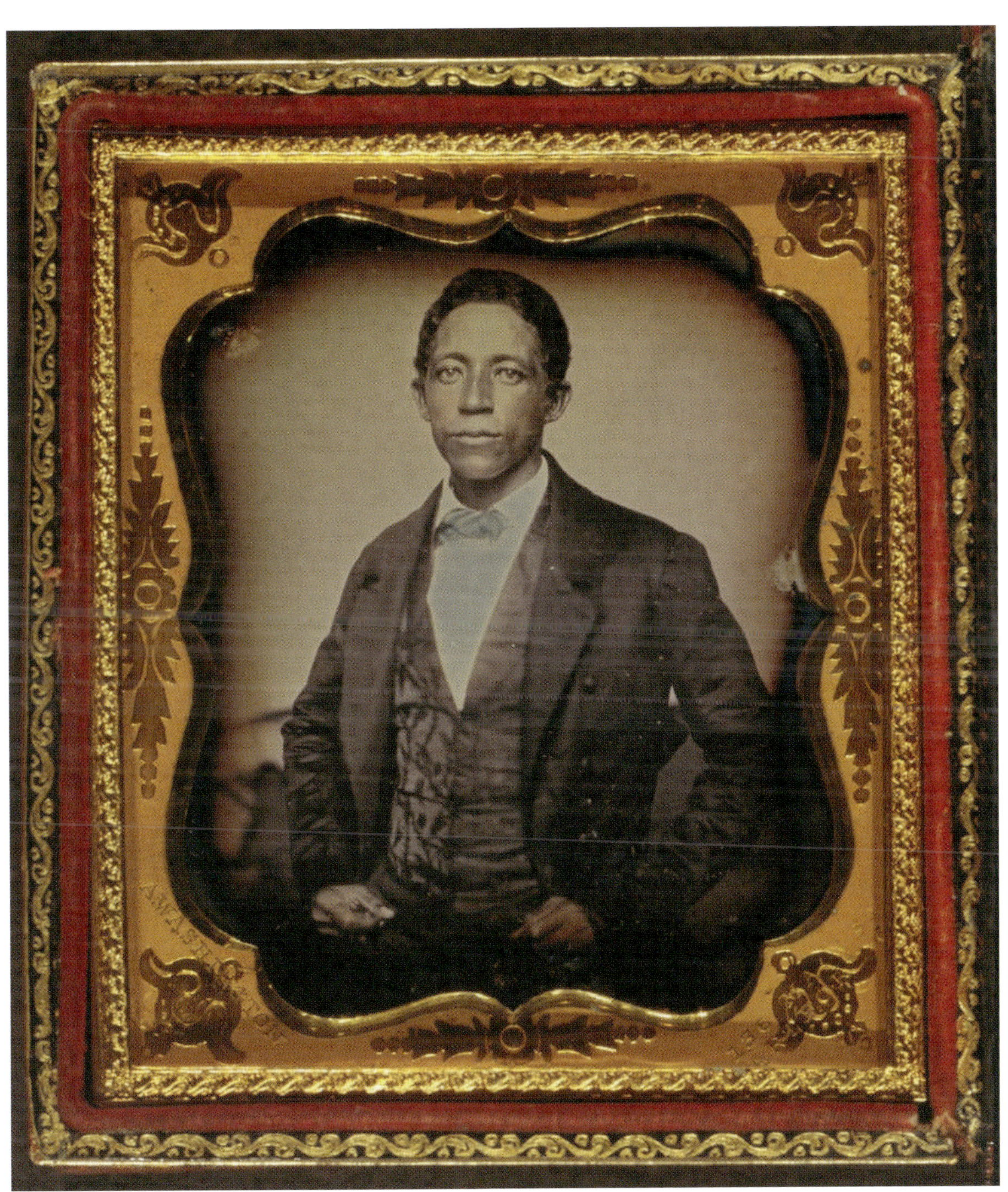

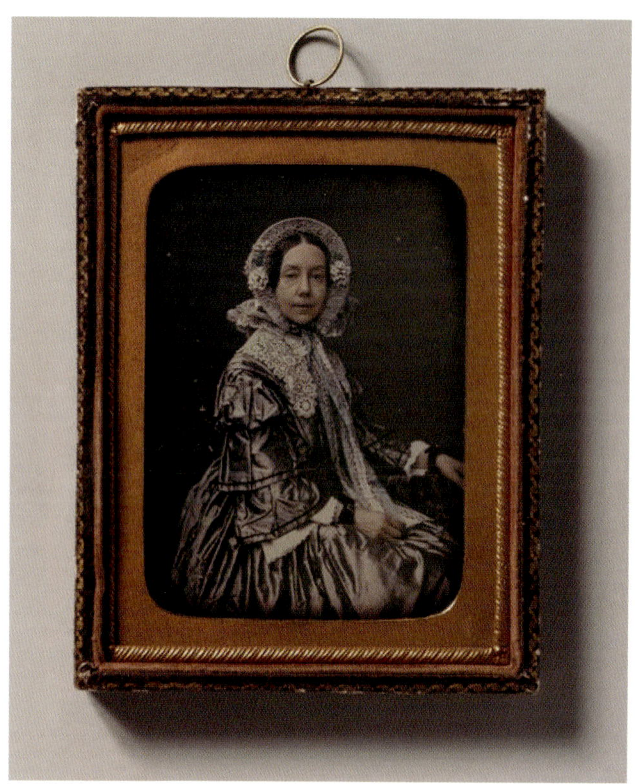

Most studios practiced an elaborate division of labor during this period, employing assistants to prepare the plates, operators to work the camera, and painters to complete the pictures after development. Only occasionally were these additional participants named, as a critic lamented following an 1857 exhibition in New York: "We regret that the artist has not been permitted to attach his name to each picture, that we might give the credit for whatever skill is evinced in its execution. . . . We cannot consider that the exhibitor should receive all the praise. It should be divided according to merit."[7] By "artist," this author meant the painter, not the camera operator or the owner of the photographic studio. As a result of this imbalance, the author concluded that hand-colored photographs should not be judged in the contest because their makers remained unnamed.

The perception of a division, or even a conflict, between the photographic and the painterly elements in pictures was common during the peak popularity of painted photographs. Many how-to authors prefaced their coloring instructions by disparaging painted photographs, claiming that they resorted to tinting photographs only to satisfy the whims of public taste. An article in *Humphrey's Journal* reasoned, "Colored photographs occupy an undeservedly questionable situation: the artist curls his lip at them, and the photographer regards them with a sneer. The one says they are no paintings, the other that they are no photographs; thus the art of photographic coloring, unrecognized by either, must seek consolation in the fact that it is embraced none the less eagerly by both."[8] *Humphrey's* even advised potential exhibitors against showing colored daguerreotypes at photographic competitions, maintaining, "There is not a skillful operator who will pronounce a colored impression equal to one with a fine, clear, brilliant toned impression untarnished by the brush."[9]

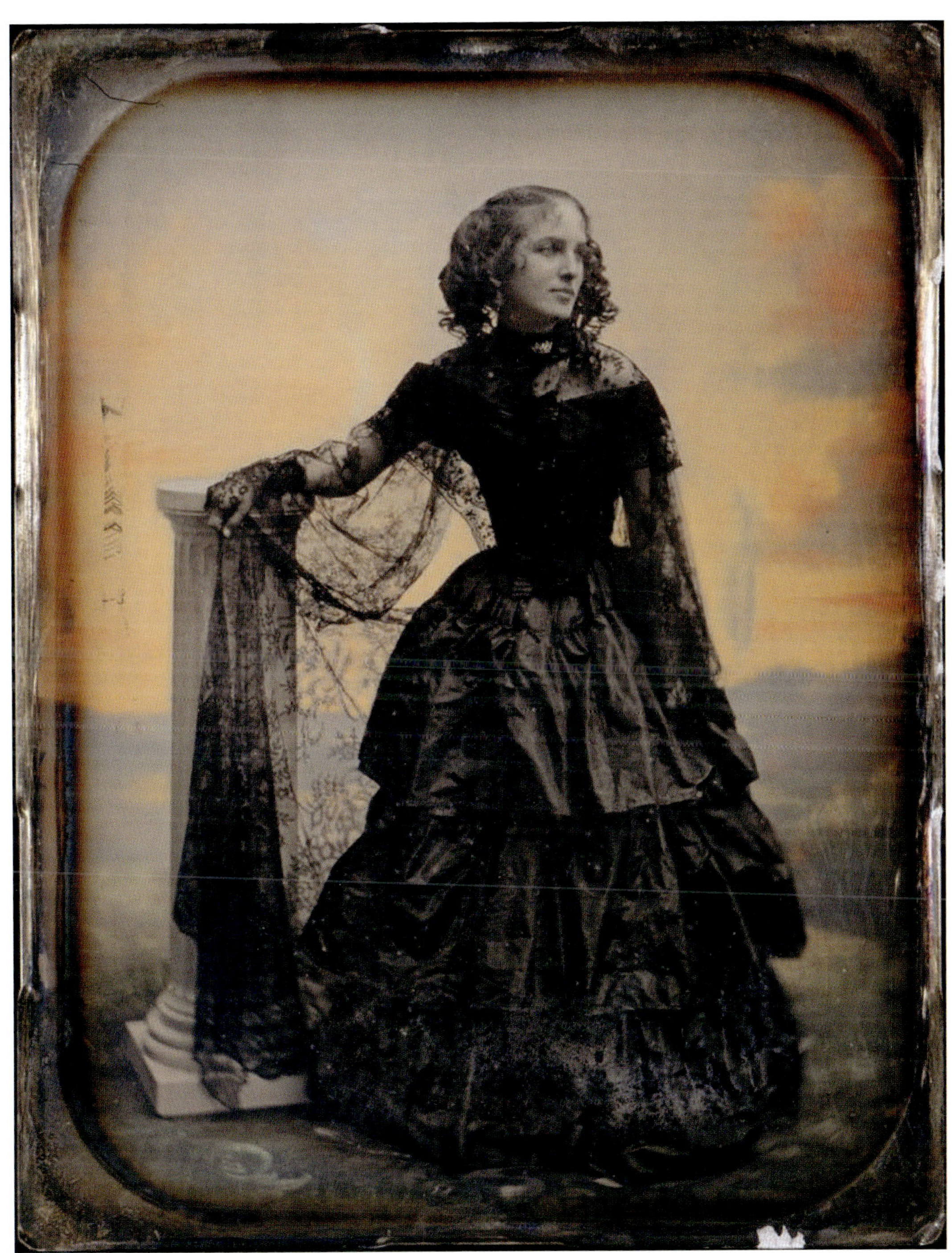

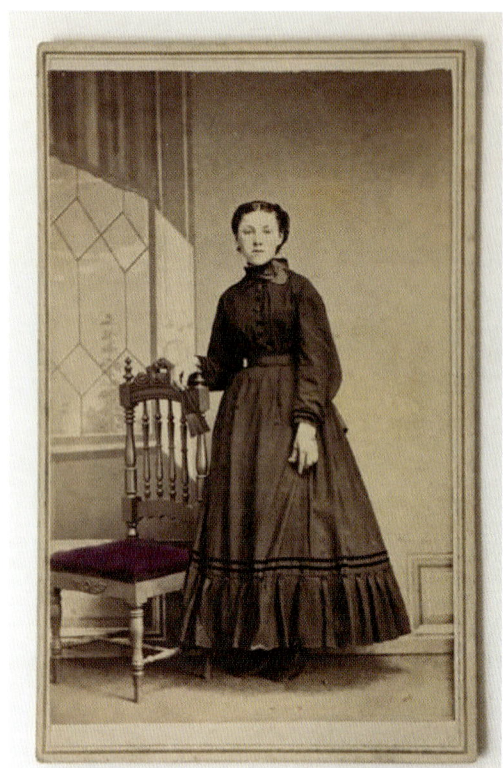

Among most photographers and critics, the chief criticism of hand painting was that it obscured the photographic nature of the image, sacrificing truth-value for artistic effects. Tasteful coloring was meant to be subtle; transparent hues should enhance, but not conceal, photographic detail. Henry Hunt Snelling, who would later become editor of the *Photographic Art Journal*, wrote in his own instructional manual, "I very much doubt the propriety of coloring the daguerreotypes, as I am of the opinion, that they are little, if any, improved by the operation, at least as it is now generally practiced."[10] Others accused less skilled studios of using hand painting to cover up photographic defects, such as poor focus or limited tonal range. A review of painted daguerreotypes at London's Great Exhibition argued, "The process of coloring photographs is, it appears to us, exceedingly detrimental to the art. Bad daguerreotypes may be painted up and passed off as tolerably successful photographs."[11]

Looking back over photography's first decade, Samuel Humphrey wrote in 1849, "Though in itself a small affair, it [the process of coloring] has created more popular clamor than all other improvements combined."[12] Coloring, tinting, painting, or "hand painting," as it came to be called after the introduction of mechanical and chemical methods of recording coloring, endures as one of the prime aesthetic markers of early photography. Despite purists' criticisms, hand coloring remained popular from the early 1840s through the craze for card portraiture that lasted into the 1880s. By 1894, however, *Wilson's Cyclopedic Photography* noted, "Formerly the demand for tinted and colored photographs was considerable; to-day, however, it can hardly be said to exist."[13] In its heyday, hand coloring was recognized with all the fervor of any fashionable trend, attracting attention and derision in almost equal measure for nearly half a century.

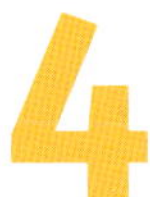

CRAYONS AND VIGNETTES

THE LONGEVITY OF MANY PHOTOGRAPHIC TRENDS makes them difficult to recognize as such. Today, for example, the difference between a portrait taken head-on and one taken from a three-quarters angle may seem negligible. In the nineteenth century, however, the three-quarters view portrait was widely understood as an aesthetic innovation in photography. Both angles are so common now that they hardly warrant a second thought. Other popular nineteenth-century visual conventions are more noticeable, though, because they remain distinct from contemporary practice. The vignette portrait, or "crayon" as it was called in the nineteenth century, is one of those orphaned trends.

The noun *crayon* refers to both drawings made on paper and drawing instruments composed of ground pigment and a binding agent. The description was first applied to photographs by a Boston-based photographer, John Adams Whipple, who in 1849 patented a method for making photographs that had the appearance of "portraits of faces taken in crayon."[1] To create his crayon effect, Whipple framed his sitter behind a large screen featuring an oval or circular cutout. During the exposure, he slightly, but continuously, moved the screen to create a soft effect around the subject. The center of the portrait remained sharply focused, but its edges were blurred by motion, like the partially rendered head-and-shoulders portrait sketches popular at the time. These photographic portraits were also later known as "vignettes," a description borrowed from the eighteenth-century term for decorative embellishments surrounding the edges of prints and manuscripts.

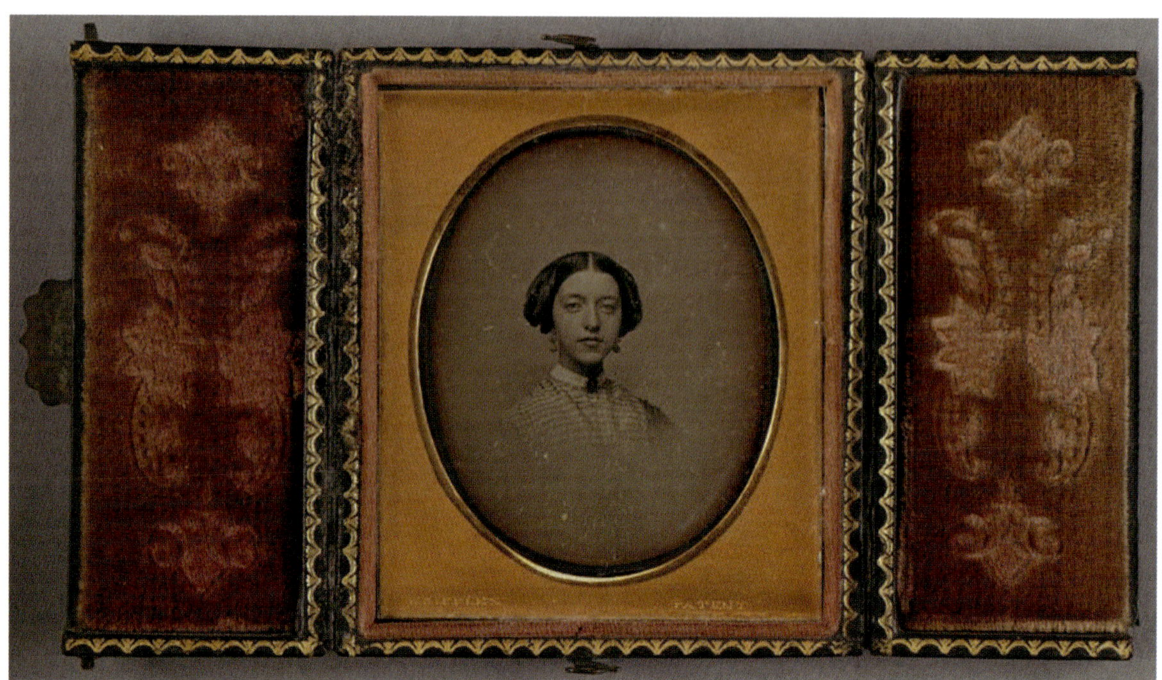

FIGURE 21. John Adams Whipple, "Vignetted Portrait of a Woman," ca. 1846–1850. Daguerreotype.

Source: J. Paul Getty Museum, Los Angeles. Digital image courtesy of the Getty's Open Content Program.

As the profession expanded, photographic journals were rife with calls to "elevate" the art and admonitions to the less skilled operators who were thought to be dragging down the public's estimation of photography. Aligning the young medium aesthetically with the history of art and handmade portraiture represented one strategy for improving the prestige of photography in the eyes of the public. By adapting the conventions of fine art, photographers like Whipple situated their productions within an established system of value.

Marcus Aurelius Root's appreciation of the crayon process underscores its artistic origin. He defined the style in his influential 1864 textbook of photography: "A vignette portrait, i.e. the head and shoulders in the crayon style, I generally find more pleasing to the true artist and connoisseur, than either full-length or half figures."[2] As in portrait painting or sketches, the unfinished effect was reserved for bust portraits, which themselves referenced the tradition of classical sculptural busts in marble or bronze.

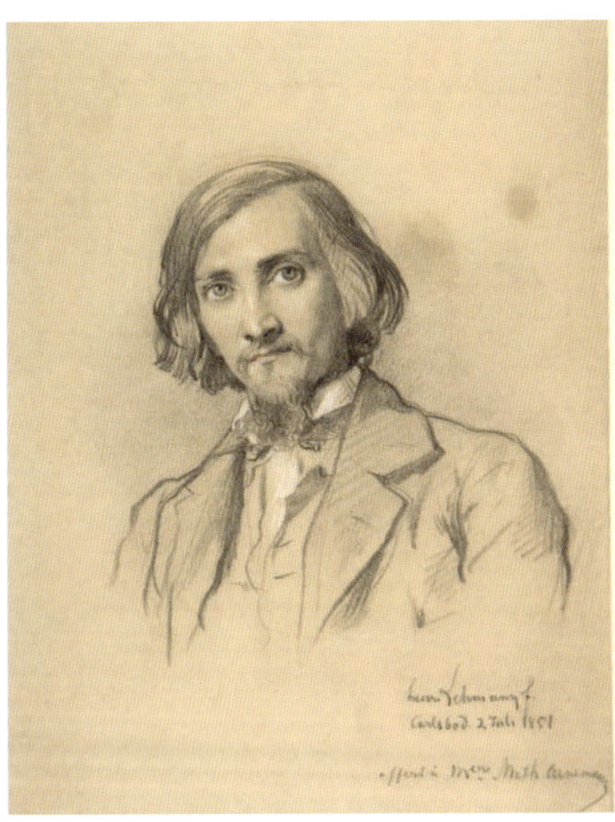

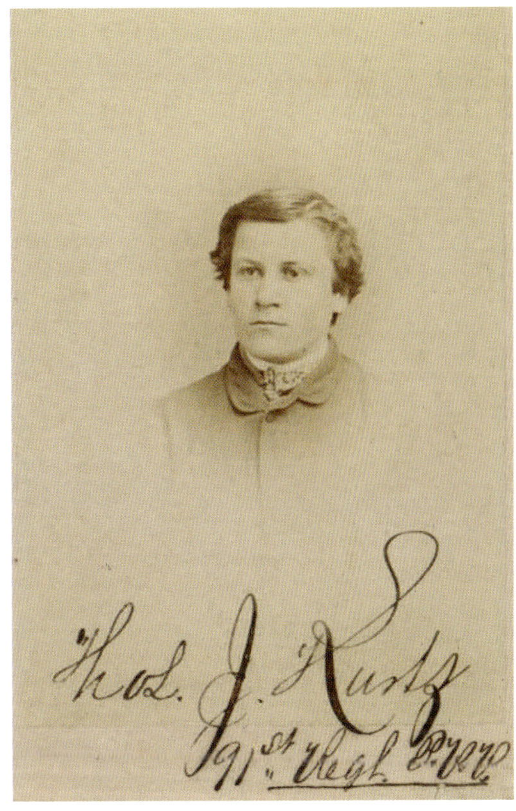

Crayons proved to be a remarkably lasting stylistic innovation in photography. They were popular throughout the nineteenth century, despite the many changes in the medium from the period of daguerreotypes to albumen prints. Several adaptations to the crayon process were developed, including one by the society photographer Oliver Sarony in 1869.[3] Sarony's "photo-crayons" called for printing the vignette photograph on tissue, then laying it on a sheet of chemically tinted drawing paper prepared with pencil hashmarks. The *Philadelphia Photographer* called it "a new and very effective style of portraiture, giving the appearance of very high artistic finish, by a cheap and easy process."[4] Sarony, the brother of the famous New York–based photographer Napoleon Sarony, claimed the finished portraits sold for twenty-five dollars each.[5] Nearly twenty years later, a critic in London was still praising Sarony's

FIGURE 22 (LEFT). Henri Lehmann, "Portrait of Anton Heinrich Springer," ca. 1850s. Graphite, with touches of red chalk, heightened with white, on tan paper. 10 11/16″ × 8 1/16″.

Source: Metropolitan Museum of Art, Gift of Alexander B. V. Johnson and Roberta J. M. Olson, 1992.

FIGURE 23 (RIGHT). Frederick Gutekunst, "Private Thomas J. Kurtz of Co. D, 91st Pennsylvania Infantry Regiment in Uniform," 1864. Albumen silver print. 4 1/3″ × 2 1/3″.

Source: Library of Congress, Prints and Photographs Division.

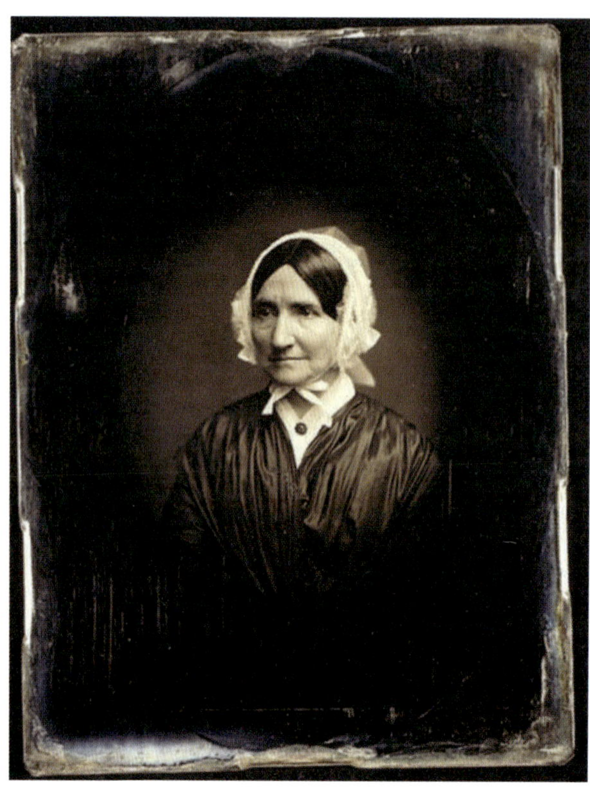

FIGURE 24. Albert Sands Southworth and Josiah Hawes, "Unidentified Woman," ca. 1850. Daguerreotype, 8 ½" × 6 ½".

Source: Metropolitan Museum of Art, Gift of I. N. Phelps Stokes, Edward S. Hawes, Alice Mary Hawes, and Marion Augusta Hawes, 1937.

photo-crayons for "exhibiting those free and 'dashy lines' and 'hatchings' so characteristic of the 'softening off' of artistic crayon drawings."[6] Crayons remained popular throughout the century, attracting none of the derision that accompanied many other popular styles in their later years.

Although Whipple's original patent recommended the use of light backgrounds and screens, dark crayons, which show the subject engulfed in shadow, were also produced. This effect would have been familiar to nineteenth-century photographers as the result of using a lens too small to adequately cover the plate, leaving unexposed corners that appeared dark in the positive image. Like many other trends, this visible shortcoming returned as an aesthetic effect, intentionally produced for artistic ends. [See also Chapter 50, "Digital Filters."] Today, the term *vignetting* refers primarily to these darkened corners in photographs, concentrating on the medium-specific failure rather than its aesthetic adaptation by Whipple or Sarony in their once-popular light-colored crayon portraits.

5

INTENSIFYING NEGATIVES

IN THE UNITED STATES, the extraordinary detail of the daguerreotype held the public's attention through the 1840s. As demand for photographs increased, however, the daguerreotype's limitations became more pronounced. The inability to create multiple prints from the opaque metal plate meant that photographers who wished to make copies had to rephotograph existing daguerreotypes. Although making positive prints from negative images had been possible since William Henry Fox Talbot's announcement of the paired calotype negative and salted paper print process in 1841, his method gained little traction in the United States. Calotype negatives were far less detailed than Daguerre's process because silver salts soaked into the paper negative, making rough paper fibers visible in the final print, unlike the smooth image surface of the silver-coated daguerreotype plate.

The invention of albumen printing by Louis Désiré Blanquart-Evrard broadened the horizon of possibility in the 1850s. By suspending silver halide crystals in a thin layer of egg white on paper, the albumen process separated the reactive silver from the paper support to create an even and unblemished image surface. In 1851, the invention of the wet collodion negative process (so named because it had to be exposed while the chemicals were still wet) enabled photographers to make finely detailed negatives on glass. In combination, the wet collodion negative and the albumen print radically transformed both the look and the reach of nineteenth-century photography.

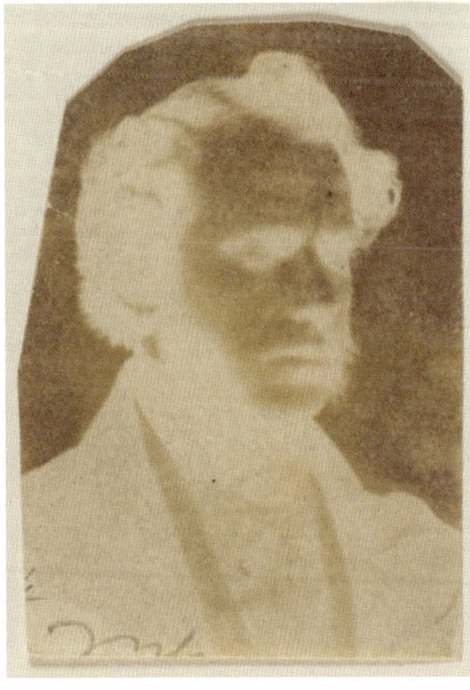

FIGURE 25. William Henry Fox Talbot, "Untitled [Nicolaas Henneman]," ca. 1841. Paper negative, 2 5/8" × 1 13/16".

Source: J. Paul Getty Museum, Los Angeles. Digital image courtesy of the Getty's Open Content Program.

40

The ability to reproduce large numbers of prints from a single negative (Blanquart-Evrard claimed he could produce "two or three hundred prints from the same negative the same day in rainy weather") enabled the production of books illustrated with tipped-in photographs and supported the growing global demand for celebrity portraits.[1] Albumen prints were mounted on cardstock, enabling the cartes-de-visite trend of the mid-1850s and the subsequent cabinet card and stereographic card fads of the 1860s through 1880s.

Albumen prints from wet collodion negatives were valued for their detail and improved tonal range. Initially, however, albumen tended to

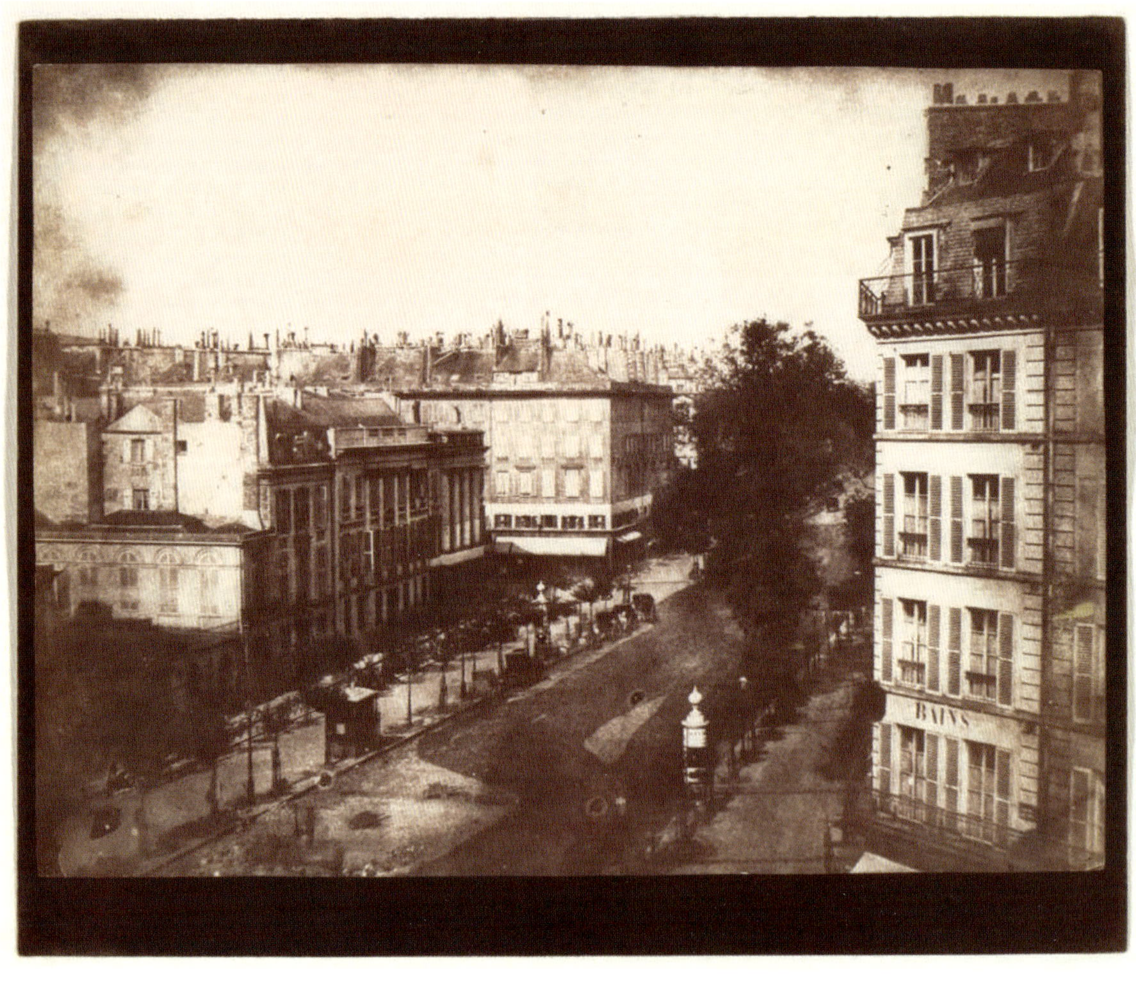

FIGURE 26. William Henry Fox Talbot, "View of the Boulevards of Paris," 1843. Salted paper print from paper negative, 6 5/16″ × 8 1/2″ (image).

Source: Metropolitan Museum of Art, Bequest of Maurice B. Sendak, 2012.

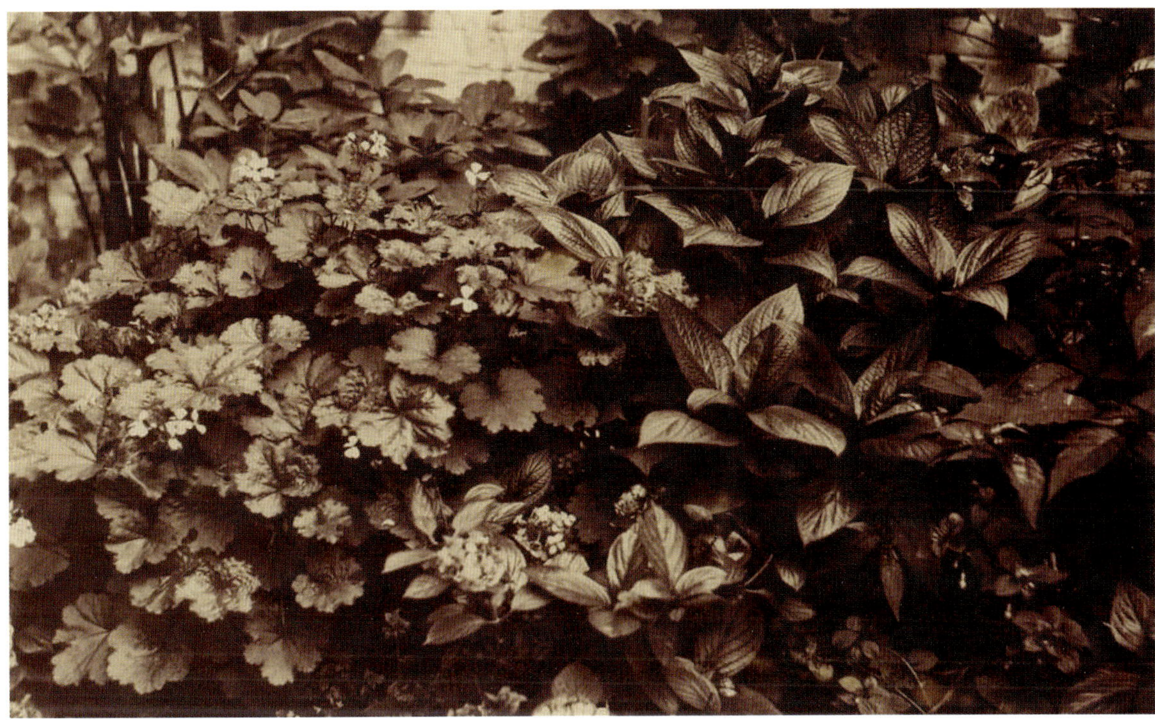

 Louis Désiré Blanquart-Evrard, "Flowers and Leaves," ca. 1853. Albumen silver print, 4 5/8″ × 7 1/2″.

Source: J. Paul Getty Museum, Los Angeles.

produce a faint image, which compared poorly with the vigorous contrasts of the daguerreotype. Collodion negatives had to be quite thick (the silver sufficiently activated by exposure to light) in order to create a more robust print, which included detail in both shadows and highlights. Before the standardization of chemicals, mass-produced plates, and printing paper made it possible to accurately predict exposures, operators often ended up with imperfect negatives. Negatives that received too little light during the exposure period were described as "thin." When printed, these negative plates would render an overly dark print because they allowed too much light to pass through to the printing paper. "Intensifying" the negative by washing it with pyrogallic acid or a sulfuric solution before printing was an easy way to improve the negative in the darkroom rather than reshooting.

By the early 1870s, this penchant for intensified negatives had attracted vocal opponents. Intensified negatives lacked detail in the highlights and shadow areas, making for prints that were just "masses of black and white," in the words of John Coates Browne, an amateur photographer and founder of the Photographic Society of Philadelphia.[2] [See also Chapter 38, "Sepia."] He maintained that "the intensifying of negatives is too often used to cover up such defects as dirty plates, under-exposure, over-worked chemicals, etc, but almost always at the sacrifice of every particle of half-tone which is the charm of all pictures."[3] Above all, Browne argued, intensifying was a lazy or uneducated photographer's last resort, and its widespread use signaled a threat to the photographic industry. He called it "a very dangerous evil, well calculated to make [photographers] careless of their work and reputation."[4]

Others opposed intensification because it made later work on pictures more difficult. The high contrast of the intensified negative posed a unique challenge for retouching or coloring artists. Looking back on the early days of albumen printing in 1870, one writer recalled, "We ignorantly thought a negative must be as opaque as a brick, to print at all on albumen."[5] The author of an important guide to hand painting, George B. Ayres, wrote, "Happily the days of 'intense' negatives—the whites too white, and the blacks too black—have nearly ended, and given place to a desire for thinner negatives intended to be printed in the shade; by which the colorist is afforded the presence and advantage of a succession of *intermediate shades* which the former order of things knew not."[6] For a painter, not only was it difficult to add color to the opaque shadow areas, but the overly bright highlights of prints made from intensified negatives also demanded that painters add in missing details. Ayres, like Browne, argued that the half-tones of the photograph "characterize the original," a point of view that would be taken up again by modernist photographers such as Edward Weston in the late 1920s.[7] Emerging in the debate over intensification is the desire for a specifically photographic style; not only should these pictures be flattering likenesses, but they must also be undeniably photographic ones.

6

CLOUDY SKIES

THE SUBJECTS OF EARLY PHOTOGRAPHS lived all their days under cloudless skies. Neither daguerreotypes nor Talbot's paper negative process could easily capture drifting clouds. One writer reflected on the daguerreotype era, noting that "the sky was represented by a dull, uniform tint of a slaty [sic] blue color, without perspective or depth, and the complete want of every living creature gave the pictures a deserted and mournful appearance."[1] Initially it was assumed that representing clouds in photographs was impossible, and some operators took to painting them in on the back of paper negatives before printing. With improvement in lenses and the invention of the collodion process, the fleecy sky seemed to be within reach by the 1850s. Collodion's color sensitivity was limited to blue light, though, so balancing the exposure for the blue sky against the lengthier one required for the green landscape remained a challenge. During this period, instructional manuals and photographic journals regularly printed recommendations for how to achieve cloud effects, "whether by natural means or dodges," as one photographer put it.[2]

Not only were photographers frustrated by the lack of clouds, which could make a stormy seascape roil beneath a paradoxically empty sky, but they also despaired of what remained in place of the clouds. When the sky was overexposed, the thin negative revealed the blotchy and streaky evidence of chemical pours on the plate. This defect was considered so grave as to completely ruin a photograph. One critic argued that such "streaks . . . often spoil fine pictures and oblige us to throw them aside."[3] Others noted that the clear negative revealed a "heavy, dingy, blotty proof"[4] or complained that the sky appeared "dirty."[5]

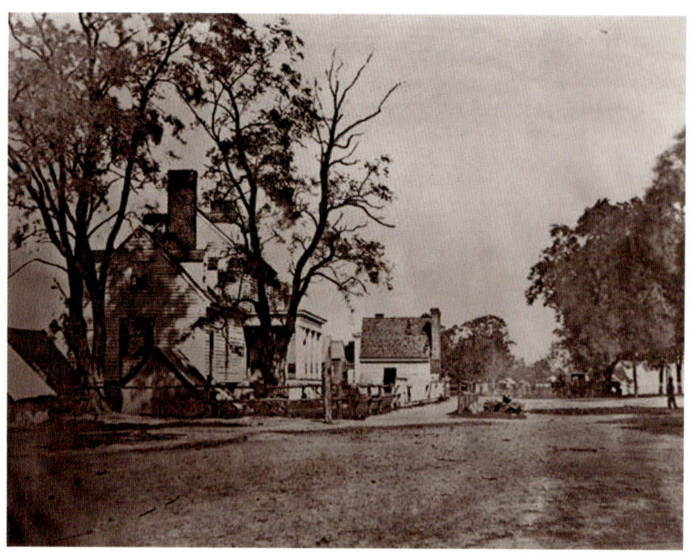

 Andrew Joseph Russell, "Headquarters of Capt. H. B. Blood, A.Q.M., at City Point, Virginia," 1861–1865. Albumen silver print, 5 1/16″ × 7 7/16″.

Source: Metropolitan Museum of Art, Harris Brisbane Dick Fund, 1933.

The first answer to these woes called for the photographer to simply paint over the offending part of the negative or black it out with india ink, so that no detail at all appeared in the positive print. This advice was popular well into the 1880s, when an article for the burgeoning class of amateur photographers suggested, "The photographer should never rest satisfied with smutty dull skies, trusting to his steady hand to block them out of the negative with opaque."[6] The technique was easily accomplished when the horizon was regular, but the introduction of any protruding bits, especially foliage, complicated the task significantly.

A still more involved solution to the absence of clouds required that the photographer make two negatives, exposing one for the landscape and the other for the sky, then combine the pair in printing. Some made cloud studies at different sites, should clouds in the original view prove unphotogenic. Occasionally writers warned that "there will always be an extreme difficulty in harmonizing these clouds with a view to which they do not belong," but combination printing, as it was called, was widely employed for landscapes throughout the nineteenth century.[7] The French photographer Gustave Le Gray was celebrated internationally for his dramatic seascapes, which featured large cloud masses, often created through combination printing (see Figure 30).

Even after the 1860s, when it became more feasible to arrest the movement of clouds with improved photographic methods, the technique of combination printing remained popular. A prominent British photographer complained that combination printing was inartistic, claiming "it is more legitimate to wait till a suitable cloud comes on the scene than to select a suitable cloud from a box and print it in."[8] An enthusiastic amateur responded in print, "Printing in clouds from a separate negative is, to my thinking, when properly done, a very artistic improvement, and I fail to see why any exception should be taken to it.

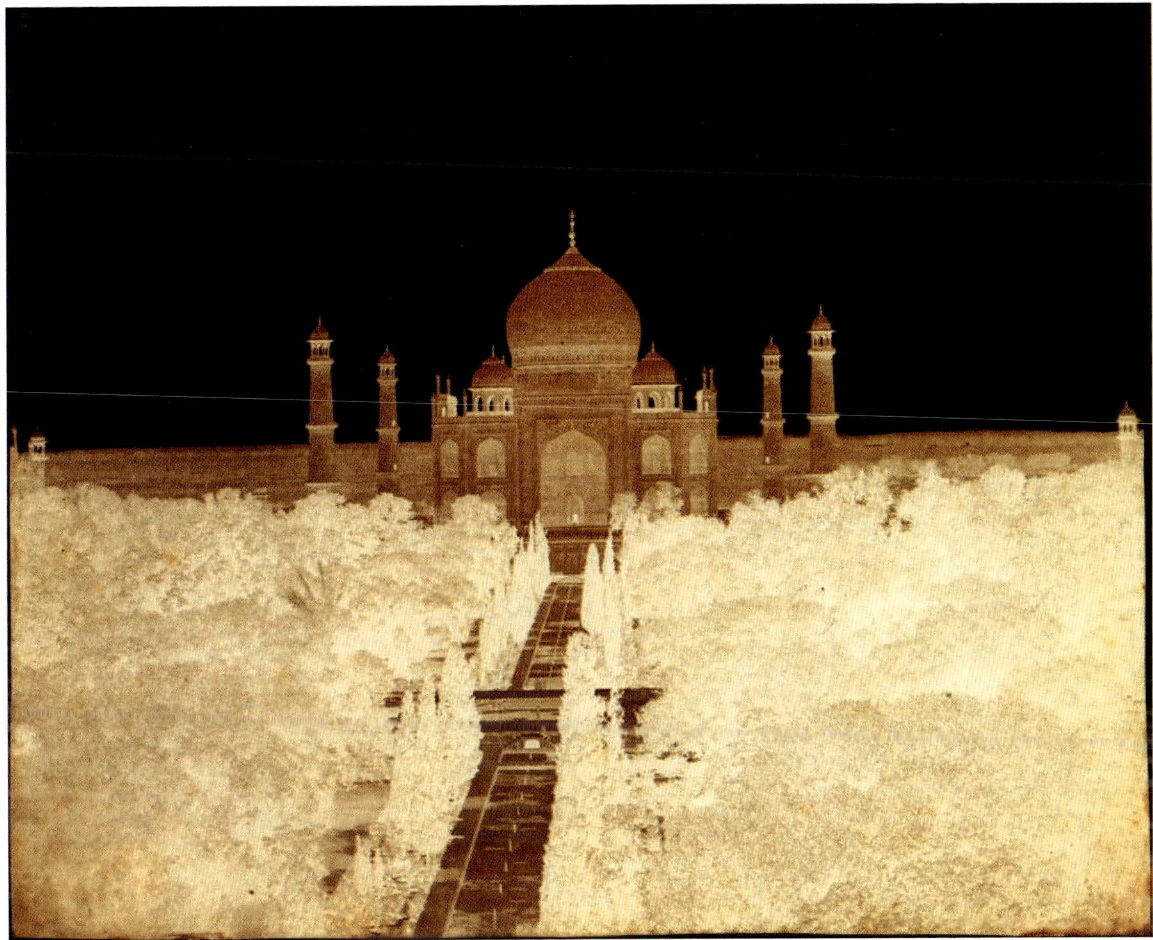

Skies utterly inappropriate may be added, and frequently are, but that is no argument against their use in a proper manner."[9] Indeed, photographers who managed to include such atmosphere in their prints were widely admired, regardless of how the effects were attained. Reporting from the 1873 international exhibition in Vienna, the critic Hermann Vogel praised a group of Yosemite photographs, noting "[Eadweard] Muybridge, above all others, is distinguished by superb cloud effects, which, in these large pictures, look extraordinary fine."[10] (See Figure 31.)

Apart from picking clouds out of a box, photographers could also mask the sky during exposure to achieve the proper balance between light and dark areas of the composition. By the mid-1880s, this was

FIGURE 29. John Murray, "Taj Mahal and Gardens," ca. 1855. Waxed paper negative, 5 3/16″ × 8 9/16″.

Source: Metropolitan Museum of Art, Rubel Collection, Purchase, Anonymous Gift and Cynthia Hazen Polsky Gift, 1997.

46

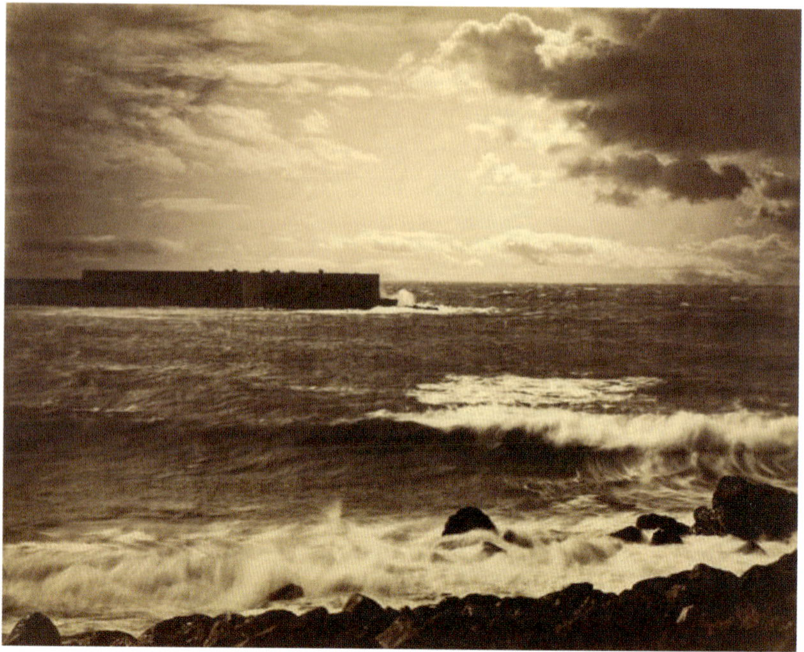

FIGURE 30. Gustave Le Gray, "The Great Wave, Sète," ca. 1857. Albumen silver print, 13 ½″ × 16 ½″.

Source: J. Paul Getty Museum, Los Angeles. Digital image courtesy of the Getty's Open Content Program.

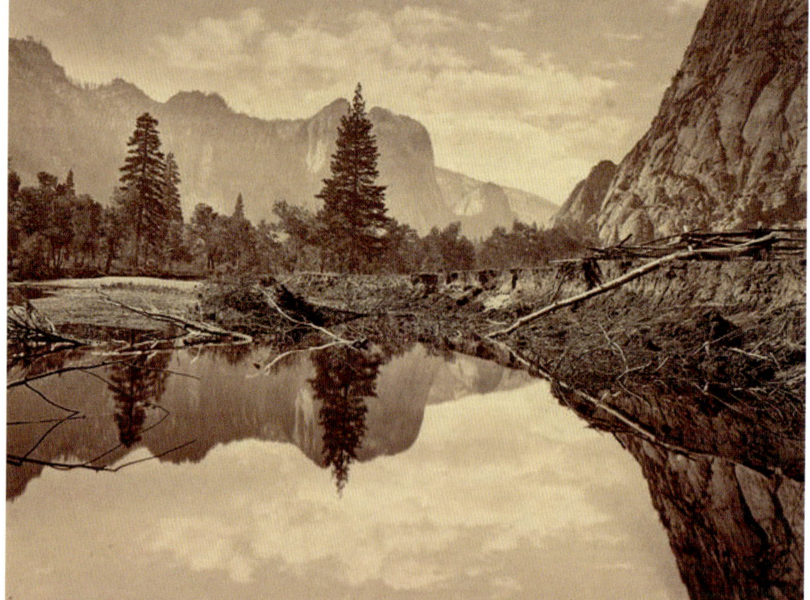

FIGURE 31. Thomas Houseworth & Company, Eadweard Muybridge (or Carleton Watkins or C. L. Weed), "Looking Down Yosemite Valley," ca. 1872. Albumen silver print, 15 ⅝″ × 20 ⅜″.

Source: J. Paul Getty Museum, Los Angeles. Digital image courtesy of the Getty's Open Content Program.

among the leading recommendations for amateurs doing landscape work: "Most operators employ the flap in front hinged from the top of the lens, which, by shading the sky, prevents it from being over-timed. Care must be taken to keep the flap in gentle motion, otherwise a rigid, distinct line will be formed on the plate."[11]

Balancing the exposure of a bright sky against the landscape remains a challenge today, as humans perceive a much wider dynamic range than even the best digital cameras. Graduated filters, which reduce the amount of light entering the top half of the lens and transition smoothly to a clear or neutral lower half, have been in use since the early twentieth century and are still popular among contemporary landscape photographers who wish to record the clouds as they are rather than picking them out a box (or digital file) later. [See also Chapter 48, "Ruin Porn," and Chapter 50, "Digital Filters."]

7

SOLAR ENLARGING

ANNOUNCING THE END OF PAINTING was one of the most popular modes of highlighting photography's ascendance in the nineteenth century. In fact, while photography did excel in the representation of detail and perspective, it also fell short of the expectations established by painted portraits in many ways. The surfeit of detail and lack of color in early photographs were both compensated for by the painter's brush. Major photo studios employed a bevy of artists to retouch and color portraits with pastel, oil, or watercolor.

Scale was another considerable, and seemingly irreconcilable, difference between the two media. Until the early twentieth century, the overwhelming majority of photographic prints were contact prints made outdoors; negatives were laid on top of printing paper and held in place with wooden print frames while they were exposed to sunlight. [See also Chapter 35, "Full-Frame Prints," and Chapter 32, "Contact Sheets."] In an 1846 photograph from William Henry Fox Talbot's workshop, more than a dozen print frames are shown arranged on tiered racks outdoors. The technique generated a positive print identical in size to the original negative. These sizes were limited by camera, lens, and plate sizes and rarely exceeded 8 ½" × 6 ½" before the 1860s. Photographs may have produced uncannily faithful likenesses, but their diminutive proportions precluded them from a real rivalry with painted portraits.

The demand for larger photographic portraits animated the efforts of several early studio owners. Following improvements in lenses and the creation of more sensitive emulsions, photographers in the 1850s began producing life-size pictures to compete with painted portraits. Initially

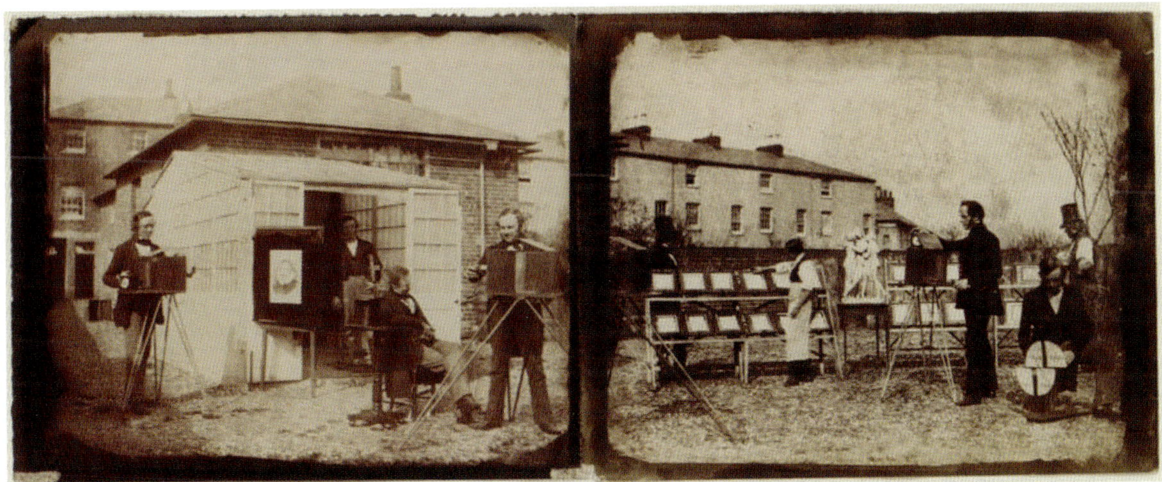

FIGURE 32. William Henry Fox Talbot and Nicolaas Henneman, "The Reading Establishment," 1846. Salted paper prints from paper negatives. 7 13/16″ × 19 5/16″ (overall sheet).

Source. Metropolitan Museum of Art, Gilman Collection, Gift of the Howard Gilman Foundation, 2005

popularized in France, where they were made with enormous cameras,[1] the earliest large-scale portraits from the United States date to 1855. These were typically enlargements, made by projecting the original negative using a copy lens onto printing paper. Some of the resulting images were truly enormous: as large as 8′ × 6′, according to the *Photographic and Fine Art Journal*, and printed on canvas.[2] The *Journal* singled out the New York studio of Murray and Jacob, claiming that they could "produce life size (or indeed any size) photographs on canvas exactly resembling the finest description of oil painting, equally durable and unperishable, with the advantage however, that these new pictures are truer likenesses than the others *can* be, and have a more life like expression."[3] *Humphrey's Journal* marveled at the prices commanded by such portraits but cautioned that their quality had more to do with the skill of the artists who colored the print rather than any inherent talent of the photographer. This criticism suggests that the life-size portraits (few of which still exist) were far more elaborately worked in paint than the subtle colorization characteristic of daguerreotypes.

In 1857, an instrument became available that consolidated operators' interest in this newly fashionable type of picture. The Baltimore-based painter-turned-photographer David A. Woodward patented a device he called the "solar camera," which resembled a camera obscura with an external mirror attachment. Positioned in a window, as is visible in this

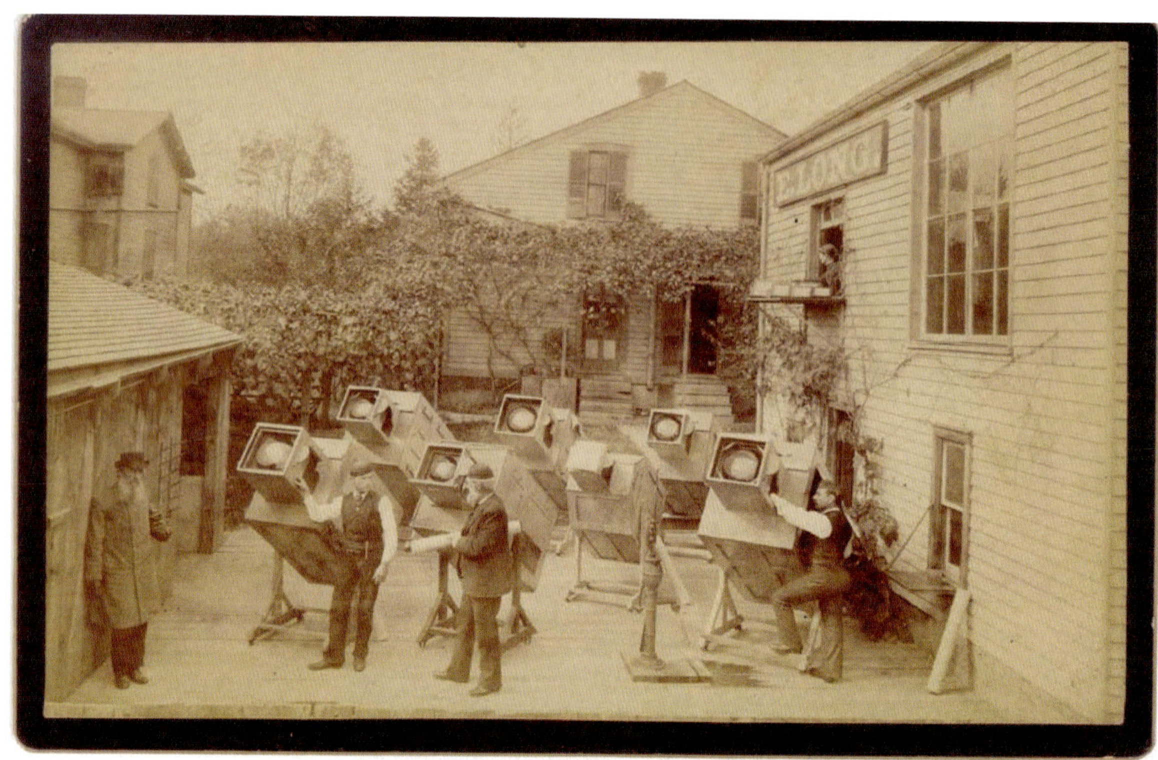

FIGURE 33. D. A. Woodward, "Woodward Improved Enlarger," n.d. Albumen print.

Source: Courtesy of Luminous-Lint.

detail from an undated photograph (see Figure 34), the solar camera's mirror directed the sun's light into a condenser lens. This light passed through a photographic negative mounted inside the box, projecting the image onto prepared paper or canvas, which was affixed to an easel in the darkened room.

Although the solar camera united all of the necessary optical equipment, enlarging remained a difficult and time-consuming process. Prints made on sunny days required exposure times as long as six hours for a life-sized bust; in cloudy weather, exposures of one to two days were required.[4] To speed things up, photographers typically developed out the printing paper in a chemical bath rather than using albumen printing-out paper on which the image appeared only by light of the sun.

Although the enlarger solved the problem of housing life-size negative plates in the camera, the process introduced its own challenges.

Woodward's model required that photographers manipulate the mirror during exposure to ensure that light reached the condenser evenly. Improvements to the solar camera in the 1860s included a heliostat to track the movement of the sun without the operator's intervention. Furthermore, the large scale of solar enlargements revealed deficiencies in everything from the silvering of the mirror to the uneven glass of the negative. One photographer suggested that only a negative in which, "the pupil of the eye can be sharply distinguished, in which the eyebrows are well defined, the hair distinctly marked out . . . is capable of producing a magnificent enlarged print."[5] As John Towler's instructional manual explained, "In order that the negative be sharp and well-defined to the very edge, and from top to toe, spare no expense, no trouble in securing a reliable lens. With this, and a moderate share of intelligence, an operator may run his career without impediment to success; whilst his neighbors, with poor lenses, whatever their amount of education, will roll down the hill to perdition."[6]

The desire for high-quality, large-scale photographs was only very partially satisfied by solar enlarging, but Woodward's device pointed at least to a new possibility. The added cost of developing out prints, in addition to the considerable time required for enlarging, made the practice impractical until the early twentieth century when more powerful electric light enlargers and faster emulsions could produce enlarged prints in a matter of minutes rather than days.

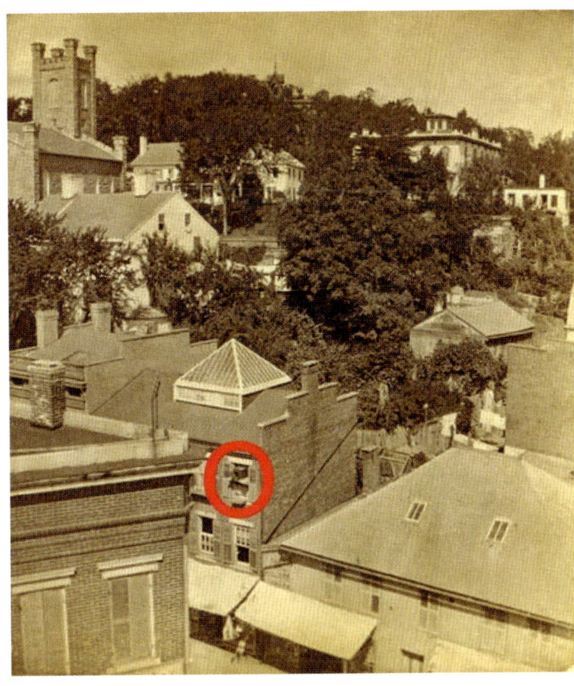

FIGURE 34. Photographer unknown, "Schtucket, Showing a Solar Enlarger," n.d. Albumen stereoview (half, detail, altered digitally).

Source: Courtesy of the National Gallery of Canada and the Archive of Modern Conflict.

PART II

1861–1900

Photography in the United States experienced enormous growth in the second half of the nineteenth century as technical innovations made the process more reliable and less expensive. At the beginning of this period, the Civil War created an unparalleled demand for portraits among all social classes. Portraits were made by traveling photographers in military encampments, rural towns, and urban centers. Styles of portraiture often followed painted precedents, but aesthetics also emerged that reflected the medium's new, more accessible status. Similarly, the professional ranks of photographers expanded beyond the educated experimenters initially involved in photography to include blacksmiths and tinkers, as well as itinerant portrait painters. The photographic press was booming during this period as well, with popular periodicals including the *Philadelphia Photographer* and *Wilson's Photographic Magazine* publishing reports of current trends in both the domestic and international markets. Subscribers around the country adopted these styles in their own practices and mailed in samples of their best work for review and possible publication.

Near the end of the nineteenth century, the medium experienced another sea change: the invention of the Kodak camera and the beginning of the photo-finishing industry. No longer did photographers have to master the chemical details associated with developing and printing their own images. Kodak included the cost of processing in the purchase price of film, transforming photography from a specialist activity into a leisure pursuit accessible to anyone.

8

FOREGROUND INTEREST

PHOTOGRAPHERS INCREASINGLY took their craft outdoors in the 1860s as more portable cameras and prepared plates unchained the apparatus from the studio. Ease of operation, however, did not guarantee artistic success. By the middle of the decade, disparaging articles appeared regularly in the American photographic press, reproaching photographers for their feckless work in the landscape.[1] While some critics allowed that at least the "early days of violent contrast—black, intense shadows, and . . . white patch for a sky"—had finally been "overcome," many lamented the chasm between American work and the views made by European photographers, particularly in Germany, Switzerland, and France.[2] Edward L. Wilson, the publisher and editor of the *Philadelphia Photographer*, wrote in dismay in 1869 of the competitions that his publication sponsored: "We are sorry to say that while there are many competitors, the average work is not good. Landscape work is particularly bad, and we hope to see great improvement in that branch during the coming year."[3] American landscape photographers were widely accused of concentrating wholly on producing a "clear, sharp, vigorous negative," which precluded any feeling of drama or depth.[4] [See also Chapter 1, "The American Process."]

Following these dismal attempts, photography handbooks and editorials began recommending to landscape photographers that they work in the low-angle light of evening or early morning. [See also Chapter 40, "Golden Hour."] They should concentrate less on attaining a perfect exposure than on one that conveys a sense of atmosphere. One popular manual advised, "The photographer cannot be too strongly enjoined not, in order to obtain a microscopic sharpness, to sacrifice the general character and expression of his view."[5] Considering the frequency with which these criticisms appeared in the 1860s, photographers must have found it difficult to adapt to the new standards after two decades of being judged chiefly according to the sharpness and clarity of their images. Making a moody image, beset by haze and long shadows, would have seemed antithetical to the standards that photography had only just achieved.

One commentator cheekily described the photographer's typical procedure in the field: "You took your photograph, packed up your apparatus, and was away in a quarter of an hour; hence you have not got the best view, and though it may be so beautifully sharp, clean, and well exposed, the photograph is still uncommonly like that taken last year by Smith, or the year before by Brown."[6] These imaginary landscape photographers Smith and Brown, the ingenuous producers of identical views, were blessed with some technical assistance in the form of the Dallmeyer Rapid Rectilinear Lens, patented in 1866. Previously, photographers had only three types of lenses from which to choose, and none that combined a wide angle of view with a small enough aperture to keep multiple planes of a landscape in focus without distortion. The Rapid Rectilinear featured a 24 degree angle of view with an aperture of f/6 or f/8 and covered a 7" × 4 ½" plate, which provided an ideal horizontal landscape view.[7]

Beyond the mechanical concerns, how-to manuals throughout this period focused on the importance of choosing an appropriate time of day and using the angle of the light to draw out depth and layers in the landscape. Emphatic, if vague, appeals to exercise the aesthetic sense by studying the work of great painters and established photographers were also regular features of the advice piled on would-be landscape photographers in the 1860s and 1870s. One publication even released a portfolio meant for study. The editor wrote,

> We have taken occasion frequently of late years to bring to the minds of American photographers the fact, that in the matter of landscape photography they were far behind their neighbors beyond the Atlantic. This did not set well on some of our more ambitious friends in this line, and finally they began to complain, saying, "Well, Mr. Editor, if

you know what better work than ours exists abroad, why do you not do as you did with portraiture, ie, import for us some of these fine landscapes, that we may procure them, and study them."[8]

Though this dialogue was certainly crafted to pique interest in the album of prints for sale by the magazine, the chorus of frustrated photographers is not hard to imagine, given the industry's relentless condemnation of their work. Still, simple study of the "good qualities" of the portfolio, made by the Scottish photographer George Washington Wilson, must have left scores of photographers curious about how best to depict subjects other than the "old ruins, marine, river, lake, architectural, pictorial, interiors, mountains, and so on" represented in the album.[9]

M. Carey Lea's 1868 *Manual of Photography* also attempted to provide nineteenth-century American practitioners with a suite of rules for landscape photography. The extensive list was beset by qualifiers:

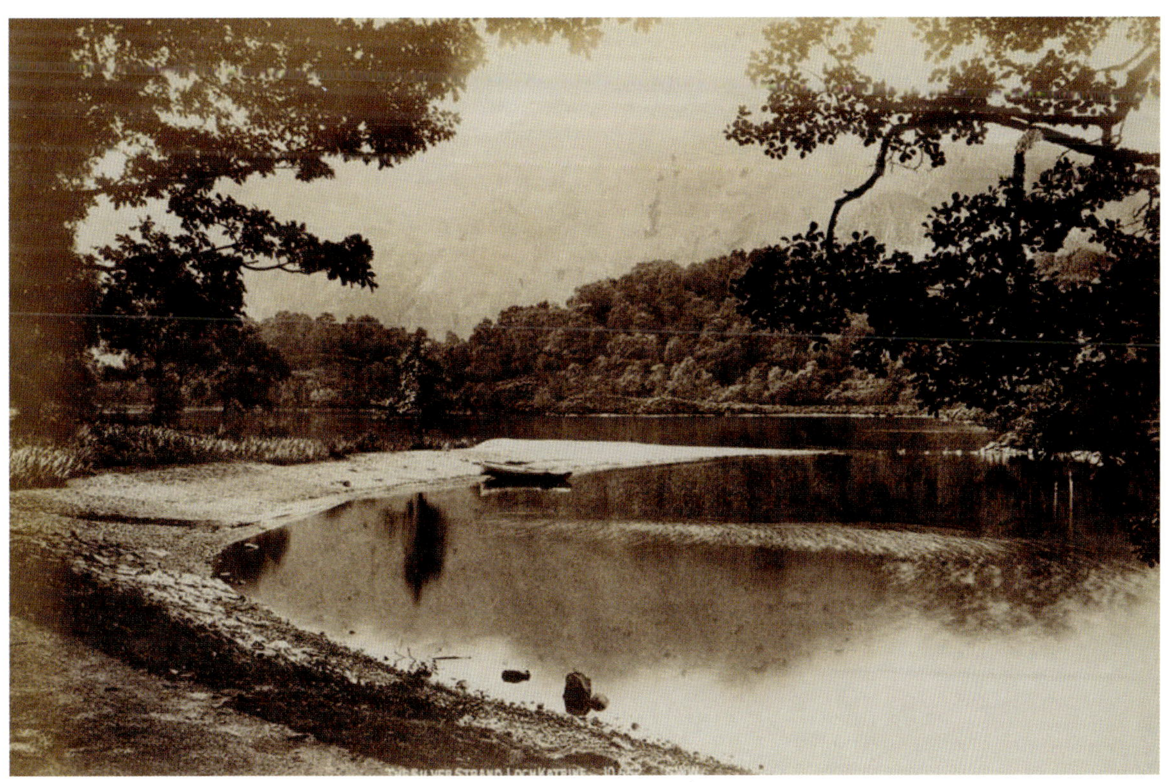

FIGURE 35. George Washington Wilson, "The Silver Strand, Loch Katrine," n.d. Albumen print, 10 cm × 15.5 cm.

Source: National Galleries of Scotland.

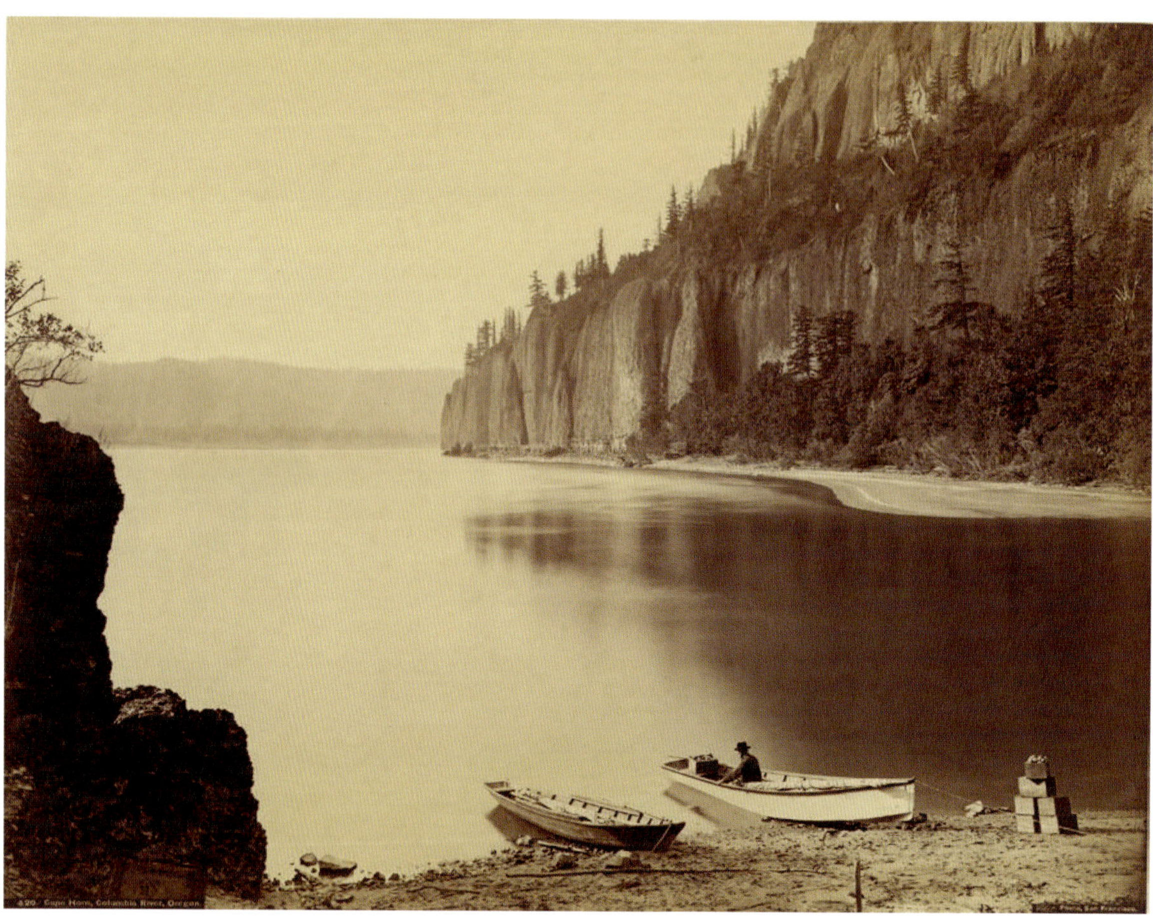

"Cultivated taste has learned that the representation of a landscape gives a completely satisfying effect to the mind most easily by complying with certain general conditions which have been reduced to fixed rules. Too slavish a compliance with these leads directly to mannerism and sameness, but some acquaintance with them cannot but be of the highest use to every intelligent photographer."[10] In other words, learn the rules and then break them judiciously. Lea summarized several compositional principles, describing how to create balance and contrast, look for repetition in shapes, and use directional lines to guide the eye. His relatively minor suggestion that photographers seek out an interesting, varied foreground would become a central tenet of photography manuals, and

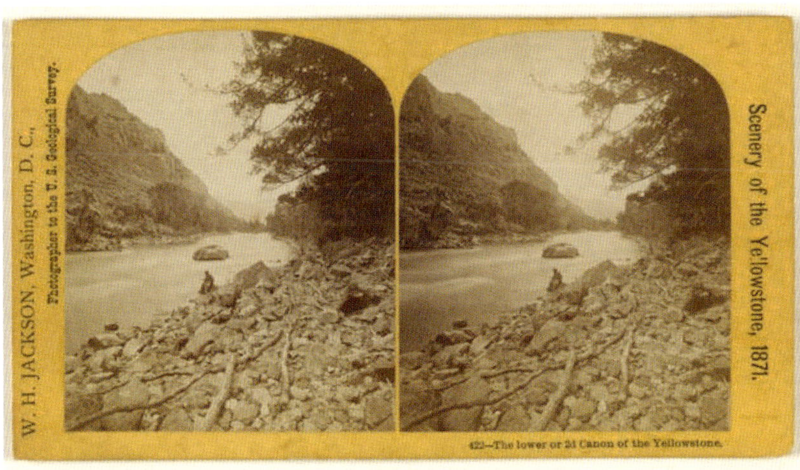

FIGURE 37. William Henry Jackson, "The Lower or 2nd Canon of the Yellowstone," 1871, albumen silver print.

Source: J. Paul Getty Museum, Los Angeles. Digital image courtesy of the Getty's Open Content Program.

its application can be seen in work by leading photographers of the nineteenth century, including Carleton Watkins and William Henry Jackson, as well as in countless amateur exhibitions and family albums. Lea wrote, "The foreground should be diversified. A level unbroken foreground of grass or meadow cannot be expected to give a good effect. It weakens the effect of the distance, and deprives the picture of much of the character that it ought to possess."[11] Instead, as one amateur guide recommended, "Bushes and vines, rocks, stones, logs, often have elements of attraction that reveal themselves only by observation and cultivation. An artificial arrangement of such objects in the foreground of a photograph lends to it an inexpressible charm."[12] Especially in stereoscopic views, foreground interest was considered essential to creating the illusion of depth, a trend that has left nineteenth-century riverbanks forever littered with logs and seashores never lacking rowboats or artfully arranged driftwood to pull viewers into the atmospheric depths of the picture.

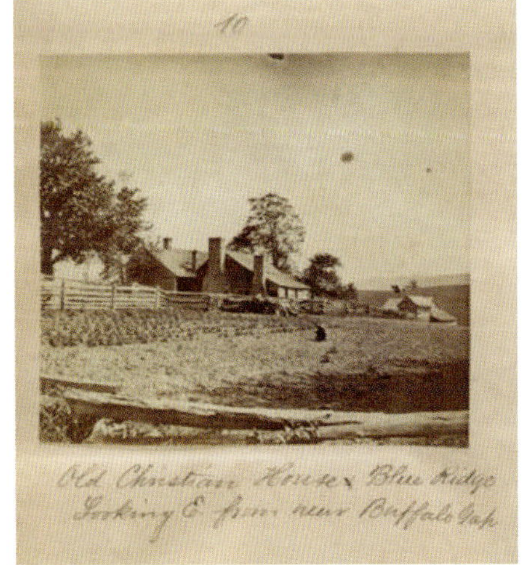

FIGURE 38. Jedediah Hotchkiss, "Old Christian House, Blue Ridge Looking E. from Near Buffalo Gap," 1871. Albumen print, 1872.

Source: Library of Congress Prints and Photographs Division.

9

STEREOSCOPIC DEPTH

WHEN QUEEN VICTORIA toured London's Great Exhibition in 1851 and pronounced her fascination with stereoscopic photographs, she began a fad that would sweep England and France and eventually cross the Atlantic to the United States. Stereoscopes combine two images taken from slightly different perspectives, which mimic the average distance between human eyes. By presenting these similar pictures separately to each eye, with the help of lenses or prisms and mirrors, the stereoscope tricks the viewer's brain into creating a single three-dimensional space from the pair of two-dimensional images. Critics of the time praised the great "roundness" and "solidity" of the pictures, effects that were sought after but difficult to achieve in ordinary photography.

The first stereoscopic viewer, invented in 1838 by Sir Charles Wheatstone, predated the public announcement of photography by just one year. Soon after, stereoscopes made from paired daguerreotypes were available in France and the United States, although their reflective surfaces made viewing difficult. The noted American daguerreotypists Frederick and William Langenheim were early producers of stereoscopic imagery, as were the Langenheims's neighbors in Boston, the photographic duo of Southworth & Hawes. The Southworth & Hawes studio even housed a cabinet-sized stereo viewer, which allowed visitors to cycle through a series of whole-plate views for twenty-five cents per session or fifty cents for an annual subscription.[1]

The stereograph viewing experience was much simplified by the invention of the albumen print process in 1850. The ability to print multiples

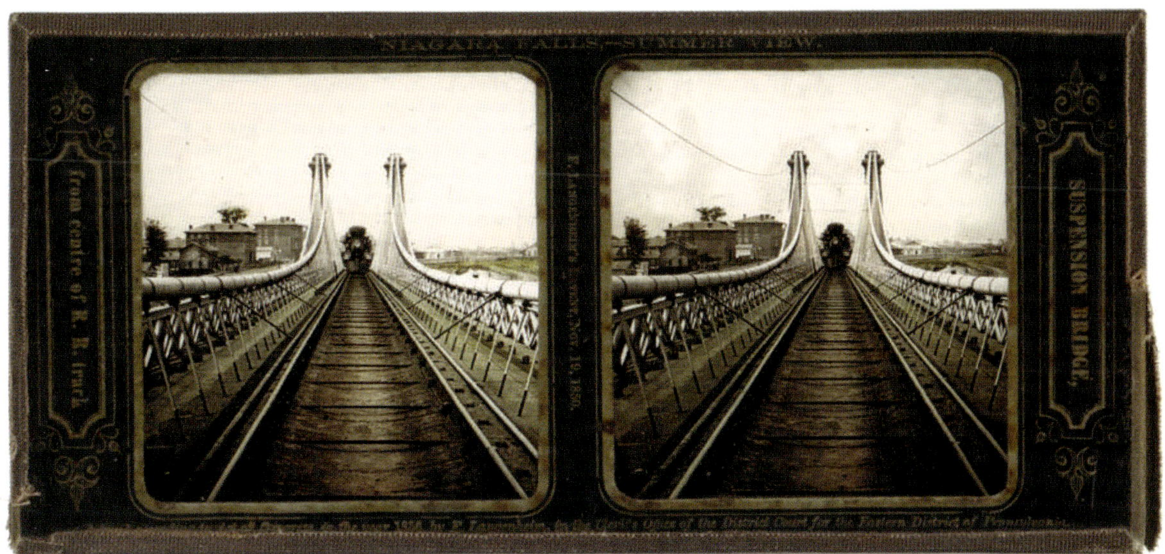

FIGURE 39. William and Frederick Langenheim, "Suspension Bridge from Centre of R. R. Track," 1856. Collodion on glass.

Source: J. Paul Getty Museum, Los Angeles. Digital image courtesy of the Getty's Open Content Program.

enabled the proliferation of stereoscopic cards, a pair of roughly 3" square prints mounted side-by-side on a 3 ½" × 7" piece of cardboard, which left room at the edges for handling and space to print the manufacturer's name and a descriptive caption. More than a quarter million stereoscopes were purchased in Paris and London in 1851 alone, and that number quadrupled by the mid-1850s,[2] though in the United States, the taste for stereo images was still emerging. As Charles Seely, editor of the *American Journal of Photography*, noted in 1858, "Stereoscopes are at last coming into vogue with us, we are actually getting up a taste for them."[3] The New York–based distributors E. & H. T. Anthony initially photographed and published their own views, offering 175 different images for sale in 1859.[4] One popular magazine described the firm's efforts: "An indefatigable array of artists are searching out all the wonderful places of Egypt, Greece, and Italy. No ruin is neglected, no grand scenery passed by, no palace hall overlooked, no work of art neglected; and the stereoscopic tourist, relieved of all expense and the wear and tear of travel, can take advantage of the labor of others and enjoy it amid the sweet associations of the home circle."[5] Anthony eventually contracted with other photographers, including Mathew Brady, to publish views from the Civil War

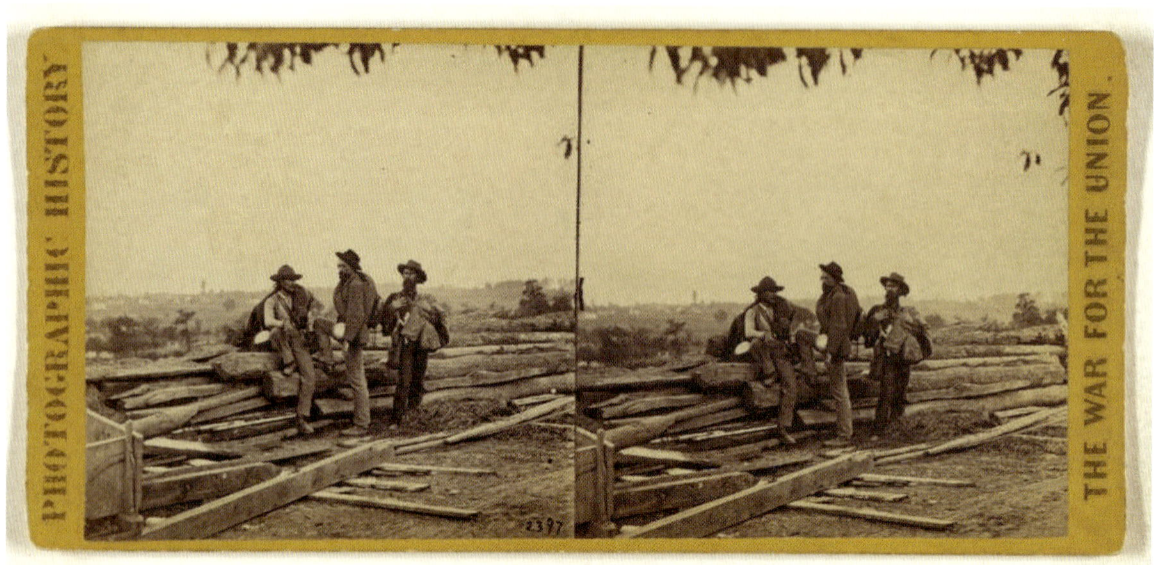

FIGURE 40. Studio of Mathew B. Brady, "Rebel Prisoners, Gettysburgh," ca. 1862. Albumen silver print.

Source: J. Paul Getty Museum, Los Angeles. Digital image courtesy of the Getty's Open Content Program.

and scenes of the western landscape, making more than eleven thousand stereoscopic pictures available by the early 1870s.[6]

Writers described the experience of viewing these highly detailed, immersive images as akin to travel, recounting the story of looking at pictures as if they traversed the landscapes themselves. The *New York Observer* maintained, "We cannot perceive wherein it is better to see the ruins of an Egyptian temple on the ground than here in Anthony's Stereoscopes. . . . You may sit for hours, if you will, and study every form and feature of this wondrous work, and the longer and more minutely it is examined, the more perfect even in imperfection comes out the representation of the original. There is the very crack in the stone."[7]

The stereoscope found fervent support in the physician Oliver Wendell Holmes. "The mind feels its way into the very depths of the picture," he wrote in an essay for the *Atlantic Monthly*.[8] The description is notable for the sense of progression it implies and the strange sense of mental physicality. Stereographs, the portmanteau term Holmes coined to describe stereoscopic pictures, display a pronounced layering and, as some critics lamented, their strongest effects appear in the foreground and midground. Instructional writers recommended that photographers exploit this limitation and always include foreground

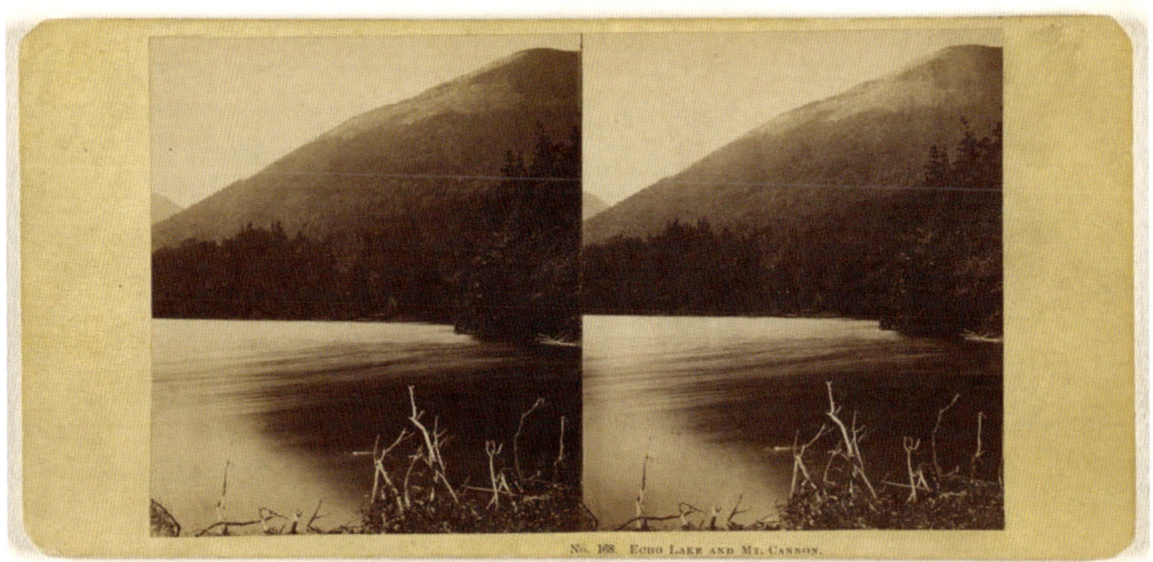

elements to provoke the illusion of depth. [See also Chapter 8, "Foreground Interest."] As one amateur handbook explained, "Some discernment is needed in selecting the subject for a stereoscopic view. If the camera points to a distant hillside, and there is no near object included in the range, the view will appear flat when seen through the stereoscope. . . . Some shrubbery, the stump of a tree, or any distant and still object will answer."[9]

Holmes offered a piece of advice to would-be makers of stereographs. He griped that stereographic pairs taken separately often revealed changes in position due to the time lag between exposures.[10] People disappeared from view in one picture to the next, or their movement appeared as a ghostly blur across the plate in one eye, but not the other. [See also Chapter 15, "Instantaneous Photographs."] Although a dedicated stereoscopic camera with binocular lenses was patented in England in 1856, many pictures were made by simply changing the angle of a single camera, often by sliding it along a level rail attached to a tripod.

Holmes also invented, but chose not to patent, an improved handheld stereoscopic viewer that was distributed widely in the United States and transformed the occasional interest into a national obsession in the early 1860s (see Figure 42). Although the format passed in and out of favor,

FIGURE 41. John P. Soule, "Echo Lake and Mt. Cannon," 1861. Albumen silver print, 3 ½" × 7" (card).

Source: J. Paul Getty Museum, Los Angeles. Digital image courtesy of the Getty's Open Content Program.

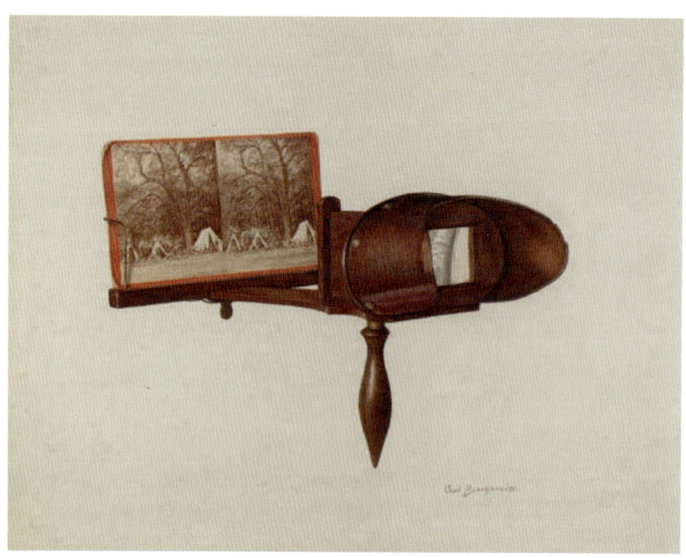

FIGURE 42. Carl Buergerniss, "Stereoscope," 1940. Watercolor, graphite, and colored pencil on paper, 14 3/8″ × 17 15/16″ (sheet).

Source: National Gallery of Art, Index of American Design.

competing with other photo fads of the nineteenth century, the famous German photographer Hermann Vogel asserted that by 1883, "there is no parlor in America where there is not a stereoscope."[11] Well into the early decades of the twentieth century, amateur guidebooks included chapters on stereography, marking it as an important photographic exploit.

Stereoscopic viewers continue to attract fans of novelty technologies: vintage View-Master reels, which premiered at the 1939 World's Fair, are still popular on eBay, and Poppy, an app and device for making and viewing stereoscopic images on a smartphone, was crowdfunded on Kickstarter in 2013. Although they never became a truly dominant form of photography, stereoscopic images, and the unique aesthetic effects that they reward, have enjoyed a persistent presence within popular image consumption since their royal endorsement in 1851.

10

TINTYPE TYPES

ALTHOUGH BOOSTERS since Daguerre claimed that photography democratized access to portraiture, in truth it was still a luxury until the invention of the tintype. This inexpensive process made visiting the photographer's studio a commonplace experience, no longer reserved for momentous life events or wealthy patrons. Tintype production, however, was almost entirely limited to the United States. Photographers may have experimented with the process elsewhere in the world, but its popularity was uniquely American.

The concept of making a photograph on a darkened metal plate was patented in Ohio in 1856, although the word *tintype* wouldn't come into use for at least another decade.[1] The earlier name, *ferrotype*, referred to the thin iron plate coated with black enamel on which the negative image was developed. Underexposing these photographs allowed the glossy black enamel to show through and darken the light areas of the negative, giving the appearance of a positive image. The photographs were also called *melainotypes*, a neologism that borrowed from the Greek word meaning "to turn black." The root's early uses in English were limited to medical literature. *Melasma* described hyperpigmentation of the skin, underscoring the fact that melainotypes were primarily portraits, photographs that depicted people. Despite the fact that darkening would affect portrait subjects of all skin tones, the adoption of such a clinical term to rationalize a sitter's altered appearance reflects the deep-seated racial anxieties of mid-nineteenth-century America. [See also Chapter 3, "Hand Painting"; Chapter 11, "The Rembrandt Effect"; and Chapter 40, "Golden Hour."]

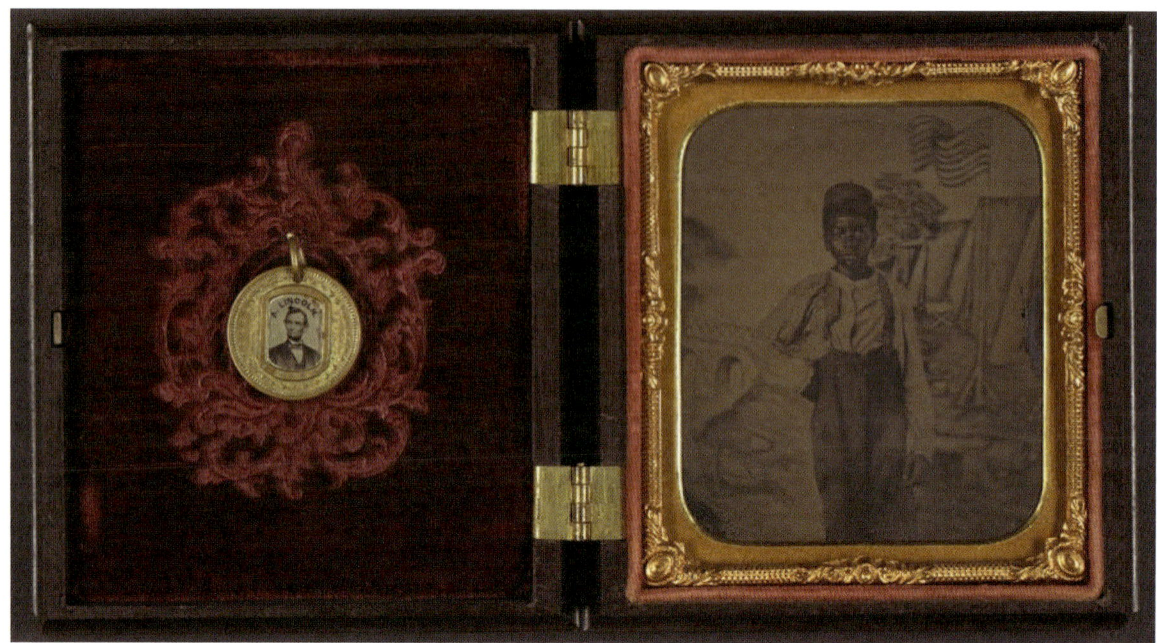

FIGURE 43. Untitled [Unidentified African American Boy Standing in Front of Painted Backdrop Showing American Flag and Tents; Campaign Button with Portraits of Lincoln on One Side and Johnson on the Opposite Side Are Attached to Inside Cover of Case], ca. 1861–1865. Tintype, 3 ¼" × 2 ¾" (plate).

Source: Library of Congress, Liljenquist Family Collection of Civil War Photographs.

The process gained popular recognition in 1860 when it was used for presidential campaign buttons. Although the pictures could be reproduced only by rephotographing them, creating a sheet of identical images and cutting them out with metal shears nonetheless proved cost-effective, highly visible, and durable campaign advertising. The outbreak of the Civil War further enhanced interest in the process. As *Humphrey's Journal* noted in 1861, "The Melainotype still holds its own, notwithstanding the war; indeed it now appears to be without a rival, and no wonder, for the great superiority of this plate for small sized pictures, especially, is acknowledged by all; for a miniature, breast-pin, or ring, it is inimitable."[2]

While carte-de-visite remained the preferred format for mass-reproduced, collectible images of "distinguished military men"[3] or celebrities, by winter 1862, the advantages of the cheap metal plate were becoming clearer: "The melainotype—we are glad to notice a demand springing up for this favorite plate among the camp-following photographers. There is nothing equal to it for beauty of finish and particularly for durability. Now a picture on glass can be accidentally dropped and smashed, but whoever heard of smashing a Melainotype?"[4] The materials were easy to prepare and transport, a necessity for the itinerant photographers who established tent studios near military encampments. There was no glass negative and no separate step for printing, as in the carte-de-visite, nor was encasing the photograph between protective sheets of glass required, as for the daguerreotype. The tintype could be developed on the spot and handed over to customers while they waited, with or without a paper mount.

Humphrey's described the emerging market thus:

> The photographer accompanies the army wherever it goes, and a very large number of soldiers get their "pictures" taken and send them to their friends. Friends at home in return send their portraits to the soldiers, and in this way an immense transportation business has been done by the Post Office. Not unfrequently a number of bags go out from the Washington office entirely filled with sun pictures, enclosed in light but bulky cases. Most of these pictures are taken on the Melainotype Plate for the reason that it is light, durable, and easily sent in a letter.[5]

At seventy-five cents to one dollar per dozen, the tintype was well within the reach of everyday folk.[6] Male farm laborers in New York were making on average a dollar per day in 1862,[7] so the tintype was not an extravagant outlay, and it was less than a quarter the cost of cartes-de-visite during the same period.[8] Although "tintype" is technically a misnomer (the pictures were made on thin iron plates), this popular name alludes to their cheapness. Traveling tinkers used thin sheets of

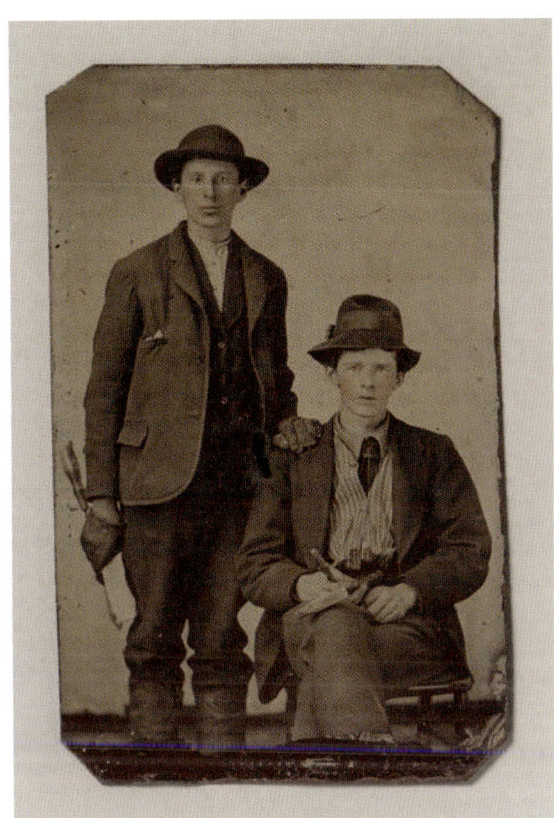

FIGURE 44. "Two Young Men, One Seated and One Standing, Holding Carpentry Tools," ca. 1870–1890. Hand-colored tintype, 3¼″ × 2″ (plate).

Source: Metropolitan Museum of Art, Bequest of Herbert Mitchell, 2008.

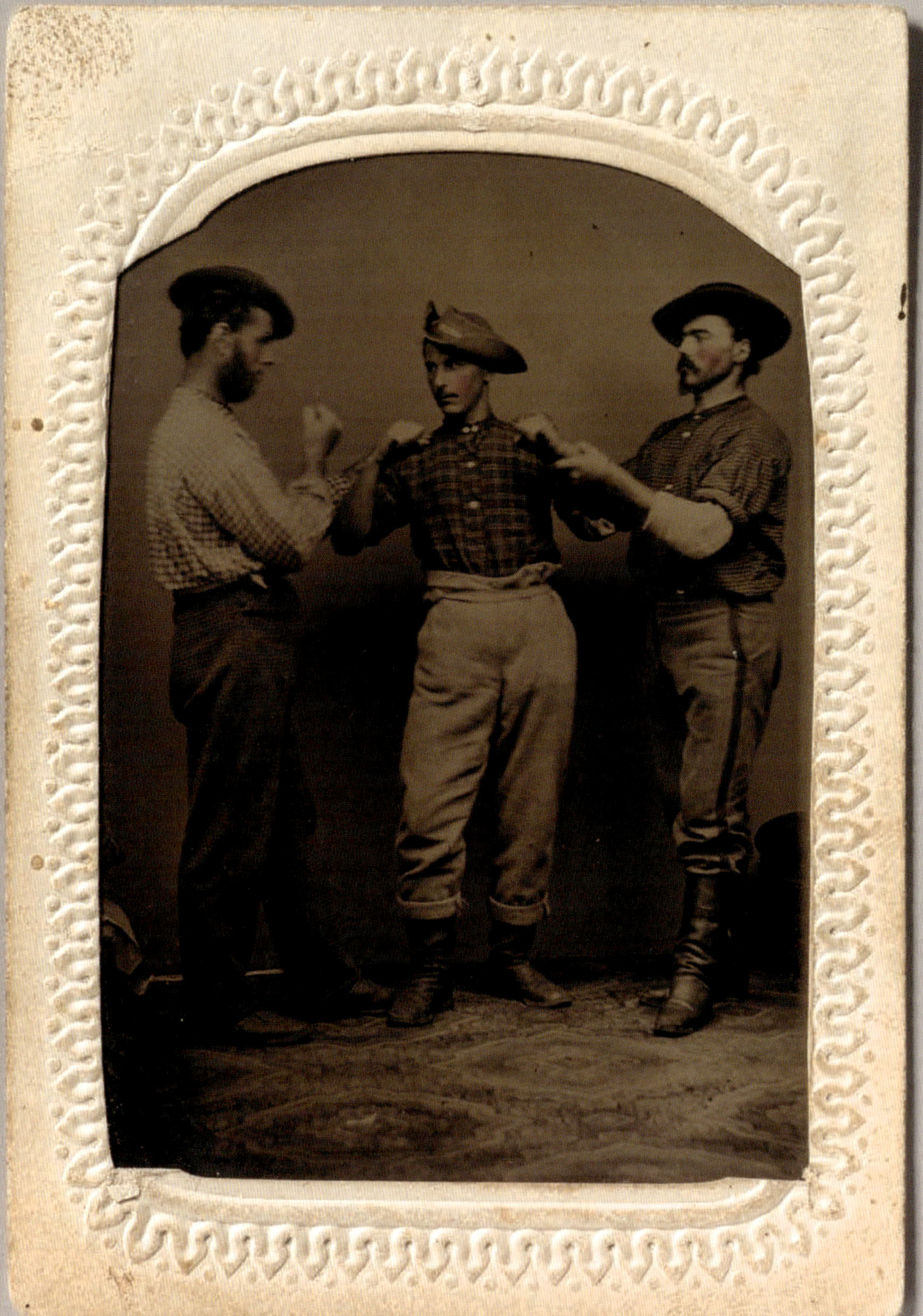

metal, or "tinplate," to repair household items. The precise origin of the name "tintype" is unknown, but the light, bendable quality of the metal-plate photographs, as well as their itinerant makers, were likely reminiscent of this widely known nineteenth-century character and his cheap tinplate repairs.[9]

The low price of the tintype made it a medium well suited for experimentation and play. Visual tropes emerged, sometimes drawn from popular theatrical entertainments or archetypal American characters, such as frontiersmen, boxers, and gamblers. Many of the playful poses that became conventionalized in the tintype were developed expressly with this inexpensive and lighthearted photographic genre in mind. Men expressed fraternal affection in double portraits by interlocking their arms or legs; groups of women displayed knee-length long hair, which was otherwise pinned up in public. Multishot sequences were popular: groups of people were pictured facing the camera, then facing away. Double-exposure trick photos turned people into twins or allowed them to display their own severed heads on platters held at arm's length.[10]

One photographer even wrote to the *Philadelphia Photographer* of the potential for tintypes to aid the temperance movement. The photographer described a man whose wife convinced him to have his tintype made during a drinking binge, which she then displayed next to their wedding portrait in the living room. In a sober state the following day, the man quietly pocketed the offending picture and never drank again.[11]

The radical accessibility of the tintype eventually led to its stigmatization. One photographer recalled a woman who came to have her portrait made and refused the tintype, saying, " 'Oh, no, that is too common; my servants get that kind.' "[12] If the carte-de-visite was a kind of social currency, as Oliver Wendell Holmes once claimed, then the tintype was a devalued one. According to the photographer G. M. Carlisle, "If one of your friends should present to you in exchange for the best card you were able to procure, a tintype or a miserable card made by one of the dollar a dozen men, that friend would not elevate himself very much

< FIGURE 45. J. C. Batchelder, untitled, ca. 1860–1880. Hand-colored tintype, 3 1/16″ × 2 1/8″ (plate).

Source: Metropolitan Museum of Art, Bequest of Herbert Mitchell, 2008.

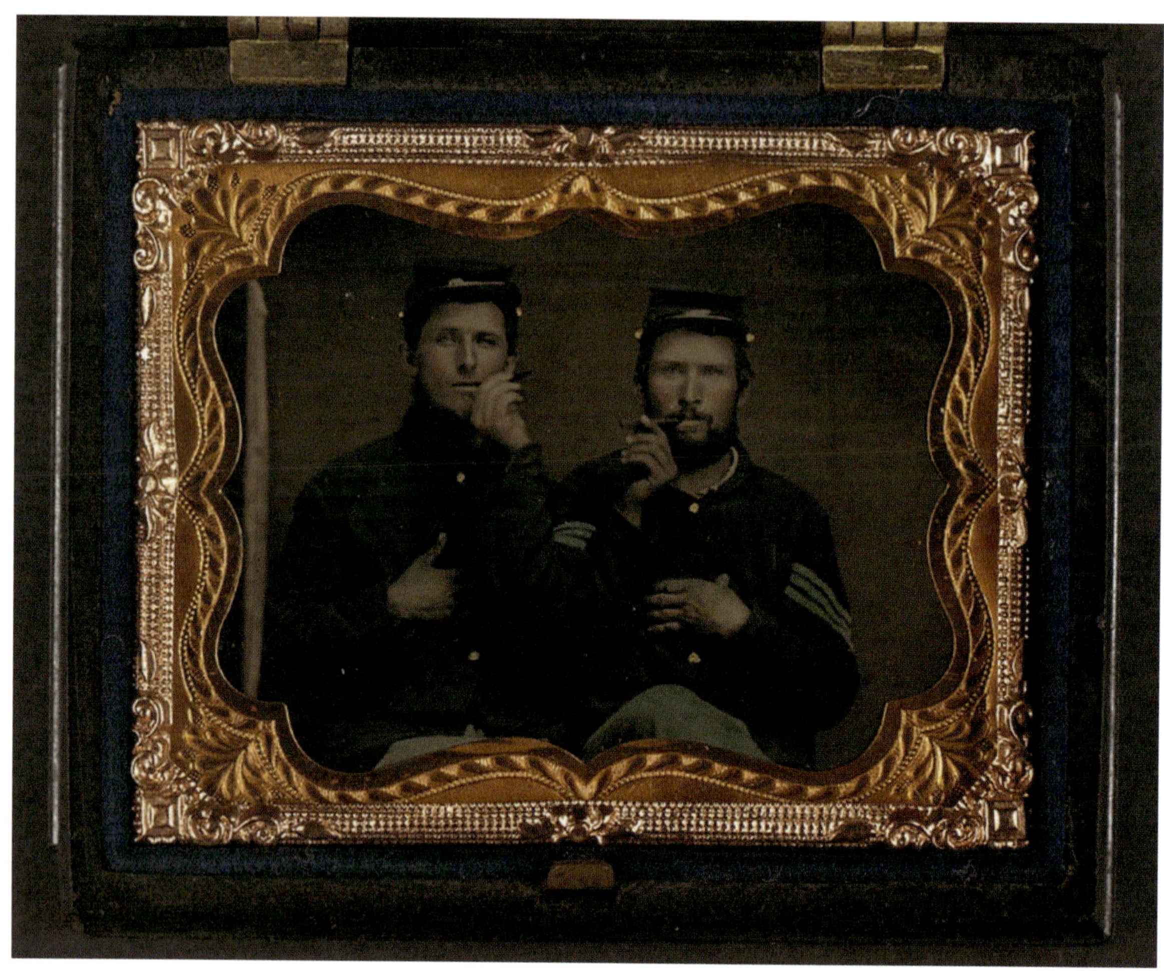

in your favor."[13] The tintype had thrown the doors of the photographic studio wide open, welcoming all of the American public and enabling a style of picture that was unimaginable only a decade earlier. [See also Chapter 2, "Portrait Props and Poses."] The advent of the tintype irrevocably changed the medium, transforming the studio visit from a serious rite of passage to a playful event with its own moods and codes, from the somber to the silly.

11

THE REMBRANDT EFFECT

THE REMBRANDT EFFECT, a portrait lighting technique developed in the late 1860s, is the longest-lasting named trend in the history of photography. Not only is the Rembrandt effect still in use today, but it established the blueprint for how the photographic community would receive trends: initial celebration and emulation, followed by derision when the style saturated the market. After the fervor died down, the aesthetic was often revived.

The term *Rembrandt effect* was coined in 1868 by the New York photographer William Kurtz. Kurtz created a sense of dimensionality in his head-and-shoulders portraits by introducing shadows, which recalled the dark paintings of the Dutch Old Master painter.[1] Since early photographic processes demanded such a prodigious quantity of light, most urban studios were located at the top of multistory buildings and lit by skylights or clerestory windows. The shadows cast by overhead lights, particularly shadows under a sitter's brow, nose, and chin, were considered defects in early photographs. [See also Chapter 2, "Portrait Props and Poses."] Portrait photographers worked hard to eliminate not just these but all other shadows on the face, in deference to clients' wishes. The Rembrandt technique called for directing the light with reflector panels that put half of the face in shadow while it maintained light in both eyes, as in Figure 48. As one would-be critic allowed of the Rembrandt effect, "Doubtless the most important gain realized by this new-style photograph, will be to crush out the old prejudices against shadows. Every provincial operator has wept over the unappreciative rustics who insist on having their faces taken like the full moon!—square

to front and in complete light—whilst others refuse a three-quarter head because it is 'too black on one side!' "[2] (See Figure 49.)From a twenty-first-century perspective, the racial implications of this complaint seem pronounced. However, the nineteenth-century photographer's appreciation of darker skin tones did not necessarily reveal a more progressive understanding of race, only a greater familiarity with the translation of colors into monochrome images. [See also Chapter 40, "Golden Hour."]

Looking back on the year 1869, Edward L. Wilson noted in the *Philadelphia Photographer* that Rembrandt effects, also called "shadow pictures," were "quite the rage."[3] Many other authors provided advice for making portraits in the highly sought-after style—"the now justly celebrated 'Rembrandt Effect.' "[4] Some suggested using the device patented by Kurtz himself: a large folding frame that focused and directed natural light. Others detailed the use of white sheets to create makeshift reflectors, a practice that is still popular today.

By the next year, however, critics of the style emerged, describing the Rembrandt effect as "unnatural and extravagant."[5] Some claimed that the technique had so completely overwhelmed the market that all portraits looked the same. On close inspection, such criticisms take aim not only at the style of these pictures, but also at their subjects, who were considered unworthy of such chic portraits. In Kurtz's published defense of the style, he argued that "commonplace or ordinary faces, when lighted in an ordinary manner, will always remain ordinary." A detractor responded, asking: "And why should they not [remain ordinary]?

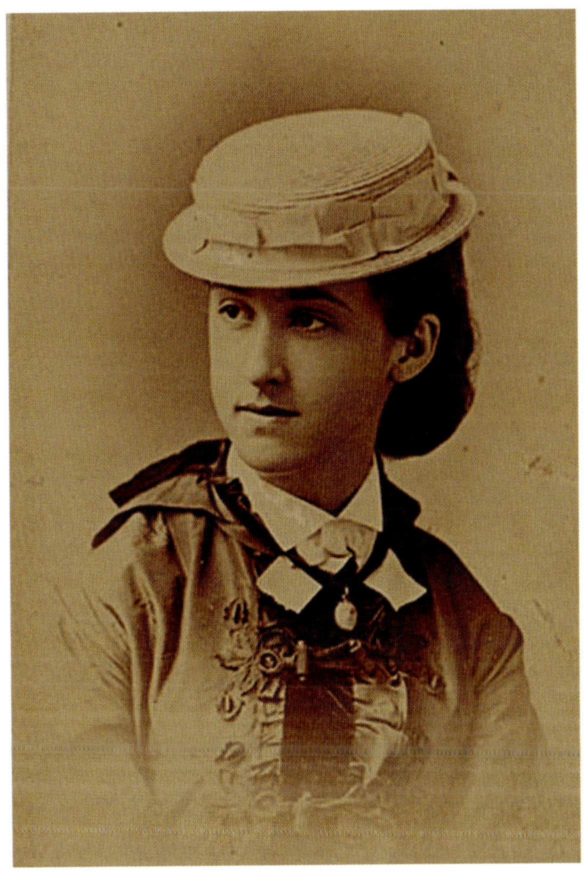

FIGURE 48. William Kurtz, "Rosina Emma Sherwood," ca. 1870. Carte-de-visite.

Source: Smithsonian Archives of American Art.

< FIGURE 47. Rembrandt van Rijn, "Self-Portrait," 1660. Oil on canvas, 31⅝" × 26½".

Source: Metropolitan Museum of Art, Bequest of Benjamin Altman, 1913.

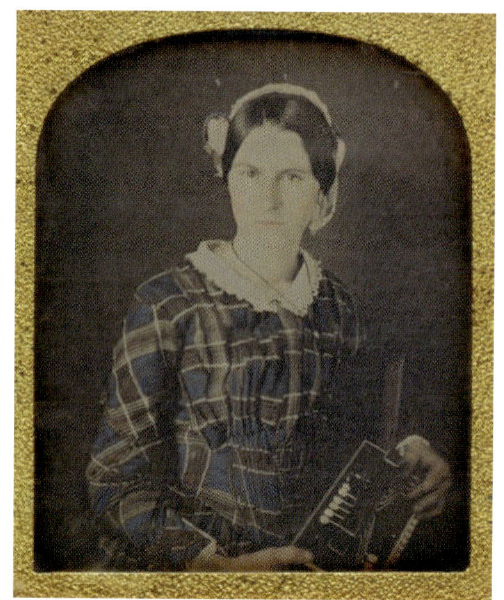

FIGURE 49 (LEFT). Ron Fasand, "Woman with Accordion," 1840s. Daguerreotype, 4¾″ × 3¼″.

Source: Metropolitan Museum of Art, Purchase, Frederick M. Lehman Bequest, 2005.

FIGURE 50 (RIGHT). "Rembrandt Reflector." In Photographic Mosaics: An Annual Record of Photographic Progress (Philadelphia: Benerman & Wilson, 1870), 79.

Source: Author's collection.

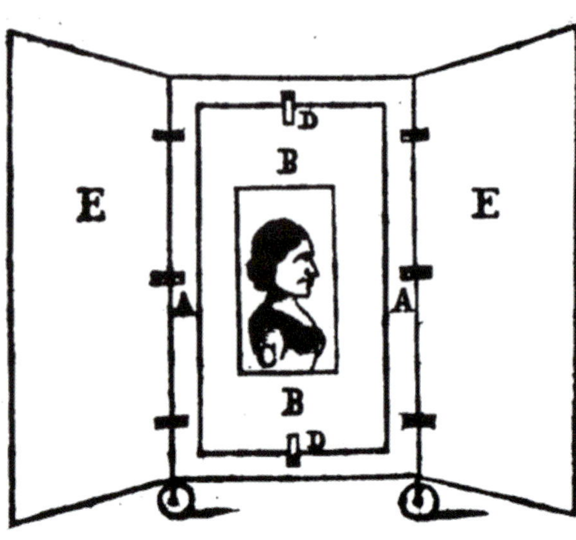

Molly the cook has a fat, chubby, good-natured face, which, lighted in an ordinary manner, will present the picture of a respectable cook; but lighted in an extraordinary manner, it may, by startling effects of light and shade, be made to suggest a Lady Macbeth."[6] This debate reveals the complexities of separating photographic style from its content, the Rembrandt effect from its effect on a particular sitter. Scorn for Rembrandt-like lighting found as much fault with the people having their pictures taken in a fashionable new style as with the style itself.

Kurtz replied to one such bitter attack by sacrificing his fellow photographers while protecting their clients: "I am led to suppose, from his very severe criticism, that he has seen only some atrocious imitations by our rural photographers, and upon which rests the sole foundation of his argument."[7] Kurtz continued, in a second published letter, "If some, in making this style of picture, overstep a certain limit, and produce work that is *simply ridiculous*, it is hardly fair to condemn the whole thing. The best of portraits can be, and are, made in this style."[8]

Trends are often accompanied by boosters' insistence that the new style represents the "best" or most natural way of making pictures. As the rise and fall of the Rembrandt effect makes clear, however, from the very beginning, trends in representation are intimately linked with what they represent. Having one's portrait made in the new style spoke as much to the yeoman's cosmopolitan aspirations as it did to his photographer's mastery of new techniques. It is little wonder, then, that American sophisticates tried to protect their tenuous hold on their newly attained social standing by volleying accusations of impropriety at the trend itself, which was less vocal in its defense than the diverse classes of people it was used to represent.

12

RETOUCHING CABINET CARDS

WHILE MANY STYLISTIC TRENDS in the history of photography seem to have been created by popular demand, the introduction of the cabinet card was a calculated business decision, intended to stoke public interest and inflate prices. During the Civil War, the market for portraits had expanded radically, especially in the cheap tintype format. [See also Chapter 10, "Tintype Types."] Correspondingly, the number of portraitists swelled and prices dropped. After the war, when interest waned, photographers were suddenly faced with the need to raise prices simply to survive.

Edward L. Wilson, publisher of the *Philadelphia Photographer*, described the situation in 1866: "Something must be done to create a new and greater demand for photographs. The carte-de-visite, once so popular and in so great demand, seems to have grown out of fashion. Every one is surfeited with them. All the albums are full of them and every body has exchanged with every body. [. . .] The adoption of a new size is what is wanted."[1] This was the inaugural editorial of Wilson's almost single-handed effort to stimulate the American market and increase prices with a new product: the cabinet-sized photograph, or "cabinet card," a 4″ × 5 ½″ albumen print pasted on a roughly 4 ¼″ × 6 ½″ board, which had recently become popular in London.[2]

In an era before enlarging was commonplace, the new size required not only different printing papers and mounts but also larger cameras, lenses, and negative plates. [See also Chapter 7, "Solar Enlarging," and Chapter 35, "Full-Frame Prints."] With the larger plate size came greater visible detail, and Wilson was quick to point out that this would make the selection and quality of backdrops, floor coverings, and accessories more important than ever before. Wilson reminded his readers that hesitant studio owners should "look back to the time when the *carte* mania began, they will recollect that it was *not great at once*; they will also remember with what reluctance they began to make that size. . . . *The new size will go*, be assured, if *you* are disposed to push it as you should."[3] New paper mounts, albums, and frames were needed to accommodate the larger prints, and Wilson praised the "enterprising dealers" (the journal's advertisers) who began producing such materials "*before* the demand arose."[4] He insisted, "There is no use of your talking new size to your customers, unless you have something to show them."[5]

Over the next several months, the *Philadelphia Photographer* featured cabinet-sized portraits as the magazine's frontispiece and offered commentary on many more. In April, Wilson noted, "We are receiving beautiful examples of this new size from all directions. Be they beautiful or not, we are much pleased to see so many making the effort to introduce them."[6] By August of that year, he proclaimed that the size was "becoming a brilliant success!"[7] Indeed, in 1873, it was so popular with the public that one frustrated photographer called on the American Photographic Society to standardize the name: Was it "cabinet cards" or "card cabinets"?[8]

The cabinet card created aesthetic problems too. Increased size and clarity of the face made the need for retouching more pronounced. While it had long been common to add color by hand-painting portraits, attention to removing "skin-spots, freckles, warts, and moles" was suddenly of paramount concern for sitters, and thus for portrait photographers as well.[9] The small size of the cartes-de-visite made this

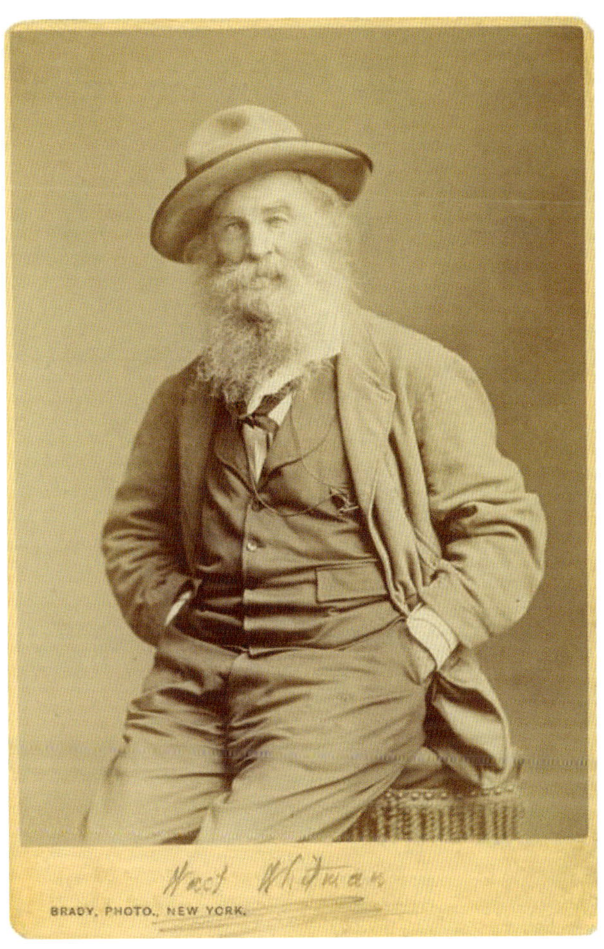

FIGURE 51. Mathew B. Brady, "Walt Whitman," ca. 1870. Albumen silver print, 5 ¾" × 4 ¹⁄₁₆".

Source: J. Paul Getty Museum, Los Angeles. Digital image courtesy of the Getty's Open Content Program.

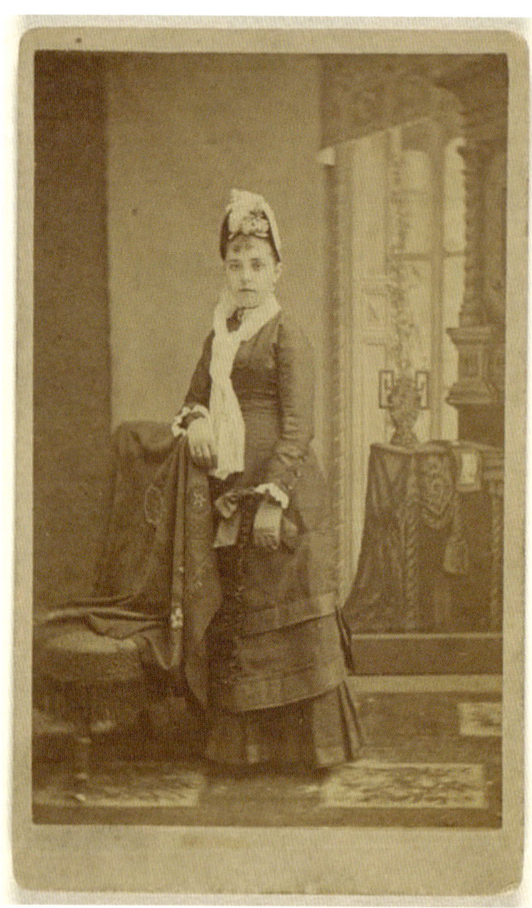

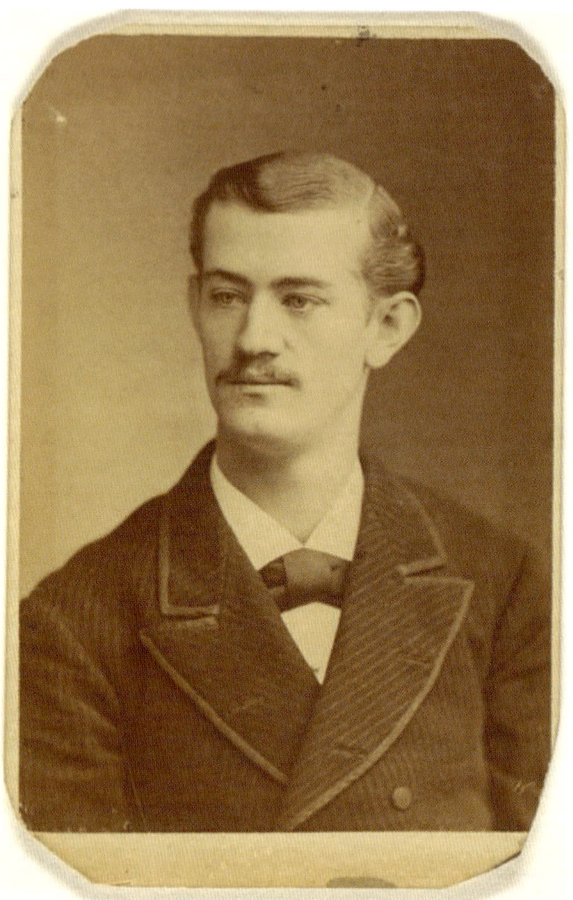

exacting handwork extremely difficult, especially at the reduced prices that such pictures commanded. Sitters expected more from the pricy cabinet card. Rather than arrange a second portrait session, photographers found retouching the negative increasingly profitable. One correspondent suggested that "an intractably stupid or surly expression may be made rather pleasing, by obliterating the puckers in the forehead, and the wrinkles between the brows, . . . more sweetness given to the mouth by altering the curve of the lips; the eye rendered vivacious, when it is too dark, by touching in a catch-light at the top."[10] As early as 1869, *Photographic Mosaics* noted that "retouching the negative is becoming quite general. Photographers no longer consider it a crime to resort to it if their work can be improved thereby."[11]

Soon, however, the growing popularity of retouching attracted ridicule. The prime targets were the so-called eggshell faces: entirely smooth, devoid of line or shadow after a thorough going-over by the retoucher's pencil.[12] The photographer W. J. Baker of Buffalo, New York, identifying European portrait studios as the worst offenders, described the face of a Parisian portrait as "so white that it almost shames the unshaded paper margin."[13] Although Baker described white faces, the practice was not limited to photographers' white clientele; any skin tone could be retouched or overexposed to hide imperfections. Baker was an early adopter of retouching, but he later became one of its most vocal critics. He conceded, "All good things have their abuse. Some photographers retouch their negatives to death. . . . Such productions are as bad as can be. They lie. They deface the glory of our beautiful art."[14] At the dawn of the Gilded Age, as wealthy industrialists rapidly consolidated their influence over local and national politics, photography's potential for duplicity was particularly vexing. Just ten years earlier, the proliferation of cheap processes had radically expanded access to what was formerly the elite art of portraiture. Now the medium was becoming stratified again, with higher-paying customers able to alter what was previously considered an incontrovertible truth. One photographer described his relationship to retouching pragmatically: "As this is the age of improvement or of misrepresentation—call it by whichever name you will—let us all equally indulge in it whilst the fashion reigns supreme."[15] Despite some early opposition, retouching is a trend whose reign since the 1870s remains unparalleled.

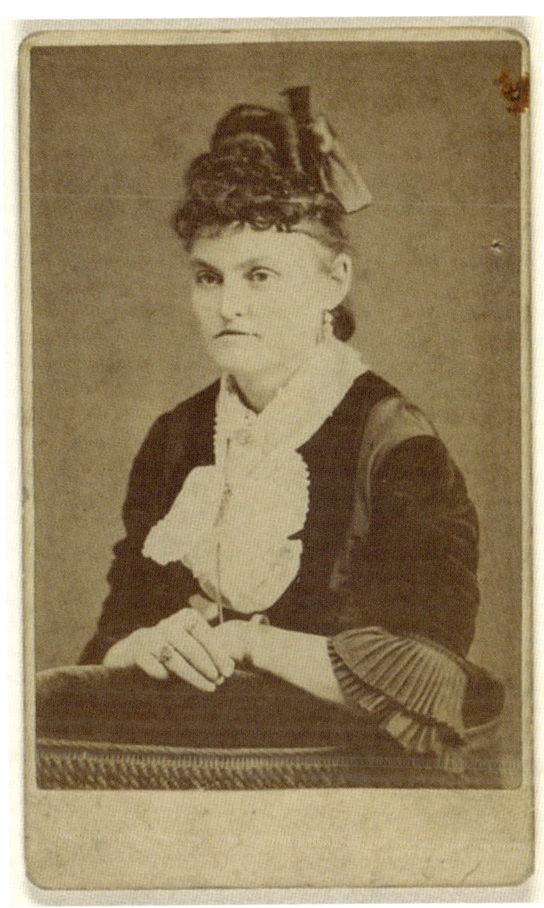

FIGURE 54. T. M. Saurman, "Unidentified Woman Seated, Leaning on Chair Arm," 1870–1875. Albumen silver print.

Source: J. Paul Getty Museum, Los Angeles. Digital image courtesy of the Getty's Open Content Program.

13

PHOTOMICROGRAPHS

PHOTOMICROGRAPHY, or the practice of recording images seen through a microscope, was one of the earliest aspirations for photography. William Henry Fox Talbot made photograms with a microscope even before the public announcement of his photographic process in 1839. Scientists on the Continent and in the United States were also eager to capture what they observed through microscopic investigation. In 1840, Andreas Ritter von Ettingshausen, an Austrian physicist, produced a daguerreian photomicrograph of a clematis; others soon followed in making photographs of plants. The technique, of lasting benefit to scientific research and education, also became a popular pursuit and skill-testing feat among serious amateur photographers in the late nineteenth and early twentieth centuries.

Most instructional guides that describe photomicrographs also take pains to distinguish them from what is nearly their opposite: microphotographs, or minuscule photographs that can only be seen with a microscope. Created in 1840 by John Benjamin Dancer, an English inventor and magic lantern slide producer, microphotographs could be useful in saving library shelf space or as spy technology. A British journal described the possibility of smuggling microscopic communications into Paris during the Franco-Prussian War via carrier pigeon.[1] Their actual fame came in a much different form: fashionable jewelry inlaid with miniature photographs.

Interest in photomicrography, on the other hand, recurs intermittently throughout the history of photography, often in relation to advances in film or printing technologies. While Talbot's early

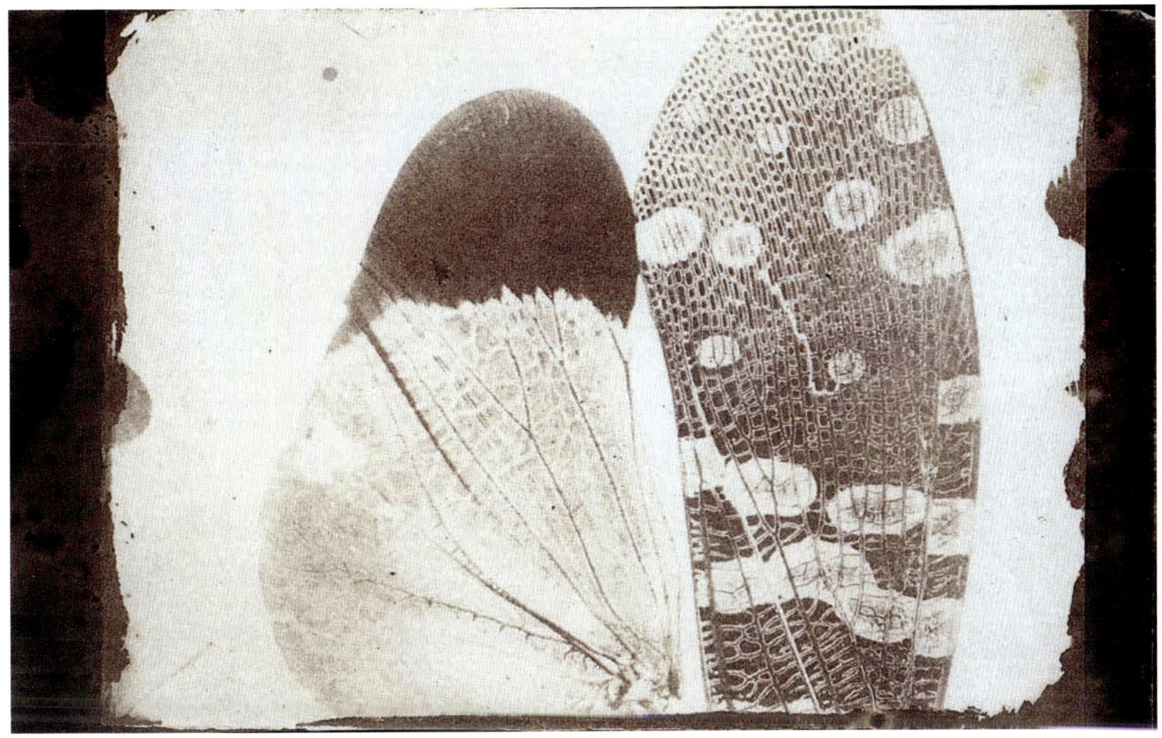

photomicrographs were reproducible, the visual interference of the paper grain in both the negative and the positive print made them less than ideal for scientific study. Daguerre's more detailed process was better suited for images that required fine resolution, but these unique images were difficult to share and could not easily accompany scientific treatises, except after translation into printed engravings, as in the 1845 book *Cours de Microscopie* by Alfred Donné and Léon Foucault.

Fascination with the discovery of microscopic organisms was widespread in the nineteenth century and not limited to the scientific community. Popular public lectures and even parlor microscopes revealed the life teeming in formerly invisible worlds. Variety was a key feature of lectures featuring photomicrographic slides projected by the magic lantern. Authors of review articles and guidebooks delighted in the laundry-list description of subjects, praising presenters for displaying microscopic views of "the siliceous deposit in guano, blood corpuscles, starch

FIGURE 55. William Henry Fox Talbot, "Salt Print of a Photomicrograph of Insect Wings," 1839–1840. Salted paper print, touches of red chalk, heightened with white, on tan paper, $10\frac{11}{16}'' \times 8\frac{1}{16}''$.

Source: Collection of National Media Museum, Science Museum Group Collection Online.

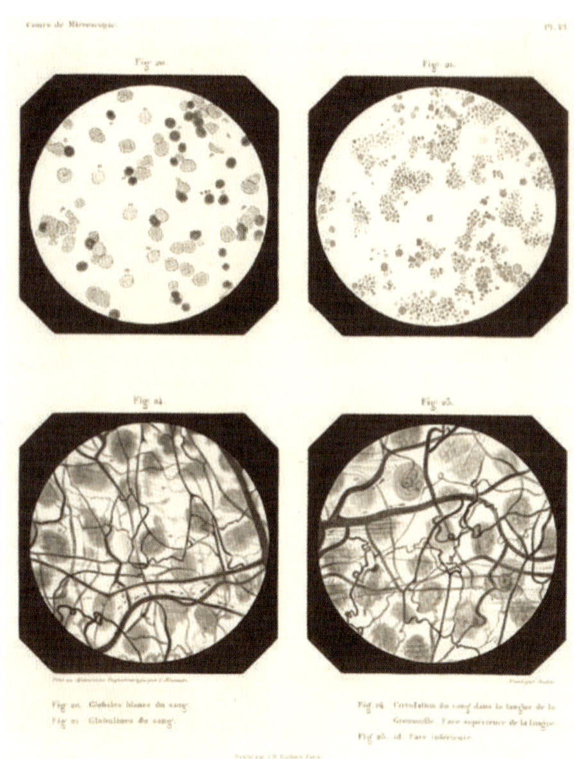

FIGURE 56. Jean-Bernard-Léon Foucault, plate VI from *Cours de Microscopie*, 1845. Engraving.

Source: J. Paul Getty Museum, Los Angeles. Digital image courtesy of the Getty's Open Content Program.

granules, itch insects, etc."[2] or "the fossil *diatom Cosciaodiscus . . .* and a transverse section oak."[3] In his early instructional guide and history of American photography, the photographer Marcus Aurelius Root dedicated fifteen pages to a history of the microscope before even touching on its application to photography. In passages laden with uncharacteristic exclamation points, Root marvels at the universes contained in everything from glacial ice to a gnat's eye or the "green scum of the wayside stagnant pool."[4] Only at the conclusion of this Lilliputian tour does Root finally point his readers to a different manual: one that contains instructions on how to make photomicrographs.

The first major advance in the field of photomicrography came with the invention of the glass plate negative process in 1851. It was this process that enabled the American physician Joseph J. Woodward to create an extensive visual inventory of soldiers' injuries and cellular pathologies after the Civil War, published as *The Medical and Surgical History of the War of Rebellion.* (See Figure 58.)

All photomicrographic instructional manuals emphasized the need to stabilize the camera and specimen together on a board in order to achieve a clear image during the long exposure time required by the microscope's complex optics. In the early 1880s, the production of dry plate negatives increased access to photomicrography even further. The first truly mass-produced photographic negative, gelatin dry plates relieved photographers of the exacting labor of mixing chemicals in a portable laboratory, since the plates came fully prepared and had a relatively long shelf life. Dry plates were also much more light sensitive than earlier processes, reducing exposure times for typical photographs to less than one second and making it easier to create sharp, finely focused photomicrographs.

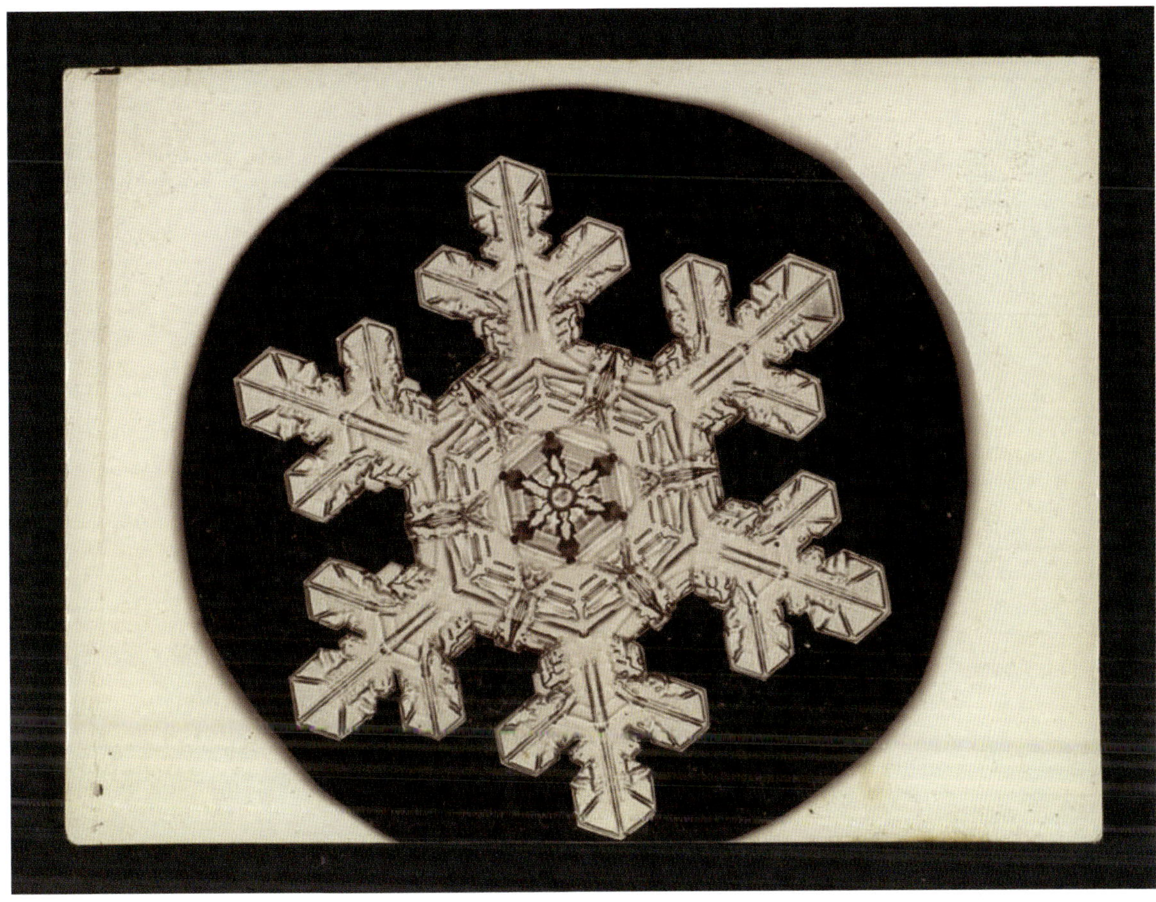

Wilson A. Bentley, a farmer and amateur photomicrographer from Vermont, enchanted the general public and the scientific community alike with his collection of snowflake photomicrographs. Aided by the dry plate process, Bentley was able to photograph snowflakes before they melted by setting up his photomicrograph station outdoors and arranging individual snowflakes on microscope slides with a feather.[5] The resulting images, which revealed the vast diversity of snowflakes, gained wide recognition through their 1901 publication in *Harper's Monthly Magazine.*

In the glut of photographic manuals aimed at the ever growing amateur market after the mid-1880s, hardly one was released that did not reference the wonders of photomicrography. T. C. Roche, in a

FIGURE 57. Wilson Alwyn Bentley, "Snow Crystal," 1890s–1920s. Gelatin silver print.

Source: Metropolitan Museum of Art, Purchase, Alfred Stieglitz Society Gifts, 2015.

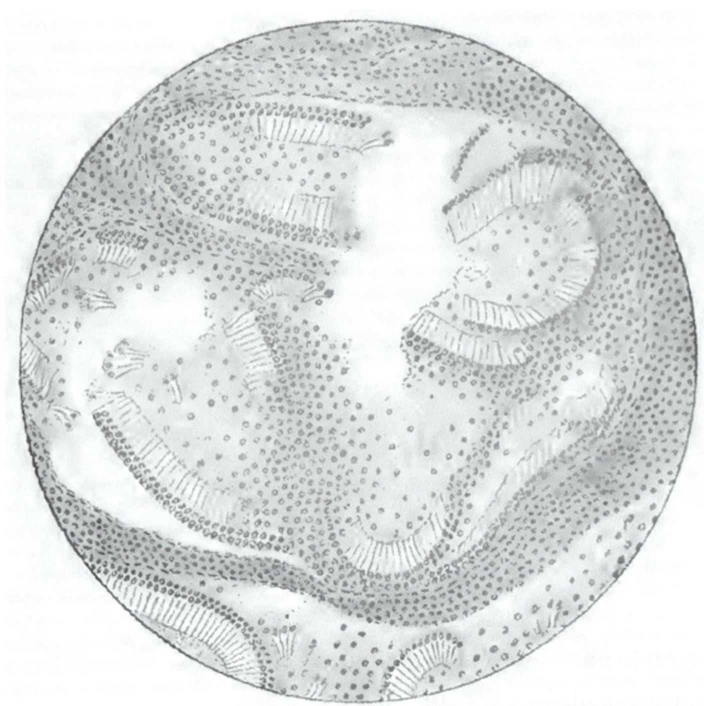

book published by the American photographic supply firm E. H. Anthony, suggested that "the photomicrographic camera may prove to be a fruitful source of pleasure to the amateur."[6] Alexander Black's *Photography Indoors and Out: A Book for Amateurs* asserted that photomicrography, and the practice of photography as a whole, had much to teach art: "The human eye is easily deceived. . . . When we know where to look for things, we begin to see them. When we learn, by other means than through the eye, about the actual forms, colors, and qualities of things, the eye begins to notice more particularly these forms, colors, and qualities."[7] The photomicrograph revealed a previously unseen world that brought about a profound change not only in how people represented nature artistically but also in how they thought about what they couldn't see.

[See also Chapter 15, "Instantaneous Photographs."]

14

PERMANENT CARBON PRINTS

AN ENTIRE GENERATION had been raised on photography before photographers were forced to come to terms with their medium's open secret: impermanence. Despite the claim of a popular advertising slogan, "Secure the shadow, 'ere the substance fade," the public knew well that with time, photographic portraits were as likely to disappear as their subjects. In 1856, a competition was held in France to hasten the development of a more permanent photographic process. The winning entry, invented by Alphonse Louis Poitevin, added carbon to sensitized gelatin in order to make prints from any negative. At first, carbon produced softer and less defined prints than albumen, but improvements in the carbon process over the next decade eventually rendered prints with exceptional tonal subtlety and clarity, as in Figure 59. The process could accommodate other pigments too, allowing photographs to approximate the red hue of Old Master drawings in crayon (see Figure 60) or traditional prints in exotic shades of green, blue, and even purple. [see also Chapter 20, "Painterly Photographs"]

Carbon printing by Poitevin's process was difficult and expensive, however. Even after Joseph Wilson Swan, an English inventor, created a simplified method, it was challenging to access his patented materials in the United States. It wasn't until 1867 when a Boston-based photographer, Frank Rowell, succeeded in making his own carbon tissue paper for printing that the process became feasible in the United States. Rowell wrote, "Our photographs, *no longer fugitive, ephemeral things,* will hereafter be as permanent as the engravings which adorn the walls of our dwellings; and *changelings no more,* they will be as enduring as the printed pages in the

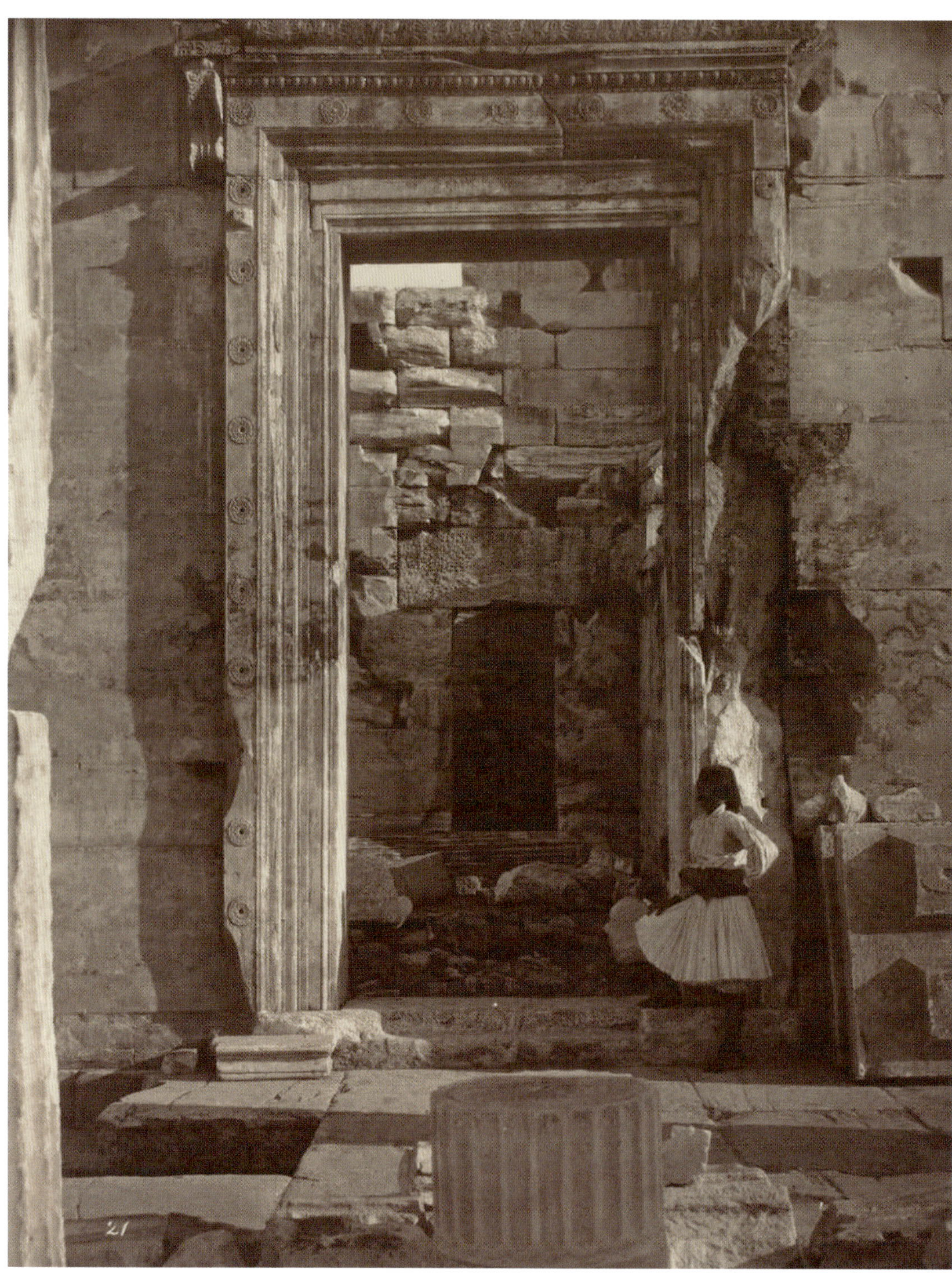

books of our libraries, for, henceforth, they will be made of the same unfading, unchangeable, and indestructible material."[1] While Rowell's faith in the quality of the image was well supported by chemical research, his prophesy that all photographs would soon be permanent ones relied on a notoriously fickle variable: public taste.

In fact, it was only with the invention of this permanent process that commentators in the United States began to boldly voice their dissatisfaction over the transience of earlier photographic methods. One critic wrote in the *Philadelphia Photographer*, "From the hour of its first discovery up to the time of the invention of the carbon process, the art of making pictures by the action of light, was but a beautiful toy, a kind of fairy-like dream, now thrilling us into misery and disappointment, exquisite pleasure from the beautiful images obtained, pain and misery as they faded from our sight."[2] Another writer detailed the stages in the photograph's demise: "[Albumen prints] gradually fade, first losing their glossy blackness and sharpness of outline; then all their early brilliancy dies away, they assume a yellow tinge, and in time entirely disappear. Any one glancing over an album can convince himself of this."[3] One photographer claimed that during the period of just one year, visitors to the Centennial exhibition in Philadelphia could observe a "radical change" in the albumen prints on long-term display.[4] The disappearance of cherished portraits almost amounted to a second death of their subjects. Despite the eloquent metaphors of the trade press, however,

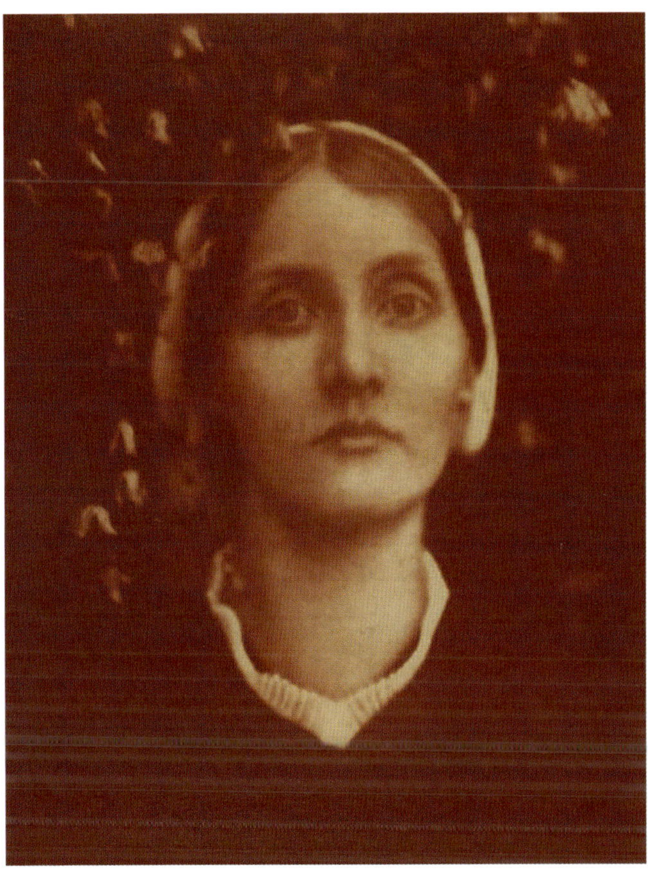

FIGURE 60. Julia Margaret Cameron, "My Niece and God Child (Julia) Mrs. Herbert Duckworth/A Beautiful Vision," 1872. Carbon print, 13" × 9 13/16".

Source: J. Paul Getty Museum, Los Angeles. Digital image courtesy of the Getty's Open Content Program.

< FIGURE 59. William James Stillman, "The Acropolis of Athens, plate 21," 1869/1870. Carbon print, 9 1/2" × 7 5/16" (image).

Source: National Gallery of Art, Robert B. Menschel Fund.

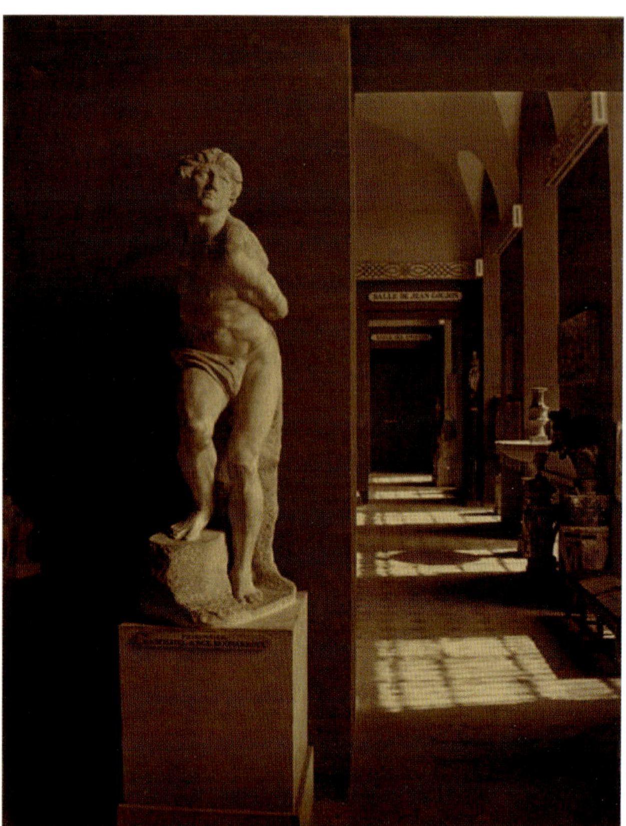

FIGURE 61. Adolphe Braun, "Rebellious Slave by Michelangelo, Musée du Louvre," ca. 1855–1876. Carbon print, 9 15/16″ × 7 9/16″.

Source: J. Paul Getty Museum, Los Angeles. Digital image courtesy of the Getty's Open Content Program.

most American photographers and their customers remained unconvinced that carbon prints were worth the price for simple portraits. Carbon was chiefly reserved for sizable printed editions, often featuring images of architecture or art of historical importance, such as the reproductions made by Adolphe Braun in France and enthusiastically collected by American museums.

In Boston, Frank Rowell continued to make carbon portraits through the late 1870s, even as other studios were working exclusively in albumen. Rowell's partner, E. L. Allen, wrote, "We do not consider [carbon] of so much importance for small pictures, because people sit often for those, but for everything designed to hang on the wall," the studio worked in carbon to prevent fading.[5] With remarkable candor, Allen critiqued the American photographic industry: "For nearly thirty years we have been making pictures that lasted indifferently well, some longer, some shorter, but a large majority of which are faded and gone. In the face of these facts we cannot expect the public to be very enthusiastic, or even take our word at par for anything new we may have to offer them, considering the amount of lies that have been told them."[6] Photographers, in Allen's estimation, were swindlers. The shadow of the portrait may last a little longer than the substance of the person, but not forever—unless it was captured in carbon.

While this history may partially explain the public's ambivalence about yet another costly new process, the Rowell studio's own use of albumen for the "small pictures" points to another factor. Cartes-de-visite and cabinet cards recorded the latest fashions or fleeting moments. Their value was bound up with their ephemerality. Each picture was destined to be replaced by a newer one at the next important occasion. The evanescence of the medium was perfectly matched to the transience of taste. [See also Chapter 46, "Selfie."]

A generation later, it was precisely those impractical, pricey elements of carbon printing—the hand labor, the variety of tone and hue—that made it appealing to art photographers of the early twentieth century. The distinctive aesthetic effects of carbon printing helped to distinguish the expressive possibilities of photography from its rote use by Kodak-carrying amateurs. [See also Chapter 20, "Painterly Photographs."] The softness of carbon prints, initially considered a defect of Poitevin's process, was reprised by these later photographers concerned with evading the medium's mechanical or technical associations in favor of creating a picture more evocative of an artist's unique sensibility.

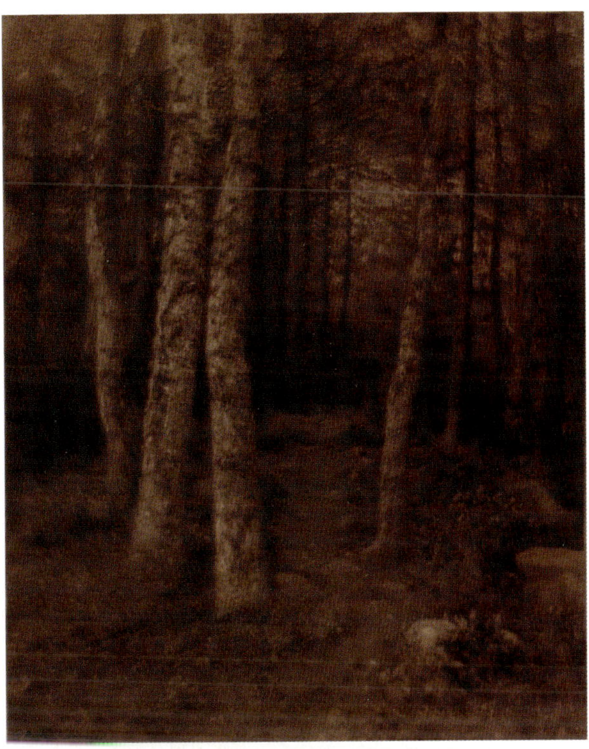

FIGURE 62. Rudolf Eickemeyer Jr., "Forest Scene," 1916. Carbon print, 14⅛" × 11¼".

Source: J. Paul Getty Museum, Los Angeles. Digital image courtesy of the Getty's Open Content Program.

15

INSTANTANEOUS PHOTOGRAPHS

CONQUEST OF THE FLEETING INSTANT had been one of the aims of photography since the public unveiling of Daguerre's process in 1839. The medium's inability to capture things in motion represented a significant shortcoming, even among its early advocates. Of Daguerre's Parisian cityscapes, Samuel F. B. Morse, who would soon introduce the daguerreotype to the United States, was forced to concede, "Objects moving are not impressed. The Boulevard, so constantly filled with a moving throng of pedestrians and carriages, was perfectly solitary, except an individual who was having his boots brushed."[1] There was nothing fast about these early photographs, which required between ten and thirty minutes for proper exposure.

The first glimpse of instantaneity finally came in 1851, when the British inventor William Henry Fox Talbot demonstrated a rapid exposure technique using an electric spark. The inaugural issue of *Humphrey's*, an American photographic journal, reported that Talbot had successfully photographed a piece of printed paper while it was spinning on a wheel. The bright flash of the spark illuminated the paper for a short period of time, appearing to freeze its motion in the resulting photograph. The editors wrote, "From this experiment the conclusion is inevitable, that it is in our power to obtain the pictures of all moving objects, no matter in how rapid motion they may be, provided we have the means of *sufficiently* illuminating them with a sudden electric flash."[2] It would be another thirty years before such illumination was readily available.

Instead, shorter lenses and faster emulsions were more immediately responsible for achieving instantaneous exposure. In the middle years of the nineteenth century, *instantaneous* was a relative term, used to describe many incremental improvements in photographic speed, not just those that revealed motion invisible to the naked eye. In the portrait studio, for example, a picture taken in a couple of seconds or fewer was advertised as instantaneous. This was highly desirable, because it allowed the sitter to assume a natural position unconstrained by the traditional posing apparatus, which had been required to hold still during longer exposures.

In the late 1850s, Edward Anthony pioneered a more radical type of instantaneous photography, capturing aspects of motion that had never been seen before with such clarity. Anthony's stereoscopic views of lively city streets were printed and widely distributed by the publishing company and photographic supply firm, E. & H. T. Anthony, which he owned with his brother. The stereoscopic camera was well suited to instantaneous work, since it needed only a short, relatively wide lens to create the pair of roughly three-inch square images that were meant to be experienced by peering through the binocular viewer. The short lens (or lenses) required less light to expose the small plates and was able to divide motion into fractions of a second. Oliver Wendell Holmes marveled at a bustling street scene that Anthony had photographed: "Every foot is caught in its movement with such suddenness that it shows as clearly as if quite still. We are surprised to see, in one figure, how long the stride is,—in another, how much the knee is bent,—in a third, how curiously the heel strikes the ground before the rest of the foot,—in all, how singularly the body is accommodated to the action of walking."[3]

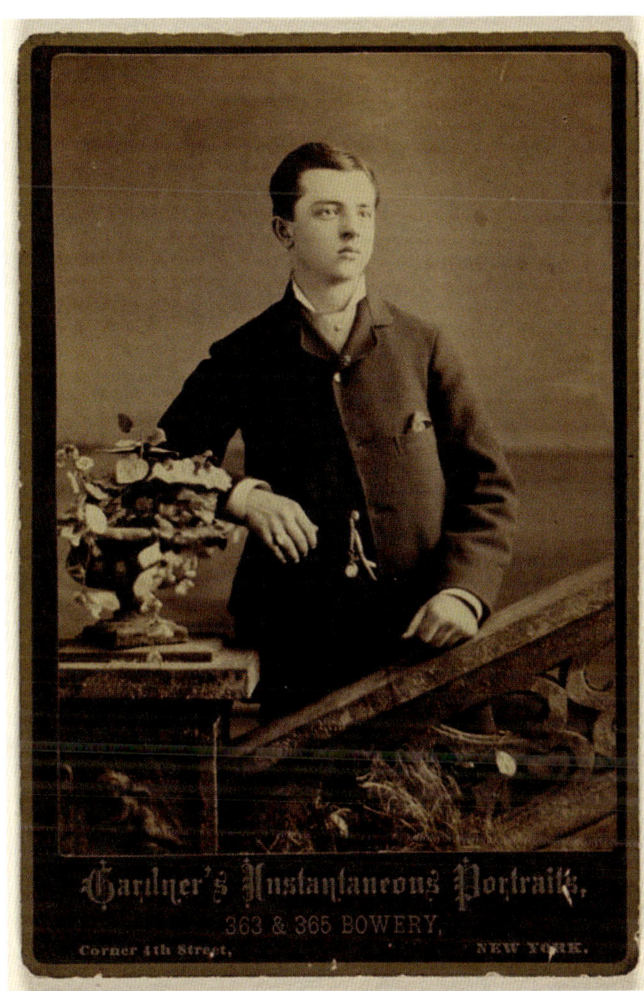

FIGURE 63. Gardner, "Unidentified Well-Dressed Young Man, Standing," ca. 1880. Albumen silver print.

Source: J. Paul Getty Museum, Los Angeles. Digital image courtesy of the Getty's Open Content Program.

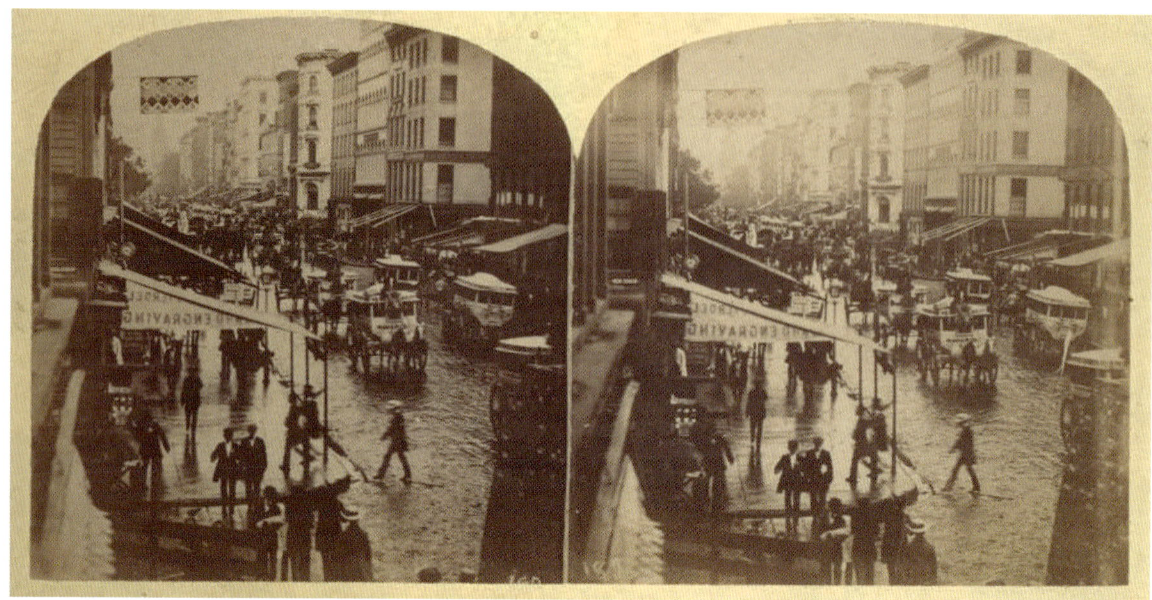

FIGURE 64. Edward Anthony, "Broadway on a Rainy Day," 1859. Albumen print (stereoscopic), 3 ¼″ × 6 ³⁄₁₆″ (card).

Source: Metropolitan Museum of Art, Warner Communications Purchase Fund, 1980

As *Humphrey's* had forecast nearly thirty years earlier, the instantaneous photograph was finally capable of fixing the "living world" in a way that even "the most practised eye could never seize."[4]

Photographers set out to document this unseen world and demonstrate their own technical acumen in the process. Instructions for creating mechanical drop shutters began appearing in the photographic press, as did advertisements for other patented shutter apparatuses, which allowed photographers to control exposure times more precisely. Earlier, less sensitive processes required only that the operator replace the lens cap to end the exposure. Although the instantaneous process made more pictures possible than ever before, it also had the effect of narrowing popular subjects. Express trains, boats under sail, and portraits of energetic children and animals dominated the instantaneous categories at photography exhibitions between 1860 and the mid-1880s.

These quotidian records of instantaneity paled in comparison to the images that the California-based photographer Eadweard Muybridge created beginning in 1872. Commissioned by railroad magnate and former governor of California Leland Stanford, Muybridge set out to document the phases of motion in a horse's gait. Using a sequence of cameras and galvanized trip wires connected to specially engineered shutters capable of operating at 1/2000th of a second, Muybridge's photographs revealed startlingly strange postures. When *Scientific American* reported the achievement and published engravings after some of Muybridge's photographs, the editors wrote, "Before these pictures were taken no artists would have dared to draw a horse as a horse really is when in motion, even if it had been possible for the unaided eye to detect his real attitude. At first sight an artist will say of many of the positions that there is absolutely no 'motion' at all in them."[5] In sharp focus and with none of the painterly ambiguity or blur that formerly suggested movement, the horses appeared stock-still. [See also Chapter 31, "Motion Blur."]

Complaints about the unnatural postures presented by instantaneous photography continued into the following decade. Highly light-sensitive gelatin dry plates became popular in the early 1880s. The plates came fully

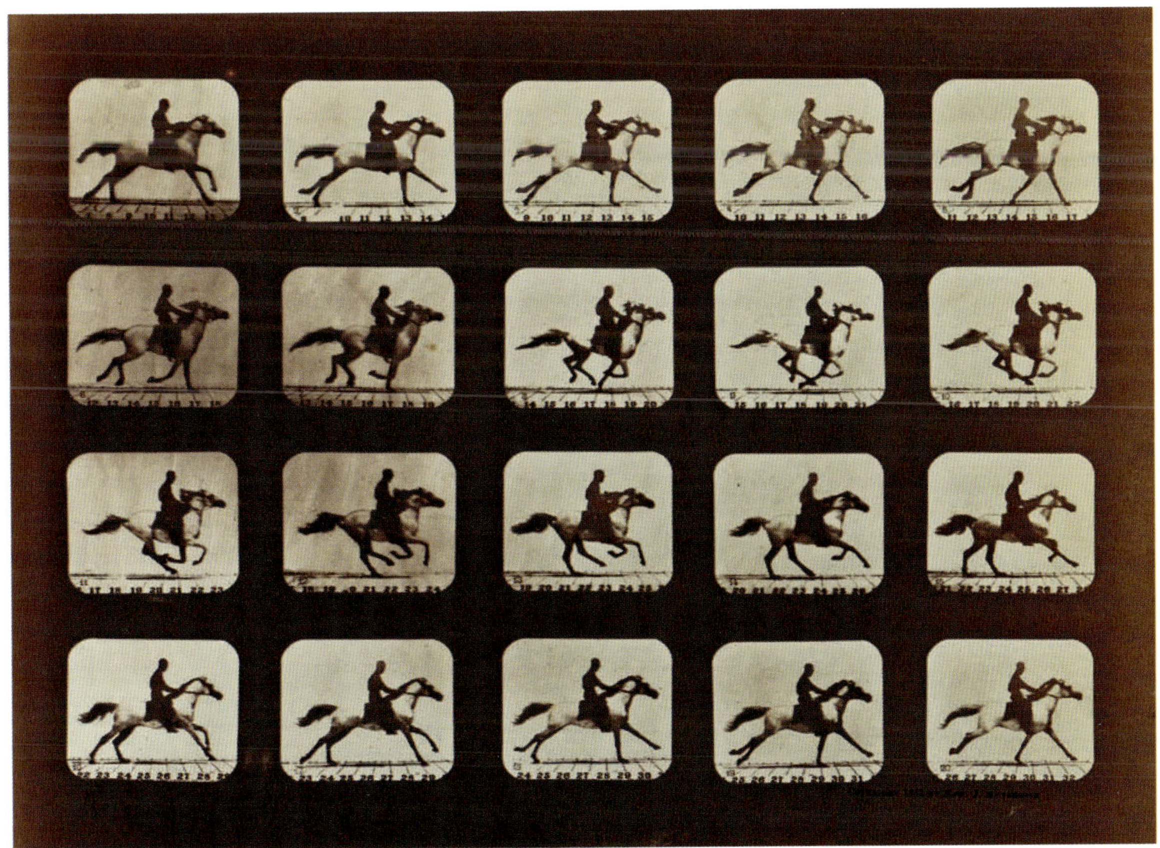

FIGURE 65. Eadweard Muybridge, "Running (Galloping)": negative, 1878–1879; print, 1881. Iron salt process, 7 7/16″ × 8 7/8″ (sheet).

Source: J. Paul Getty Museum, Los Angeles. Digital image courtesy of the Getty's Open Content Program.

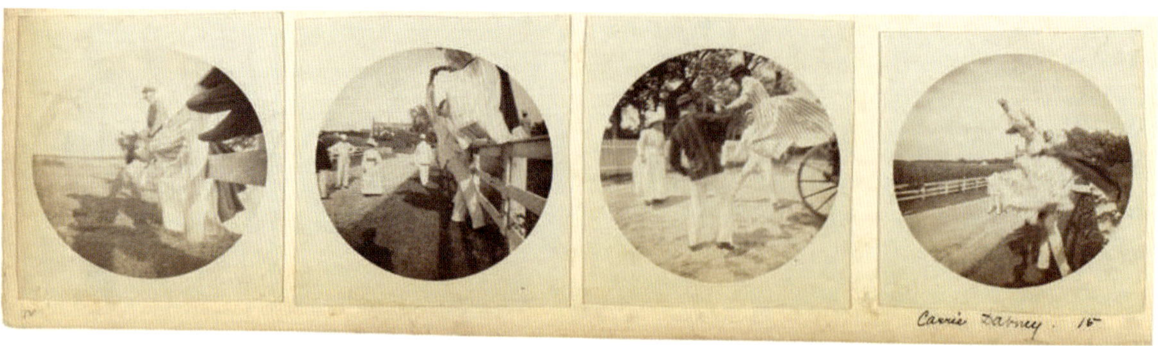

FIGURE 66. Unknown American photographer, "Charles Walter Amory Family Album (Detail)," 1888–1897. Album of gelatin silver and albumen prints, 10 5/8" × 12 3/16" (page).

Source: National Gallery of Art, Gift of Robert E. Jackson.

prepared and ready to expose, opening up photography to a growing class of amateurs who proved eager to experiment with instantaneous pictures. One amateur handbook noted, "Instantaneous photography possesses a fascination peculiar to itself; the amateur feels a peculiar desire to 'take something' and if the 'something' be an animate object . . . so much the better."[6] Just a few years later, Charles Taylor, author of the illustrated guide *Why My Photographs Are Bad*, cautioned readers, "Many amateurs seem to desire only instantaneous work, because there is more excitement in it; yet in most cases this very excitement is the cause of the failure to make a good picture."[7] Taylor explained that anticipating where the subject would pass through the frame and carefully timing the release of the shutter were two of the most difficult aspects of making instantaneous photographs. This was especially true when working with one of the original Kodak box cameras, which did not have viewfinders. Despite these challenges and critics' initial disdain, stilling a moving subject in an unlikely pose remains one of popular photography's lingering attractions.

16

MAGNESIUM FLASH

BLINDING LIGHTS, "fearful" volumes of irritating and noxious smoke, as well as the threat of death all attended the use of artificial light for photography in the nineteenth century.[1] Even for an already dangerous profession or hobby, these outcomes were severe. Judging from the space dedicated to magnesium flash in the photographic press during the second half of the nineteenth century, however, its danger didn't dissuade many photographers.

Although William Henry Fox Talbot had demonstrated the possibility of making photographs by the light of an electric spark as early as 1851, his experiment illuminated just a small piece of printed paper. To light an entire scene, a single spark was hardly sufficient. The element magnesium was first isolated in 1808 but became useful for photography only in 1859, following the invention of magnesium wire, which could be slowly passed through a flame to produce a bright, white light. An editorial in *Humphrey's* described magnesium light as "so bright that a person will instinctively shade his eyes."[2] In 1864, specially engineered "burners" were introduced, which combined a reflector with a clockwork mechanism that fed the wire automatically through the flame, creating a more constant intensity of light that lasted as long as a minute.

Magnesium wire was in the news repeatedly in the 1860s, particularly after the Scottish astronomer Charles Piazzi Smyth used it for photographs inside an Egyptian pyramid in 1865. Of the images he made, Smyth wrote that "all persons, whether travelers to the land of Egypt or not" will be able to experience the impressive scale of the pyramid's chambers.[3] Armchair travelers in the United States could also see in

96

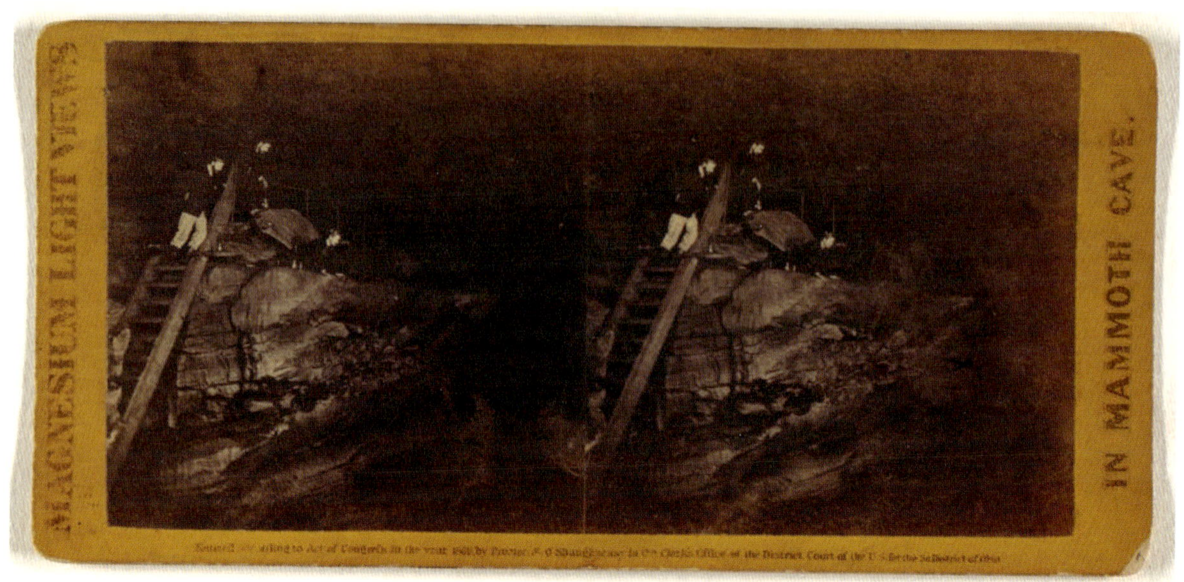

FIGURE 67. Charles Waldack, "Cliffs over the Dead Sea," 1866. Albumen prints, 3 ¼" × 6 ¾".

Source: J. Paul Getty Museum, Los Angeles. Digital image courtesy of the Getty's Open Content Program.

the dark closer to home. The American photographer Charles Waldack made a series of stereoscopic views in Kentucky's Mammoth Cave in 1866. Previous work in dark places had been accomplished with electric batteries, such as the photographs made by Nadar (Gaspard-Félix Tournachon) in the catacombs of Paris in the early 1860s, although the size and heft of batteries limited their use.

The dogged interest in magnesium, despite its formidable dangers and expense, underscores one of the most basic limitations of photography in the nineteenth century. There was, as late as 1900, a season for photographing. Winter, with its weak light and early dusk, was inhospitable, especially to studio work. As many authors noted, making better use of the hours of the day—even during more favorable seasons—was critical for photographers seeking to increase profits. Even eager amateurs wanted to be able to pursue their hobby when their salaried work was done. None of this could be accomplished without artificial lighting.

Winter and inclement weather were instead times for experimentation or copy work, photographically duplicating cartes-de-visite or other artworks that didn't require the rapid exposure times demanded by live sitters. Edward L. Wilson recalled visiting Boston during winter 1865 for research on an article about the city's photographers. Caught in a storm, he was forced to seek refuge in John Adams Whipple's studio, where the photographer was experimenting with magnesium wire. The unsuspecting writer became Whipple's portrait subject. Wilson wrote later, "We endured three minutes' exposure with the light glaring in our face, and the wire crackling and sparkling like electric sparks or infantile pyrotechnics."[4] Ever the booster, Wilson nevertheless was quick to qualify the experience: "The light produced is very beautiful, exceedingly bright, though not dazzling or painful to the eyes, and no doubt will be applied in many useful ways to photography."[5] Wilson and other members of the photographic press often struggled to describe the power of the light without making the experience seem unpleasant.

The photographic columnist and medical doctor John Towler was optimistic about the impact that magnesium light could have on the industry. He wrote a series of recommendations for making portraits (still the most lucrative area of photography) with magnesium wire. The concentrated light of the material introduced new challenges, however, and Towler warned, "If the background be placed very near the sitter, his shade or ghost will be strongly depicted on the background, which will tend to spoil the picture."[6] Towler suggested three ways of "exorcising" this ghost, including a three-point lighting system, which called for an assistant to light a small portion of magnesium between the sitter and the backdrop. This aesthetic aversion to the hard, dark shadows produced by flash light lasted well into the twenty-first century. [See also Chapter 43, "On-Camera Flash."] Towler concluded, "It is natural to expect that nocturnal galleries will soon be opened in our large cities for the accommodation and amusement of parties, who during the day are either too busy with the fabrication of dollars, or during the long evening crave after recreation or dissipation. Such a recreation would be the most innocent of our city dissipations, and besides the least expensive."[7]

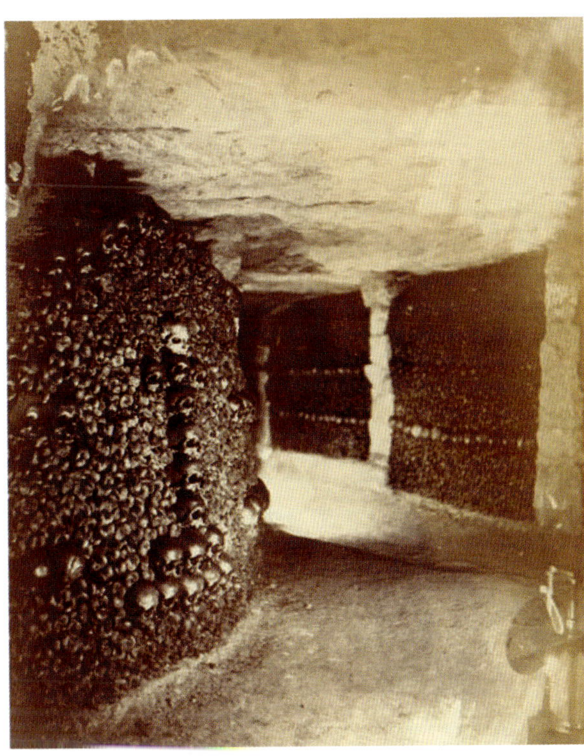

FIGURE 68. Nadar (Gaspard-Félix Tournachon), "View in the Catacombs," 1861. Albumen print, 8 7/8″ × 7 1/8″.

Source: J. Paul Getty Museum, Los Angeles. Digital image courtesy of the Getty's Open Content Program.

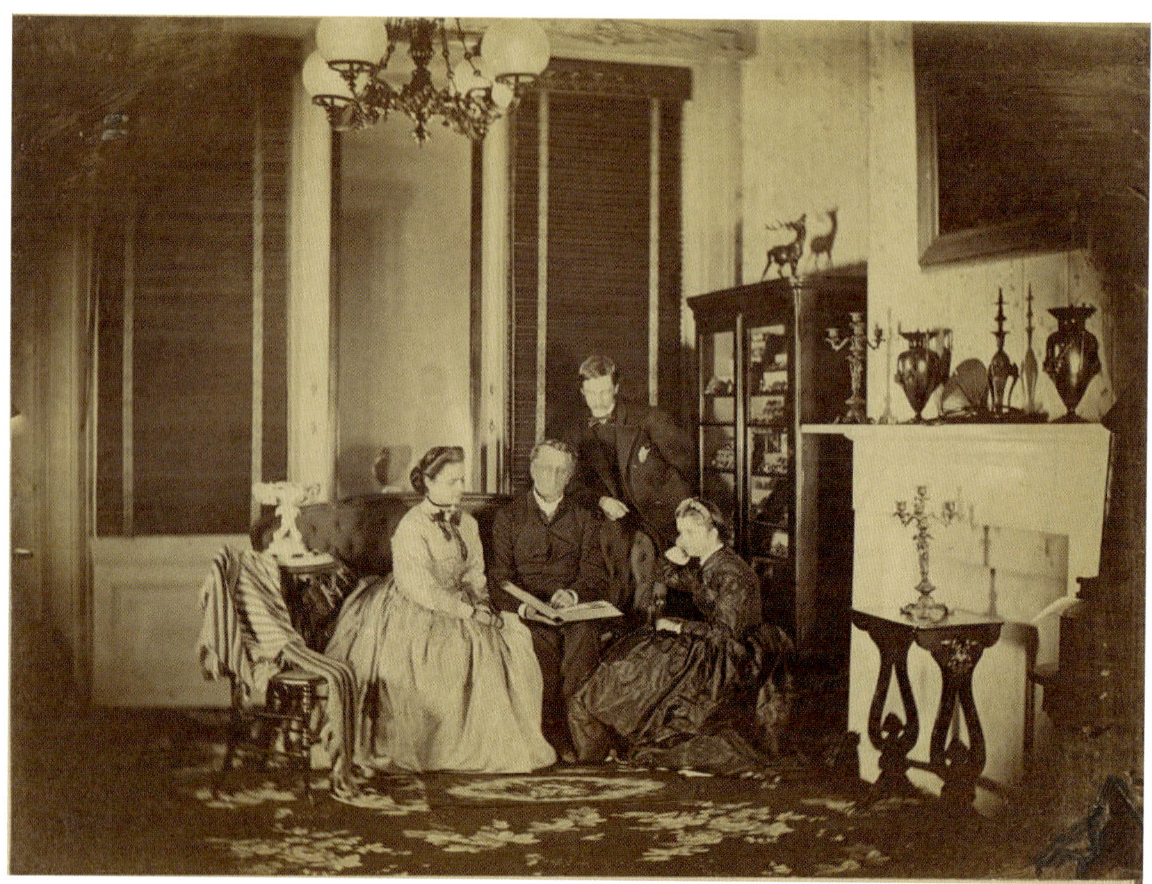

As the price for magnesium dropped and safer systems were engineered, magnesium-based flash powder became popular in the 1880s. *Anthony's Photographic Bulletin* suggested that the trend was well established by 1888, reporting paradoxically, "Nocturnal photography is still the order of the day."[8] Jacob Riis, a New York–based journalist-turned-social reformer, attributed his recognition of the need to photograph in the city's tenements to a newspaper announcement about the new, commercially manufactured German flash powder.[9] Riis's experiments not only illuminated the grim lives of New York's immigrants and laborers but also the dangers of flash powder: during one photo session, he set a building on fire.[10] Even the *Philadelphia Photographer* was forced to concede, "As to the danger attendant upon these flash-powders, it is well

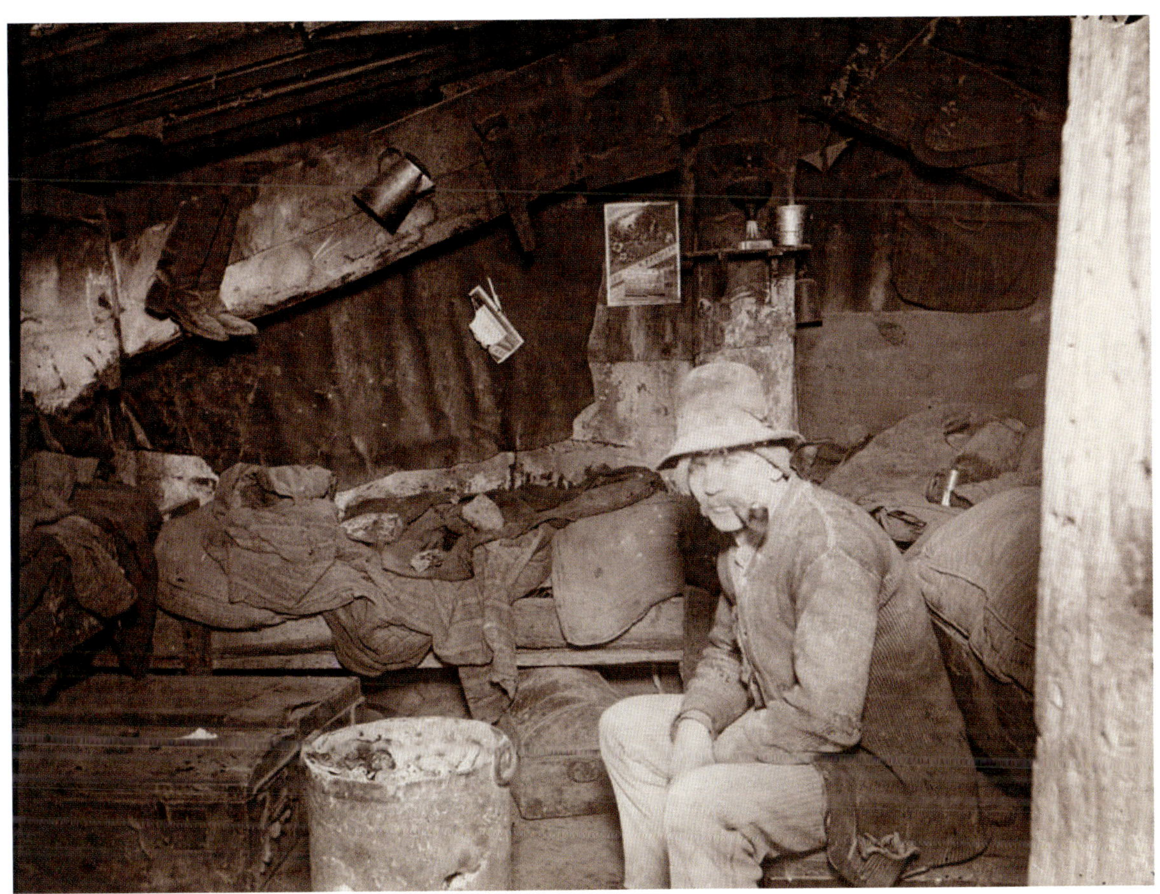

known, it is not chimerical or imaginary, and any representations to the contrary are reprehensible. Serious accidents have occurred with them, even to the loss of life."[11] Regardless, flash powder remained popular among amateur photographers until 1929, when single-use flash bulbs became widely available. So long dependent on the sun, photographers were finally able to dispense with the notion of a photographic season or time of day after the development of artificial lights.

FIGURE 70. Jacob A. Riis, "An Italian Home under a Dump," ca. 1888–1898. Gelatin silver print.

Source: Museum of the City of New York.

17

THE KODAK

TO KODAK, KODAKER, KODAKERY: the little box camera with an invented name changed much more than the language of photography.[1] Kodak transformed the very meaning of what it was to photograph and who could do it. During summer 1888, the black rectangular box became a familiar sight everywhere from city streets to picturesque country parks and on all the railway lines in between. In a newly minted photography column, the *New York Times* described the Kodakers: "On any pleasant Saturday afternoon now they may be seen almost everywhere, with the little boxes jauntily thrown over their shoulders."[2] The amateur market had been growing since the commercialization of the gelatin dry plate, but the introduction of the Kodak camera marked the beginning of an even more substantial social shift. Only a few weeks after the Kodak's arrival in stores, its inventor, George Eastman, wrote without overstatement, "From present indications it will be the most popular thing of the kind ever introduced."[3] Later that autumn, *Photographic Times and American Photographer* remarked, "This ingenious and convenient little instrument is now too well known to need much explanation or description from us."[4]

The Kodak was a simple box camera that measured 6 ½″ × 3 ½″ × 3 ½″ and was covered in black leather. For twenty-five dollars (about three weeks of an average salary in the United States), the would-be photographer received a camera preloaded with a roll of film, capable of making 100 exposures.[5] Upon completion of the roll, the entire camera was mailed back to the manufacturer for processing. The 2 ½″ round negatives were contact-printed, the camera reloaded with film, and all was returned to the user for ten dollars.

The company's advertising slogan, "You press the button, we do the rest," was not only catchy but also accurate. The longstanding technical challenges of photography (chemical preparation, printing, and even the loading of negative plates) were all resolved by the Kodak. Within the year, the Eastman Company released a new Kodak model, which made rectangular negatives, and still more options were slated for production through the end of the decade. In 1900, the introduction of the much cheaper Brownie camera, which sold for just one dollar and could be out-fitted with a roll of film for fifteen cents, surpassed all previous expecta-tions. Marketed to children as well as adults, more than 150,000 Brownie cameras were sold in their first year of production alone, more than all the cameras the company had sold since the original Kodak's first decade.[6]

The photographic fad gripping the nation during these years was often described as a kind of affliction. One sufferer noted, "The photo-graphic fever made many victims in my neighborhood before it marked me for its own. Indeed, I might have escaped it altogether, but for the Kodak."[7] There are dozens of mentions of "Kodak fiends"—photographic obsessives—in the popular and specialist press between 1888 and the

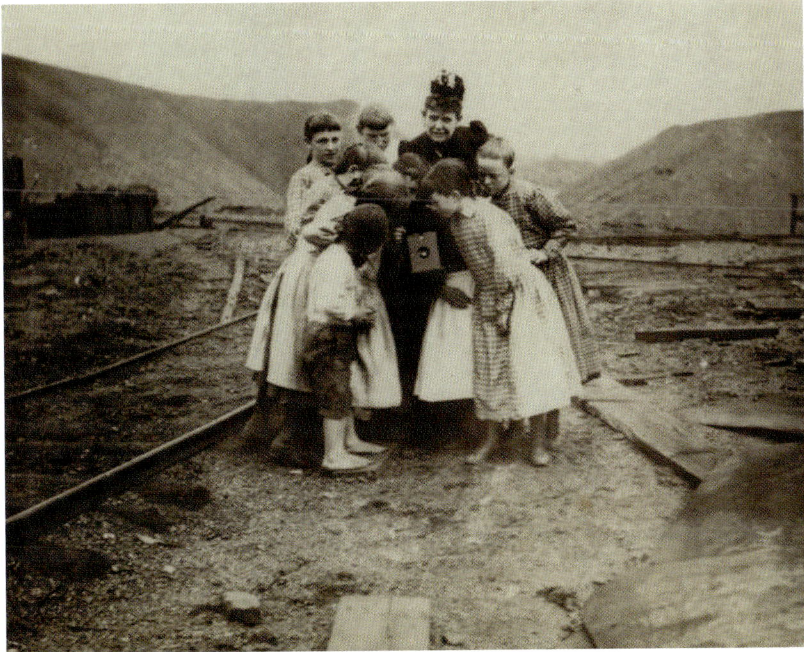

FIGURE 71. Photographer unknown, "A Kodak Creates a Sensation," ca. 1890–1900. Albumen print.

Source: Library of Congress Prints and Photographs Division.

turn of the century. While many used the language of addiction in jest, sometimes this epithet revealed real disdain for the Kodak's sudden and pervasive disruption of public life. Enterprising amateurs sold pictures to the press, usually without the consent of their subjects, who were as likely to be public figures as attractive young women caught unawares in sporting costumes or at the beach.[8]

FIGURE 72. Unknown maker (American), "Amateur Snapshot Album," ca. 1890–1892. Cyanotypes, 11 1/8" × 14 1/2" (album).

Source: Metropolitan Museum of Art, Funds from various donors, 1997.

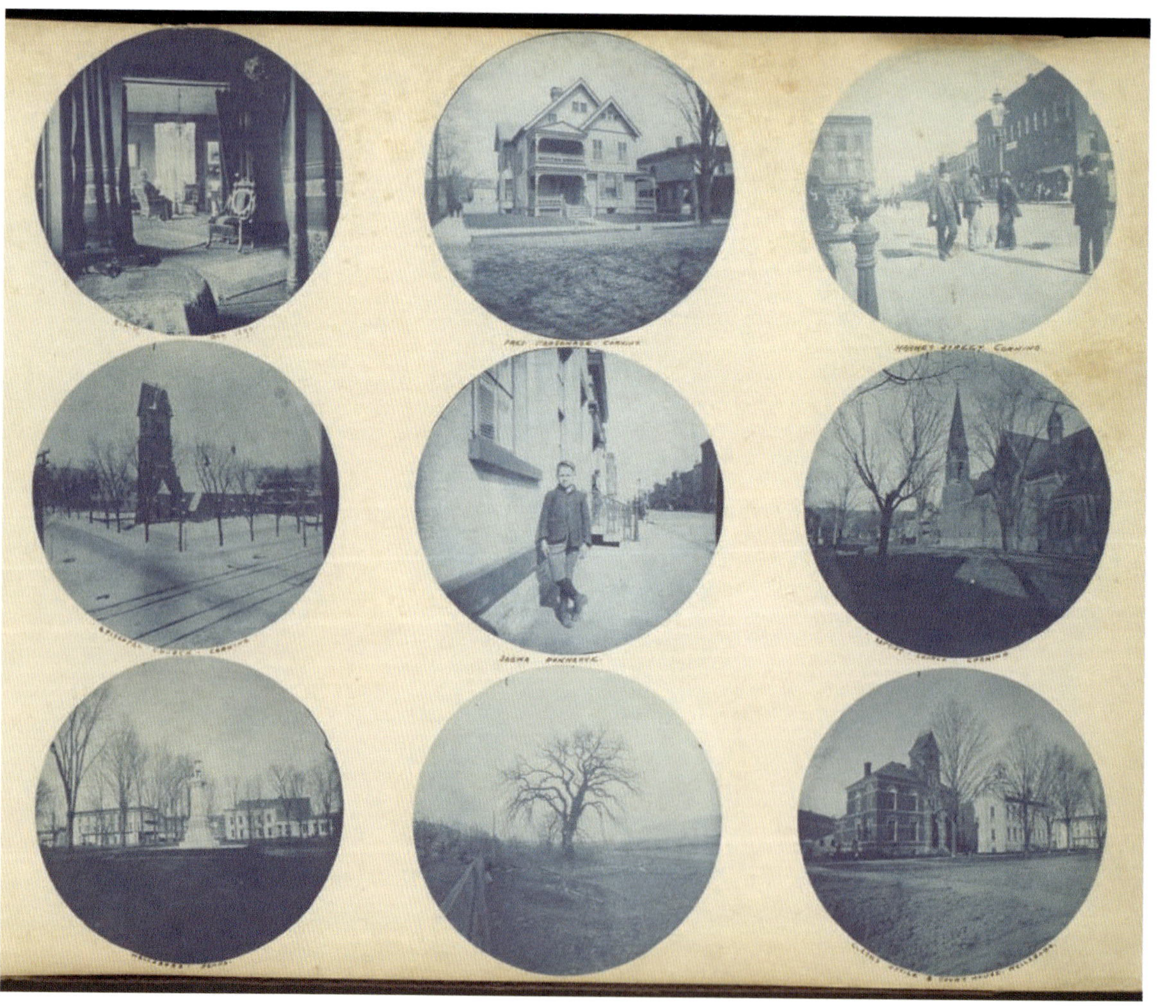

> FIGURE 73. Photographer unknown, "Snapshot: Dog and Man," ca. 1890. Gelatin silver print, 3 7/16" × 15 1/6" (card).

Source: Metropolitan Museum of Art, Purchase, Horace W. Goldsmith Foundation Gift, through Joyce and Robert Menschel, 1993.

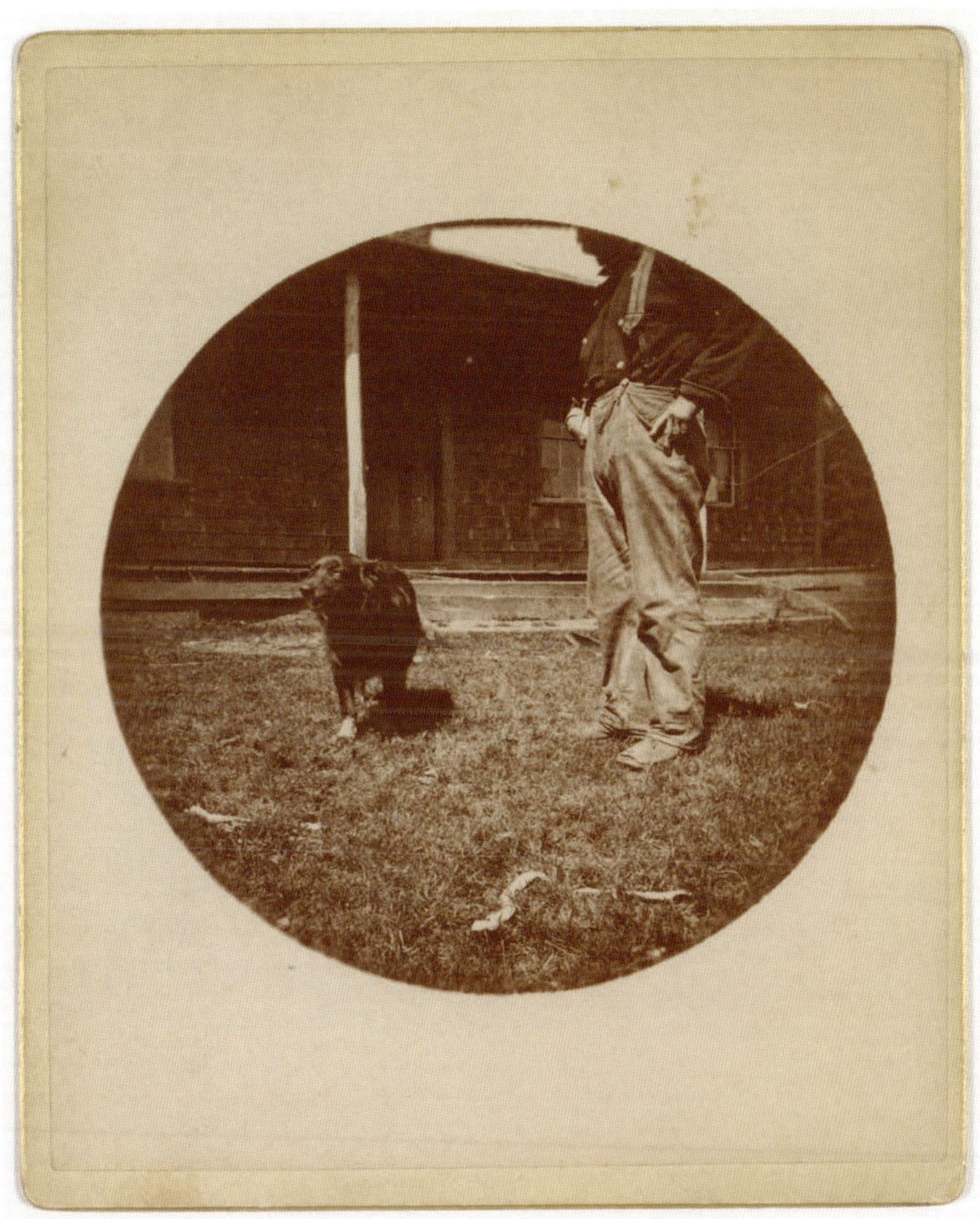

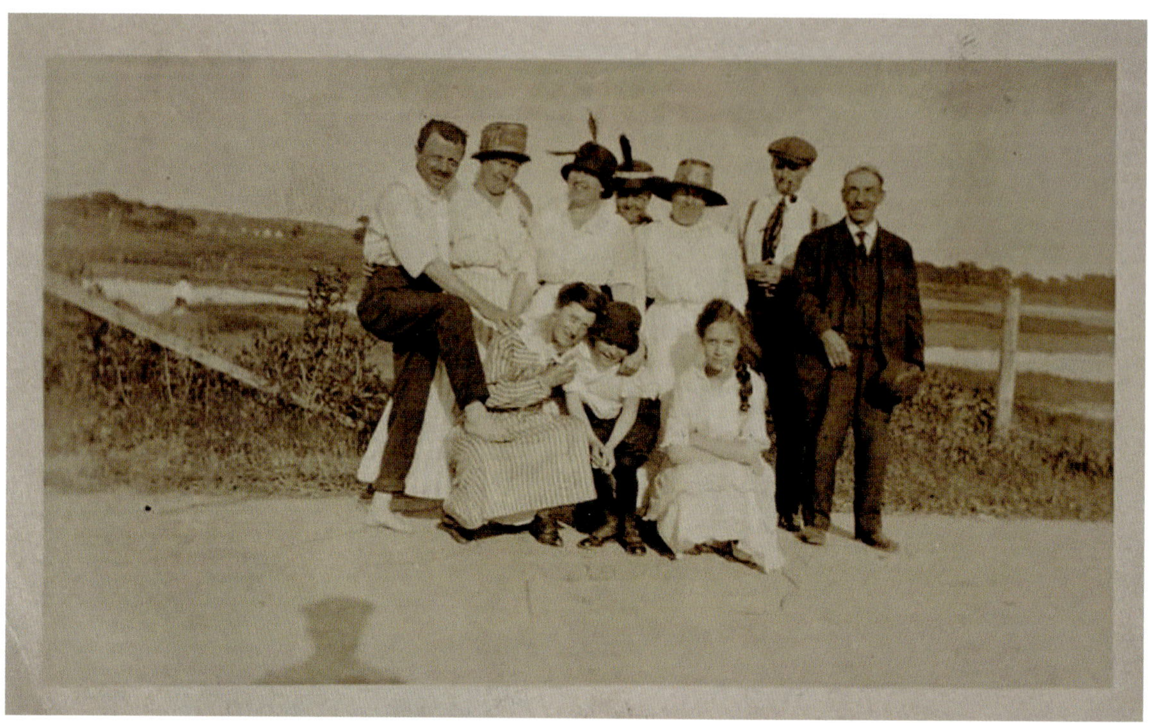

The original Kodak lacked a viewfinder and focusing ring, technical details that contributed to its pictures' distinctive look. Although some cameras were sold with a chart to calculate focal distances, blurry pictures, whether due to subject proximity or movement, were early aesthetic hallmarks of the Kodak. These stylistic features were soon associated with the broad class of amateur pictures, which came to be known as snapshots. The noun *snap-shot* had been in use since the early nineteenth century to describe a hunter's hasty rifle shot, made without careful aim, often at moving prey.[9] Although early photographers occasionally referred to pictures as *snap-shots*, it was the popularity of the Kodak that vaulted the term into wide circulation at the end of the nineteenth century. The haphazard nature of photographing with the small, handheld box was known to create vertiginously tilted horizons or abruptly cropped subjects or include the photographer's shadow in the foreground of the wide-angle lens. [See also Chapter 26, "New Angles," and Chapter 36, "Close-Cropped Portraits."] Without the ability to frame and focus the view, critics grumbled that the Kodak also inspired experienced practitioners to "sacrifice . . . *picture making* to the facilities for procuring a rapid succession of 'snap shots.'"[10] Even before these unconventional aesthetics were adopted by modernist photographers as evidence of an authentically photographic vision, they represented the dramatically expanded scope of photography that the Kodak enabled. By the turn of the century, anyone could be a photographer.

PART III

1901–1929

CONCERN OVER THE ROLE OF AMATEURS in the photographic community marked the beginning of the twentieth century, as new camera technologies made the process easier and more affordable. People could now make their own pictures, without the aid of a professional photographer. The Kodak Brownie camera led this revolution in access. Not only was the Brownie inexpensive, but its small scale also meant that the camera was exceptionally portable. The newfound ubiquity of cameras also fueled debates over privacy and critics began to question photography's limits in daily life.

Many amateurs were content to make casual snapshots, but others enthusiastically sought out technically challenging subject matter, from wildlife photography to candids and night scenes. These advanced amateurs participated in camera clubs and entered their photographs in regional competitions. The photographic literature swelled to meet the new demand as camera and film manufacturers, photo clubs, and many individual authors published handbooks designed expressly for amateur photographers.

In reaction to this rapid expansion and democratization of photographic practice, established photographers endeavored to reinforce aesthetic rules and define the tenets of photographic art. They adopted previously abandoned technologies for creative ends, displaying a preference for the handmade aspects of nineteenth-century photography in contrast to the uniformity of commercial photo finishing, which developed film and printed photographs for the mass of amateur users.

18

FIGURES IN THE LANDSCAPE

THE POPULARITY OF LANDSCAPE PHOTOGRAPHY surged at the turn of the century as amateurs armed with hand cameras sought worthy subjects. A Seneca Camera Company manual explained, "The amateur is advised to begin with landscapes. Not only are the results very pleasing, but the chances of success for the beginner are greatest, and the lack of experience is not so keenly felt in this as in other classes of work."[1] Other how-to books recommended landscapes because photographing outdoors was a healthy antidote to the workaday life. "The value of the Photographic Camera in tempting forth those who lead confined lives into the fresh air of the woods and fields is becoming more and more felt every day," one author noted.[2] So many amateurs set out to the countryside on weekends that the *New York Times* suggested that hotels provide darkrooms on-site. The newspaper assured proprietors that "they will make a host of friends, and, besides, the views of their hotels and places of natural beauty in the vicinity will prove not a bad advertisement."[3]

With this expansion of the practice came rules to tame the new, untutored class of photographers. One piece of advice was uncontested in both the professional and amateur photographic literature for more than a century: do not let subjects look at the camera, unless making a portrait. Even before the vogue for "candid" photographs, how-to manuals recommended that subjects learn to ignore the photographer taking their pictures. [See also Chapter 25, "Candids."] Arthur Hope wrote in the *Amateur Photographer's Hand Book,* "Many landscape views are failures, through the introduction of people in the immediate foreground, staring at the camera as if they had rushed in where they did not belong and were not wanted, to

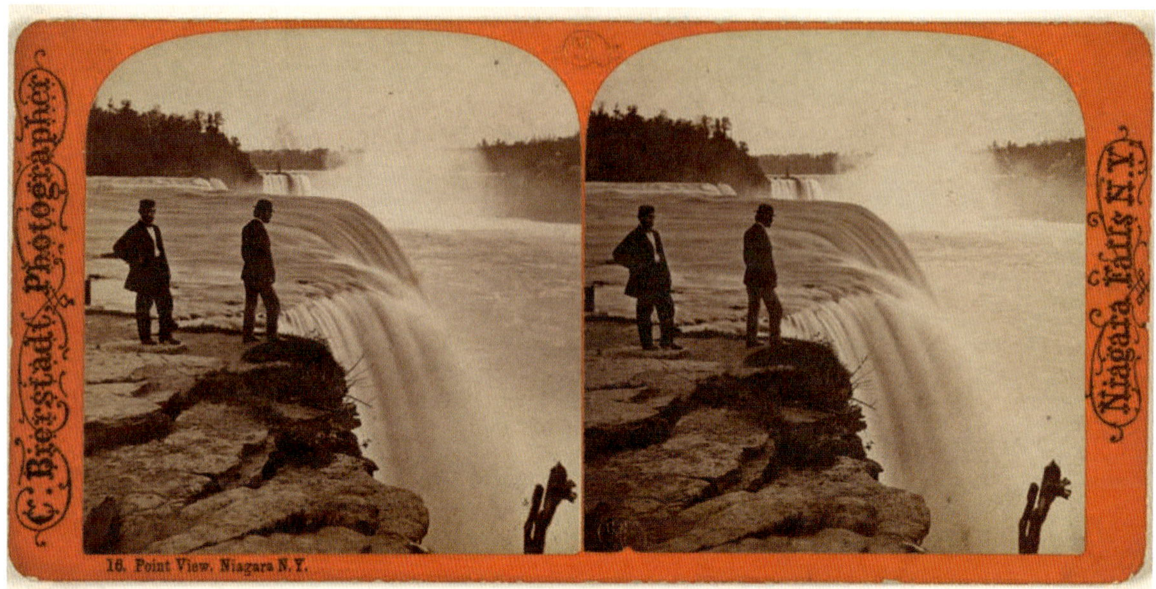

FIGURE 75. Charles Bierstadt, "Point View, Niagara, N.Y.," ca. 1870. Albumen silver print.

Source: J. Paul Getty Museum, Los Angeles. Digital image courtesy of the Getty's Open Content Program.

'get their pictures taken.'"[4] He conceded that this was not always the fault of the photographer: "Those who have tried to take views of charming bits of scenery in our public parks, know what a desire some people seem to have to get into the view; and stop where they are entirely out of place."[5] The guidebook author W. F. Carlton concurred: "In composing a scene where figures are introduced, it is bad taste to represent the figures as looking at the camera; this is a very common mistake among beginners, and naturally, as the camera being the central point of interest, all persons in sight, unless cautioned by the photographer, just previous to the exposure will invariably gaze at that instrument."[6] He offered a solution that was common practice among professional photographers: "In many cases the effect is better if the figures are placed with the side or back to the camera."[7]

Earlier photographic manuals demanded only that subjects appear to belong in the scene. In his widely read 1864 guidebook, Marcus Aurelius Root maintained, "Whatever be the species of picture which the photographer aims to produce, he must follow the great law of unity; i.e. the composition should have but one decided point of interest."[8] He provided an example: "In a composition representing inanimate nature; e.g. a group of deer—by introducing hunters, horses, &c., you destroy the unity of interest and infringe a law of art."[9] Following the established conventions of landscape painting in the picturesque tradition, early photographers included figures who could be found "naturally" in the landscape and provide some sense of life or scale, although it didn't much matter where they were looking. Preferably these were farmers, herdsmen, and peasants: a cast of characters unambiguously distinct from the late nineteenth-century guidebook author's own social class.

By the turn of the century, the picturesque convention was united with the preference for unposed figures. *Photography Indoors and Out* noted,

> A farm scene is generally improved by a glimpse of cattle, of the milkmaid, of the cowboy, of the farm hand at the hayrick or the farmer himself at the bars. A picture of a roadside spring is improved, perhaps, by a figure with cup stooping to drink. But every figure should be carefully introduced, so as to look entirely natural, and not posed, or it is better to leave out such an attempt altogether.[10]

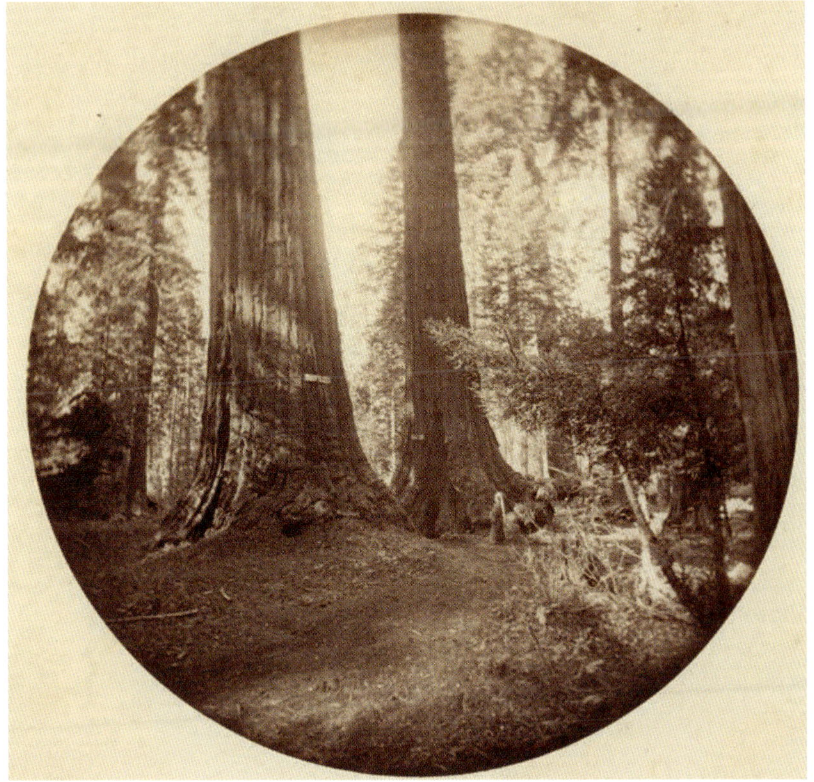

 Carleton Watkins, "Old Dominium and Uncle Tom's Tavern. Calaveras Grove," ca. 1878. Albumen silver print, 4^{15}/$_{16}$" × 4^{15}/$_{16}$" (image).

Source: Metropolitan Museum of Art, Gilman Collection, Gift of the Howard Gilman Foundation, 2005.

The effect of naturalness was often achieved through the inclusion of props or by engaging the subject in a relevant activity. One author warned, "Perhaps there is no more certain way to spoil an otherwise good picture, than to pose your cousin or best girl in the picture center, with nothing to do but stare at the camera. If you must place her in the range of the lens, give her some appropriate employment, such as picking daisies, golden rod, or other wild flowers."[11]

The Kodak manuals were particularly adamant about the role of figures in the landscape. With annotated illustrations, Kodak's *How to Make Good Pictures* detailed the appropriate positioning of a figure in the middle or foreground of a scene. [See also Chapter 8, "Foreground Interest."] The guide directed readers, "Take a good look at the picture on the next page (at left). Now place the tip of your finger over the image of the man. Quite a change, isn't it? Something happens; the scene becomes a bit desolate, though all the beauty of Nature is still there."[12] The natural scene no longer required the picturesque "rustics" of old, since the early twentieth-century

FIGURE 77. Photographer unknown, "Woman Standing in a Field," n.d. Gelatin silver print.

Source: Collection of Barbara Levine/ Project B.

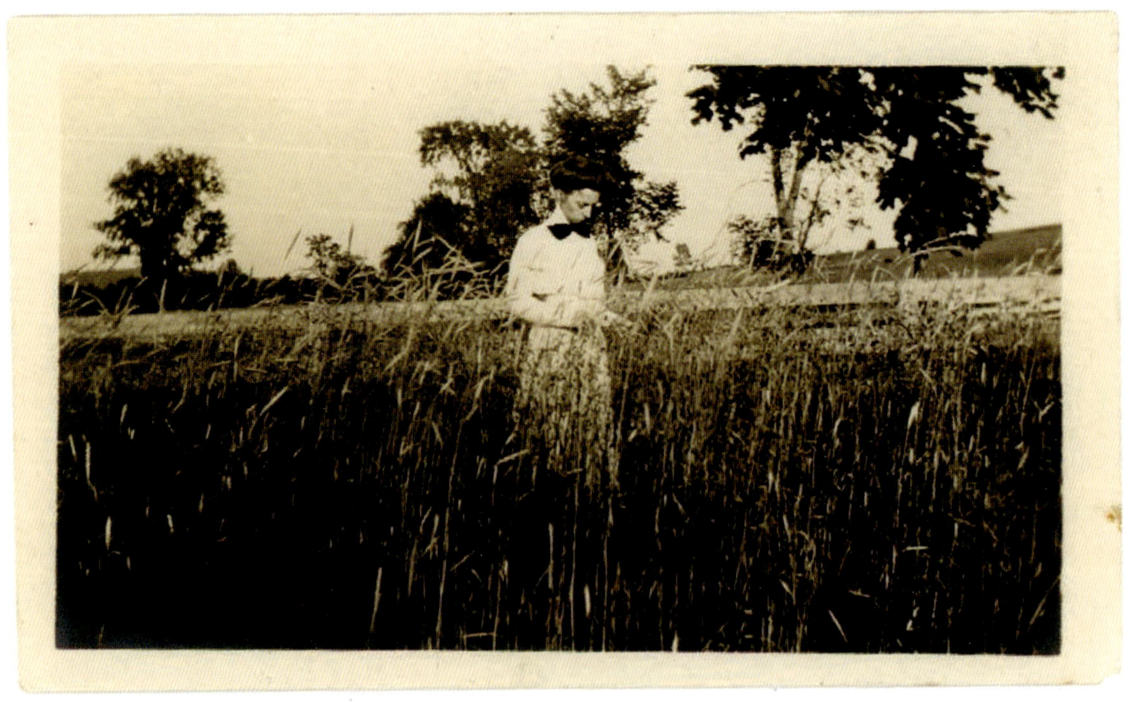

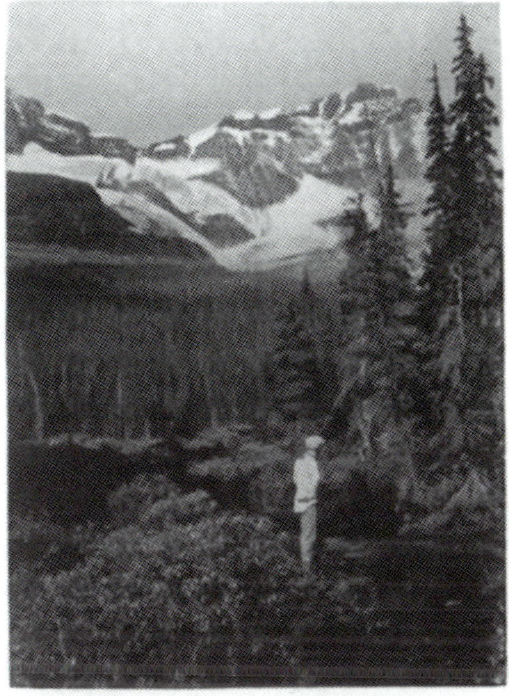
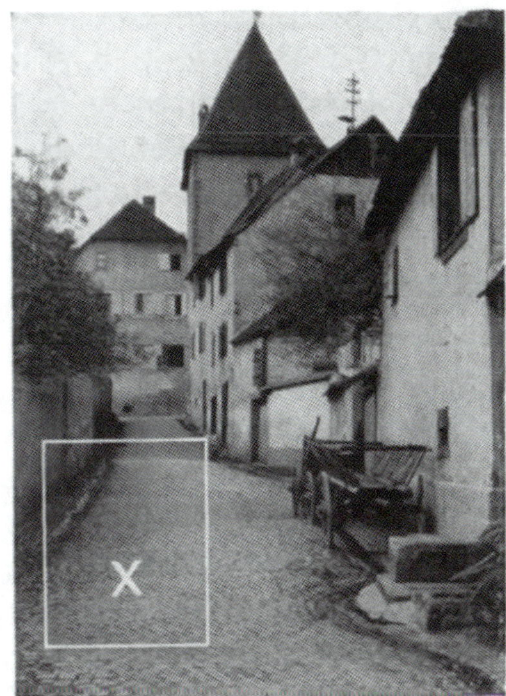

Does the figure help the picture?   *Would a figure at X help this?*

landscape was full of photographers and their willing apprentices.[13] Still, the admonition followed in the Kodak handbook too: "Of course it is a mistake to have the subject you use as an incidental figure in such a picture too near or looking at the camera."[14] Throughout the twentieth century these stringent rules and the near-constant exhortation of "don't look at the camera!" shaped the experience of being in photographs as much as the practice of making them.

FIGURE 78. Photographer unknown, "The Human Interest Element," from *How to Make Good Pictures* (Rochester, NY: Eastman Kodak, 1936), 74–75.

Source: Author's collection.

19

WILDLIFE PHOTOGRAPHY

AN EARLY KODAK guide deadpanned, "Every year hundreds, almost thousands, of Kodak photographs of deer are made, and in nearly every instance the owner of the camera is surprised, often disgusted, at the insignificance of the animal, frequently a magnifying glass being necessary before its whereabouts can be discovered."[1] The author's solution was to simply wait until the deer came closer. Buried further in the chapter is a note about telephoto lenses, although even Kodak admitted that they weren't very useful for animal pictures because of their slow shutter speeds.

The first telephoto lens was invented in 1840 and went into production in the 1850s.[2] The lens was recommended for landscapes because it was still far too slow to photograph animals in the wild. One photographer described a typically frustrating experience outdoors: "A cow, that has been ruminating among the grass, forming a fine point in the middle ground, gets up slowly, takes a quiet look at the strange three-legged thing that is standing in the field, and walks away deliberately, giving us a fine landscape, with a continuous cow of many heads, much body, and centipedian legs, through the centre!"[3]

During most of the nineteenth century, portrait lenses were the most highly engineered lenses on the market. Since their subjects demanded minimal distortion, portrait lenses were longer than wide-view landscape lenses, but they also required significant depth of focus at fast speeds. [See also Chapter 21, "Soft Focus" and Chapter 39, "Fish-Eye."] The quest for a true telephoto lens wasn't taken up again until the end of the nineteenth century, when several entered production at the leading optical supply manufacturers. Still, these were chiefly recommended for technical work. An article on the Parvin telephoto suggested that the lens would be most useful to geologists and travelers aiming to identify distant features of the static environment.[4] As the amateur market expanded, interest in the telephoto also increased, though these pictures were still relegated to specialist or technical categories in exhibitions rather than the general landscape classification. Some even argued that the telephoto lens could not be considered a naturalistic view, since it reproduced an image unattainable by human vision alone.

Photographic hunting with the telephoto was still a rarefied pursuit until its popularization by *National Geographic Magazine*. In the early twentieth century, the magazine published long articles accompanied by extensive photographic documentation, introducing readers to exotic places, as well as unexpected views of nature in their own backyards,

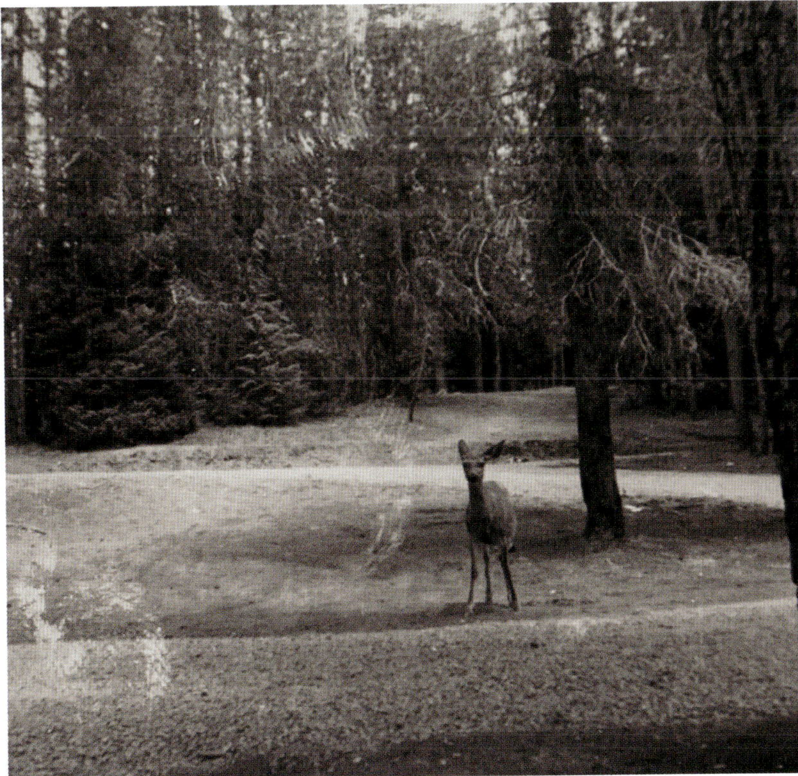

FIGURE 79. Karen Magnuson, "Doe—Yosemite," 1957. Gelatin silver print.

Source: Courtesy of the artist.

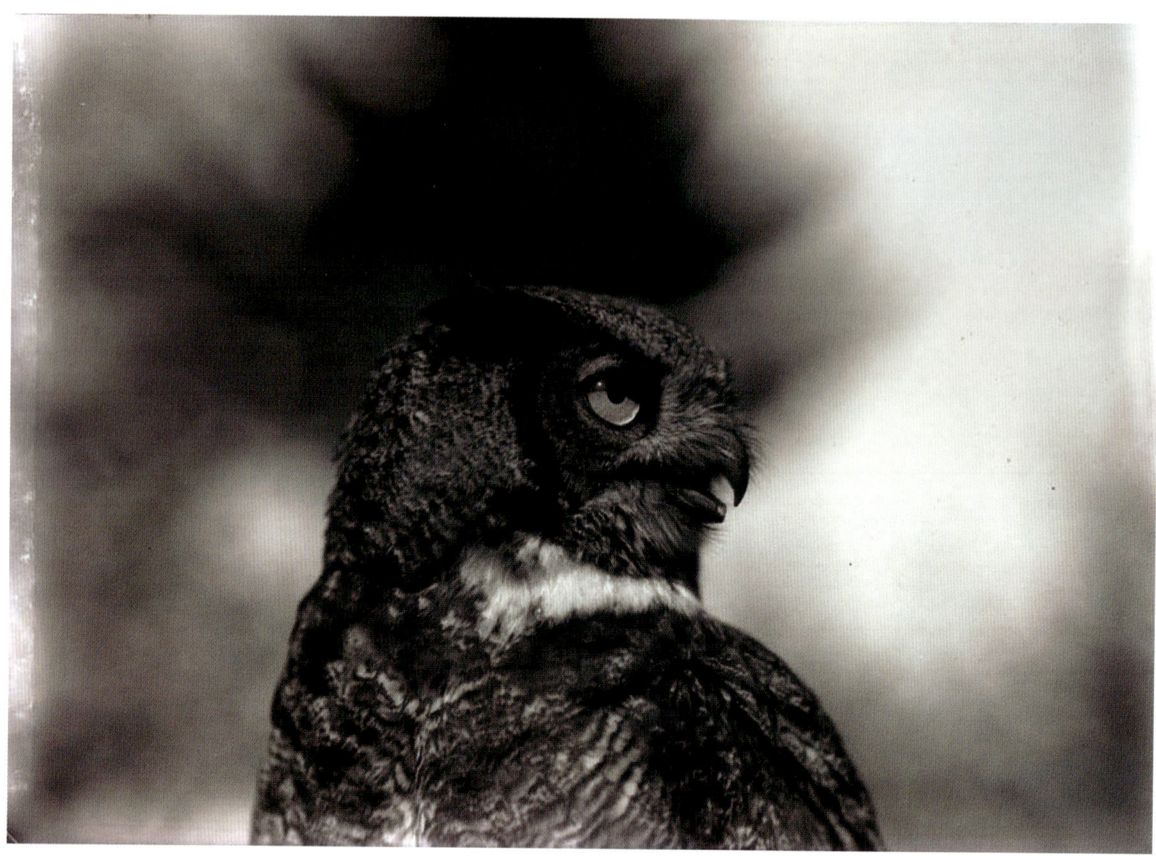

FIGURE 80. William L. Finley, "Dusky Horned Owl," 1909. Glass plate negative, 5″ × 7″.

Source: Oregon Historical Society Library.

often with the aid of the telephoto lens. The emphasis of such stories was divided equally between the animals and their photographer, highlighting the perseverance and technical acumen required to obtain wildlife views. *National Geographic* stories frequently exploited the "shooting" euphemism, arguing for preservation of wildlife through the humane hunting of animals with cameras rather than rifles. [See also Chapter 17, "The Kodak."] US Congressman George Shiras, also a passionate nature photographer and friend of Theodore Roosevelt, argued in the magazine, "It is not necessary to convert the wilderness into an untenanted and silent waste in order to enjoy the sport of successfully hunting wild birds and animals."[5]

>FIGURE 81. Unknown photographer, "Bohlman and Finley Photographing Ducklings," 1901. Glass plate negative, 7″ × 5″.

Source: Oregon Historical Society Library.

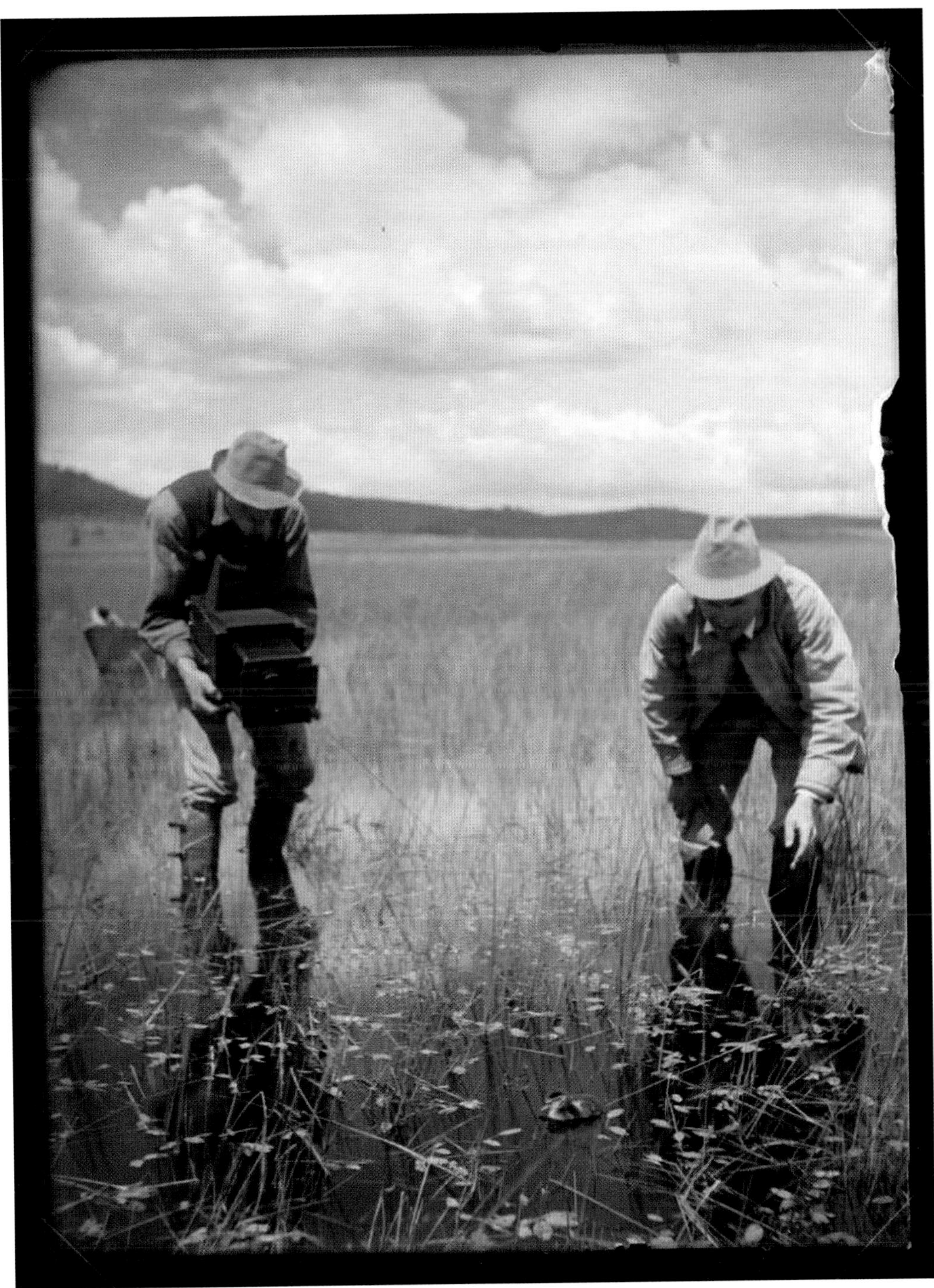

118

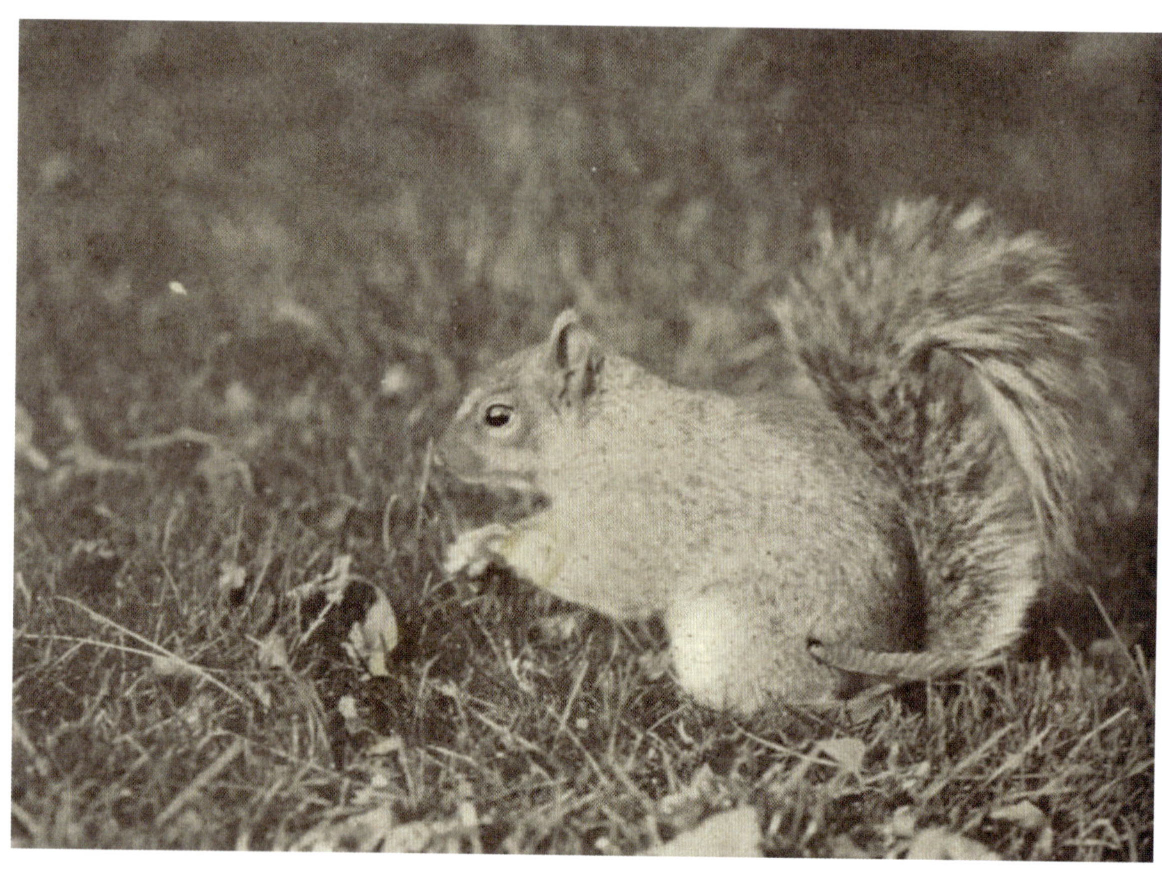

William Finley, a young birder who would later become president of the Oregon Audubon Society, was a prime advocate for wildlife photography in support of conservation. In 1923, *National Geographic* published a portfolio of Finley's vast body of work, which he created with his wife, Irene Finley, and his childhood friend Herman Bohlman. Finley described in detail the elaborate setups required to create artistic and useful photographs of birds in their natural habitats. Following precedent, he wrote, "Behind the years of hunting lies an eagerness for the chase that has been fully satisfied in hunting and shooting with the camera."[6] Pictures of the Finley group engaged in the hunt reveal the supreme difficulty of photographing nature during these years; perching on ladders, wading in marshes with giant cameras, and rigging remote triggers with string were regular activities for the Finleys and Bohlman. Few enthusiastic amateurs could afford a similar outlay of effort and expense. The Naturalists' Graflex camera, which could accommodate a 26" inch focal length lens, cost nearly $200, without the lens, in the 1910s.[7]

Despite these limitations, how-to manuals eventually began to instruct amateurs in the creation of wildlife photography in the early twentieth century. In the "Bird Pictures" chapter, *Practical Notes on Photography* advised concealing the camera, or the entire photographer, in a "bower of bushes and leaves" and lying in wait near a nest.[8] Another photographer suggested a similarly low-tech solution: "Did you ever try standing upon the shoulders of a companion while making a photograph?"[9] The sample photographs in these guides differed markedly from professional productions, not least because the animal subjects were common ones, such as squirrels, pigeons, turtles, and frogs. Amateur photographers in the early twentieth century were wholly consumed by capturing an animal—any animal—in complete stillness at a scale large enough to fill the frame. The stylistic elements, which might later read as trends, such as shallow depth of field, were considered necessary sacrifices. [See also Chapter 42, "Boke."] The rules of good photography were willingly traded for the satisfaction of hunting with a camera.

20

PAINTERLY PHOTOGRAPHS

IN REACTION TO THE KODAK'S straightforward simplicity, turn-of-the-century art photographers embraced the limitations imposed by earlier photographic processes. [See also Chapter 17, "The Kodak."] Alfred Stieglitz, the art photographers' great champion, described the impact of the Kodak camera in *Scribner's Magazine*: "Placing in the hands of the general public a means of making pictures with but little labor and requiring less knowledge has of necessity been followed by the production of millions of photographs. It is due to this fatal facility that photography as a picture-making medium has fallen into disrepute in so many quarters."[1] Stieglitz and others in his circle aimed to elevate photography's reputation for artistry. These self-proclaimed "pictorial," or art, photographers sought to transform the medium from a purely mechanical pursuit into one that favored ideas and emotion over the direct transcription of visual facts.

Pictorialists accomplished this goal by rejecting the "fatal facility" of modern photography and returning instead to vintage printing processes, such as gum bichromate. [See also Chapter 14, "Permanent Carbon Prints."] The process called for mixing pigment with a layer of gum arabic made sensitive to light in combination with potassium bichromate. When exposed to light beneath the negative, areas of the image that received more light were hardened. The print was then finished by brushing on warm water, enabling the photographer to selectively dissolve areas of the hardened gum, resulting in a print that resembled a watercolor or wash drawing (see Figure 84).

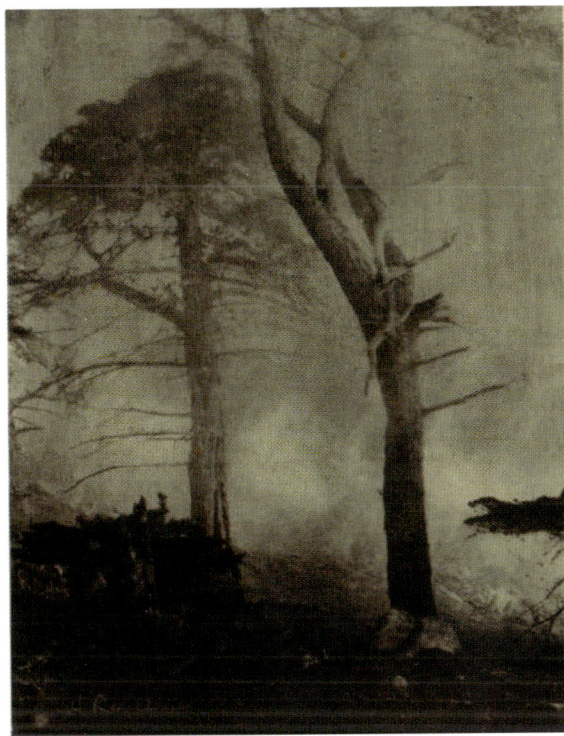

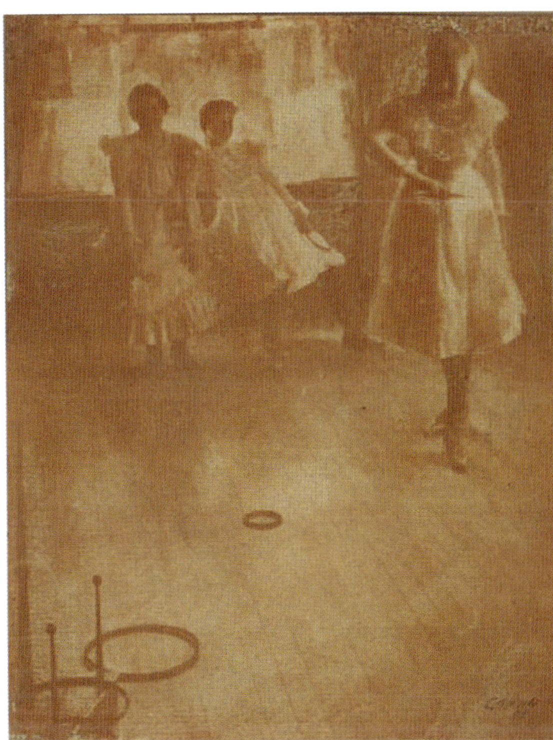

There was little room for any such creativity in the burgeoning photo-finishing industry launched by Eastman Kodak. One critic complained, "The snap-shot artist who, without much consideration, presses the button and sends his negative to a dealer or professional to be developed and printed, receives in return a photograph in which, so far as he is concerned, there is the least possible trace of his individuality."[2] Stieglitz and other artistic photographers preferred the gum bichromate process to modern techniques because it gave the photographer greater control and emphasized handwork. A book review in the *American Amateur Photographer* pointed to an instructional guidebook that found the variability of the gum process troublesome, citing the difficulty of making multiple identical prints. Yet the reviewer countered, "To a professional photographer who does business by the dozen the objections may have some weight, but to the artist it is surely one of its

FIGURE 83 (LEFT). Henry Ravell, "Fog and Cypress Trees," 1910s. Gum bichromate print.

Source: Metropolitan Museum of Art, Gift of Mrs. Florence D. R. Lothrop, in memory of her brother, Henry Ravell, 1930.

FIGURE 84 (RIGHT). Clarence H. White, "The Ring Toss," 1899. Gum bichromate print, 7 1/16″ × 5 1/2″.

Source: Metropolitan Museum of Art, Alfred Stieglitz Collection, 1933.

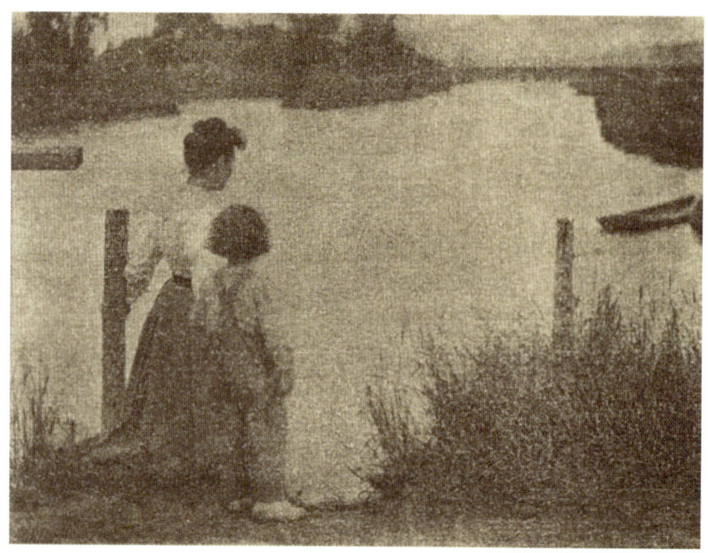

FIGURE 85. Gertrude Käsebier, "[The Still Water]," 1904. Gum bichromate print, 5 7⁄8″ × 7 3⁄4″.

Source: J. Paul Getty Museum, Los Angeles. Digital image courtesy of the Getty's Open Content Program.

advantages."[3] For pictorial photographers, the uniqueness of the print signaled the artist's individual vision, or, what one photographer described as "the personal element."[4]

In instructional articles and reviews, authors frequently rehearsed the history of gum bichromate, taking care to describe it as a long-outmoded process introduced in the 1850s. A typical instructional article began, "Although this method of printing was introduced nearly half a century since, it was not much followed until the last year or two."[5] Establishing gum bichromate's archaism and, by extension, the oppositional stance of the photographers who used it, these writers positioned themselves as neo-Luddites within the otherwise highly technologized and increasingly professionalized discourse of photography.

While advocates of the process might seem historically minded, in fact their embrace of photography's past was limited. Turn-of-the-century art photographers rejected the medium's longest-standing aesthetic tenet: the demand for a "sharp, crisp and clear" image.[6] [See also Chapter 1, "The American Process."] One critic wrote of the changing fashion, "Now it is no longer the photograph full of detail, sharp in outline, technically perfect, that pleases. What is aimed at is breadth of effect, the subordination of detail to the point where the picture represents the landscape as the artistic eye would see it."[7] The celebrated photographer Edward Steichen, known for "getting painter's results" in his photographs, agreed.[8] He wrote, "It is evident that the greatest lesson the average photographer has to learn is to unlearn, and one of his first lessons would be to overcome the idea of a 'sharp, brilliant' photogram."[9] The gum bichromate print was celebrated instead for its soft, painterly effects and the ability it afforded to restrict detail through localized development. In an article on pictorial landscape photography, one photographer contrasted artistic work with professional productions: "The photographer . . . should have the same liberty as the painter to simplify details, and since the lens gives him everything he should exercise a wise discrimination. He is not a commercial view-man, but is trying to make his print convey a message."[10]

Gum bichromate and other painterly effects soon became omnipresent at the pictorialist exhibitions. Critics warned that gum was not suitable for every type of picture and suggested other printing techniques, especially platinum, which was revered for its softness and wide midtone range.

Even as the popularity of the gum print declined in the 1920s, the distinction that it helped to illustrate between objective, commercial photography and the individual, artistic print would remain. In an early article on pictorial photography, Stieglitz wrote in favor of handworked artistic printing processes, echoing the language of late nineteenth-century French painting: "As no two people are ever impressed in quite the same way, no two interpretations will ever be alike."[11]

FIGURE 86. Alfred Stieglitz, "Spring Showers—The Coach," 1899–1900. Platinum print, 3 3/8″ × 1 13/16″.

Source: Metropolitan Museum of Art, Gilman Collection, Gift of the Howard Gilman Foundation, 2005.

21

SOFT FOCUS

IN 1867, the *Philadelphia Photographer* bemoaned the shallow depth of field possessed by most portrait lenses. The author attributed the overwhelming use of stock poses to this technical limitation, which forced photographers to arrange subjects in a narrow plane to keep all of their features in sharp focus. "How disagreeable the effect of the blurred outline of the further shoulder," the writer lamented. To remedy the effect, he suggested drawing in lines with india ink to give definition to "cloud-like masses of hair and clarify the "projecting end of the nose."[1] [See also Chapter 2, "Portrait Props and Poses."]

A complete reversal of aesthetic recommendations came at the end of the nineteenth century when photographers began using shallow depth of field intentionally to separate subjects from backgrounds. Commenting on a reader's pictures, the editor of *American Amateur Photographer* was unsparing in his criticism: "The greatest fault . . . lies in the fact of all the planes being of equal value, everything is equally sharp and prominent."[2] The editor's solution was to "try this picture over again," make the central figure more pronounced, and "throw everything else decidedly out of focus."[3] Following improvements in lenses during the second half of the nineteenth century, photographers increasingly returned to older lenses of limited focal range to create these aesthetic effects. [See also Chapter 42, "Boke."]

Soft-focus techniques were especially popular among turn-of-the-century art photographers who aimed to produce a sense of atmosphere, mood, and emotion in their prints. They sought to distinguish art (or "pictorial") photography from the work of Kodak snapshooters.

[See Chapter 17, "The Kodak."] The photographer Alfred Stieglitz became the artists' most vocal advocate. In exhibitions and in the journals published by two prominent New York–based amateur camera clubs, Stieglitz set forth his ideals for the new art photography. These aims were richly illustrated with photographs by Stieglitz and his contemporaries, as well as the work of early nineteenth-century photographers, including Julia Margaret Cameron and David Octavius Hill. Forty of Hill's photographs from the 1840s were included in an exhibition organized by Stieglitz in 1910 in New York. The catalog introduced Hill thus: "At the very threshold of the new art of photography there was a worker who realized its possibilities—restricted though they were technically—for pictorial and individual expression."[4] In

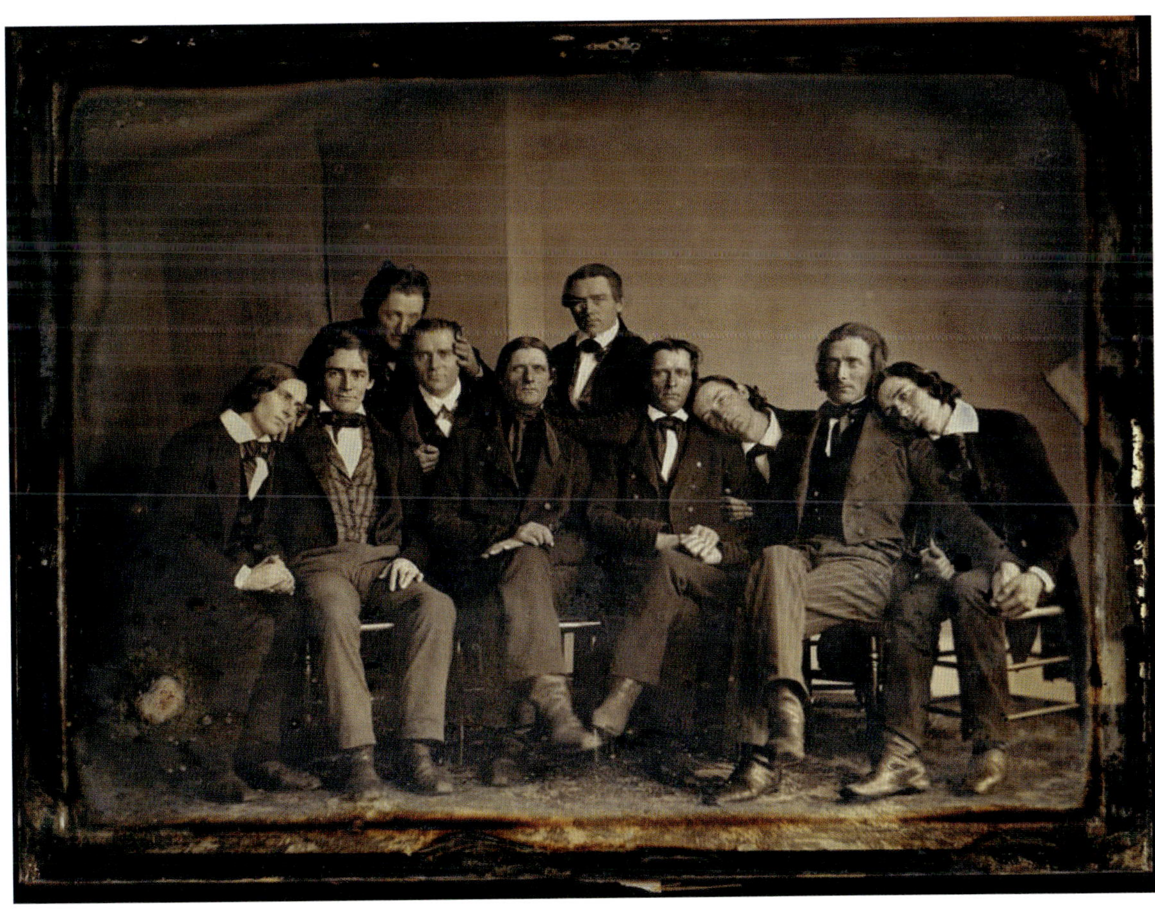

FIGURE 87. Unknown photographer, "Hutchinson Family Singers," 1845. Daguerreotype, 5 11/16″ × 7 3/4″.

Source: Metropolitan Museum of Art, Gilman Collection, Gift of the Howard Gilman Foundation, 2005.

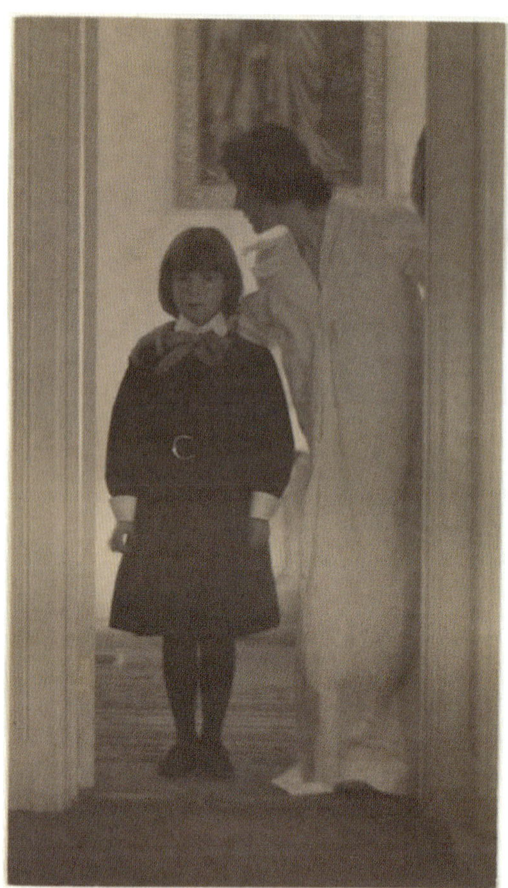

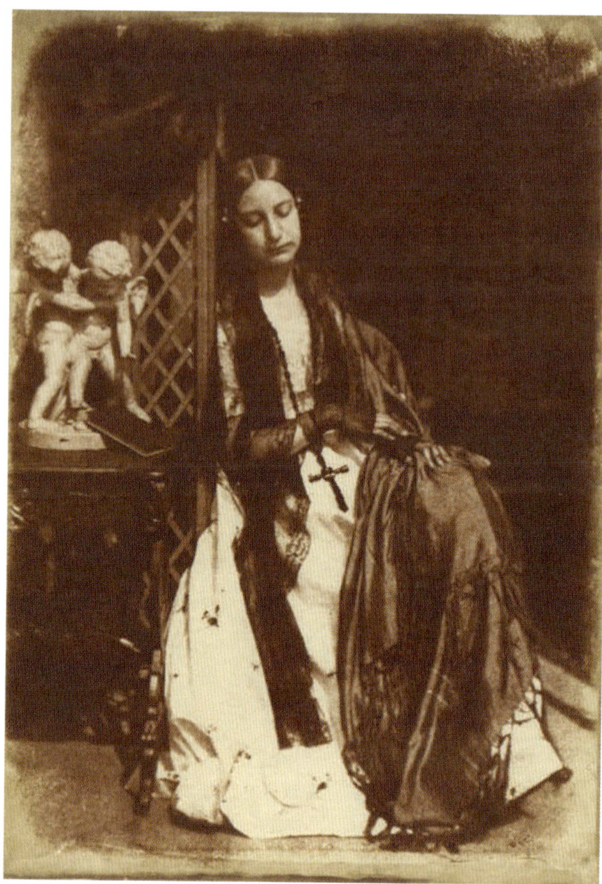

 Gertrude Käsebier, "Blessed Art Thou among Women," 1899. Platinum print, 9 1/16″ × 5 3/16″.

Source: Metropolitan Museum of Art, Alfred Stieglitz Collection, 1933.

 David Octavius Hill and Robert Adamson, "Elizabeth Rigby [Lady Eastlake]," 1843–1847. Salted paper print from a paper negative, 8 3/16″ × 5 5/8″

Source: J. Paul Getty Museum, Los Angeles. Digital image courtesy of the Getty's Open Content Program.

the pictorialists' estimation, these technical limitations were also vital sources of aesthetic feeling.

The soft-focus effect could be created either in-camera by the lens or later in the printing process. At the turn of the century, photographers deconstructed or intentionally misused contemporary lenses to achieve the desired out-of-focus effect. Some relied on lenses that produced chromatic or spherical aberrations, optical effects that were once the bane of the photographic industry. By the 1910s, companies responded to this aesthetic trend by manufacturing lenses that allowed photographers to introduce varying degrees of softness into their negatives.[5] One of the most popular of these was the Struss Pictorial Lens, designed by the young American photographer Karl Struss and used in his own work for many years; it was made commercially available in 1915.

With the growing accessibility of the soft-focus style, some publications issued strident warnings about its overuse. An article in *Wilson's Photographic Magazine* rebuked readers: "The lens does not supply brains. It must not be imagined that the mere fact of using a soft-focus lens will of necessity make the pictures artistic. Softness of definition *per se* is not art, and if the photographer is not an artist, and has no ideas, no individuality, to put into his pictures, the lens will not supply them."[6] The *Photographic Journal* published an article entitled, "Soft-Focus Lenses—Their Use and Abuse," which similarly decried the overuse of soft-focus lenses: "Discard the idea that all it is necessary to do in order to become a photographic artist is to get a soft-focus lens and take pictures as blurry and indistinct as possible. 'Mush' is not impressionism;

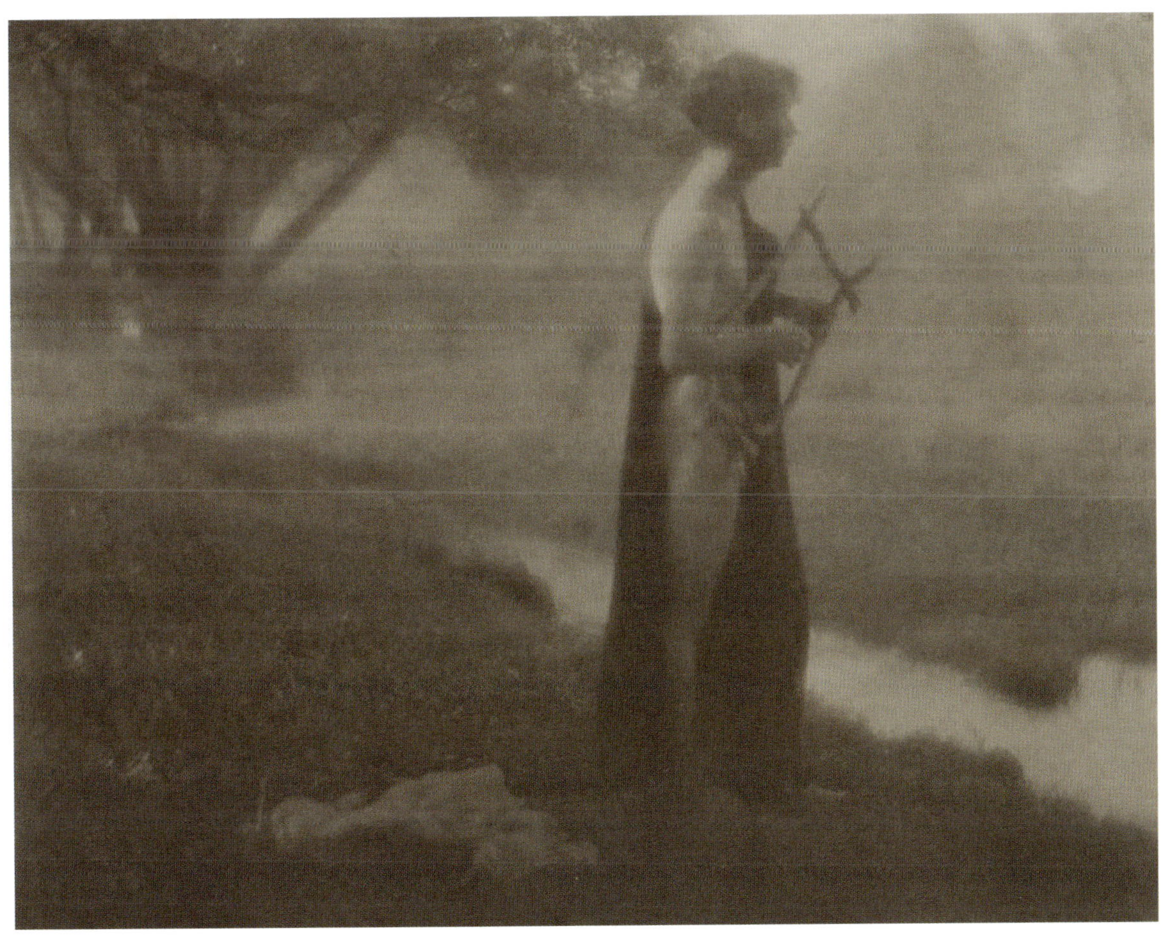

FIGURE 90. George H. Seeley, Untitled, ca. 1903. Platinum print, 7 9/16″ × 9 9/16″.

Source: J. Paul Getty Museum, Los Angeles. Digital image courtesy of the Getty's Open Content Program.

mystery is not obscurity and disintegration; suggestion suggests something."[7] Even Stieglitz's philosophy was changing. The final issue of *Camera Work*, published in 1917, featured Paul Strand's radically simplified and abstracted photographs of plates and bowls, tables and shadows. In his accompanying essay, Strand argued that photographers should celebrate the medium's objectivity without recourse to "tricks of process or manipulation."[8]

While the soft-focus style was short-lived, the principles espoused in its support had a lasting impact. Growing interest in the photographic artist's unique vision and emotion was opposed not only to Kodakers' snapshots but also to much of the history of photography, which largely suppressed a photographer's personal aesthetics in favor of principles that celebrated the technical advancement of the medium. Although some previous trends called for the repurposing of mechanical limitations, this adaptation of photographic history was often accomplished without overt recognition. [See also Chapter 4, "Crayons and Vignettes," and Chapter 44, "Squares."] With the popularization of soft focus, however, the valorization of past defects was described explicitly. In a manual for pictorial photographers, Paul Anderson enthused, "The Struss Pictorial Lens, especially designed for pictorial work, [is] such a lens possessing all possible errors, and giving, as a result of its optical defects, a very soft and pleasing quality of definition."[9] The ability to reevaluate these former faults as uniquely photographic effects would become one of the medium's most enduring artistic moves in the twentieth century.

22

STRAIGHT PHOTOGRAPHY

THE CONCEPT of "straight photography" emerged in the very late nineteenth century in contradistinction to the painterly effects then in vogue among art photographers. [See also Chapter 20, "Painterly Photographs."] The straight photograph described a print made from a single, unaltered negative, without extensive manipulation in the darkroom. Pictorial photographers had recently adopted labor-intensive printing processes, such as gum bichromate, to counteract the impression that photography was a purely mechanical medium. The visible handwork of gum bichromate and other antiquated printing methods made these photographs look like wash drawings and, thus, in the pictorialists' estimation, more worthy of consideration as art. The proponents of straight photography also argued for the medium's artistic merits, but suggested instead that photographers underscore the technical or lens-based effects of their work rather than borrowing from the established aesthetics of painting.

The criticism of pictorial photography was often vitriolic. One photographer wrote, "Apparently it has become the style—and fashion rages as much in photographic circles as in society—to delve into the abstract, to confuse, to mystify. This has been carried to such an extent that the commonplace admirer of pure photographic work must ask in fear and trembling if yonder conglomeration of bichromated mass is representative of landscape, marine, portrait or interior. The subject is shrouded in deepest mystery."[1] The influential critic Sadakichi Hartmann was also dismissive of the painterly photographs then popular in exhibitions

FIGURE 91. Fred Holland Day, "Vita Mystica," ca. 1900–1905. Gum bichromate print, 9" × 4 13/16".

Source: J. Paul Getty Museum, Los Angeles. Digital image courtesy of the Getty's Open Content Program.

organized by Alfred Stieglitz, Edward Steichen, and others associated with the new art photography. In a scathing review, Hartmann wrote:

> As was to be expected of an exhibition, selected and arranged by three pictorial extremists, who lay more stress on "individual expression" than on any other quality, the majority of pictures showed a certain sameness in quality and idea. . . . It is only a general tendency towards the mysterious and bizarre which these workers have in common; they like to suppress all outlines and details and lose them in delicate shadows, so that their meaning and intention become hard to discover.[2]

Numerous pleas for straight photography presented the movement as an essentially conservative one that harked back to the origins of photography and away from the recent modern distractions of painterly abstraction. As one writer described a pictorialist exhibition, "Distortion rages rampant, reason is trampled under foot, fidelity to true photographic principles is crushed."[3] Hartmann instructed would-be straight photographers to "compose the picture which you intend to take so well that the negative will be absolutely perfect and in need of no or but slight manipulation. I do not object to retouching, dodging or accentuation as long as they do not interfere with the natural qualities of photographic technique."[4] Despite the vigor of these written appeals, a concrete definition of photography's "natural qualities" took more than a decade to crystallize.

In 1917, the photographer Paul Strand published an essay advocating for straight photography in the final issue of *Camera Work*, the journal

> FIGURE 92. Paul Strand, "Abstraction, Porch Shadows, Twin Lakes, Connecticut": 1915 (negative), 1917 (photogravure).

Source: Philadelphia Museum of Art: The Paul Strand Collection, from the Collection of Dorothy Norman, 1967, 1967-285-266. Copyright: © Aperture Foundation, Inc., Paul Strand Archive.

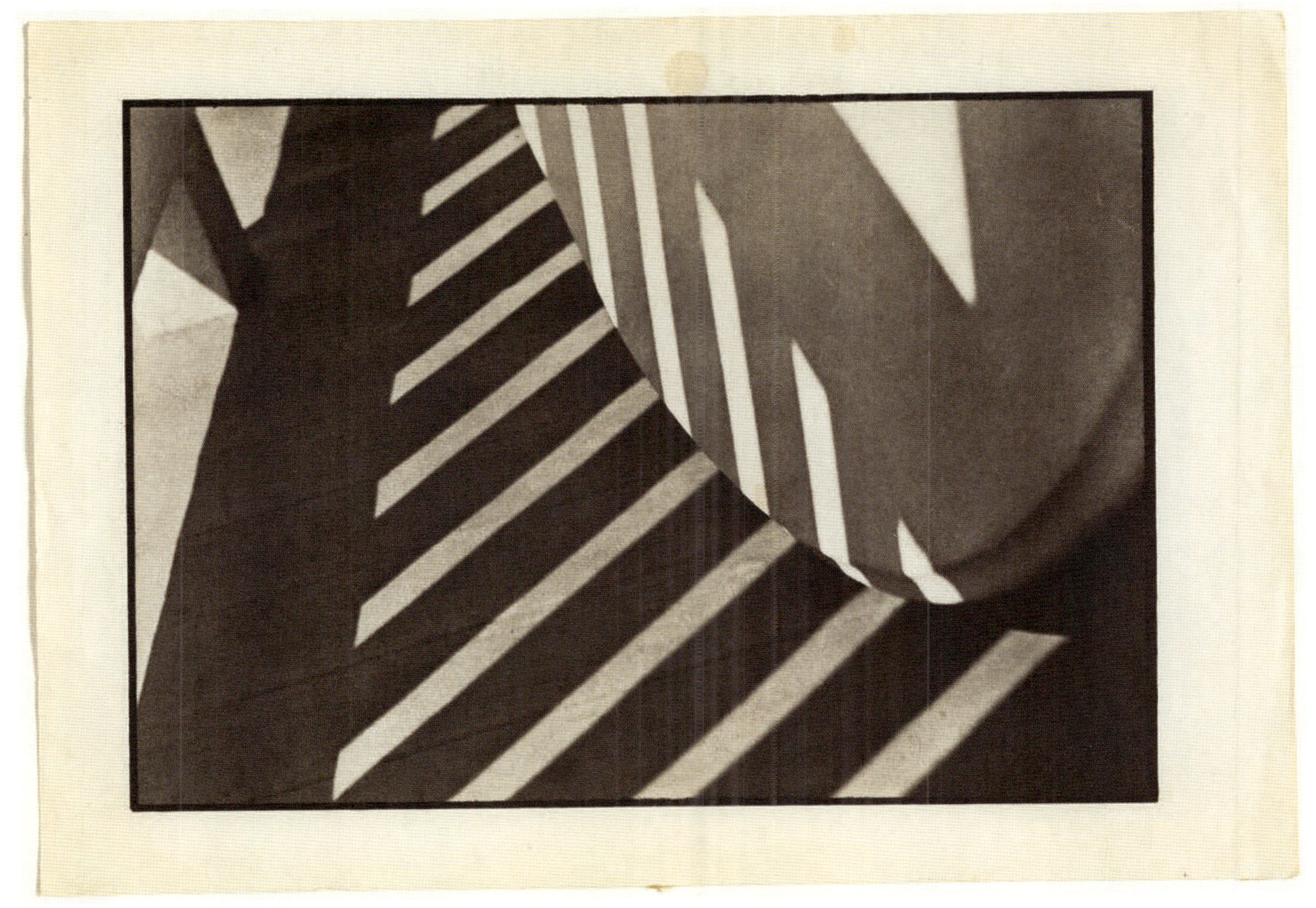

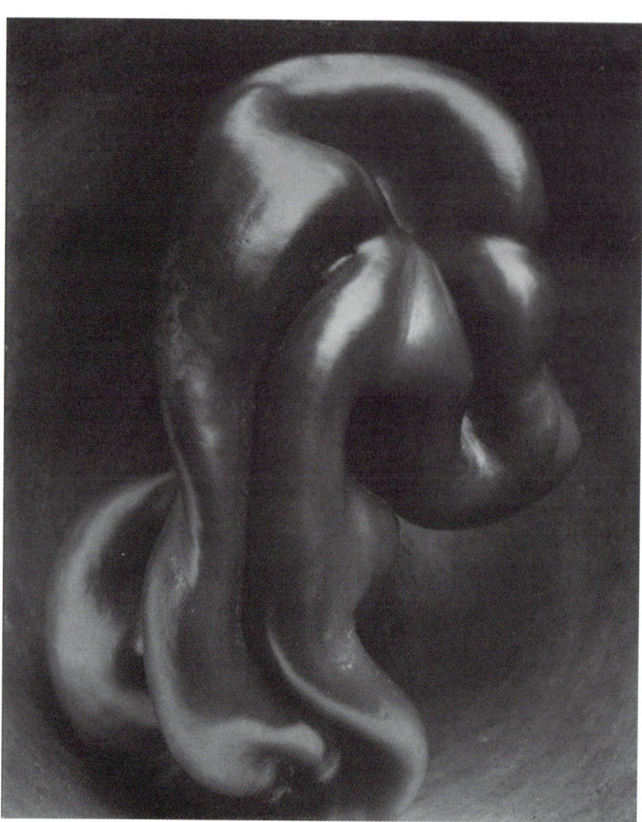

edited by Alfred Stieglitz. In an unabashed disavowal of the photography once championed by the journal, Strand wrote, "The full potential power of every medium is dependent upon the purity of its use, and all attempts at mixture end in such dead things as . . . the gum-print, oil-print, etc., in which the introduction of hand work and manipulation is merely the expression of an impotent desire to paint."[5] But Strand went further than other critics to describe those purely photographic effects as the medium's ability to represent "almost infinite tonal values which lie beyond the skill of human hand."[6] Instead of relying on painterly handwork to legitimate photography, Strand argued that photographic artists should emphasize elements unique to the medium.

Other writers also began to define the aesthetics of straight photography at this time. To Strand's list of photography's inimitable qualities, they added texture and detail.[7] One critic noted, "We must confess there was a great charm in the old direct whole-plate or 10 × 8 work," contrasting the remarkable amount of detail visible in nineteenth-century large-plate photographs with the small negatives produced by miniature cameras of the early twentieth century.[8] [See also Chapter 7, "Solar Enlarging," and Chapter 35, "Full-Frame Prints."] Another defender of straight photography concluded, "It is in the technical quality of the print that the beholder will find the greatest appeal."[9] The popularization of straight photography required that makers and critics be able to name and identify the particular aesthetics of photography, especially those elements that set the medium apart from other art forms.

The distinction between these two factions of artistic photographers is perhaps more pronounced in their writing than in their photographs, however. To viewers familiar with straight photography as practiced by Edward Weston, Ansel Adams, and others associated with the aesthetic from the 1930s through the 1950s, the straight photographs of the early twentieth century still appear fairly soft and sketchy, begging the question of just how intrinsic to the medium any style can be.

23

NIGHT PHOTOGRAPHY

DARKNESS WAS LONG ANTITHETICAL to photography. The medium was described poetically as "sun painting" and photographs as "sun pictures." Writers took noms-de-plume that played on these associations, fashioning themselves "Sol" or "Lumiere." With the popularization of the more light sensitive dry plate process in the 1880s, intrepid photographers set off to explore a new frontier: the night.

The early years of night photography focused on using artificial illumination, such as magnesium flash powder, to bring light to dark places. [See also Chapter 16, "Magnesium Flash."] By the turn of the century, however, artistic photography could be accomplished at night without the aid of the blinding, explosive flash. Photographers in the United States took to the streets in the late 1890s, inspired by a series of nocturnal views of London by the British photographer Paul Martin. At the end of 1897, the photographer and art impresario Alfred Stieglitz described night photography as "the novelty of the year."[1]

Most instructional articles recommended working in cities with street lamps, revealing the modern fascination with electric light and a newfound appreciation of the urban environment, as well as the perceived necessity of maintaining some bright light in the scene. Still, Martin's nighttime exposures required thirty minutes or more. One American photographer recommended measuring such long exposures by counting the number of times he had to refill his pipe.[2] Working on a well-lit street, Stieglitz was able to reduce his own exposures to just one minute.

Inclement weather conditions were also prized, as reflections in the wet streets or brilliant white snow shortened the exposure times and increased visible detail in otherwise dark areas of the composition. The rainy-night trend was well established by 1910 when the critic Sadakichi Hartmann wrote in a pamphlet dedicated to night photography, "We are the slaves of tradition, and so, for most of us, photographing at night seems to call for rain and snow, with their attendant discomforts."[3] In a summary of the limitations of nocturnal photography, one author acknowledged, "It is held by some photographers that night photography has few pictorial possibilities. To a certain extent this is so; for of the one thousand and one subjects by day we have perhaps only one that may be suitable by night."[4] He tried to supplement this paucity by providing exposure guidelines for other suitable subjects: fireworks displays, "conflagrations," iron foundries and blast furnaces, storefronts,

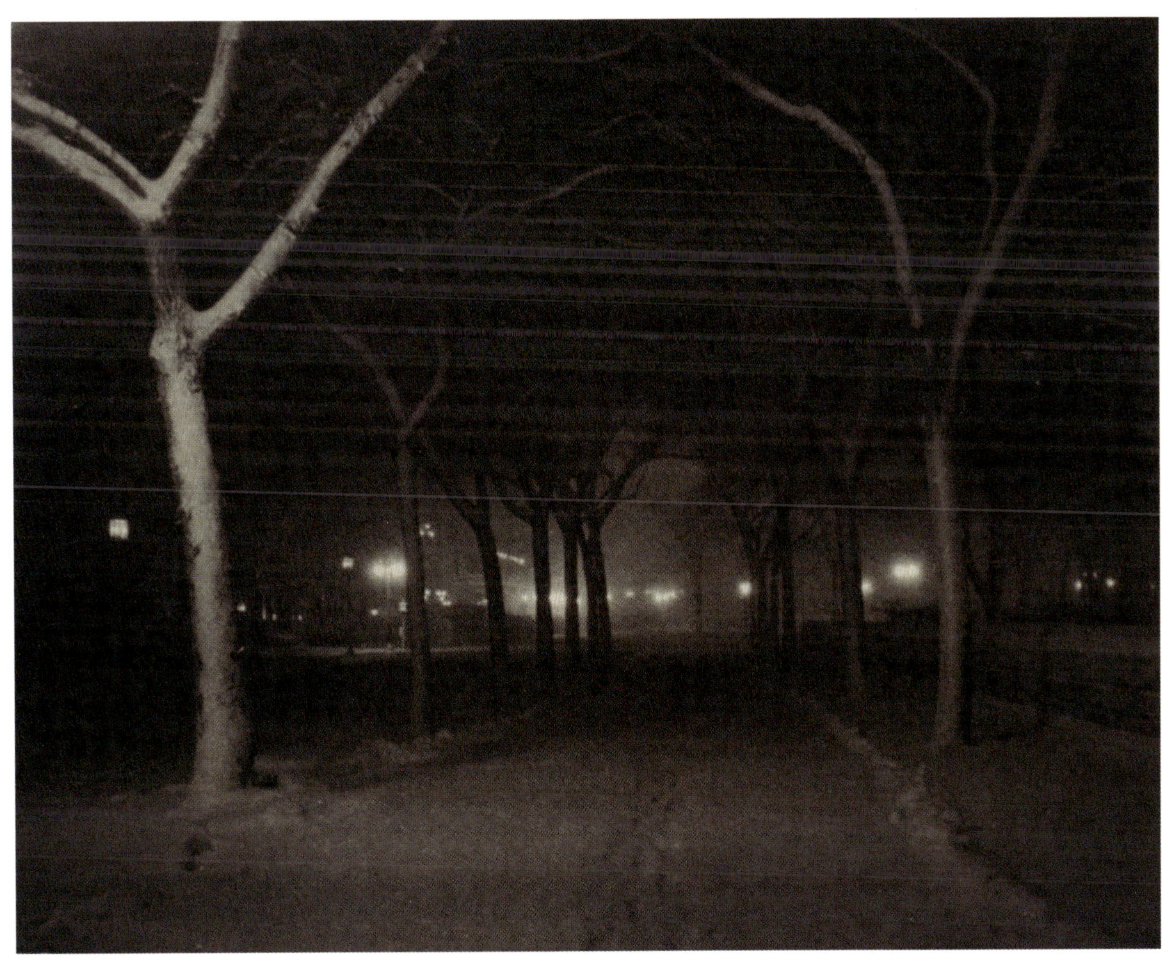

FIGURE 94. Alfred Stieglitz, "An Icy Night," 1898, printed 1920–1939. Gelatin silver print from glass negative, 3 5/8″ × 4 5/8″.

Source: Metropolitan Museum of Art, Alfred Stieglitz Collection, 1949.

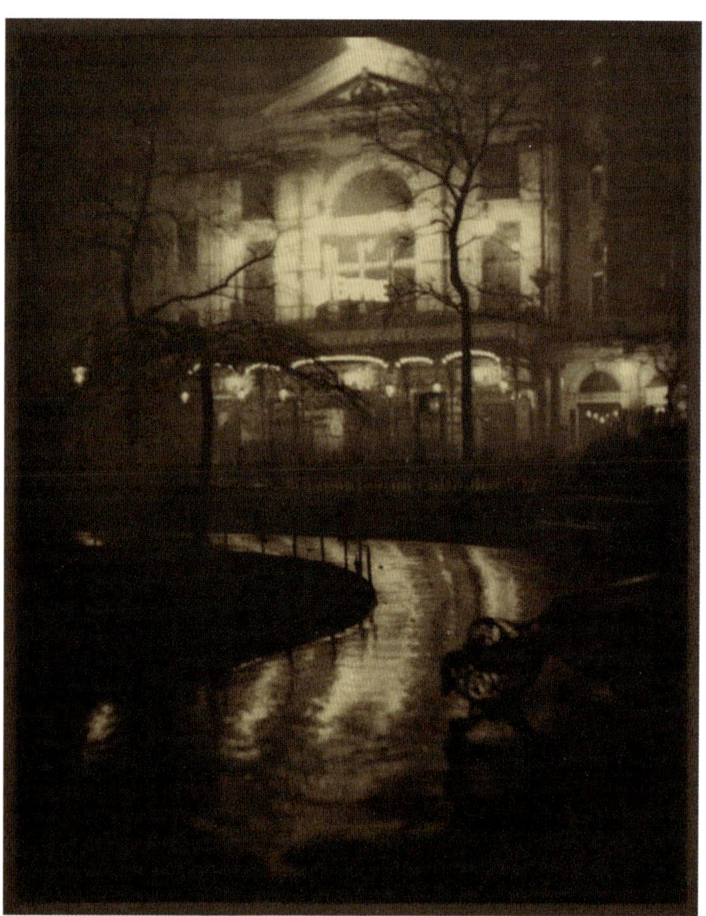

churches by night, railroad stations by night. Given this list, it is easy to sympathize with Stieglitz's complaint about the genre: "The impression conveyed is one of sameness, although the subjects presented may vary considerably."[5] [See also Chapter 8, "Foreground Interest."] Night photographs all tended to look like night photographs: some bright lights surrounded by darkness.

The procedure for making night photographs was also highly regularized. Many commentators recommended that the photographer block lights from directly entering the lens in order to limit halation, a localized overexposure surrounding the light source that occurs when light passes through the plate and is reflected back into the image layer. (See Figure 96.) Trees and telephone poles served as ready-made shades.[6] Anti-halation plates, made with a backing to prevent reflection, were also invented in this period. [See also Chapter 34, "Lens Flare."]

How-to manuals struggled mightily with balancing the technical and aesthetic demands of night photography. The photographer Charles Smyth noted, "A little halation around the brighter lights, if it is not too sharply defined, is not altogether objectionable, as a little haze gives a truer appearance of what is really seen with the eye."[7] Hartmann agreed: "Halations, and light seen in drizzling rain or spreading on the mist, really add to the pictorial effect. Those who are enamored with the artificial light of the night want it as it is, with all its breaks, supernatural radiance, hectic glow and gleam amidst opaque recesses and intensest darks."[8] As with other techniques of the pictorialist era, photographers

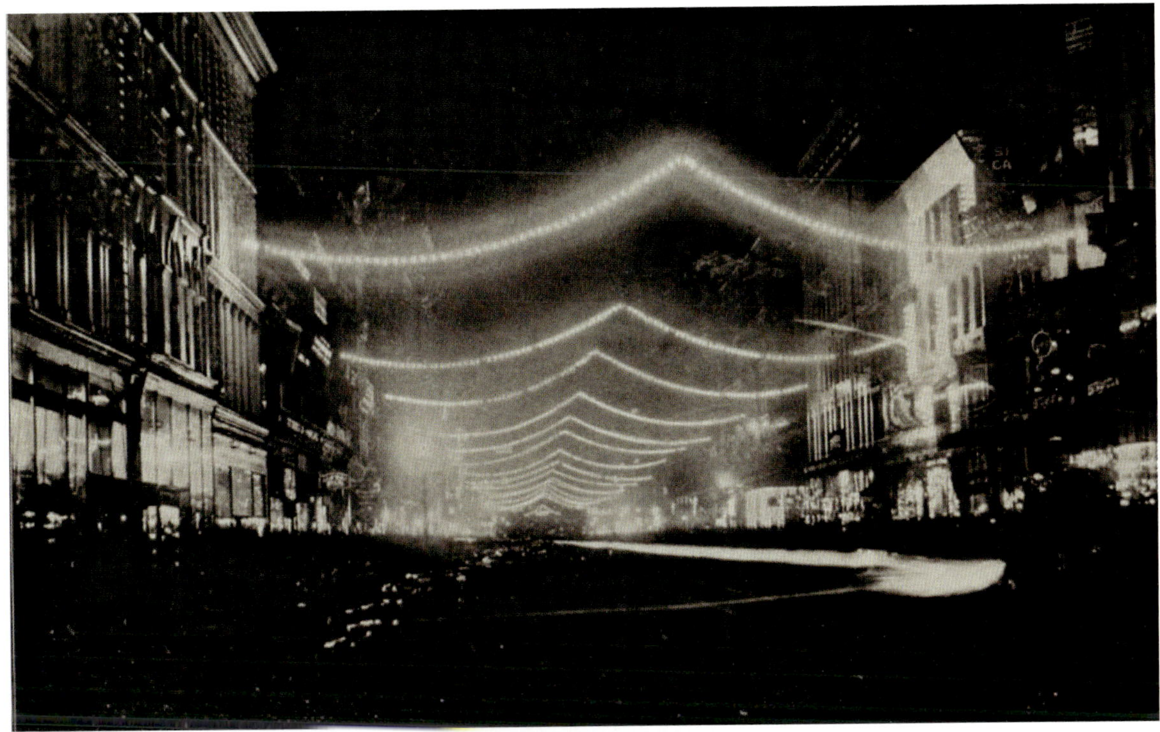

were starting to embrace the limitations of the medium in search of artistic effects.

The aesthetic battle also hinted at an ideological one: Why take photographs at all? Was photography a technical achievement or an artistic practice? Criticism of night photography often highlighted this ongoing debate. One naysayer wrote, "Let us be artists of the night by all means, but why expose plates at night for merely scientific enjoyment?"[9] Another critic enumerated the differences between pictures made for aesthetic appreciation versus those intended to display technical virtuosity:

The photographer who is interested mainly in the science and the technical difficulties of his medium will show this in his choice of subjects. . . . He will not seek to evade difficulties; he will not endeavor to cover up the lights in his picture with a convenient tree or a telegraph post, but will glory in rendering as many lamps as possible with the minimum of halation and other technical faults. The artist [on the other hand] will include

FIGURE 96. Henry Abbott, "Imperfect Night Scene," *Modern Photography in Theory and Practice* (Chicago: George K. Hazlitt, 1899), 176a.

as few lamps as possible in his picture. . . . A little halation, too, will not be regarded as a grievous fault, for on a misty night, such an effect is seen in nature; each lamp has a little halo around it.[10]

Even after arguing eloquently for the picturesque effects of technical failures, such as halation, many instructional books provided a caveat: technical proficiency must be achieved before it can be abandoned for artistry. These authors maintained that only when "so-called errors are not accidental but . . . intentional" could they be considered art, thus cementing a trend within the rhetoric of twentieth-century instructional manuals.[11] Technical errors are to be prized by the creative photographer, but only when they are deliberately introduced, not accidentally obtained.

24

PANCHROMATIC

IT WAS LONG AN ACCEPTED FACT of photography that the world's colorful hues were translated to black-and-white tones in a somewhat irregular manner. Early processes were responsive only to blue light, leaving skies bright white due to overexposure, while leafy green landscapes appeared only as shadowy masses. [See also Chapter 6, "Cloudy Skies."] Subjects wearing red seemed to be dressed in the black of mourning. Still-life pictures featuring baskets of fruit displayed this uneven light sensitivity potently: jet black strawberries alongside dark gray plums belied photography's realism. Aside from the frustration with clouds, however, these shortcomings were rarely cited in print during photography's first fifty years. Instead, writers praised the process for its perfect representation of the "variations of shade," likening the photograph's monochromatism to a mezzotint or engraving.[1] Few of these early notices mentioned the strange tonal relationship between the varied shades, however. Early photography's uneven receptivity to the spectrum was one of its key visible characteristics, although paradoxically this shortcoming remained nearly invisible in period commentaries.

Concern over relative tonality emerged in print only when this limitation could be corrected. The first step in this endeavor came in 1873 with the discovery of a method

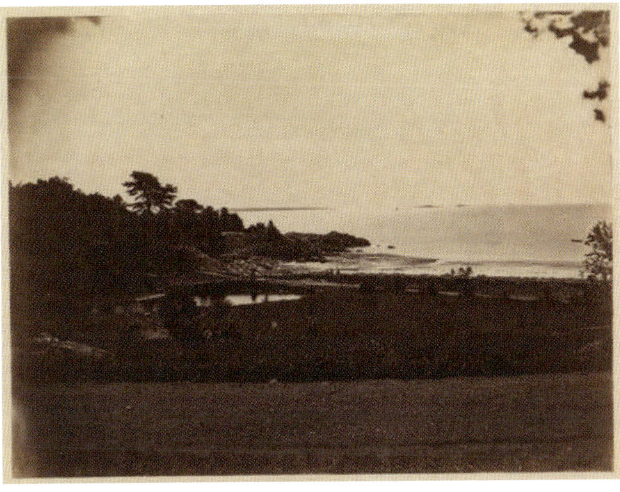

FIGURE 97. Samuel Masury, "Pride's Crossing," ca. 1856. Salted paper print from paper negative, 10 1/8″ × 12 1/2″.

Source: Metropolitan Museum of Art, Gilman Collection, Museum Purchase, 2005.

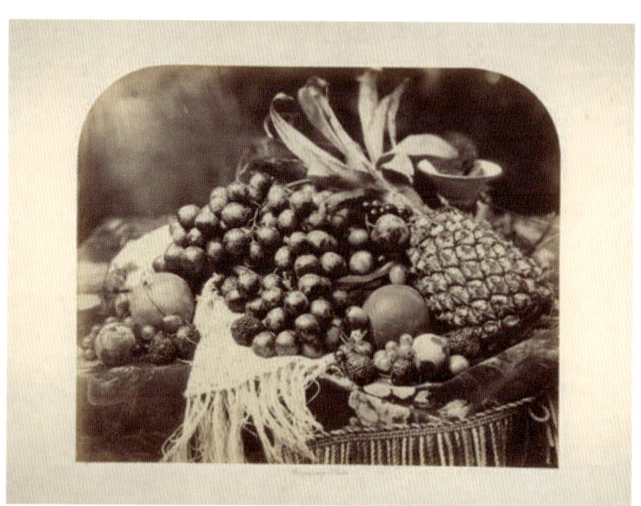

to make plates sensitive to green and yellow light, in addition to blue. Using a yellow filter, the photographer was instructed to balance the exposure, reducing blue and green equally, in an attempt to capture any small quantity of light reflected from predominantly red or orange objects. The new process promised orthochromatic or "correct color." But the process would not be widely used for more than a decade. The editor Edward L. Wilson complained in 1885, "The highly interesting, useful and promising orthochromatic process has, in spite of all writing, talking and printing, remained a terra incognita."[2] Photographers were likely discouraged by the necessity of adding a step to the already cumbersome process of sensitization, as well as the fact that orthochromatic plates were less sensitive to light overall. The small gains of the process only outweighed its shortcomings in a few areas of photographic practice.

Orthochromatic plates were recommended for the technical work of copying paintings and colorful decorative objects, such as wallpapers, rugs, and stained glass.[3] The annual publication *Photographic Mosaics* advocated for the implementation of orthochromatic plates in landscape work, explaining, "The whole beauty of a view lies in its composition, and often the key to the whole picture is a white cloud or a green slope. If the former is to be entirely lost, or the latter to appear as a black blotch, it is better not to take the picture at all."[4] Other guidebooks agreed: orthochromatic plates "should always be used when there are varied colors in the view, especially in autumn, when the leaves have changed to purple and red, and in photographing flowers."[5]

Beyond these specialized uses, orthochromatic photography also had a large impact on portraiture. An article in the *Photographic Times* noted, "Retouching, indispensable with negatives taken on ordinary plates, is almost entirely dispensed with [orthochromatic plates], frequently not at all needed."[6] Retouching had become widespread during the 1870s with the rise of the cabinet card. Especially for sitters with light complexions, the insensitivity of collodion to red exaggerated blemishes and wrinkles, rendering these areas darker in the portrait. (See Figure 100.) In articles that inadvertently highlighted the industry's racial prejudice, authors recommended orthochromatic plates for sitters (assumed to be white) who possessed "very florid, sunburnt, or brunette complexions" in order to avoid a "dusky appearance" in the portrait.[7] Orthochromatic plates used with a yellow filter came closer to representing the tonal values as seen by the eye and preserved the white sitter's sense of racial identity. [See also Chapter 40, "Golden Hour."]

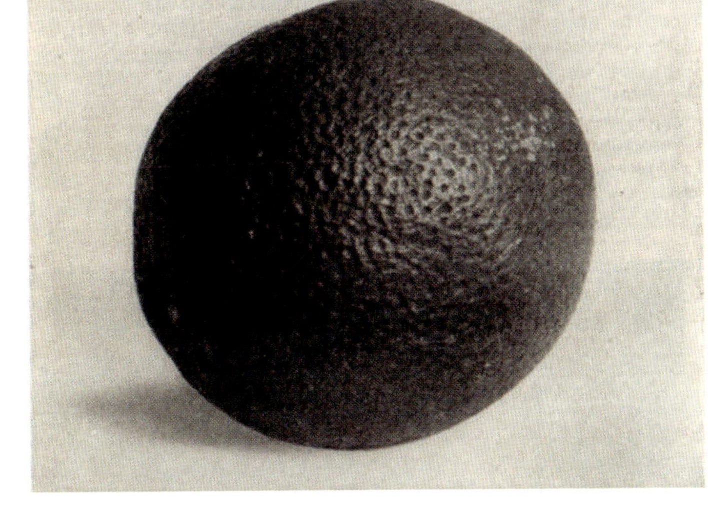

FIGURE 99. Unknown photographer, "Picture of an Orange on Blue Cloth."

Source: C. E. K. Mees, *The Fundamentals of Photography* (Rochester, NY: Eastman Kodak, 1920) 101. Author's collection.

With the availability of mass-produced orthochromatic plates in the mid-1880s came a willingness to criticize what had formerly been accepted as an inevitable shortcoming: the medium's persistent limitation with regard to red light. As one article hedged, "Orthochromatic plates reproduce the tone value of natural colors *almost* correctly [emphasis added]."[8] Even Kodak admitted that orthochromatic plates gave a "*truer* color value [emphasis added]."[9] The industry's typical boosterism was tempered by the sudden recognition of this persistent imperfection.

Panchromatic film, or film that was responsive to all wavelengths of the visible spectrum, was introduced in 1902 and widely available by the late 1920s. Shortly afterward, in the 1930s, a new style emerged that capitalized on the full-spectrum receptivity of panchromatic film, but not for naturalistic effect. Photographers began using red filters with panchromatic film to exaggerate contrast, especially in landscape pictures and cloud studies. The author Jacob Deschin pointed to the growing interest in this filter-film pairing in his 1936 amateur guide, stating, "This is the combination that gives us those dark skies we sometimes like to show."[10] Kodak's *How to Make Good Pictures* provided instructions for achieving the style, warning that it created "a greatly exaggerated contrast, but if the form of

142

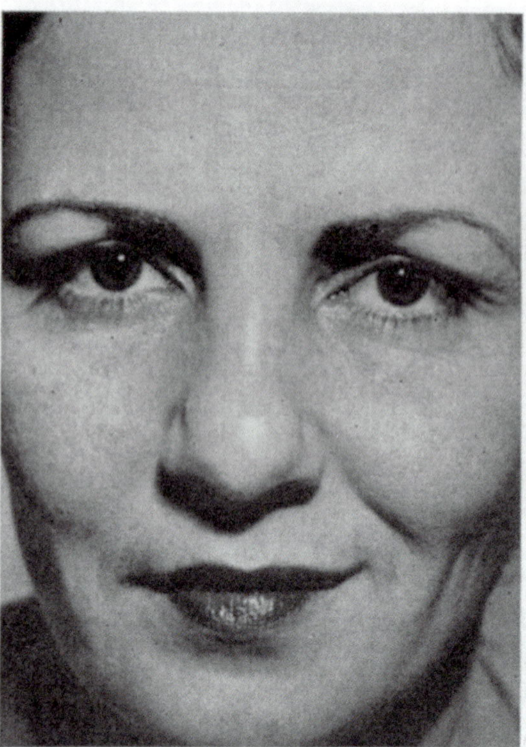

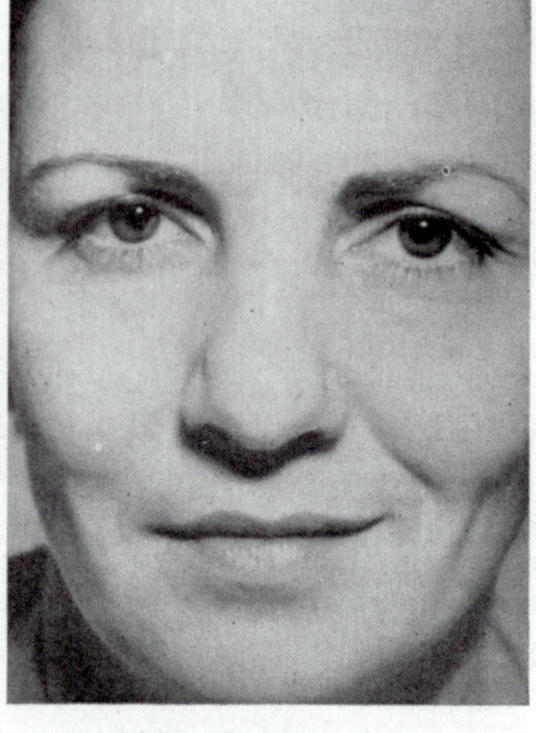

FIGURE 100. Unknown photographer, "Skin Texture with Orthochromatic Film and Skin Texture with Panchromatic Film." Paul Louis Hexter, *Make Your Pictures Sing* (San Francisco: Camera Craft Publishing, 1946), 91.

Source: Author's collection.

the clouds is all that is required, such an exaggeration is to be desired."[11] Ansel Adams, one of the first to popularize the effect, put it in context in his 1948 guidebook: "Since the beginnings of photography, rendition of color and brightnesses have been conventionalized by the limitations of the negative material. In early days, with the color-blind plates sensitive only to blue light, we became accustomed to white skies, dark lips, and very dark foliage."[12] He explained that "dark skies (exaggerated by the use of filters) . . . have become as 'conventional' as those of earlier times."[13] Like so many other trends, the new style became possible only when it could be described as an intentional effect rather than an inherent limitation of the medium.

25

CANDIDS

THERE HAD BEEN PUBLIC OUTCRY over photographers' snapping of sly pictures since the popularization of the Kodak, but the term *candid* wasn't applied to this practice until 1929. The design of small, handheld cameras became possible in the 1880s following the invention of the faster dry plate process. Cameras no longer had to be positioned on a steady tripod in order to make sharp exposures. The new handheld instruments were dubbed miniature or "detective" cameras for their unobtrusive size, as well as for the speed at which they could be set up and photographs taken.[1] Specialty cameras pushed this association with the surreptitious; cameras were concealed in dozens of small articles from vests, canes, cravats, and pocket watches to books and handbags.[2] (See Figure 101.) It wasn't until the release of the Leica and Contax, however, that hand cameras could produce pictures of suitable quality for reproduction and enlargement. Adapting 35 millimeter film, which had been recently standardized by the motion picture industry, these roll film cameras could make thirty-six pictures without reloading. They even worked indoors owing to their exceptionally fast, and eventually interchangeable, lenses.

In 1929, the British periodical the *Graphic* ran a hand-camera shot made by the society photographer Erich Salomon at a Royal Academy dinner. Salomon's picture revealed such dignitaries as Prince George in decidedly informal poses, radical departures from their official portraits. The magazine described Salomon's photograph as "an unconventional snapshot, taken with an intensely powerful pocket-camera." The author also pointed out the dean of St. Paul's Cathedral, who was

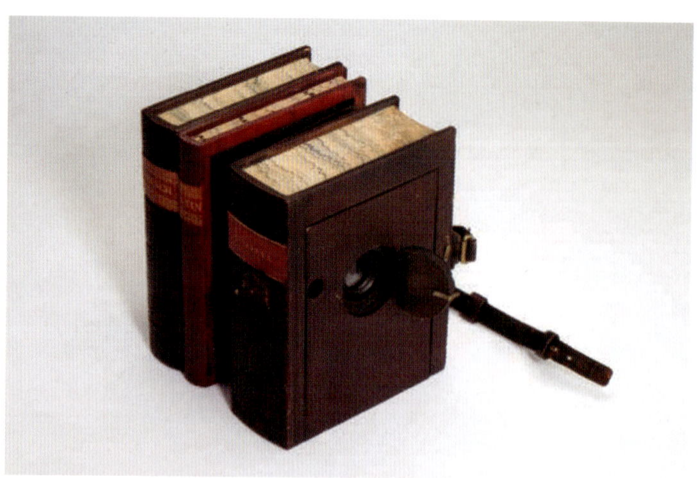

unceremoniously chewing on a cigar in the foreground, "unaware of the proximity of the candid camera."[3] This inaugurated a series in the *Graphic*, all described as "candid camera," and soon this style of unposed photographs, as well as the description of such pictures as "candid," made its way into international publications.

Initially "candid" referred to the truthfulness or directness of the camera itself, but soon the plural form, candids, came to describe the honesty of the photographs made by these cameras. For the first several years, the term remained in quotes, but it quickly became mainstream. *Life* magazine, which began publication in 1936, immediately adopted the term, describing a series of (rather unflattering) pictures made of First Lady Eleanor Roosevelt as candids.[4] Instructional manuals had long advised that when including figures in a landscape, photographers should instruct their subjects to feign ignorance of the camera, since catching them truly unaware was nearly impossible considering the bulky camera and tripod required by earlier processes. [See also Chapter 18, "Figures in the Landscape."] The aim of a candid picture was to relieve models of the need to act unaware, catching people in their natural state rather than in the stiff or contrived poses associated with studio portraiture.

By the mid-1930s, candid picture making had become so popular that the owner of a Chicago nightclub dedicated one night each week to these cagey photographers. A *Life* magazine photographer recorded the amateurs in action, especially the contorted facial expressions typically found behind the small cameras' new eye-level viewfinders. The spread illustrated the reductio ad absurdum by which "the candid photographer, in taking curious expressions on other people's unguarded faces, makes his own face the perfect candid camera subject."[5] The hand camera also transformed the iconic silhouette of the photographer from

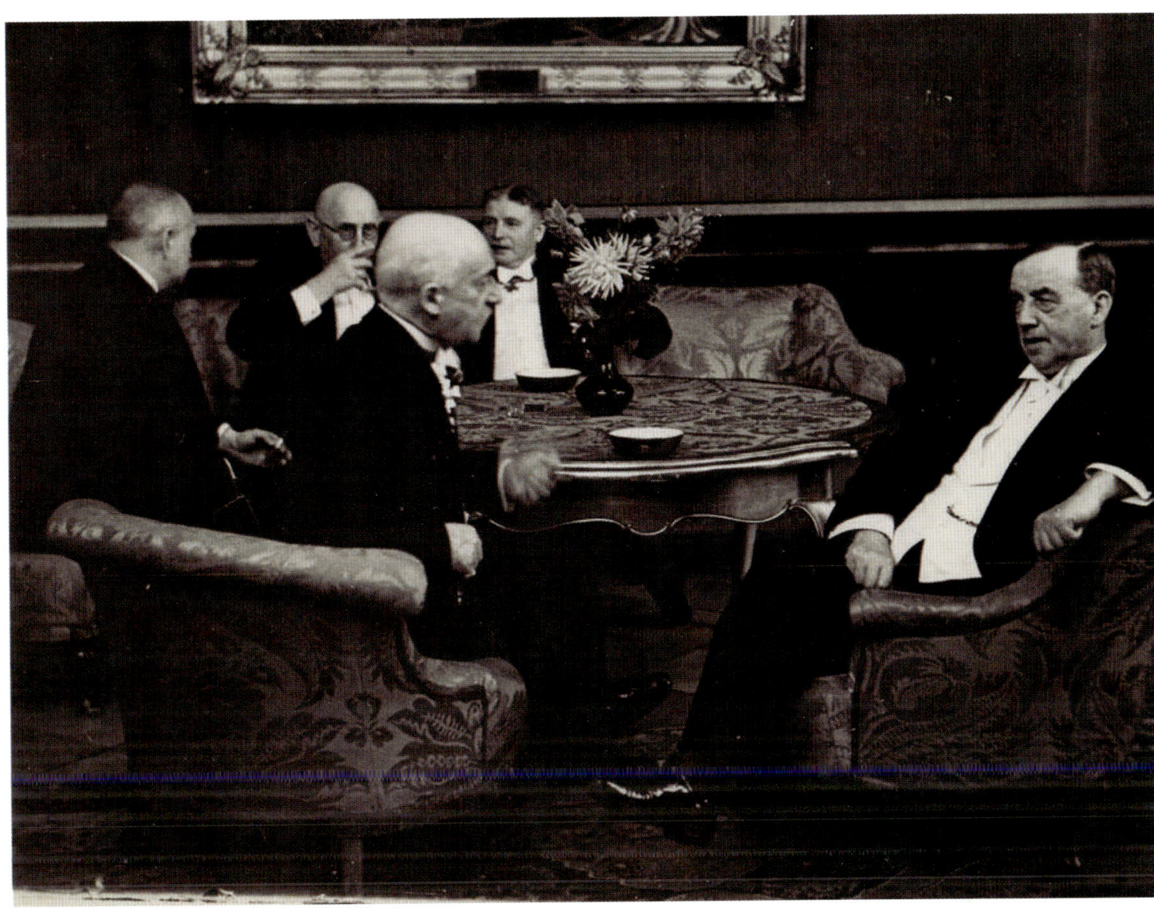

a person hunched under the shroud of the black focusing cloth into a person standing upright with a rectangular box held to his or her face.

Despite the popularity of candids in the picture press, the practice of making such pictures was fraught; the anxiety inspired by the "Kodak fiend" at the turn of the century was still palpable. [See also Chapter 71, "The Kodak."] One how-to author warned, "Don't try to sneak up on people with your camera unless you are 100 per cent sure you can get away with it."[6] Most guides acknowledged the bad reputation of candid picture makers but arduously defended the practice nonetheless. The *New York Times* photography columnist, Jacob Deschin, conceded, "All this

FIGURE 102. Erich Salomon, "[Five Gentlemen Conversing around Table]," 1920s–1930s. Gelatin silver print, 6⅞" × 9⅛".

Source: Metropolitan Museum of Art, Ford Motor Company Collection, Gift of Ford Motor Company and John C. Waddell, 1987.

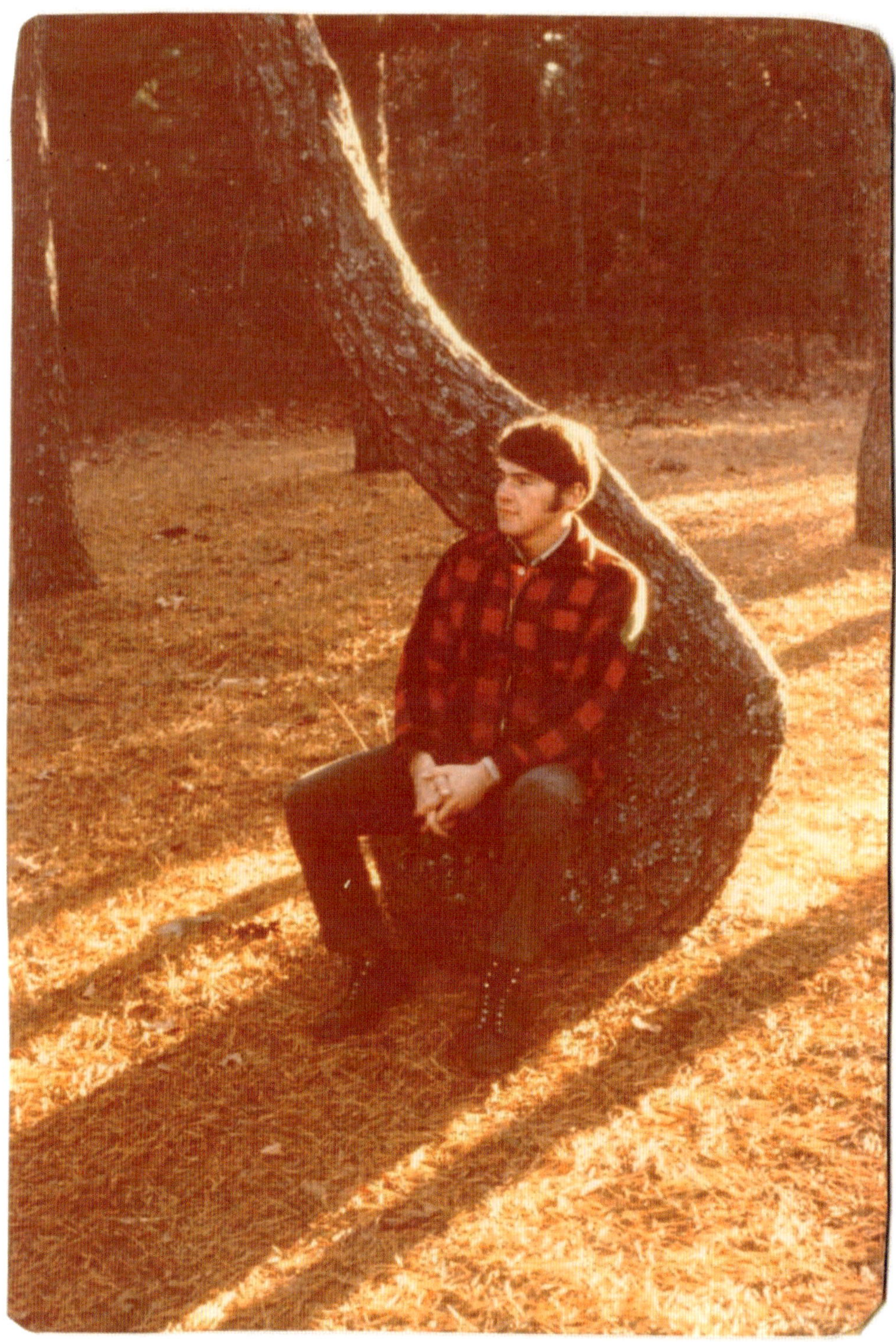

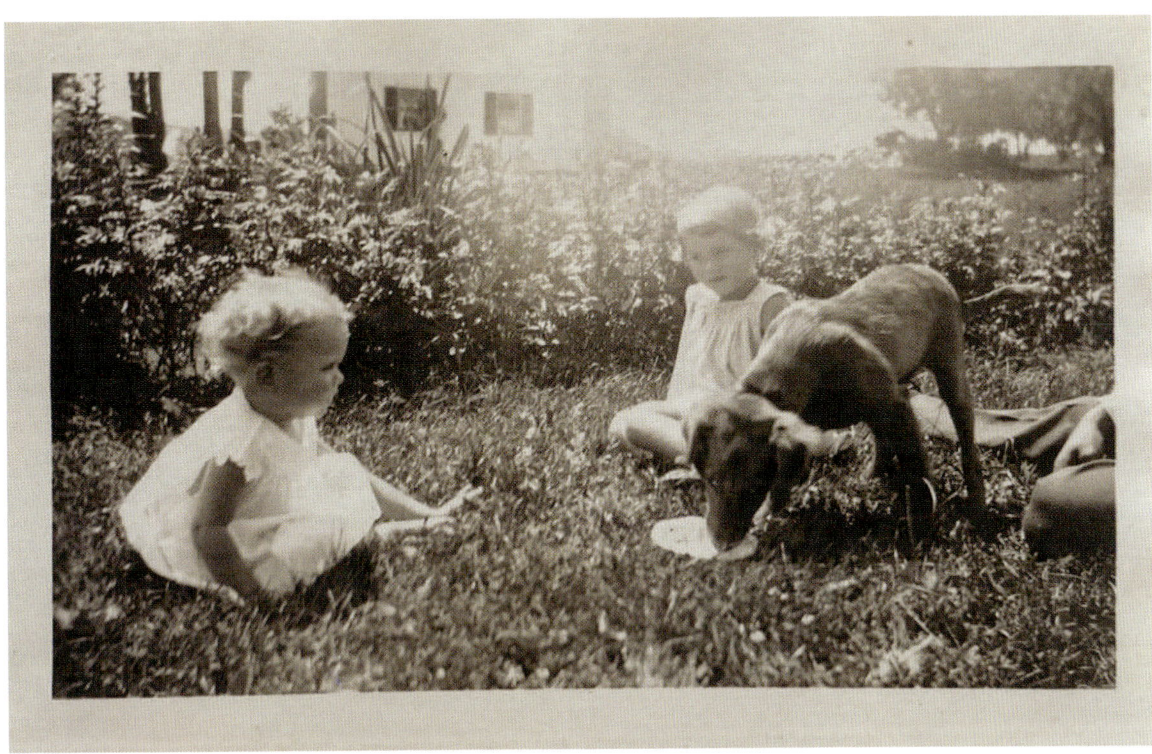

may sound to some people . . . a bit unfair, but one must consider that no one is harmed thereby and that the essence and value of the candid picture lies in just such off-guard 'slices of life,' not possible to obtain in any other way."[7] Deschin and other authors argued that candid photography rendered "human vignettes of lasting and incalculable interest and value."[8] Nearly a century after photography's invention, it could no longer capture human truths without subterfuge.

FIGURE 104. Photographer unknown, "Untitled," n.d. Gelatin silver print.

Source: Author's collection.

< FIGURE 103. Karen Magnuson, "Untitled," 1970. Chromogenic print.

Source: Courtesy of the artist.

PART IV

1930–1965

PHOTOGRAPHY AT MIDCENTURY in the United States was defined by the picture magazines, especially *Life*, which began publication in 1936. Although best known for its staff photographers' extensive photo essays, the magazine also published shorter one-picture stories and columns. These often provided behind-the-scenes accounts of the photographers' work or described new trends and technologies related to the medium. The photographic styles that were pioneered in *Life* and other picture magazines of the period, including *Look* and *Fortune*, were soon described in detail by how-to guides.

Other nationally distributed magazines dedicated to the instruction of photography also emerged, the most popular of which were *Popular Photography* and *U.S. Camera*. These magazines featured detailed reviews of new products, as well as articles on do-it-yourself photographic projects and ways to cheaply approximate the effects of sophisticated camera accessories. The glut of wartime technology also made its way into photographic production. By the end of the 1950s, electronic flashes, high-speed film, and ever-more miniaturized cameras became widely accessible. With the arrival of these innovations, how-to guides initially celebrated the medium's mastery of formerly difficult subjects, whether it was making pictures in low light, of fast-moving subjects, or in out-of-the-way locations. However, soon after the widespread adoption of these new technologies, they were quickly put to uses that were unintended by their inventors and manufacturers. Once technical success was assured, photographers backtracked and intentionally incorporated one-time failures, such as motion blur or pronounced film grain, into their pictures. The instructional manuals did not discard the rules wholesale, though; they continued to insist that photographers learn proper technique before abandoning it to create artistic work.

26

NEW ANGLES

TILTED, TWISTED, AND TURNED: unusual camera angles dominated the photography of the 1920s and 1930s. Since the advent of the hand camera in the late nineteenth century, when the instrument was first unmoored from its stable tripod, instructional guides had warned of the distorting effects of photographing at an angle. Pointing the camera up at tall buildings created an exaggerated sense of height. A failure to level the camera against the horizon made boats appear "to sail downhill," according to one author.[1] (See Figure 105.) These strange perspectival effects were associated with amateurism. For most of photography's history, textbooks aimed to correct rather than encourage such unconventional visions, but the embrace of the unusual angle marked a turning point in instructional practice.

Charles Taylor's 1902 glibly titled manual, *Why My Photographs Are Bad*, provided an illustration of an offending angle. Taylor explained, "I have known amateurs to overcome all the early difficulties in photography, and yet to fail repeatedly in their pictures, because they forgot to make sure that the camera was perfectly level while focusing."[2] Katharine Stanberry listed inappropriate angles among the most common beginner's troubles in her 1911 handbook. She warned, "The camera should be held level with the subject, not pointed up or down at it, whether the subject be a tall building or a clump of fern by the brookside."[3] Angled pictures like these were broadly scorned by instructional authors throughout the nineteenth and early twentieth centuries.

In the mid-1920s the avant-garde photographers Aleksandr Rodchenko and László Moholy-Nagy sought out these supposed failures.

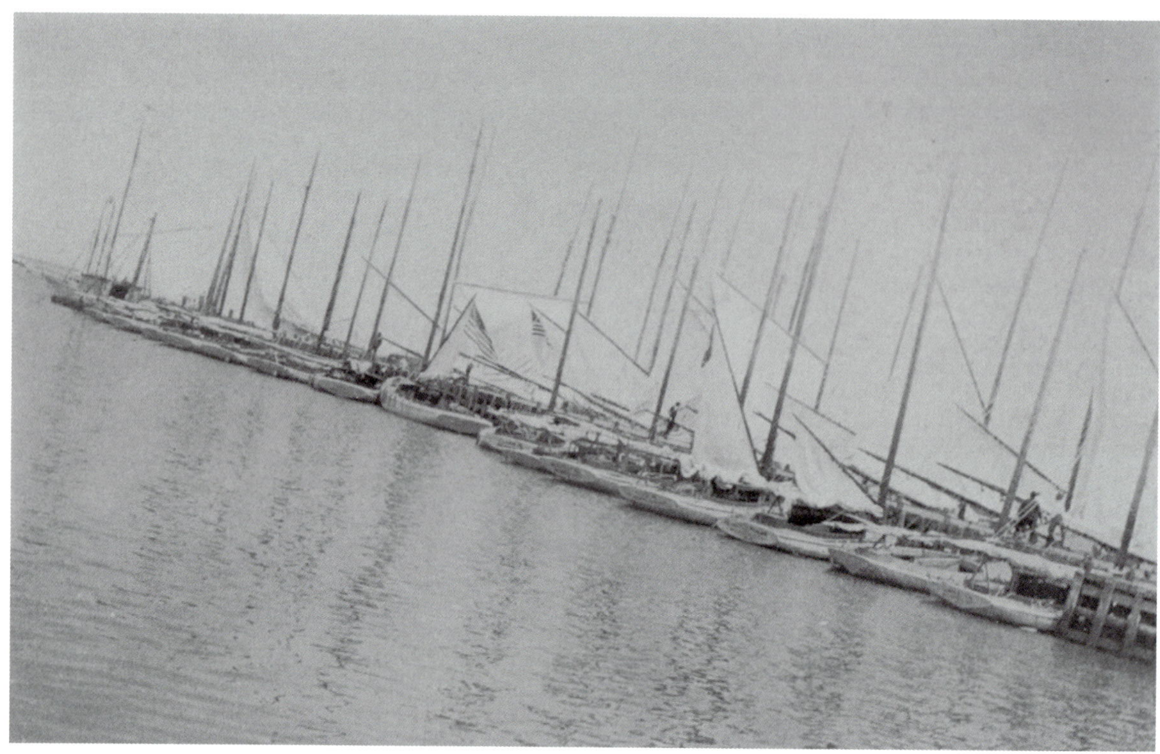

They intentionally aimed their cameras up at apartment buildings and down on people in the street. They tilted their cameras to transform horizontal lines into dramatic diagonals. The handheld camera's size and maneuverability freed them from the static perspectives long naturalized by painting. Rodchenko argued that these new angles were critical tools for modernity. He wrote, "We who are accustomed to seeing the usual, the accepted, must reveal the world of sight. We must revolutionize our visual reasoning."[4] Widely published in the nascent picture magazines in the United States and abroad, angled shots quickly became associated with the energy and unconventional ideals of modernism.

Even typically stodgy instructional guidebooks featured vertiginous perspectives by the 1930s. Kodak suggested that "interesting and odd views are obtained from the windows of high buildings, pointing the camera down."[5] Looking down on the chaotic arrangement of urban street traffic counterbalanced by hard shadows became a popular trope. (See Figure 107.) Graphic compositions gazed up at skyscrapers, exaggerating their converging orthogonal lines. Jacob Deschin, the photo-editor of the *New York Times* recommended that amateurs seek out angled shots either in the midmorning or late afternoon, when an "idle walk about town . . . should yield a good harvest" of photos.[6]

While Kodak's *How to Make Good Pictures* had long eschewed the leaning effect created by aiming the camera upward at tall buildings, by 1939 the company's popular handbook included a new section, "The Unusual Viewpoint." The editors wrote, "Expert photographers are to-day finding new angles from which to make their pictures, and for the most part the results are pleasing, as well as attractive and unusual. Many amateurs are also finding a new interest in seeking and achieving something different. They, too, are 'shooting' from positions that are daring and new."[7] The Kodak guide finally sanctioned the "worm's-eye" view,[8] reasoning, "After all, if you look up at a tall building your eyes do actually see the vertical lines converging towards the top, so why should not a photograph of the building show the same effect?"[9]

By the 1950s, many handbooks also taught readers how to successfully deploy the canted horizon effect. *This Is Photography*, a popular guide, explained, "The same subject is given enhanced interest and vitality by slightly raising and tilting the camera to produce a more dynamic compositional scheme."[10] (See Figure 108.) Ever the disciplinarians, though, the Kodak editors warned, "There is all the difference in the world between deliberately tilting your camera to obtain some novel or unusual effect and accidentally holding it slightly out of the straight, when the resulting picture merely looks carelessly composed."[11] As with many

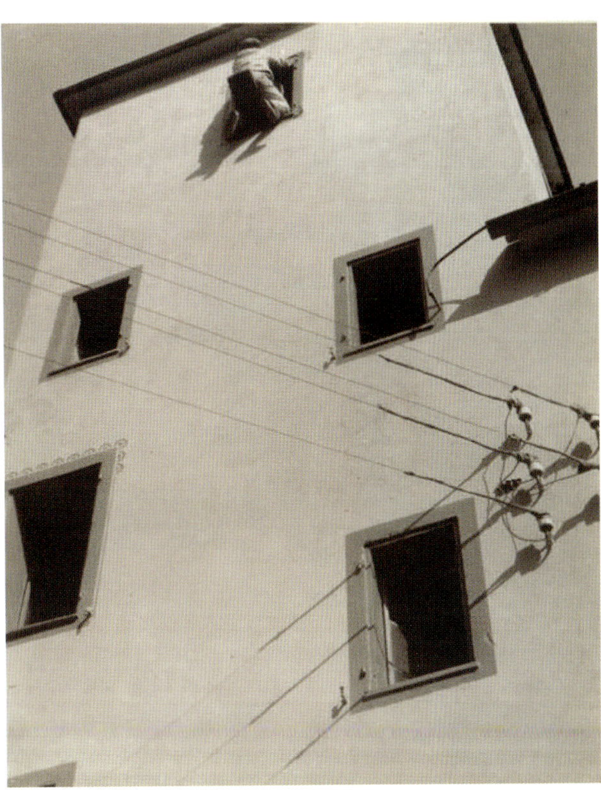

FIGURE 106. László Moholy-Nagy, "Decorating Work, Switzerland," 1925. Gelatin silver print, 19^{15}/$_{16}$ × 15^{13}/$_{16}$".

Source: Metropolitan Museum of Art, Gilman Collection, Purchase, Robert Rosenkranz Gift, 2005. Image source: Art Resource, NY.

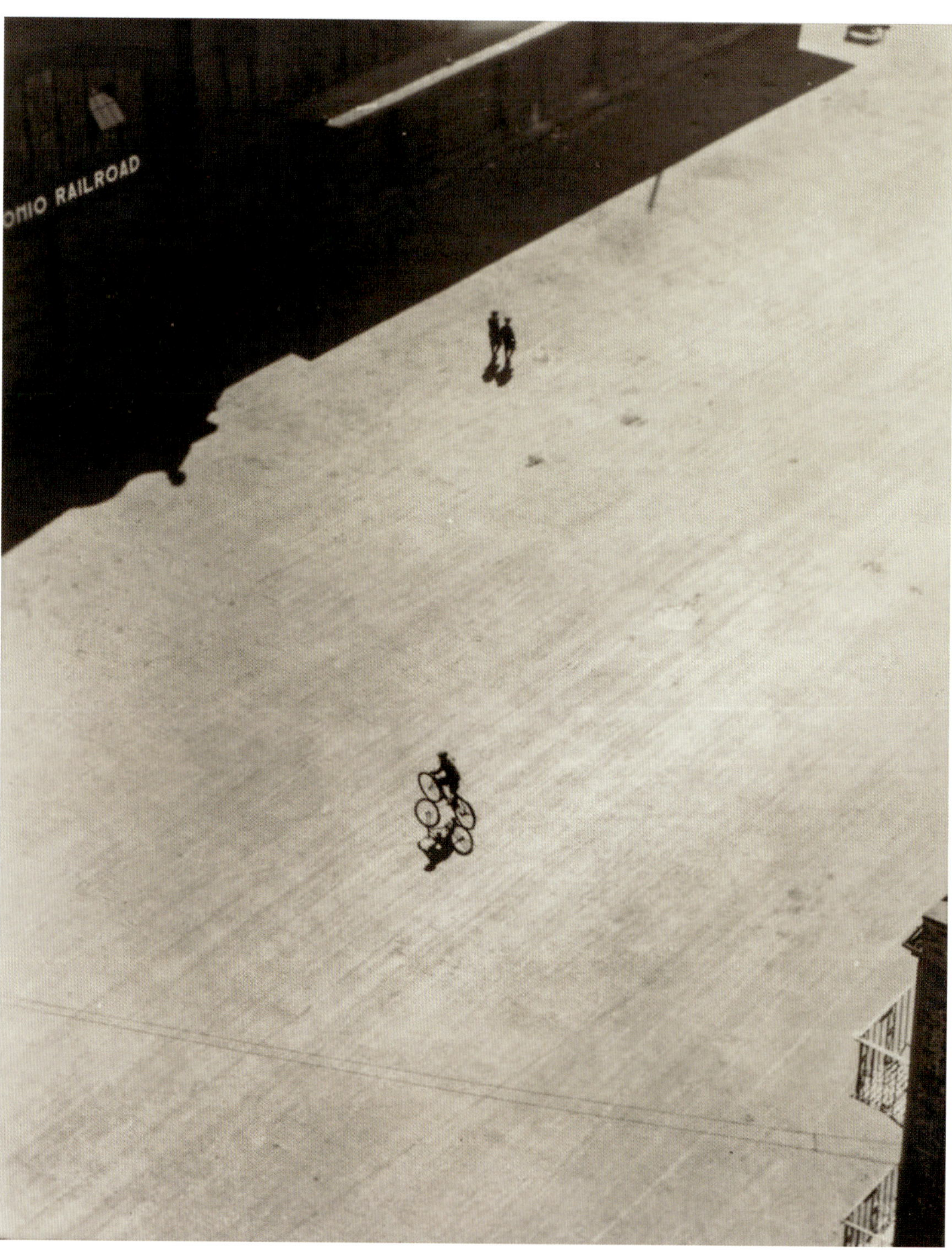
OHIO RAILROAD

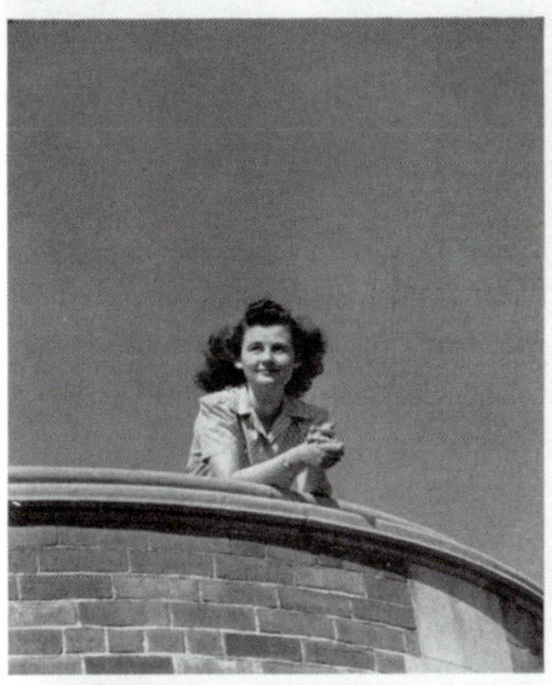 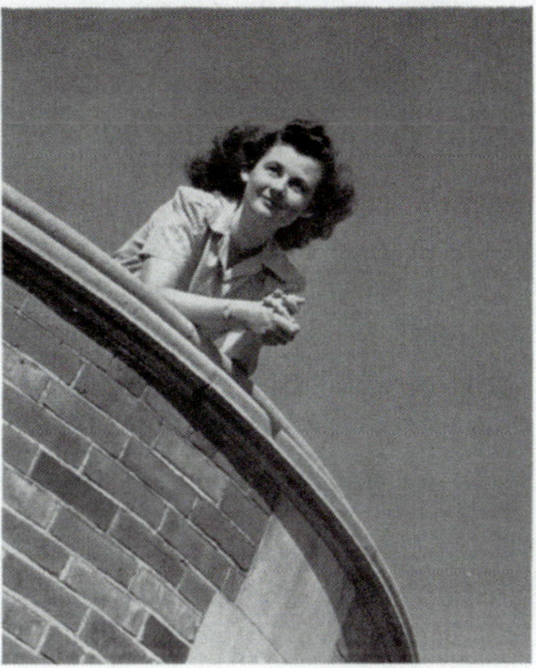

other trends that repurposed accidental effects or technical errors, the instructional literature was adamant about the need to apply such effects intentionally rather than haphazardly.

With the sweeping popularity of the unusual angle there also came criticism. Arthur Hammond, editor of *American Photography* and the author of a textbook on composition, was skeptical. He wrote:

It seems to me that the wave of modernism that is sweeping over present-day pictorial photography is very largely due to a natural desire to "get ahead" of the other fellow. Someone makes a picture showing some interesting curves of part of a spiral staircase, and

<FIGURE 107. Ralph Steiner (American, 1899–1986). *Boy on Bike*, 1921 (printed 1981). Gelatin silver print; image: 12.7 x 9.7 cm (5 x 3 ¹³⁄₁₆"); paper: 12.7 × 10.1 cm (5 × 4"). Courtesy of the Estate of Ralph Steiner and the Cleveland Museum of Art, Gift of Murray and Therese Weiss 2016.321

someone else does him one better by placing his camera on the floor in the center of the spiral, looking up, and thus getting the entire corkscrew effect. Then the only thing to do in order to be different is to get as similar view of a spiral staircase, looking down from above instead of up from below.[12]

The faddish currents of modern photography seemed to move at a dizzying pace compared with nineteenth-century trends, which relied on the passing of photographs hand-to-hand or infrequent visits to studio exhibitions. But Hammond's rant also hints at a concern for the future of the medium and for the instructional genre in particular: What happens when the established compositional rules no longer apply? What happens when "bad" photographs suddenly become art?

27

MODERNISTIC COMPOSITIONS

IN THE LATE 1920s, a new style appeared in picture magazines and on the walls of amateur exhibitions. Broadly defined, they might be called simply still-life pictures, but unlike the historical genre of still life, these told no story. They did not purport to represent a person through his or her possessions or warn of life's ephemeral nature. Instead, the new images focused on geometric shapes, picturing everything from industrial forms in glass and metal to quotidian household objects. Critics struggled to define these new photographs. Reviewing a photograph selected for *Photo-Era Magazine*'s regular competition, one critic wrote, "If the term 'modernistic' may be used as applying to art in photography, we have it in 'Salts and Angles,' by Carl H. Moulton. A drinking-cup, two salt-cellars, and some triangular pieces of cardboard would seem to be rather meager materials from which to work out a picture, yet Mr. Moulton has done it by effective arrangement and lighting."[1] These still-life pictures transformed the "meager" into the modern.

Photographers created graphic compositions out of mundane props using strong, directional lighting, high camera angles, and sharper focus than the pictorialist work that was still popular at the time. [See also Chapter 20, "Painterly Photographs," and Chapter 21, "Soft Focus."] In a review of an amateur exhibition, one critic described the scene: "A distinctly modernistic tendency was evident in some prints, one being a somewhat symmetrical arrangement of steel taps on a white ground strongly side lighted by artificial light to cast long shadows." He concluded, "The pattern was very striking and one which might be adapted to use in textiles or in fancy cover-papers, and so on."[2] This pronouncement would

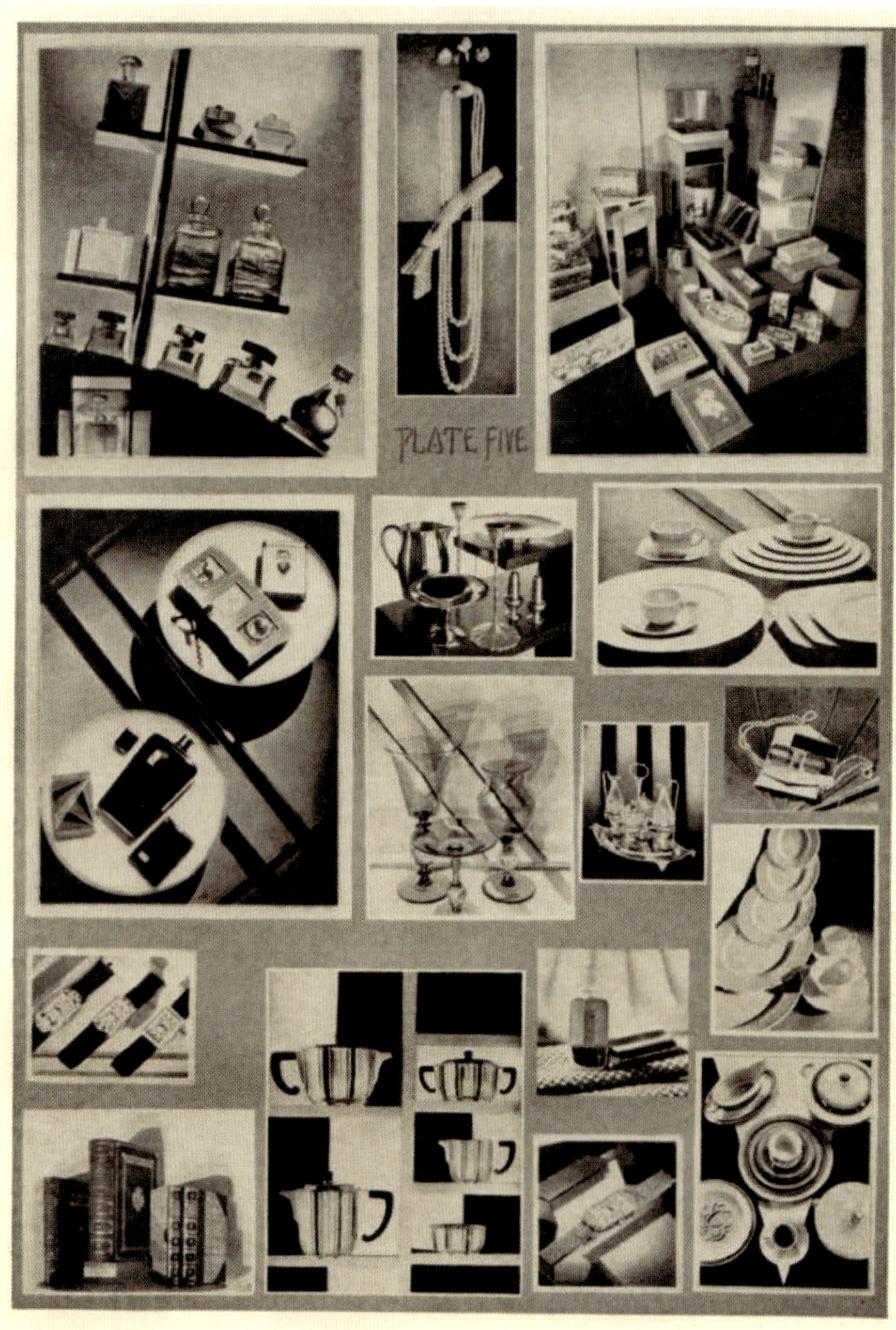
PLATE FIVE

have been harsh criticism for some pictori-alists who valued the disinterested status of the amateur. But modernist photographers, especially the reformed pictorialist Edward Steichen, were actively redefining the rela-tionship of art and commerce.[3] Advertisers and industry were the new patrons of art.

The impact of commercial imagery is readily identifiable in exhibition reviews of the period. The use of hard lighting and the diagonal arrangements then popular in product photography was widespread. In a portfolio for the industry publication *Arts and Decoration*, the photographer Paul Outerbridge included pictures of a half-filled wine glass on a checkerboard, a saw and a box, and eggs in a bowl, among sun-dry other items. He explained his catholic choice of subject matter: "I was not taking a portrait of these objects, but merely us-ing them to form a purely abstract composition."[4] Soon, however, these seemingly arbitrary objects began appearing regularly in oth-er photographs. The newly appointed Condé Nast art director, Me-hemed Fehmy Agha, wrote cuttingly in 1929 that "modernistic pho-tography is easily recognized by its subject matter: Eggs (any style). Twenty shoes, standing in a row. A skyscraper, taken from a modern-istic angle. Ten tea cups standing in a row. A factory chimney seen through the ironwork of a railroad bridge (modernistic angle) . . . . The interior of a garbage can. More eggs."[5] Popular criticism echoed Agha's judgment. An amateur photographer writing in defense of pic-torialism admitted, "Still-life studies of eggshells in kitchen-sinks are very clever, and I admire the work of many pattern-makers; yet I don't think that such efforts are suitable in a frame in the living-room. I have done several of these modernistic things, myself, purely for amuse-ment. I just cannot take them seriously."[6]

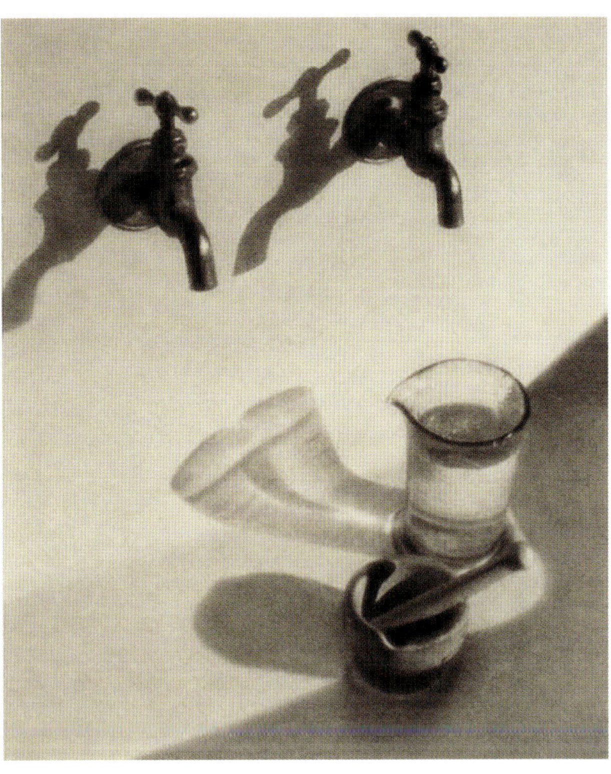

FIGURE 110. Akira Furukawa, "Untitled (Faucets, Beaker, Mortar & Pestle)," c. 1930. Bromoil print, 9.75" × 7.85".

Source: Dennis Reed Collection. Courtesy of the Furukawa Family.

< FIGURE 109. Photographer unknown. Leonard A. Williams, *Illustrative Photography in Advertising* (San Francisco: Camera Craft Publishing Company, 1929), 79.

Source: Author's collection.

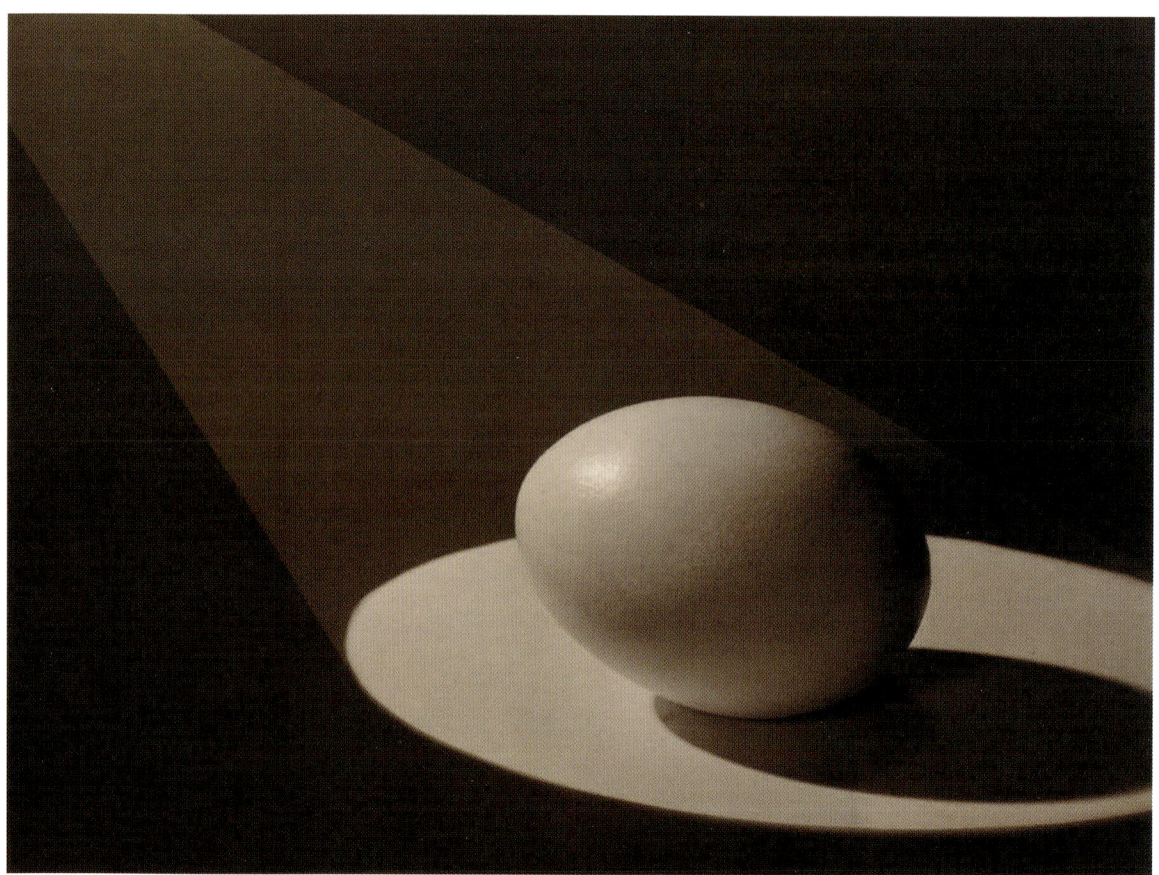

New subjects were introduced in the 1930s, but soon these too became widely stereotyped. The critic A. H. Beardsley wrote, "Of late, many studies of glassware in all manner of shapes and sizes and composition have appeared in the photographic press and at salons."[7] Another writer for *Photo-Era* praised a glass still life in the New York Camera Club's annual show, but noted his bias: "Possibly this selection was made because I like to photograph glass myself, and I know just how difficult it is to correctly render the texture and the life that is to be found in this subject."[8] Beardsley tried to understand the subject's new-found popularity: "Probably the selection of various kinds of glassware has become rather a welcome change from the basket of fruit or the bouquet of flowers." He signaled the ongoing pictorialist tendency, writing, "There are those who fail to understand and appreciate the pleasure which many obtain

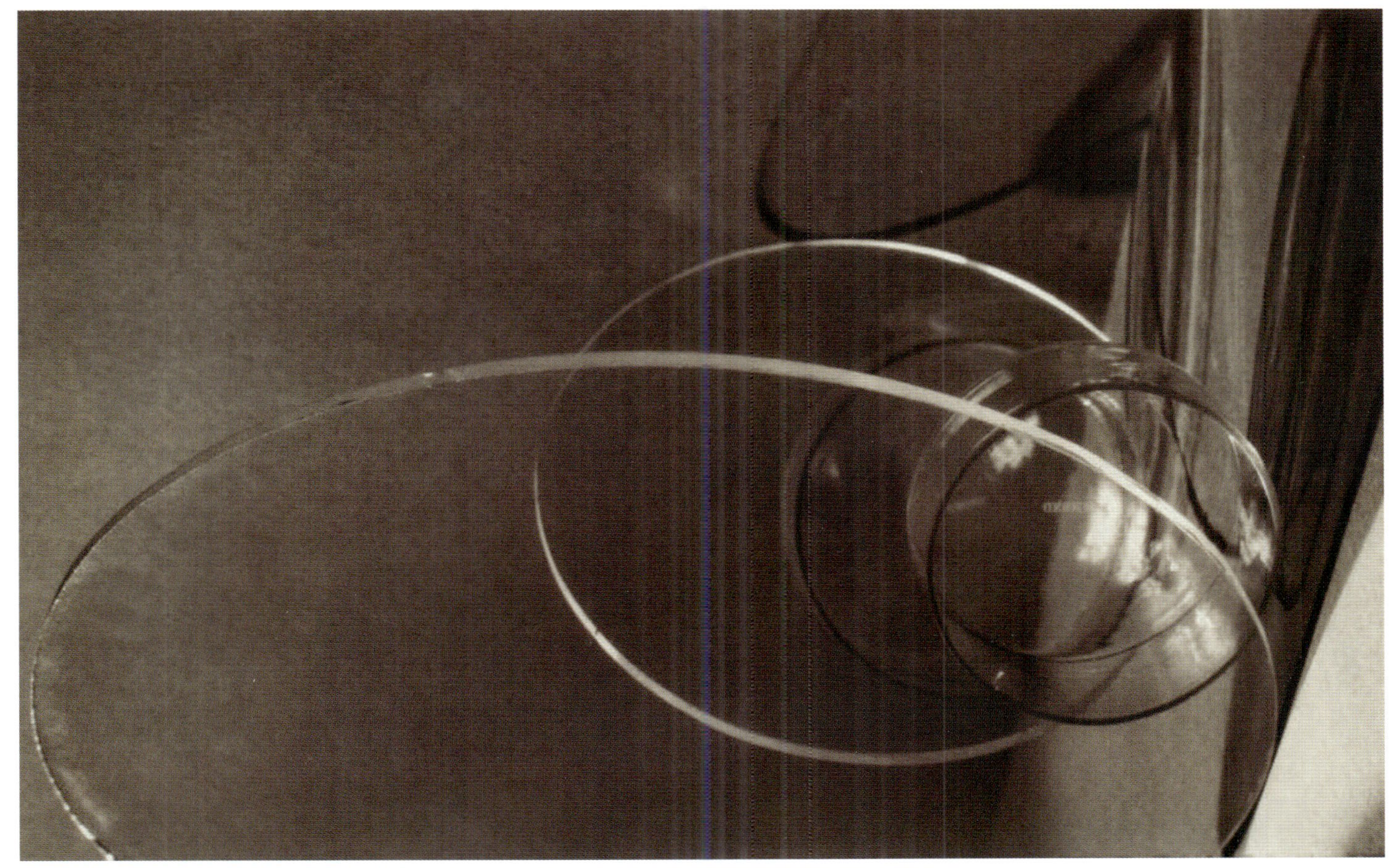

162

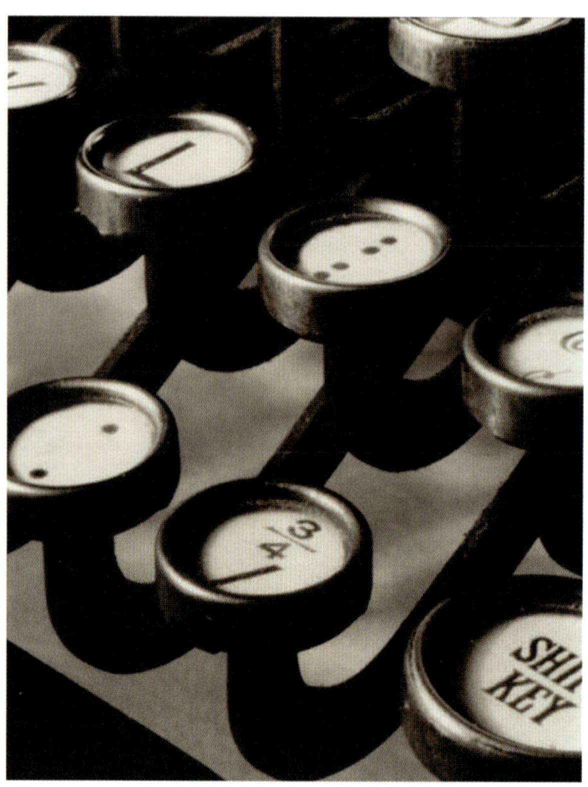

FIGURE 113. Ralph Steiner, "Typewriter Keys," 1921. Gelatin silver print, 8 ⅙″ × 6″.

Source: Library of Congress, Prints and Photographs Division.

from the creation of angles, curves, light and shadow, and patterns, by the use of any article which may come to hand . . . but when its shadow is projected on a background, a curious and perhaps attractive effect is obtained and we have a so-called modern photographic design or pattern."[9] Beardsley, a gentle critic, could barely tell what genre these pictures represented, let alone whether he found them successful.

Still life was only an occasional subject for photographers in the nineteenth century, whose work mainly recreated the established genres, such as fruit and flower pictures or after-the-hunt scenes. Amateurs later recorded arrangements found in their homes with the early Kodak cameras: a collection of pictures and objects on a mantle or sideboard. The new, "modernistic" still life carried none of the sentimentality or philosophical weight of these precedents. Instead, the modern still life concentrated on the photographic abstraction of light and shadow. These pictures promised to transcend the ordinariness of their subjects through the new perspectives afforded by photography, even as such pictures underscored the regularity and proliferation of mass-produced goods. Some writers cited the impact of the German "Neue Sachlichkeit," or "new objectivity" of photographer Albert Renger-Patzsch. A popular American guide quoted Renger-Patzsch's description of his quest, which was to discover "new viewpoints, the unusual in the usual, the extraordinary in the ordinary."[10] The newness of these pictures was tempered by the fact of their rapid ascendance to pervasiveness. Like many other trends, once they saturated the visual field, their sense of naturalness dissipated, leaving behind an image of the trend itself.

28

HOLLYWOOD GLAMOUR

SINCE THE DEVELOPMENT of the Hollywood studio system, which consolidated production and distribution of motion pictures in the late 1920s, advertising and public relations duties fell to the studios rather than individual movie theaters. Essential to this enterprise were the studio portrait photographers and "stills men," the (mostly male) photographers who worked on set. In the era of the sound film, photographers had to work quickly, either at the end of a shot or during filming by enclosing their cameras in a large soundproof bubble to eliminate the noise of the shutter. Their work was entirely subordinate to the director's creative vision.

Portrait photographers had more freedom. They worked in separate portrait studios, sometimes with actors in costumes related to upcoming roles, but often in other situations devised by the photographer. These were the glamour shots. Featured in Hollywood magazines, on advertising posters, and as 8" × 10" prints mailed to fan club members, this style of portraiture was widely known and imitated.

Movie magazines and photographic guides were full of recommendations in the 1930s and 1940s for making one's subject—or oneself—look like a Hollywood star. Famous portrait photographers, including Clarence Sinclair Bull and George Hurrell, offered tips for creating successful home portraits or preparing for a visit to a photo studio. One article promised, "You've seen their names in italics below the portraits of every single one of your favorite movie stars. Stay with us and they will—in effect—put their names under your picture."[1] Often these guides were written in the form of advice to a Hollywood starlet learning how to

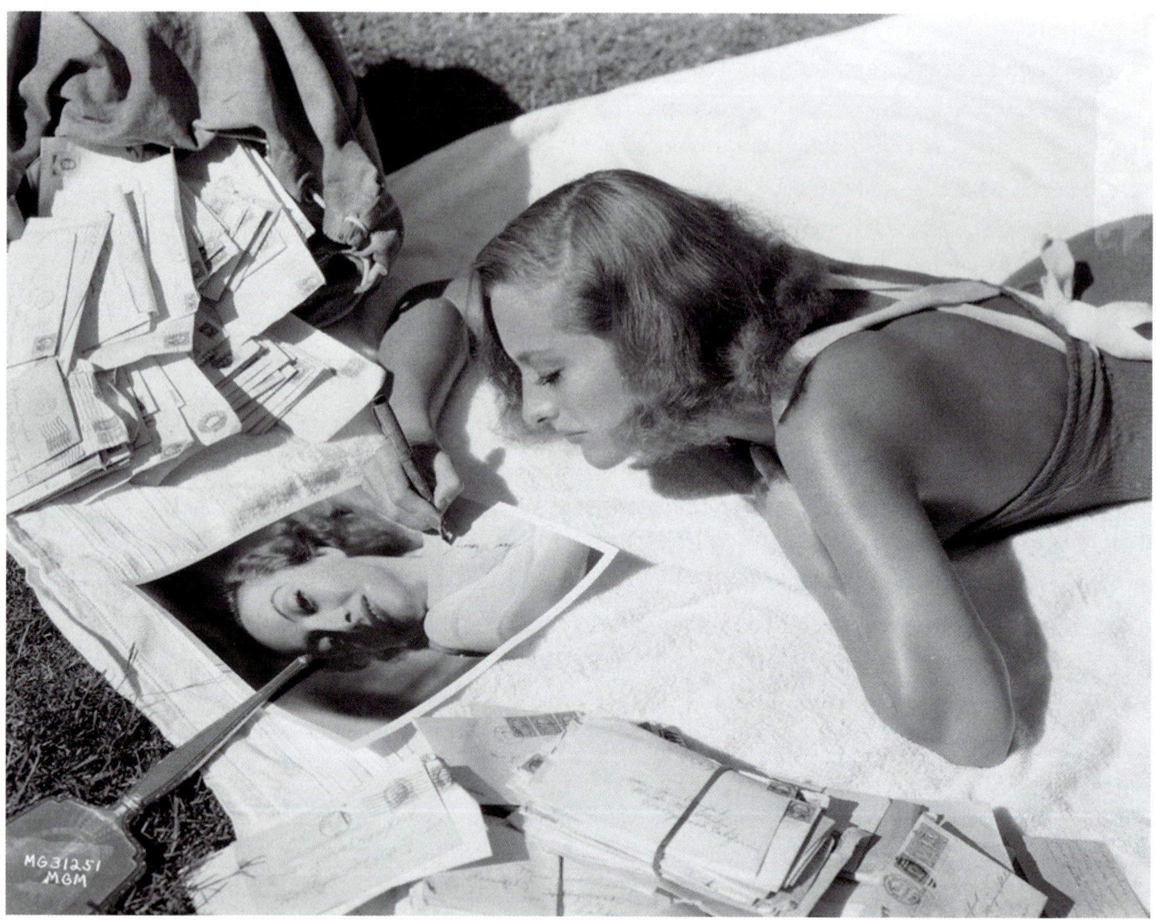

take her own pictures, with the implication that if even an actress could make photographs, anyone could.[2] These condescending conversations reinforced Hollywood's objectification of women and echoed photographic advertising in the popular press, which, since the introduction of the Kodak Brownie, suggested that photography was so easy that even a woman could do it.

The Hollywood glamour shot was defined by two elements: lighting and pose. How-to guides offered detailed advice on recreating the new effects, which were radically different from earlier portraiture. Most articles acknowledged that amateurs wouldn't have access to powerful motion picture lighting equipment. Instead, authors provided do-it-yourself instructions for adapting window light with the use of homemade reflectors. Bull, known popularly as Greta Garbo's preferred photographer, explained, "Take a piece of board—compo board, part of a box, whatever you can get—paint it with aluminum paint or cover it with aluminum paper and there you are! At a pinch, you can save the silver paper that comes wrapped around your films and paste this on your board. It makes a satisfactory reflector."[3] When using strong, directional light, the reflector filled in dark shadow areas with detail.

Although portrait photographers had long used lighting to correct imperfections, the Hollywood portraitists exaggerated the lighting and introduced severe camera angles to emphasize actors' distinctive features. In an interview, Hurrell noted, "Few people realize the fact that most motion picture stars deliberately call attention to their striking facial characteristics."[4] Hurrell described one star's strong jaw and another's round face, while the article's author also provided notes on how to "fix" these features by shooting downward to taper and thin the face. Turning the body away from the camera to narrow the hips, as well as pointing the toe to lengthen the leg, were common—and widely adopted—suggestions. [See also Chapter 46, "Selfie."]

In contrast with the largely eye-level view of nineteenth-century portraits, glamour shots relied on a new, more intimate relationship between the camera and the subject. One star described her role in a typical portrait session from "getting zipped into a slinky off-shoulder garment, lounging dangerously on an Empire sofa," then finally, "peering through half-closed lids at a photographer whose instructions are limited to two words—'Look sexy.'"[5] Even during the chaste years of the Motion Picture Production Code, when studios self-censored sexual content, glamour shots continued to rely on these suggestive poses to entice theatergoers. One of the studio photographer's beloved props

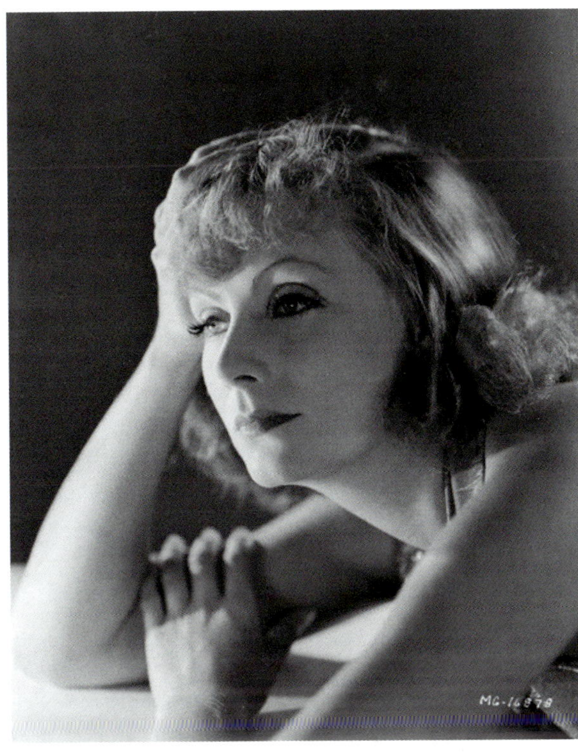

FIGURE 115. Clarence Sinclair Bull, "Greta Garbo," 1931. Gelatin silver print.

Source: Courtesy of John Kobal Foundation/Getty Images.

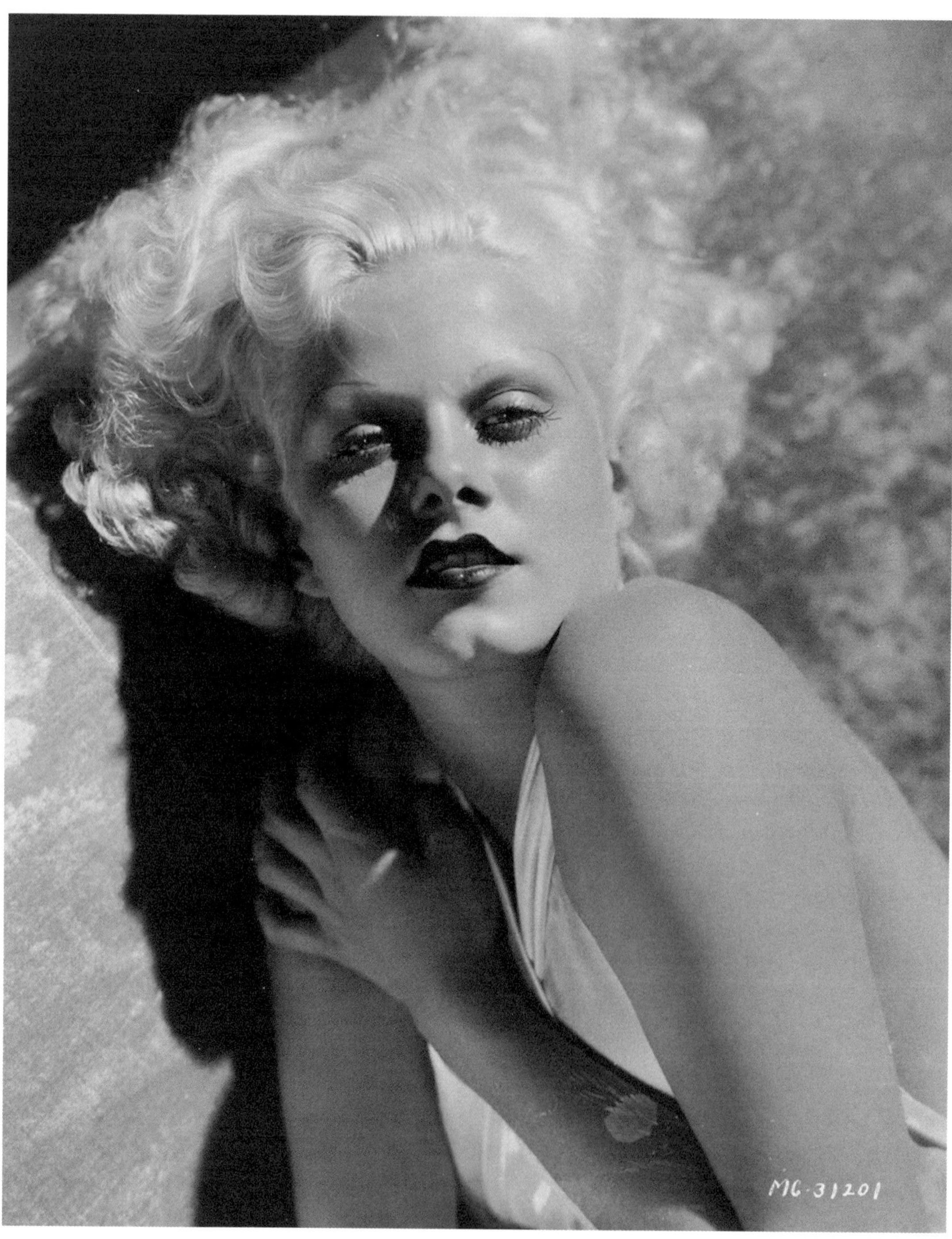
MG-31201

was the "Hollywood bed," an adjustable posing lounge.[6] The photographer could easily shoot from above this low-reclining platform to create a wholly new style of pose that featured the star in a prone position. Reclining shots also allowed photographers to display women's hair. Sometimes these shots were shifted from a horizontal to a vertical orientation, creating unusual antigravity effects, which intensified the star's otherworldly character. Even in more conventional poses, photographers recommending paying special attention to lighting the star's hair. The Paramount photographer Eugene Robert Richee said, "The best pictures are made with loose hair to catch light and give life and abandon to the subject."[7] Bull recommended backlighting blondes, and *Silver Screen* magazine promised "the subject's hair will truly become her crowning glory."[8] [See also Chapter 34, "Lens Flare."]

   With the decline of the Hollywood studio system in the late 1940s, however, the formal glamour studio shot gave way to more natural locations, even as the poses and lighting remained highly regimented. An article by the Hollywood photographer Sam Wu revealed that a natural look for women was still a long way off, even in the late 1950s. Wu wrote, "Today's concept of glamor is that women should look glamorous not only in the photographer's studio but also at home, at work, and in other surroundings. . . . The 35-mm camera helps catch candid glamor as no other camera can."[9] [See also Chapter 25, "Candids."] By the 1960s, fans' fascination with the carefully constructed photographs of Hollywood's Golden Age shifted to an interest in actors as real people going about their daily lives, caught by the long lenses of the paparazzi.

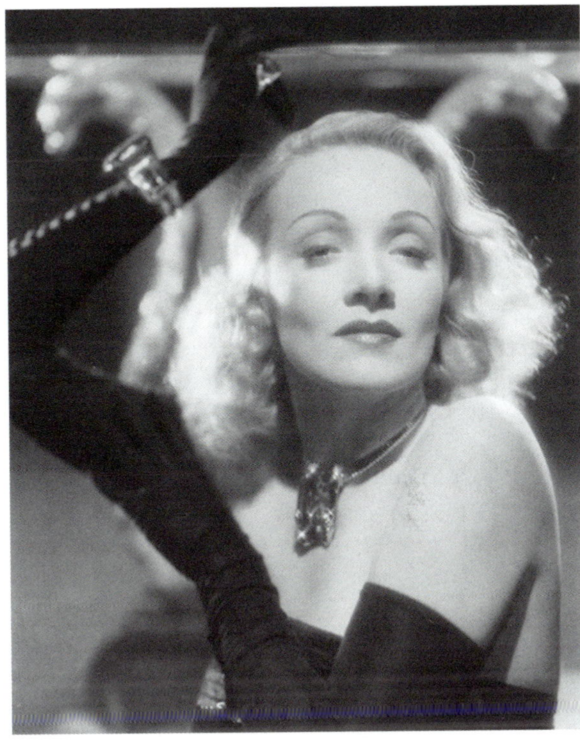

FIGURE 117. A. L. Whitey Schafer, "Blonde Venus [Marlene Dietrich]," 1942. Gelatin silver print.

Source: Courtesy of John Kobal Foundation/Getty Images.

< FIGURE 116. George Hurrell, "Hollywood Goddess [Jean Harlow]," 1933. Gelatin silver print.

Source: Courtesy of John Kobal Foundation/Getty Images.

29

DISTRACTING COLOR

FIGURE 118. Cover of *Kodachrome: A Data Book on Photography in Color* (Rochester, NY: Eastman Kodak, Company, 1941).

Source: Author's collection.

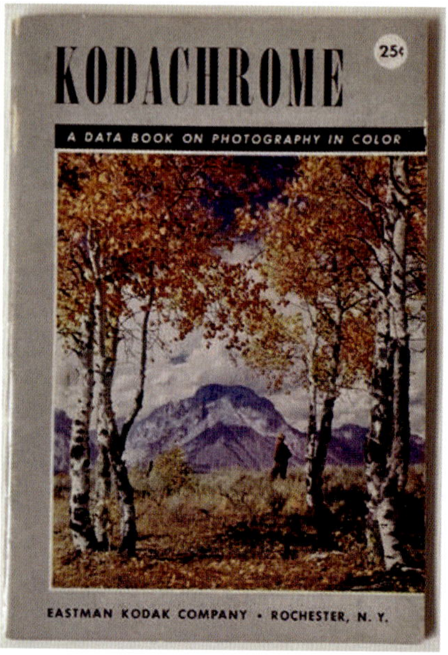

THE 1936 RELEASE of Kodachrome was described as the most important advance in photography during the medium's first hundred years.[1] Earlier twentieth-century color processes, such as Autochrome or Dufaycolor, were prohibitively complicated. With the cost of processing included in the purchase price of all Kodachrome film, color photography was finally available to amateurs who did not have access to darkrooms or color processing chemicals.

However, limitations of the process—including the slow speed of the original Kodachrome film, its small size, and the difficulty of creating lasting prints with an internegative—were quickly identified. In interviews and amateur guides, it was common to praise the new film in one breath, then quickly disassociate oneself from it in the next. The photographer Berenice Abbott explained that in addition to the film's "technical problems," color photography failed "to satisfy critical taste" because photographers lacked judgment in selecting subject matter that would play to the new medium's strengths.[2] A number of articles addressed these technical limitations and tried to turn weaknesses into advantages. Color film was best used with "miniature" cameras, as 35 millimeter single-lens-reflex and rangefinder cameras were then widely known. These cameras, with their smaller lenses placed closer to the film, required less light than medium- and large- format cameras and therefore could use color film in more diverse lighting situations. The difficulty of creating prints from Kodachrome color positives was rerouted into an appreciation for the brilliant colors and the lack of pronounced grain when viewed as projected slides.[3]

One criticism of color photography, however, had little to do with technical limitations of the medium and was instead blamed on photographers' inexperience with color composition. Photographers had to learn to see the world in terms of hue and color contrast rather than just tonal values. Where light and shadow easily created separation between objects in black-and-white photography, contrasting colors had the tendency to stick out of an otherwise subdued background, collapsing the appearance of depth and overwhelming the composition's subject. This had the greatest impact on portrait photography, where it was necessary to separate the subject distinctly from the background. Instead of receding into a shadowed or out-of-focus background, contrasting colors became prominent regardless of their relative sharpness or brightness.

The 1941 booklet, *Kodachrome: A Data Book on Photography in Color*, included more than fifty pages of detailed advice on exposures in a variety of situations, from interior portraits and architectural shots to fireworks displays, sunsets, and tropical scenes. The solution to the problem of color contrast and distracting backgrounds for Kodachrome users was simple according to guidebooks like this: shoot everything against the sky. More than half of the portraits in *Kodachrome and How to Use It* made use of a low angle to frame subjects against a simple blue sky background. As the author and principal photographer, Ivan Dmitri, explained, "The greatest fault in the use of Kodachrome by amateurs is that the photographer fails to approach his subject from the proper angle, and has a tremendous affinity for improper backgrounds."[4] By tilting the camera upward, especially in combination with a polarizing filter, Dmitri argued, "the eye remains concentrated upon the figure and is undisturbed by any distraction in the dark blue background."[5] [See also Chapter 26, "New Angles."] Also the subject of a *Life* magazine "Speaking of Pictures . . ." spread, the lessons and images from *Kodachrome and How to Use It* were widely seen in the early 1940s.[6]

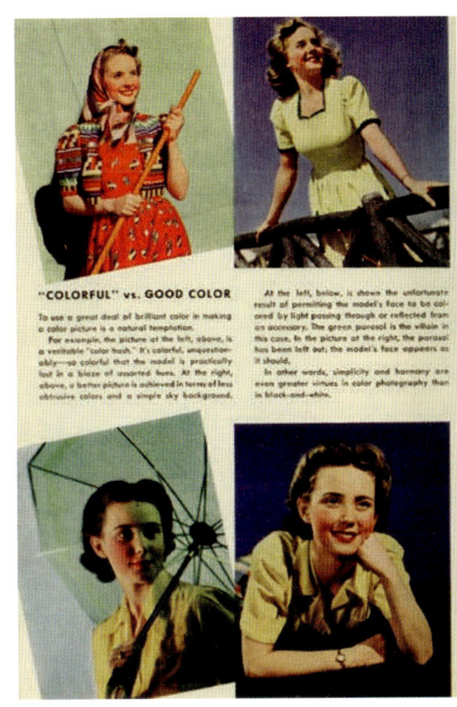

FIGURE 119. "'Colorful' vs. Good Color," in *How to Make Good Pictures* (Rochester, NY: Eastman Kodak Co., 1943), 208.

Source: Collection of the Prelinger Library.

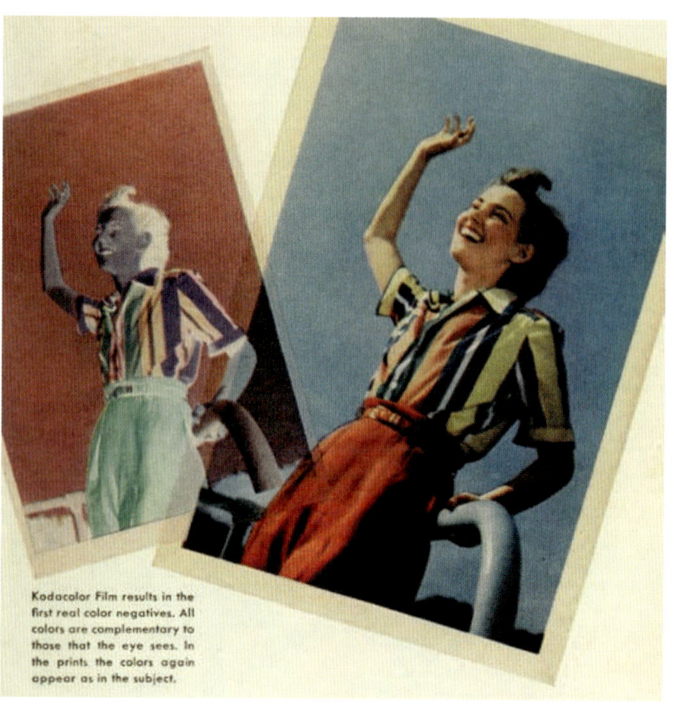

FIGURE 120. "Kodacolor Film Results in the First Real Color Negatives," in *How to Make Good Pictures* (Rochester, NY: Eastman Kodak Co., 1943), 35.

Source: Collection of the Prelinger Library.

These recommendations abruptly discarded decades of advice that warned against the use of unconventional angles for portrait photography. The consensus among earlier American guidebooks was that for portraits, "an extreme camera angle had best be avoided, since it conveys the impression of unnaturalness."[7] Yet by 1950, amateur photographers struggling to simplify their work in the newly colorful medium were regularly encouraged to point their lenses upward at their subjects for the simplicity of the background and the improved angle of view. One guidebook explained, "The sky is about the finest of all backgrounds, because it is unobtrusive and infinitely varied, and because it usually forces you to use a fairly low camera angle, an angle that gives your subjects a psychological advantage, thereby giving you a better picture."[8]

While today viewers are likely to associate this camera angle and posture with monumental socialist realist worker portraits and propaganda posters of the 1930s and 1940s, the adoption of the low angle by amateur photographers in the United States was motivated by formal rather than rhetorical concerns. As photographers became comfortable with color contrast and film was made more responsive to subtleties of color tonality and saturation through the second half of the twentieth century, these dramatic low angles waned in popularity, allowing the aesthetic to remain cemented within the tradition of political propaganda rather than with Americans' first casual pictures in color.

30

TELEVISION PICTURES

IN 1944, *LIFE* MAGAZINE forecast that television would be one of the largest industries to arise in the postwar period. The article stated baldly, "Its impact on U.S. civilization is beyond present prediction."[1] In 1950 only 9 percent of households owned a television. That figure skyrocketed to nearly 90 percent in just ten years, far outpacing the adoption of radio in the preceding decades.[2] With characteristic editorial hyperbole, *Life* asserted, "[Television] has a power to annihilate time and space that will unite everyone everywhere in the immediate experience of events in contemporary life and history."[3] The practice of photographing the television screen, which emerged in the 1950s, celebrated this newfound proximity to events and celebrities of international renown.

Popular Science announced in 1950, "There's a new hobby awaiting you these days—making a scrapbook of TV scenes. Sitting comfortably before a television set, you can snap photos of celebrities, sports events, and pin-up girls."[4] As the media historian Lynn Spigel has argued, television watching was highly gendered in the 1950s, although popular representations of TV often reversed the traditional codes of feminine passivity and male activity. In advertising of the period, men were depicted as fully, even comically, relaxed in front of the television, while women busied themselves with domestic labor, serving snacks, or multitasking with other chores. Advising men in how to actively engage with the television may have been designed to dissipate the threat of passivity that had come to be associated with their television watching.[5]

Instructional articles pictured men perched close to the television set with an elaborate camera set up on a tripod. How-to features emphasized the quick reflexes and specialized knowledge required to achieve the best television pictures. In an article on photographing televised boxing matches, the author cautioned, "Shooting fights is a little more tricky than other types of TV photography. For one thing, you must try to beat the fighters to the punch with your shutter finger—just as news photographers do."[6] Photographing the television was pitched as a dramatic, skillful activity. [See also Chapter 15, "Instantaneous Photographs."] To recreate the thrill of street photography while still getting guaranteed shots of well-known personalities, another author suggested photographing at movie theaters, where "obstacles like adamant theater managers keep cropping up. You either learn how to hurdle them or go around them, getting your pictures in either case. The pictures are the goal, of course, but there's a lot of fun to be had while going after them."[7]

For readers of *Popular Science*, the practice of TV photography had an educative potential too. The magazine warned, "To take such photos, you must know the tricks. A simple box camera won't do."[8] Articles published in *Popular Science* in the early 1950s used the new photographic pastime as an opportunity to describe the mechanics of the cathode-ray-tube television. Contrary to most modern photographic practice, photographing the television required a relatively slow exposure, since the TV's scanning beam illuminated the full image only thirty times per second. Shutter speeds more rapid than 1/30th of a second would reveal only a partial image.

Capitalizing on the new trends in both TV watching and photographing, *Popular Science* sponsored a contest in 1951 that promised fifty dollars to the maker of the best TV photos. The five hundred entries were judged according to their "subject matter and technical quality."[9] The winning photos fell into categories that would remain consistent

> FIGURE 121. R. P. Stevenson, "How You Can Photograph the Fights Via Television," *Popular Science* 158, no. 2 (February 1951): 214.

How images are produced on your television set.

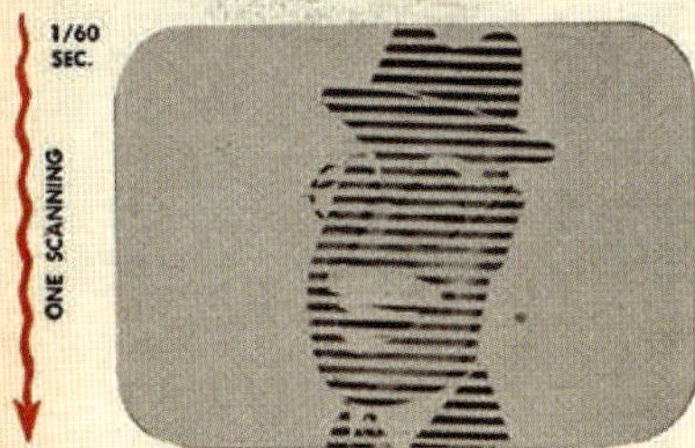

Each 1/60 second the scanning beam, a pin point of light, moves in slanting zigzag lines from top to bottom of tube. This produces a "field." As it moves, the beam momentarily records an image made up of tones ranging from black to white. In a single field, your eye could see a recognizable image, but with spaces between lines picture would be incomplete.

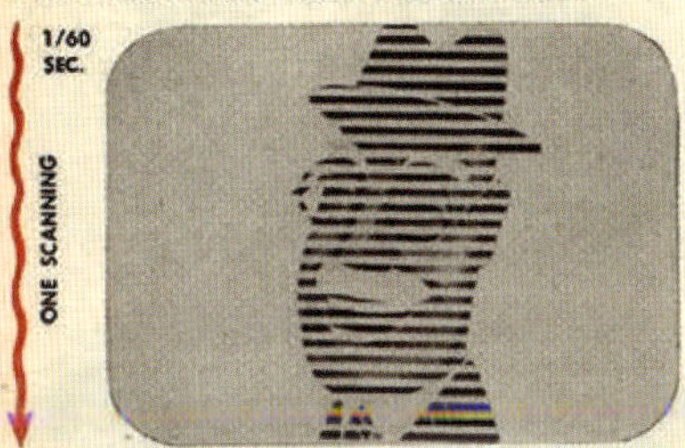

A second scanning, also taking 1/60 second, is needed to give a full image. This is called the "interlace." Scanning beam moves back and forth over spaces not covered first time. Consequently, the interlace lets you see parts of image you didn't see in first field. Sketches are exaggerated. Actually, there are at least 250 scanning lines in one field.

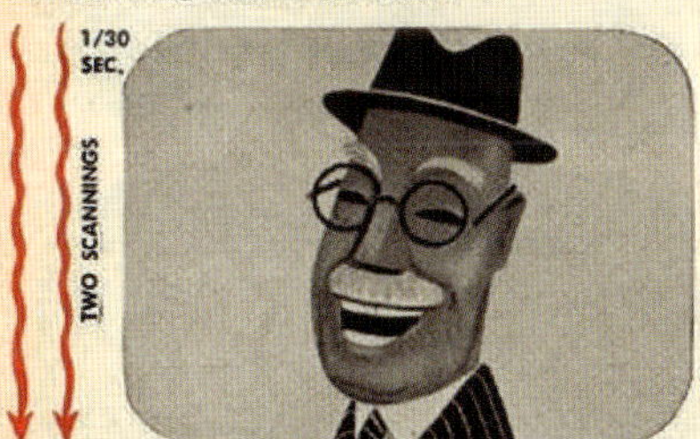

Complete TV image consists of two fields, one interlaced with the other. This is called a "frame." A new one is produced each 1/30 second. A succession of frames, one following the other without measurable delay, creates action you see. In effect, each frame is a still picture. Actually, there may be slight movement of image from one field to next.

POPULAR SCIENCE. At that speed he found it next to impossible to get satisfactory TV photos of fights, dancing, and other fast action. So he set out to experiment with faster speeds—specifically 1/50 and 1/100 second.

And here are the results. Eventually he found that 1/50 second at f/3.5 gave him what he wanted—a good image with little or no movement. To compensate for the underexposure that results at these settings, even with Super XX and other film of equal speed, he overdevelops all his shots. Using D-76 developer, he gives his film 45 or 60 minutes of development instead of the customary 15. This formula causes no chemical fog in prolonged development, and in moderate enlargements his 2¼" by 2¼" negatives give no trouble from grain.

Turn brightness above normal. For all his TV shots Bill uses a 2¼" by 2¼" reflex fitted with a portrait attachment and moved in close to a 10" screen. While shooting, he turns the brightness a little above normal—but not enough to wash detail out of the highlights. He shoots with the lens open wide at f/3.5.

If your camera has an f/4.5 lens, you still can probably get good fight photos by developing your film longer, say to 75 or 90 minutes. Should you be using sheet film, you can of course buy film that is far faster than the Super XX type. This will not require such long development.

Sketches show what happens. Why 1/50 second shutter speed is the most practical for stopping TV action is shown in the accompanying sketches. First, study how a TV image is formed. Then see what happens at different shutter speeds.

(This explanation refers only to between-the-lens shutters. Focal-plane shutters are sometimes used for TV shooting, but most photographers do not favor them because of their different action—a slit sweeping across the film.)

Even though some scanning lines are missing at 1/50 second, this makes very little difference. In moderate blow-ups, you'll never notice they aren't there. Best of all, the one scanning field and part of another enables you to get many shots without the blurs that come from fast action.

What about 1/30 second? In theory, a shutter opening of 1/30 second might be considered ideal, especially if the shutter could be synchronized to open and close with the beginning and completion of in-

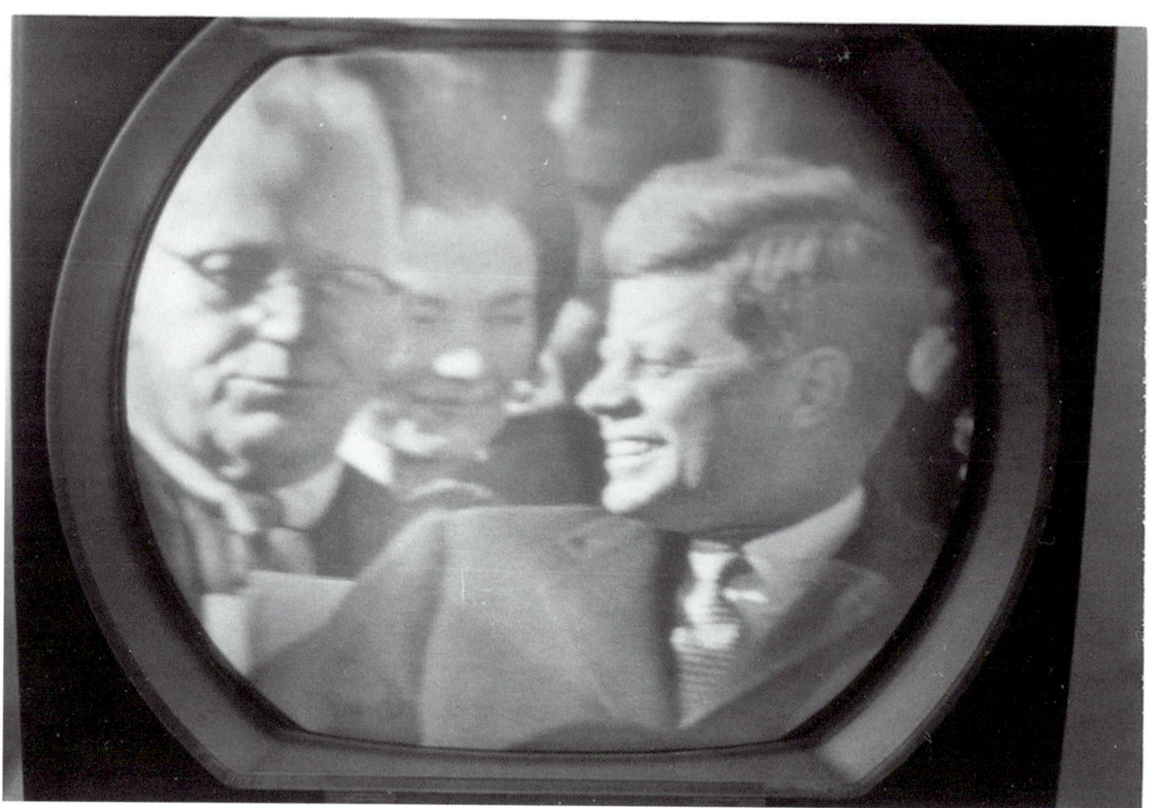

among amateur TV photographers through the 1960s: "history in the making," popular entertainers and other celebrities, and sports.[10] The contest also privileged photos that were tightly cropped, showing just the screen rather than the entire television cabinet. The close-up aesthetic seems to have been rooted in a desire to erase the television's mediation and claim the photographer's presence at the scene, or at least to secure a good picture of it for posterity. Like nineteenth-century albums featuring mass-produced cartes-de-visite of celebrities, the television photograph brought global events into the domestic realm. As one guidebook author described a friend's collection of television photos, "He didn't bother himself with technicalities but concentrated on getting the best possible likenesses of President Eisenhower, Winston Churchill, Gina Lollobrigida, Queen Elizabeth, and others for his personal picture gallery."[11] Through the screen image, even amateurs earned privileged access to people and events far from home.

A handbook by the photojournalist Arthur Rothstein reveals the professional photographer's wariness of television's ascendance. Rothstein wrote, "Some members of the press have begun to view with alarm the type of news and feature coverage given to events by television. These extremists see the eventual end of the still photograph in favor of the instantaneous and immediate transmission of the electronic image."[12] While Rothstein was more optimistic about the future of photography, the professional concern he cited was widespread. Nonetheless, television pictures represented a significant aspect of amateur practice in the 1950s and 1960s. The dearth of information on television pictures in the photographic press may be related to the nervousness that Rothstein identified among his colleagues. Not only did television's immediacy threaten to replace news reporting, but by taking pictures of the screen at home, even amateurs could create a permanent record of noteworthy events.

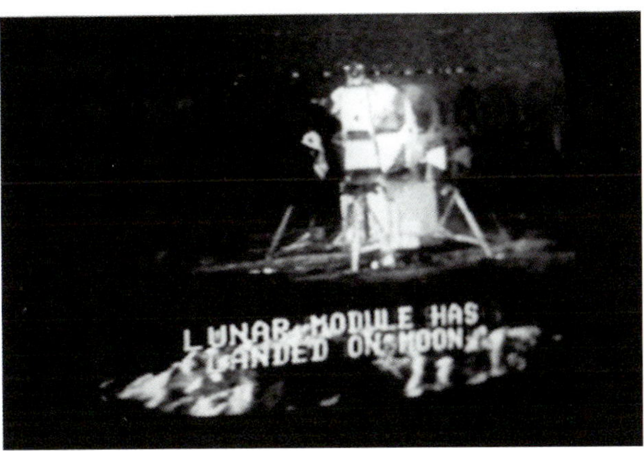

FIGURE 123. Photographer unknown, "Lunar Module Has Landed on Moon (Snapshot Made of a Television Screen)," 1969.

Source: Collection of Barbara Levine/ Project B.

31

MOTION BLUR

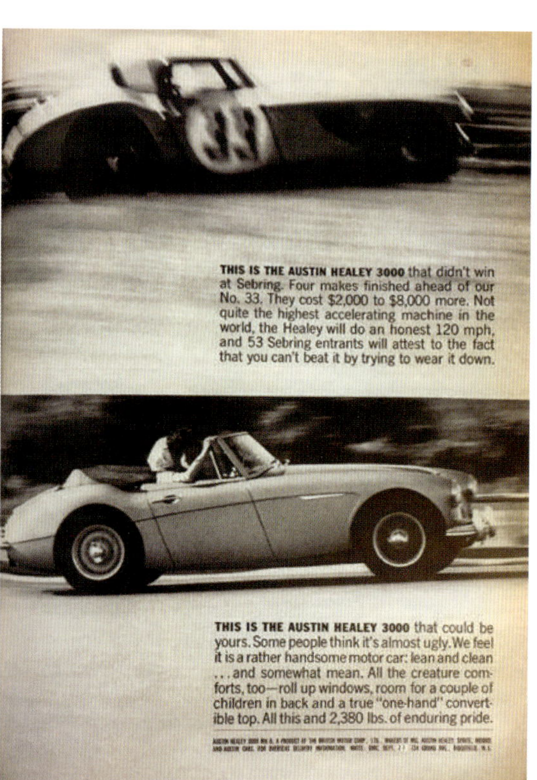

FIGURE 124. Austin Healey, "This Is the Austin Healey 3000," *Road and Track*, September 1963.

IN THE LATE 1950S AND EARLY 1960S, American photographic journals were anxiously trying to position themselves in relation to a new photographic trend: blur. In advertising and editorial work, professional photographers used slow shutter speeds combined with camera movement to create the dramatic effect. By panning, or following the moving subject with the camera, photographers inverted the appearance of motion. Speeding race cars appeared still in relation to the camera while the scene behind them blurred, as if passing by at high speed. Even comparatively slow movement seemed fast using this technique. While athletes and racehorses streaked across the pages of popular magazines, so too did fashion models' windswept hair or elegant dresses.

The author of a 1957 article in *Popular Photography* warned that the fad threatened a deskilling of photography: "To blur or not to blur . . . is *not* the question if you are still toddling through the first steps of photography."[1] To combat this possibility, the magazine had offered elaborate tutorials almost annually since 1955, which emphasized the expertise required to create a sophisticated blur.[2] In 1962, *Popular Photography* would ask, "Are Photographers Going Blur Crazy?"[3] By this point the photo magazines were fully complicit in the trend. A *U.S.*

Camera article published at the same time invited readers to weigh in on the debate, asking, "The Battle over Blur: Creative Tool or Sloppy Technique? You Tell Us!"[4]

Some of these publications welcomed blur as an antidote to the ubiquity of highly sharp photographs, like the pictures of speeding bullets popularized by Harold Edgerton in the 1930s. With portable flash units newly available on the consumer market, stop-action photographs dominated amateur publications from the early to mid-1950s. [See also Chapter 15, "Instantaneous Photographs."] Beyond this stylistic backlash, popular magazines also tried to explain the appeal of blur in terms of psychology and perception. Articles in *Popular Photography*, *American Photography*, and *Petersen's Photographic* attributed interest in blur to the 1960's relaxed state of mind or claimed that it was a better approximation of the human visual experience in cases of high speed.[5]

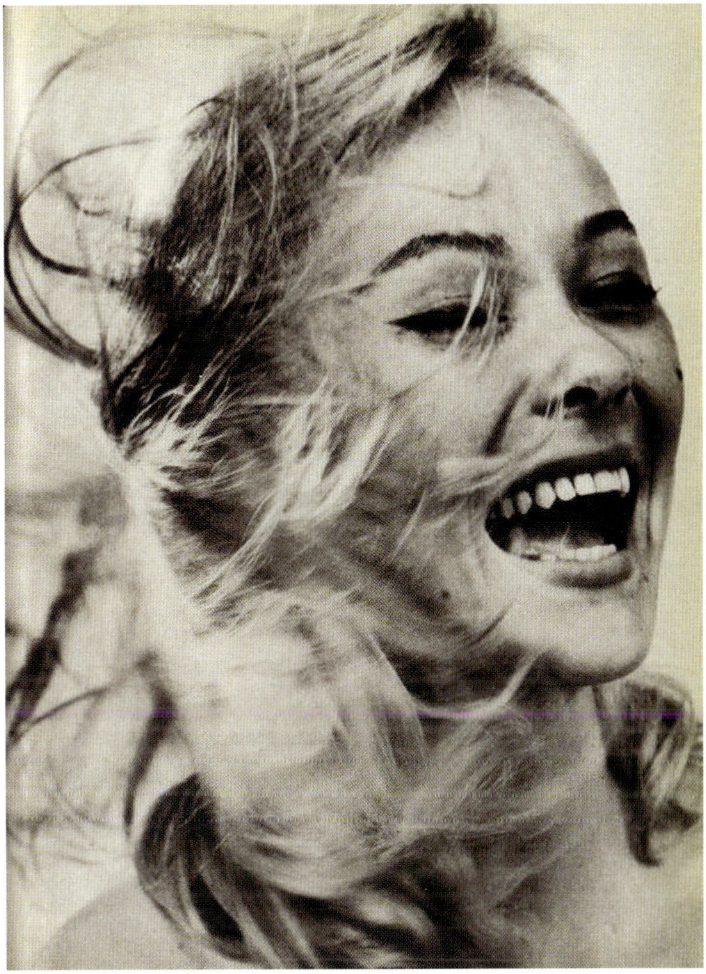

The confusion between human and camera vision had been at the heart of debates over blur since the invention of photography, when any movement at all resulted in blurring during the minutes-long exposures. [See also Chapter 2, "Portrait Props and Poses."] Initially considered a gross failure of the apparatus, by the end of the nineteenth century, blur was reevaluated and transformed into a necessary signifier of speed. When more sensitive dry plate technology finally made it possible to arrest rapid motion in the 1890s, photographers had quickly realized that without at least partial blurring in the image, fast-moving objects

FIGURE 125. Ulf Cronberg, "Are Photographers Going Blur Crazy?" *Popular Photography*, February 1962, 51.

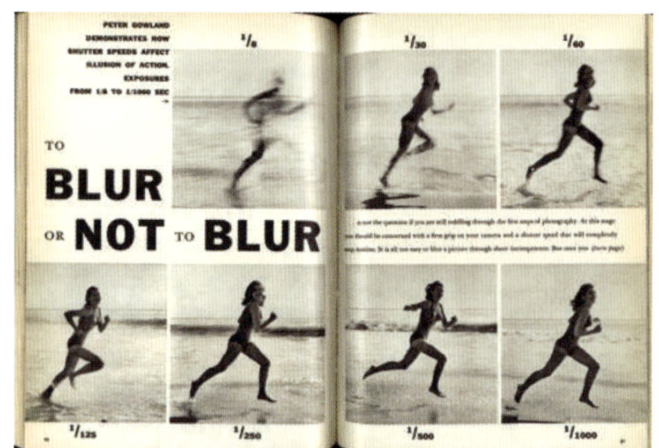

FIGURE 126 (LEFT). Peter Gowland, "To Blur or Not to Blur," *Popular Photography*, April 1957, 86–87.

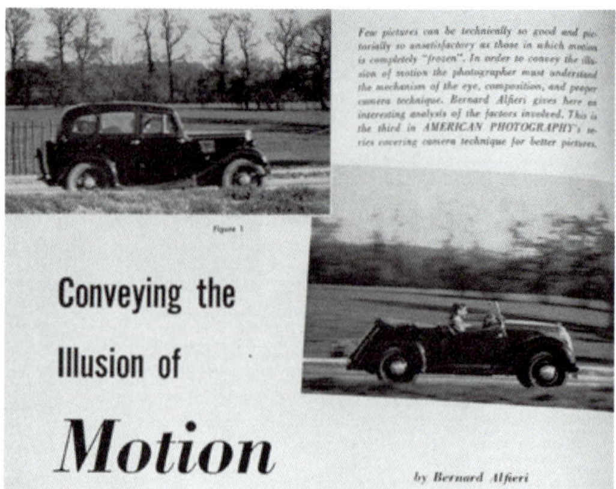

FIGURE 127 (RIGHT). Bernard Alfieri, "Conveying the Illusion of Motion," *American Photography*, April 1950, 40.

Source: Author's collection.

appeared entirely still. To represent the high speeds reached by the powerful new steam engines, photographers allowed the movement of spokes and crank arms to blur, counteracting the stilling effect of the dry plates and fast shutters.[6] Formerly understood as an accident of the medium, blur was now laden with interpretive significance.

Building on these associations, photographers in the 1960s inverted the markers of speed and motion. By panning with slow shutter speeds, they created a dynamic contrast between pervasively blurred backgrounds and sharply focused, though moving, subjects. The technique was seized on by sports photographers and the automotive industry to convey experiences of speed. The pictures seemed to transform viewers from distant observers into participants in the action. Rationalized by popular photography guides, these methods taught amateur photographers of the 1960s to imbue their photographs with a sense of excitement and viewers to read the markers of motion as they never had before.

32

CONTACT SHEETS

PRINTING CONTACT SHEETS became a necessary step in photo editing and archiving after the adaptation of motion picture roll film to still photography. Miniature cameras using the 35 millimeter format could make up to thirty-six exposures per roll, resulting in an apparent glut of pictures for photographers accustomed to taking only one or two pictures at a time. [See also Chapter 7, "Solar Enlarging."] To quickly review the surfeit of negatives, photographers and photo editors cut the developed roll into strips, laid them out on a sheet of 8″×10″ photo paper flattened under a piece of glass, and contact-printed them, creating a page of unenlarged positive images. These contact sheets, immediately useful for editing and archiving, also provide crucial insight into a photographer's shooting process since they reveal the original framing and the complete numbered sequence of pictures.

Contact sheets came into common use at the newly established photo agencies of the postwar era and served as tools for communication between editors and photographers, who were often working on the road. Still, the general public rarely—if ever—saw contact sheets during these years. While some magazines printed motion picture film strips in the early twentieth century as illustration or graphic decoration, the horizontal grid of the contact sheet was not recognized for its aesthetic quality for several decades. In a behind-the-scenes look at photojournalism, the former executive photo editor for *Life*, Wilson Hicks, included positive-printed negative strips, oriented vertically and without sprocket holes, as was common for motion pictures in print.[1] Henri Cartier-Bresson anticipated the eventual interest in negatives and contact sheets

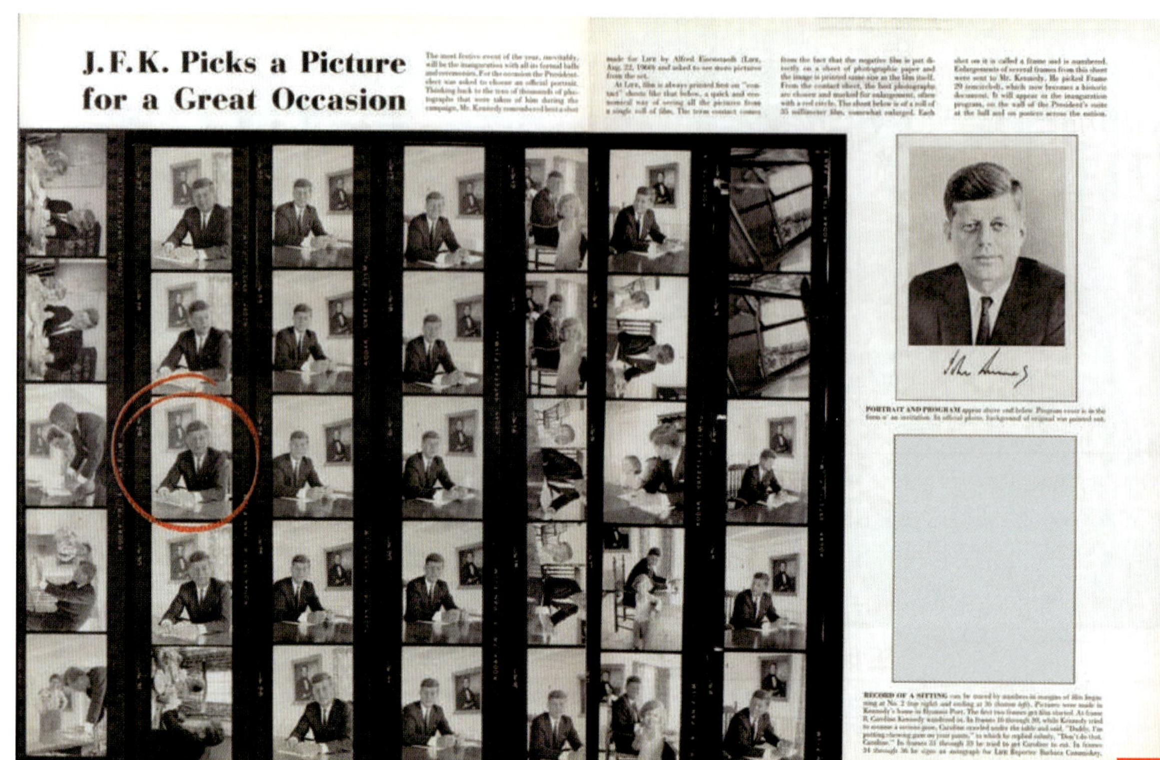

FIGURE 128. "JFK Picks a Picture for a Great Occasion," photographs by Alfred Eisenstadt.

Source: From the pages of *Life Magazine*, January 20, 1961, 89. © 1961 The Picture Collection Inc. All rights reserved. Images by Alfred Eisenstaedt. Reprinted/Translated from LIFE and published with permission of The Picture Collection Inc. Reproduction in any manner in any language in whole or in part without written permission is prohibited. LIFE and the LIFE logo are registered trademarks of TI Gotham Inc. used under license.

and took to carefully editing his own archives, separating individual negative frames and even discarding some, beginning in 1939.[2]

It wasn't until the 1960s that 8" × 10" contact sheets achieved public notice in print and in museum exhibitions. A *Life* magazine story photographed in 1960 and appearing on newsstands on the day of John F. Kennedy's inauguration featured a two-page spread of the new president's first portrait session for the magazine. The article focused on the editing process as much as on the subject of the pictures. The magazine explained, "The sheet below is of a roll of 35 millimeter film. . . . Each shot on it is called a frame and is numbered. Enlargements of several frames from this sheet were sent to Mr. Kennedy. He picked Frame 29 (encircled), which now becomes a historic document."[3] This story was not only an early example of a contact sheet in print, but it also featured one of the prime aesthetic markers of later published examples: inclusion of the editor's red grease-pencil marks.

Contact sheets were increasingly included in photography exhibitions of this period as well. A 1965 Museum of Modern Art show in New York City traced the development of photo essays from the German illustrated magazines of the interwar years to their peak in the American magazines *Life*, *Look*, and *Fortune* from the late 1930s through the 1940s. The curator, John Szarkowski, wrote on a wall label, "During the decade after World War II, the photographer became an individual observer, and emphasis shifted to the quality of his personal vision. The subject of these essays was often not the exterior event but the photographer's reaction to it."[4] Display of the contact sheets provided evidence of each photographer's unique process and way of working the scene. The format, which began as a private communication, was quickly going public.

Specialist publications, such as *Popular Photography* and *U.S. Camera*, began running stories in the mid-1960s instructing amateurs how to make and use contact sheets.[5] One tutorial, "How Pros Edit Contact Sheets," described the editing and notation process, advocating for the contact sheet as a money- and time-saving step for amateur photographers as well as pros.[6] Even as contact sheets gained visibility everywhere from museums to amateur darkrooms, they still conveyed a sense of privileged access both to the photographer's perspective, as well as to models or celebrities caught off guard. The photographer William

FIGURE 129. Installation view of the exhibition, "The Photo Essay," Museum of Modern Art, New York, March 16, 1965 through May 16, 1965.

Source: Museum of Modern Art Archives, New York. Photo: Rolf Petersen. The Museum of Modern Art, New York, NY, USA. Digital Image © The Museum of Modern Art/Licensed by SCALA/Art Resource, NY.

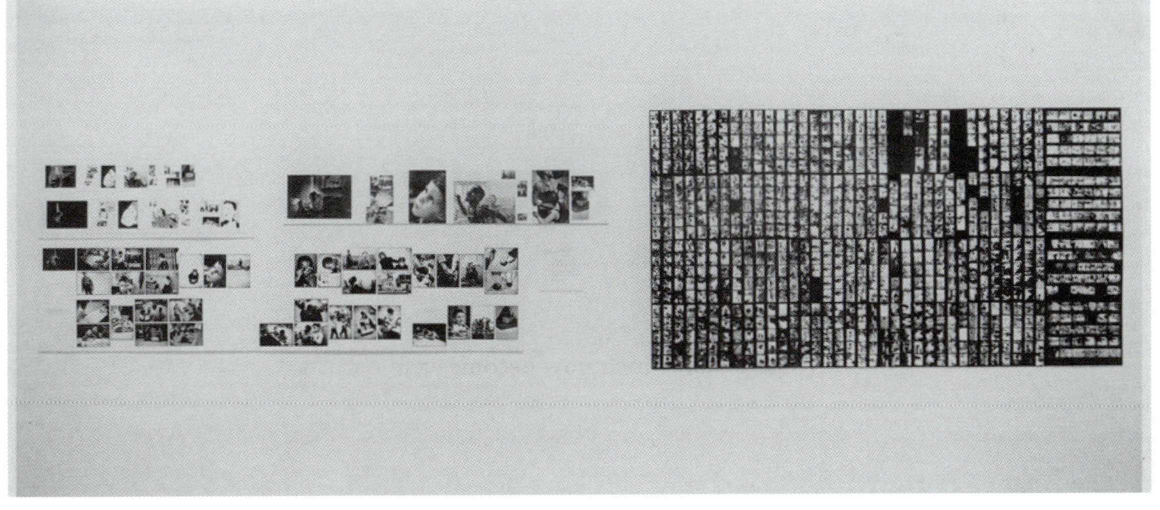

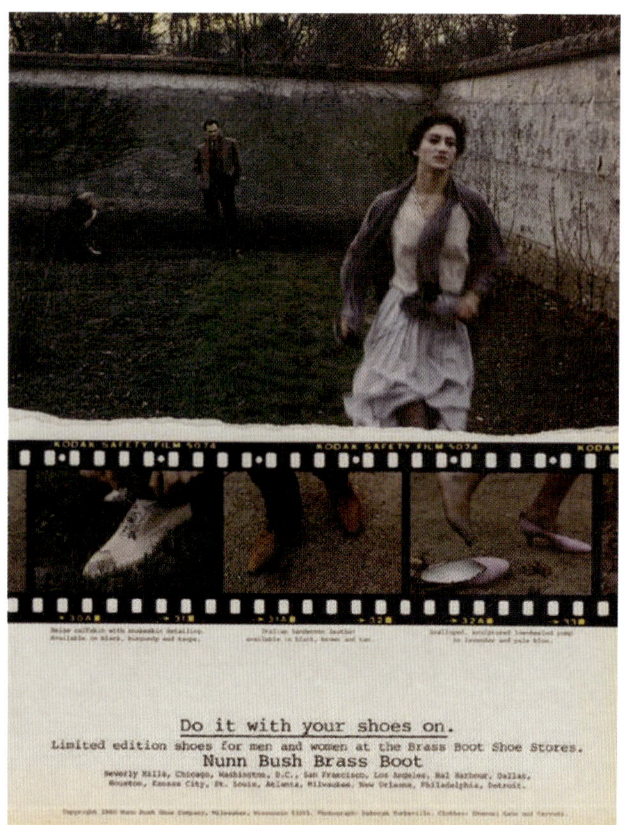

FIGURE 130. Nunn Bush advertisement photographed by Deborah Turbeville, 1980.

Source: Courtesy of the Deborah Turbeville Foundation.

Klein directed a television documentary featuring his own marked-up contact sheets in 1986, talking viewers through the story of famous shots from his legendary work in New York, Paris, and Tokyo in the late 1950s. The aesthetic was taken up by advertisers in the 1980s, applying the filmstrip's sense of presence and authenticity to a brand experience.

Following the shift to digital in the early 2000s, interest in contact sheets has more often been related to their historic analog nature. Landmark museum exhibitions of Robert Frank and Diane Arbus both prominently featured contact sheets as evidence of these photographers' exceptional work in-camera, before the possibility of postprocessing, or the sly use of a delete key on the camera back.[7] While contact sheets once threatened the mythology of the "decisive moment," today they celebrate the restraint and craft of photographers working in the predigital era.

33

GRAININESS

JACOB DESCHIN, the longtime *New York Times* photography columnist, grudgingly admitted in 1963 that "grain, blur and distortion are becoming gradually acceptable as legitimate, and sometimes effective, techniques of an increasingly venturesome medium."[1] [See also Chapter 31, "Motion Blur."] Most other commentators who addressed the emergence of these styles also took care to note their formerly debased status and offered justification for their current appeal. Unlike the long-time bugbears of blur and distortion, graininess had become a problem only in the late 1920s. Following the popularization of the miniature camera, whose small negative sizes necessitated enlargement, individual silver particles suspended in the negative's emulsion were made more prominent in the final print. Most nineteenth-century photographic processes were either contact printed or were unique negative processes that didn't allow enlarging, such as the daguerreotype, ambrotype, and tintype. Clarity and detail were the prime assets of these techniques, even if they were also slow and cumbersome. In the 1920s and 1930s, the increased speed and portability of the miniature camera required a trade-off with image quality: more light-sensitive films required larger silver particles, which were more visible when enlarged.

The descriptive term *graininess* was coined to refer to the undesirable visual result of this new technology. One manual's glossary described grain as "an unsightly mottled effect found in films which have been improperly developed or which have an inherent 'graininess.'"[2] Fine-grain films and developing solutions were created to counteract the problem, and guidebooks suggested other ways to mitigate the appearance of grain, from avoiding large masses of undifferentiated

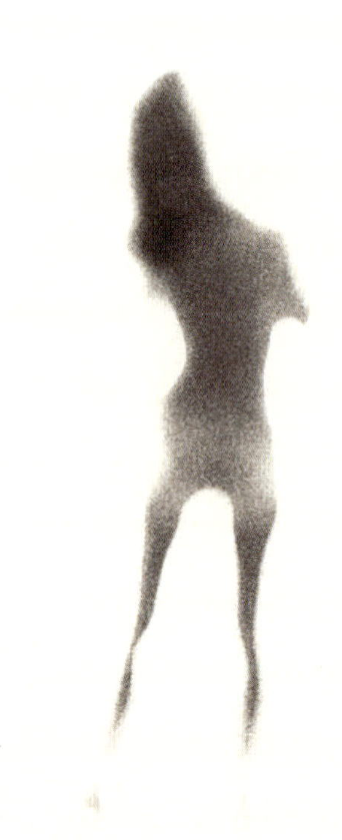

midtones to printing on textured paper for camouflage. [See also Chapter 6, "Cloudy Skies."]

In instructional manuals written specifically for the miniature camera, authors initially insisted that enlargements from small negatives were passable. Deschin contended, in a handbook dedicated to miniature camera work, "Fine grain does not present such a great problem in the larger miniature negative when the full or almost full negative is being enlarged."[3] But amateurs showing in camera club exhibitions often enlarged their negatives to 16" × 20" inches, increasing the image area more than two hundred times from the 35 millimeter frame. During the first few years of the miniature camera's popularity, many amateur photographers willingly accepted this shortcoming in exchange for its ease of use. [See also Chapter 35, "Full-Frame Prints."]

Reflecting on newspaper photographers' adoption of the 35 millimeter format, one writer argued, "Grain is not as important as a great many writers and manufacturers of fine-grain developing solutions would have it appear," noting that a newspaper's halftone screen would eliminate some grain before printing anyway.[4] This pronouncement was optimistic, to say the least. While fast film and 35 millimeter cameras were increasingly valuable in reportage for candid and natural light situations, photographers for *Life*, the premier picture magazine, continued to use the 2 ½" Rolleiflex and 4" × 5" Graflex cameras, which used larger film sizes to produce sharper images that could sustain enlargement and the photo editor's cropping. As a result, the occasional publication of a grainy photograph suggested that its content was prized over and above these aesthetic rules.

Deschin wrote in the mid-1950s of the trade-off between picture quality and authenticity: "The natural-light photographer sacrifices fine

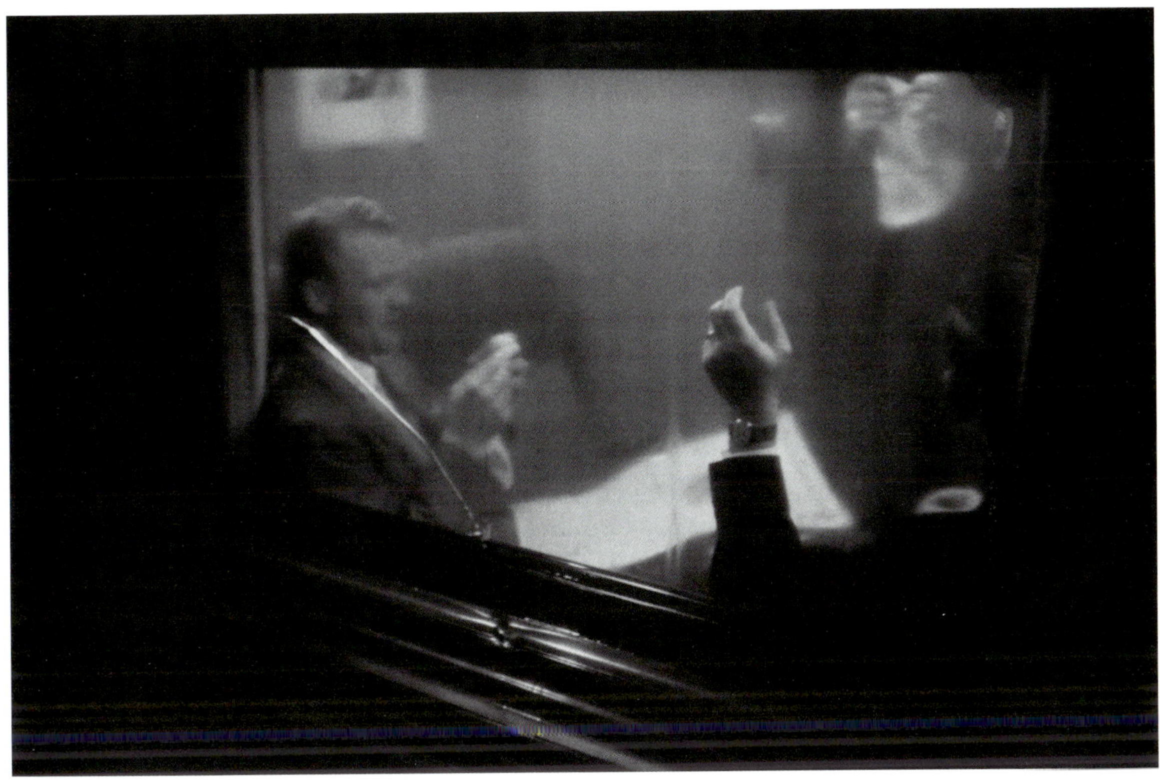

FIGURE 132. Louis Stettner, "Card Players, Penn Station, New York," 1958. Gelatin silver print.

Source: © Estate of Louis Stettner.

grain and sharpness to gain atmosphere and a sense of truth."[5] The photographer Louis Stettner agreed: "At times grain will give your photograph a sense of spontaneity and immediacy not obtainable otherwise."[6] Grain, when it did appear in print, signaled truthfulness and immediacy, in contrast to the staged and frozen quality of photographs made with the artificial lighting of flash. Robert Capa's grainy, blurry 35 millimeter photographs of Allied troops landing on Omaha Beach, which ran in *Life*, are a case in point.[7] (See Figure 133.)

By the 1960s, grain had come to signify a more generalized feeling or "mood."[8] It was a visual rejection of conventional values. How-to authors who rehearsed the history of grain in this period invariably situated its use as oppositional. An article in *Popular Photography* explained, "For many years 'grain' was almost a dirty word to the salonists [sic] and other

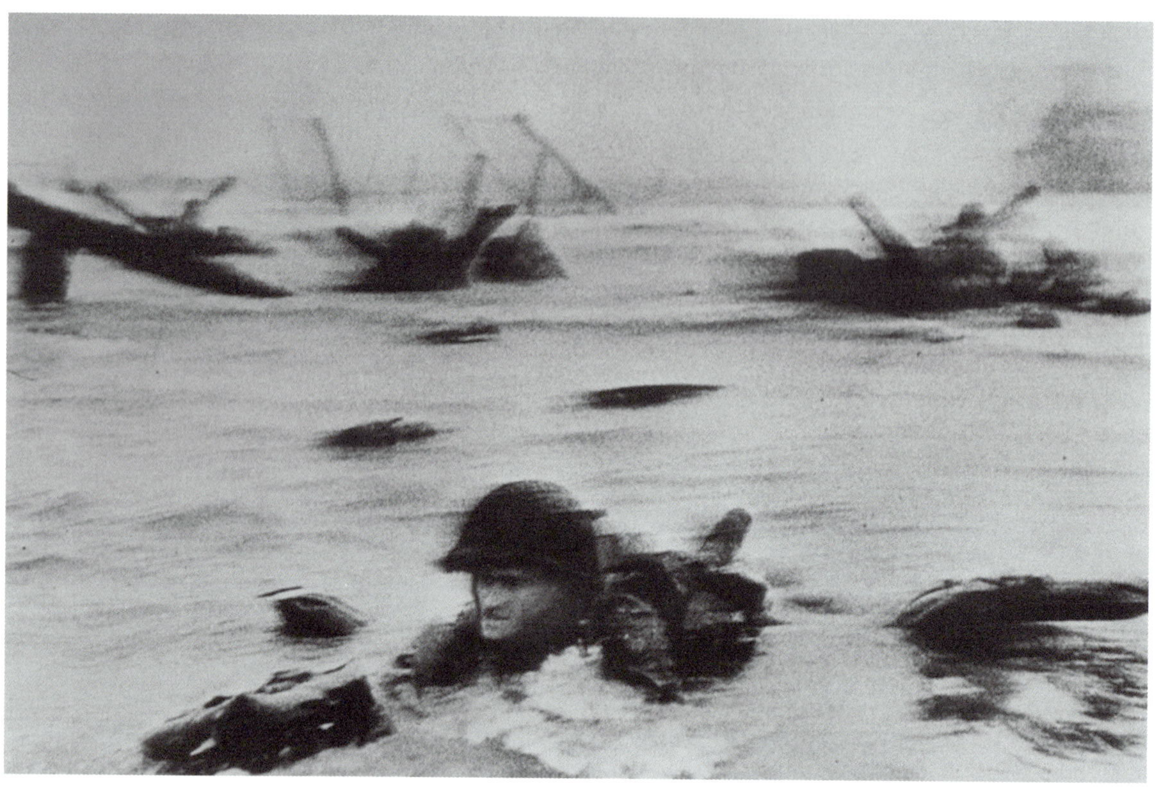

FIGURE 133. Robert Capa, "American Troops Landing on Omaha Beach, D-Day," France, Normandy, June 6, 1944.

Source: Photo by Robert Capa © International Center of Photography/ Magnum Photos.

photographic purists who dominated the field. But then came available-light shooting with a rush—and with it came big grain. Soon art directors began clamoring for it, and any grainy picture suddenly became acceptable. Photographers began selling their mistakes and looking for ways to give their pictures that grainy look."[9] [See also Chapter 22, "Straight Photography."] Dozens of articles and guidebooks offered recommendations on how to create the ideal graininess, which was widely used in fashion, advertising, and journalism through the 1980s. Coarse-grained fast films and extreme enlarging were common techniques, but overdeveloping or using a developer like Dektol undiluted by water were also popular ways to achieve "controlled" grain.[10]

Despite its eventual cooption by commercial interests, the intentional use of grain in the late 1950s and early 1960s forged an artistic revolution in photographic aesthetics. The comparison between this countercultural style and social movements of the time was not lost on period writers. One photographer derided the "traditionally oriented" critics of grain who saw graininess as a cheap "trick" rather than a legitimate photographic technique. He contended, "This method of working is no more of a trick than the sharp, large-camera approach of Edward Weston or Ansel Adams."[11] By questioning the long-reigning dogma of straight photography, this photographer and many others saw the appropriation of the medium's former limitations as a powerful challenge to convention.

PART V

1966–1995

ADAPTING FORMER FAILURES to artistic ends was a hallmark of popular photographic practice in the middle of the twentieth century. Technical limitations and entrenched aesthetic tenets were all subject to reevaluation during this period. Golden hour lighting, for example, became widely used in commercial photography and was eventually taught in amateur how-to guides, abandoning decades of warnings about the extremes of early morning and late evening light. Technical accidents, such as lens flare and cross-processed film, were also recast as intentional aesthetic choices. Many of these reversals hinged on the achievement of technical proficiency. As soon as photographers were able to avoid these effects when desired, they began mining past mistakes for creative potential.

Digital cameras and computing arrived at the end of this period. Like earlier innovations, such as color film, cost and quality were significant limitations during digital photography's first decade on the commercial market. Although important for its rapid transmissibility, digital photography was low in quality and expensive, accessible only to major media outlets through the early 1990s. Nonetheless, its promise also inspired a return to analog aesthetics as photographers watched as 150 years of darkroom practice threatened to disappear with the digital revolution.

34

LENS FLARE

THE 1941 EDITION of Kodak's *How to Make Good Pictures* offered some unusual advice: "Many amateurs are . . . finding a new interest in seeking and achieving something different. They . . . are 'shooting' from positions that are daring and new."[1] After nearly fifty years of establishing and enforcing photographic rules, Kodak began pointing out the creative value of breaking them. Among the guidelines they jettisoned was the practice of keeping the sun to one's back when photographing. As early as 1932, the Kodak guide began suggesting that photographers shoot into the sun to create "backlighted" pictures. By hiding the sun behind the subject, the photographer could allow the edges to become overexposed, while the subject itself was properly or slightly underexposed.[2] The bright backlight created a glowing halo effect. The editors wrote, "Notice the illustrations in newspapers and magazines. Bold, odd, forceful, fantastic,—*different*!"[3]

The advent of *Life* and *Look* magazines in 1936 accelerated the dissemination and proliferation of photographic styles, including ones that broke the rules. Where previously Americans saw relatively few photographs and in limited genres—portraits, landscapes, news, advertisements, and their own snapshots—magazine photojournalism took the camera, and photographic style, to new places. [See also Chapter 26, "New Angles."] Nonetheless, Kodak located the origin of the

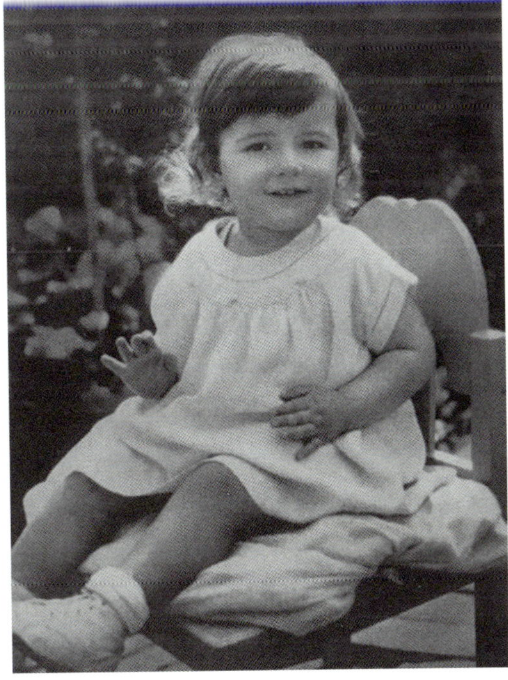

FIGURE 134. Photographer unknown, "A Garden Portrait," in *How to Make Good Pictures: A Book for the Amateur Photographer* (Rochester, NY: Eastman Kodak Company, 1932), 74.

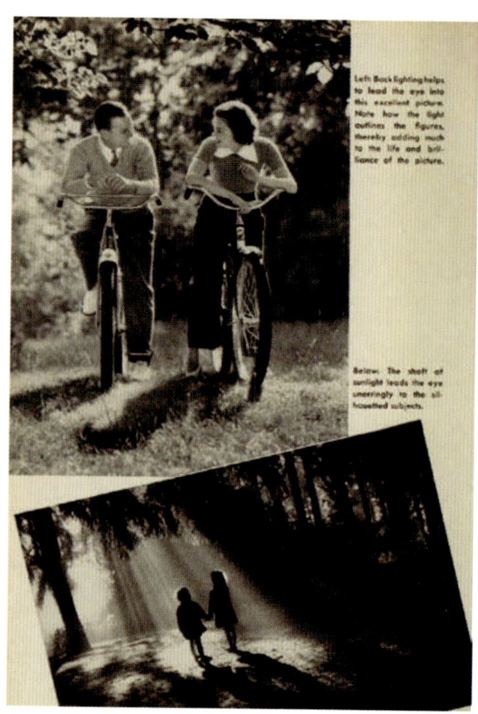

FIGURE 135. Photographer unknown, "Backlighting Helps Lead the Eye into This Excellent Picture," in *How to Make Good Pictures: A Book for the Amateur Photographer* (Rochester, NY: Eastman Kodak Company, 1943), 92.

backlighting trend even further afield, in cinematography: "This radical departure was probably first due to the professional motion picture camera man, who ignored all previous 'rules of the game.' The first thing he did was to 'shoot' into the light."[4]

Through the 1960s, as guidebooks advocated for more latitude in the direction of light, expectations for proper exposure also shifted. The availability of in-camera light meters made a balanced exposure relatively simple, but professional photographers writing in photo periodicals and their own guidebooks suggested straying from the happy medium in order to create more striking pictures. Photo editor Michael Edelson counseled photographers to use meter readings, "not as compensation for unusual light conditions, but rather as a method of producing photographs that possess imagination, and possibly, artistry."[5] The photographer Ron Harris wrote in *Popular Photography* that backlight "can lift a picture out of the ordinary class and give it snap and sparkle."[6] Edelson concluded, "Be daring . . . do something wrong for a change. Learn when it's wise to make deliberate photographic errors."[7]

Breaking the rule of shooting with one's back to the sun opened photographers up to other challenges, most notably lens flare, which is the result of bright light sources reflecting off multiple glass elements within the lens. Lens flare started appearing intentionally in major motion pictures of the late 1960s, such as *Cool Hand Luke* (1967) and *Easy Rider* (1969), where it was a marker of realism and on-location filming, signifying a rejection of the highly controlled studio films of classical Hollywood.

In the 1990s, flare transitioned from a lens-based effect to an element added in postprocessing to motion pictures, still photographs, and even animations. The ability to recreate lens flare through computer-generated effects led to its use in science-fiction films, where it was meant to validate fantastic and futuristic environments. As one critic explained, "If early flare said, 'these feelings are real,' now it could

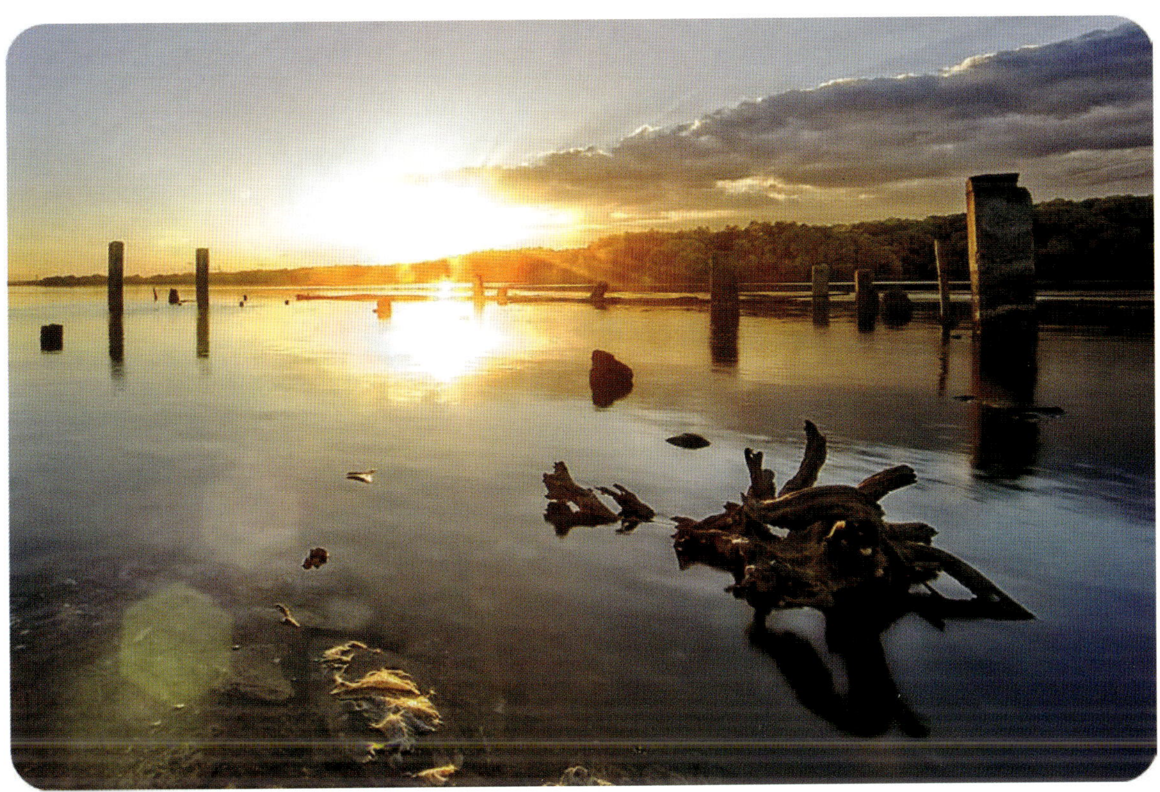

Source: https://flic.kr/p/7CVP96.

say, 'These spacemen and explosions are real too.'"[8] Although flare was widely used in film through the end of the twentieth century, audiences reacted vociferously to its apparent overuse by the director J. J. Abrams in 2009. Abrams famously offered an apology for his abuse of the technique after a fan created a compilation of the more than seven hundred instances of lens flare in his first *Star Trek* movie.[9]

The lens flare backlash was not felt so powerfully in still photography, however. This tempered response may be related to the fact that photographs more frequently depict realistic environments rather than the distant planets of *Star Trek*. In still photographs, lens flare reads as an inevitable product of the shooting situation, familiar even to amateur photographers from sunset snapshots. Audiences' acceptance of lens flare in still photographs seems to indicate a belief in the fallibility of cameras, despite the fact that these aberrations can be avoided or removed almost as easily as J. J. Abrams adds them.

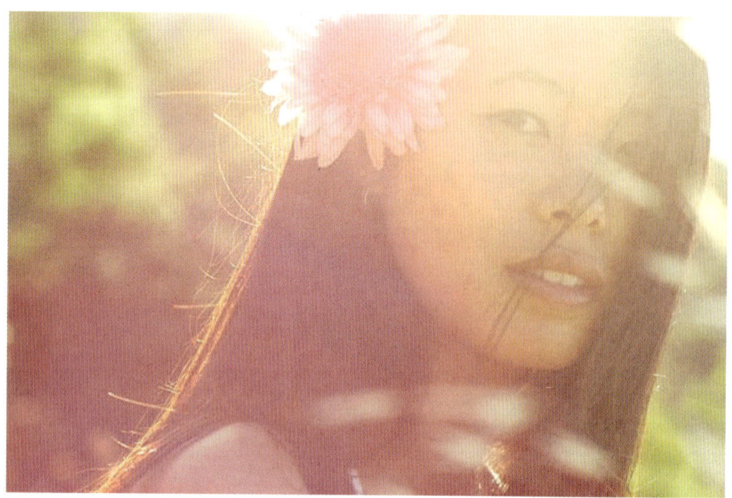

Still photographers were also slower to embrace intentional lens flare than their counterparts in motion pictures. Guidebooks continually warned photographers against lens flare, especially as the backlighting trend grew through midcentury. A 1946 guide, *35 mm Photographic Technique*, cited flare among the "most common technical problems" in 35 millimeter photography, which the author recommended remedying with a lens hood or shade.[10] The pocket-sized *Golden Guide* to photography, published in 1964, cautioned, "With back lighting, always screen your lens from direct sunlight with a lens shade or cardboard, or you'll get glares of light that spoil your picture."[11] The tide began to turn in the 1970s. In 1972, the Bauhaus photographer Andreas Feininger listed several technical effects, formerly considered errors, as the "first requirement of any 'good' photograph," among them perspective distortion and flare.[12] Feininger described these as elements that create "visual stopping power" in a photograph: bold, graphic effects that arrest a viewer's attention.[13]

The lens flare trend has continued to grow in still photography, in advertising and fashion photography, as well as in amateur images shared online. Lens flare suggests that the urgency of the moment overrides all concern for the rules; inclusion of the camera's limitations certify the spontaneity, authenticity, and candor of the photograph. Paradoxically, though, lens flare creates this experience through the introduction of an effect not seen with the human eye and, increasingly, not seen by the camera either, but added digitally later.

35

FULL-FRAME PRINTS

WITH THE POPULARIZATION of miniature cameras, enlarging became a regular step in the photographer's practice. It also offered creative possibilities. Katharine Stanberry wrote in her 1909 amateur guide, "The error of thinking that the print must include the full subject of the negative is one in which none but the veriest tyro is likely to fall."[1] Pictorialist photographers in the early twentieth century began experimenting with new compositions in the darkroom. They made unusually scaled prints by enlarging and cropping, a practice that had been impractical during the nineteenth century when most prints were contact-printed from standard-sized plates. [See also Chapter 7, "Solar Enlarging," and Chapter 20, "Painterly Photographs."]

By the late 1930s, a new term was coined to describe this increasingly important part of the photographer's workflow: *cropping*. The *New York Times* photography column took care to define the word in an early use as "the selection of only a certain part of the negative for enlargement."[2] As late as the 1950s, cropping was still considered a specialized term requiring explanation, even in photographic manuals. To this day, its photographic meaning is not defined by the *Oxford English Dictionary*, which focuses instead on agricultural cropping: the practice of cutting back the heads of plants to encourage new growth. Initially photographic cropping also suggested some degree of literal cutting or trimming the negative, but soon how-to guides advised photographers to preserve the entirety of the negative and crop only by enlarging or masking when making the print.

FIGURE 138. Alfred Stieglitz, "The Flatiron," 1903. Photogravure, 6¹¹⁄₁₆" × 3¼".

Source: J. Paul Getty Museum, Los Angeles. Digital image courtesy of the Getty's Open Content Program.

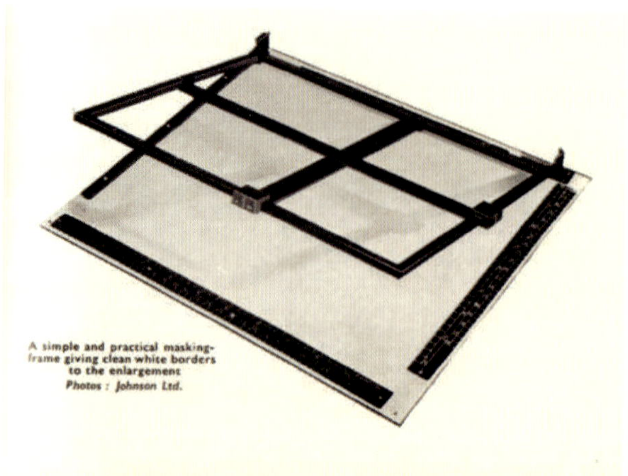

FIGURE 139. Johnston Ltd., "A Simple and Practical Masking-Frame Giving Clean White Borders to the Enlargement."

Source: Author's collection.

Andreas Feininger, a former *Life* photographer, cautioned amateurs in 1949, "Nothing looks more sloppy and 'don't give a damnish' than lint spots and raggedy edges."[3] Darkroom tools were manufactured to support the practice of cropping prints, including adjustable print frames, easels, and masks, which could be used to block out extraneous areas of the negative and create uniform white margins around the printed image.

Eventually critics began to find fault with the reduced quality of enlargements made from small sections of 35 millimeter negatives. In his famous 1952 book, the photographer Henri Cartier-Bresson set out his rules for composition, underscored by the sanctity of original framing.[4] By the mid-1950s, other mainstream guides were also recommending that photographers pay more attention to framing while shooting in order to limit the enlarging and cropping done later in the darkroom. A handbook for "ultraminiature" photography cautioned, "If you have to crop (cut out) extraneous negative areas from your final picture, you will need to enlarge more, with resulting loss of image definition. Do your composing right in the viewfinder whenever possible, rather than on the enlarging baseboard."[5]

In a guidebook published by *U.S. Camera*, the photographer Louis Stettner warned, "It is advisable not to be creative with a pair of scissors. Composition should be resolved at the moment of picture taking."[6] Stettner allowed that sometimes composition could be improved in the darkroom, but photographers should guard against the possibility that they "rely on the trimming board as a substitute for finding the right angle of view and position in [one's] 35 mm camera technique."[7] Cropping had come to signify lazy, amateurish work.

In the 1960s a new style emerged among American art photographers that could be easily distinguished from these amateur productions. By including the borders of the negative in their prints, photographers such as Diane Arbus and Richard Avedon verified that their images had been composed in-camera and were printed full frame. Negative carriers, which hold the negative below the light in the enlarger, were produced in standard sizes, usually slightly smaller than the dimensions of the film. Photographers took to filing out these metal holders in order to reveal the edges of the film. The clear, unexposed area around the frame of each image printed solid black, slightly blurred by the irregular edges of the filed-out carrier. The L-shaped arms of the printing easel could cover this over entirely, or they could be adjusted to expose a hairline black border around the print. Although initially these edges were cropped out by book designers and editors, they began appearing in print in the early 1970s. Danny Lyon's 1971 photobook *Conversations with the Dead* included hairline black borders. Arbus's 1972 monograph reproduced full-frame prints with thick, black borders, regardless of the fact that she had abandoned the black border style in her art prints in 1969, when she began to feel that "everyone" was printing this way.[8]

Magazines such as *Vogue* and *Rolling Stone* were using black borders widely in photographic layouts by the mid-1970s. An article in *Popular Photography* eventually identified the spread of the trend, stating, "There is a current fashion for using a broad, sloppy black line, not trimmed by the easel at its outer edges."[9] In 1986, an advertising industry publication described the prevalence of black borders in an article entitled, "Close to the Edge: Will the Real Full Frame Photo Please Stand Up?" As the title suggests, the style was still used to connote authenticity but no longer guaranteed it. Art directors and photographers often improved

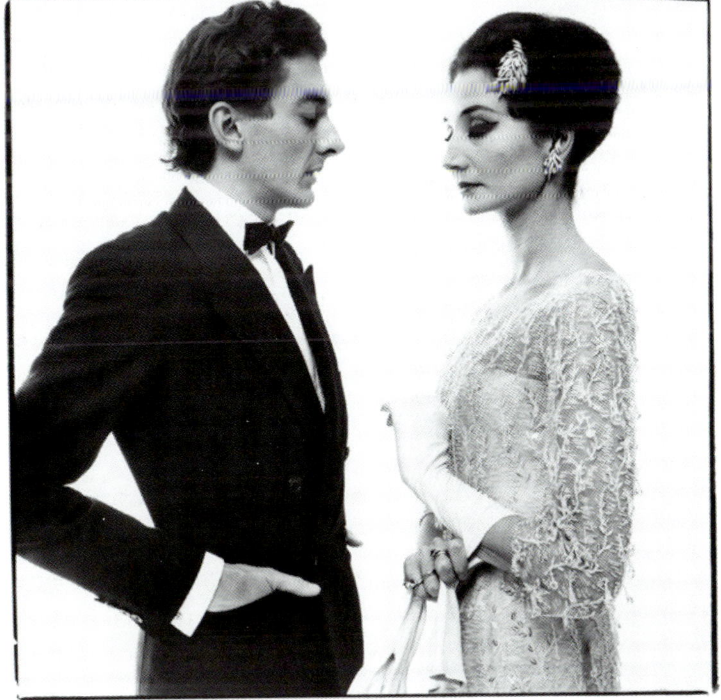

FIGURE 140. Richard Avedon, "The Vicomtesse Jacqueline de Ribes and Raymundo de Larrain, New York, May 16, 1961," 1961. Gelatin silver print. Source: © The Richard Avedon Foundation.

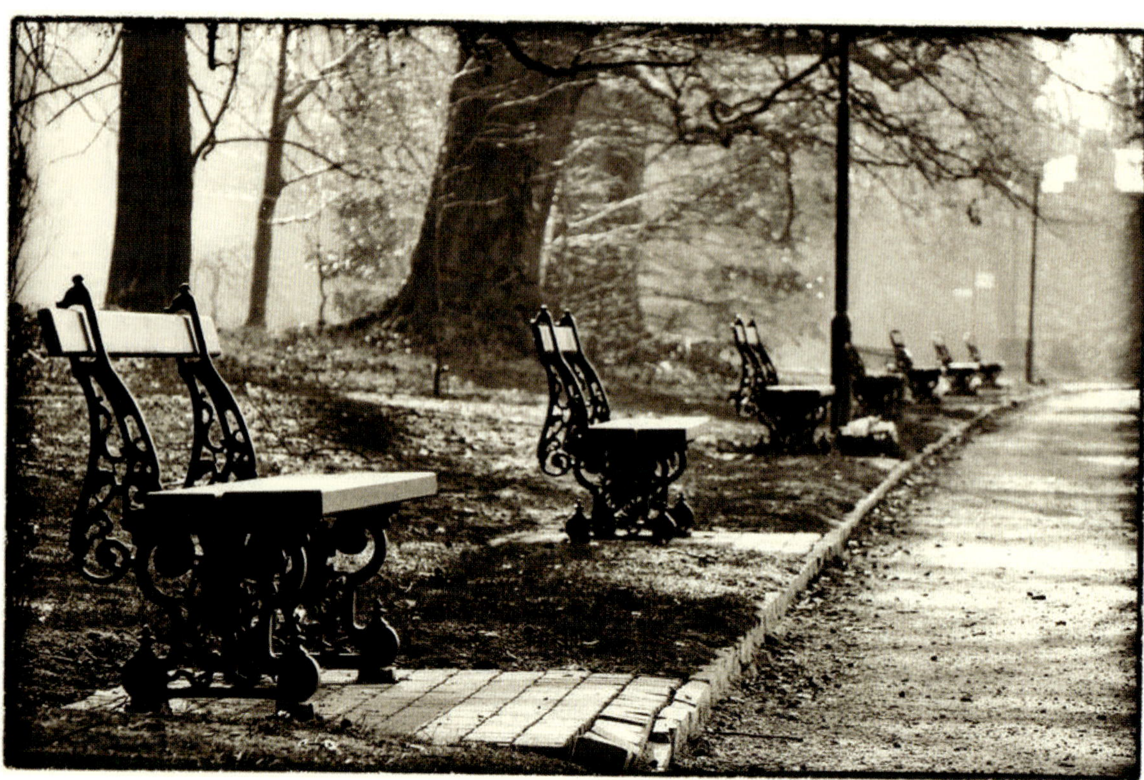

FIGURE 141. Alan E., "Park Bench," 2014. Flickr. CC BY-ND 2.0. https://creativecommons.org/licenses/by-nd/2.0/.

Source: https://flic.kr/p/kUP3QX.

their borders by combining several images, borrowing the edges from one photograph and superimposing it onto another in printing.[10] A writer for *Popular Photography* explained, the black border would "magically bestow the aura of a cropped-in-the-camera image, regardless of your picture's crop status."[11] By the late 1990s, full-frame borders could be added digitally to any print. Commercial print labs declared themselves "sloppy borders" specialists.[12] At the dawn of the digital revolution, inclusion of the negative frame, long considered evidence of an amateur's messy failure, signified nostalgia for the days of the handmade photographic print.

36

CLOSE-CROPPED PORTRAITS

ONE OF THE PIECES OF ADVICE doled out regularly to photographers, especially after the invention of the Kodak, was to avoid "subject surgery."[1] In deference to painterly conventions, cutting off the top of a person's head or part of their feet in standing portraits was strictly prohibited. Instructional authors attributed these mistakes to a lack of careful framing. Charles Maus Taylor, author of the 1902 amateur manual *Why My Photographs Are Bad*, explained that "the result is sometimes a grotesque appearance."[2] Taylor advised readers to step back from the subject to ensure that part of the subject's body was not inadvertently cropped out of the frame. Although some art photographers, among them Paul Strand and Alfred Stieglitz, produced intimate, tightly framed portraits in the 1920s, the technique was not yet widespread.

At midcentury, how-to guides continued to cite this error as one of the most common amateur mistakes, although there was still no consensus on how to refer to it. A handbook published by *Popular Mechanics* warned, "It's easy to 'scalp' your subjects especially at close range, if you are careless in aiming the camera. Make sure that you frame all of the subject."[3] Another guide joked, "Who is that man with no head? That's Uncle Harry, because you never learned to point your camera."[4] Still another advised bluntly, "Heads and ears should not be chopped off by photographers."[5]

The violence of the language used to describe this compositional error suggests concerns that ran deeper than aesthetic preference. These partial views seemed to exhibit uncanny

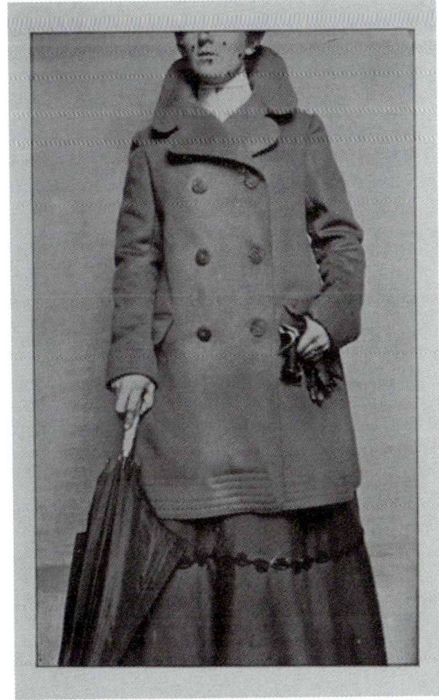

FIGURE 142. Charles Maus Taylor, "Placing a Picture," from *Why My Photographs Are Bad* (Philadelphia: G. W. Jacobs & Co., 1902), 31.

Source: Author's collection.

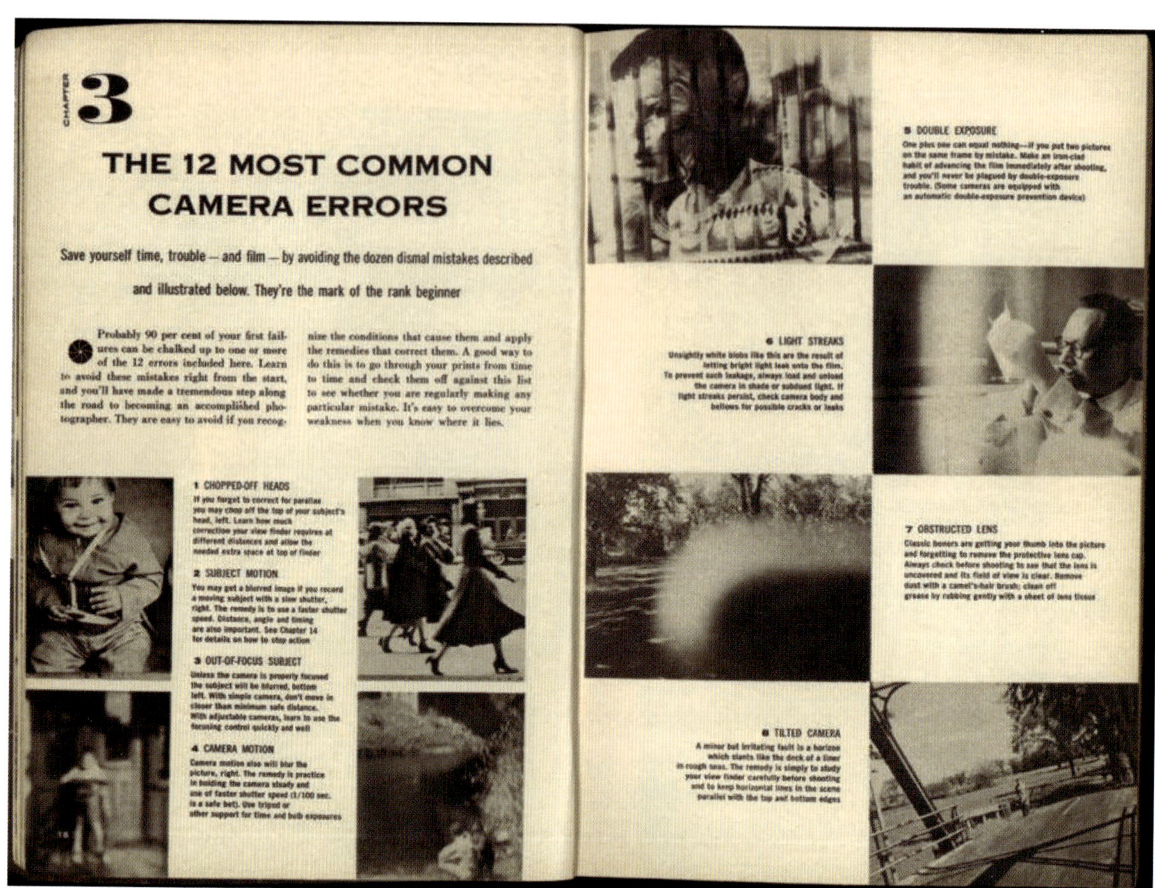

CHAPTER 3

THE 12 MOST COMMON CAMERA ERRORS

Save yourself time, trouble — and film — by avoiding the dozen dismal mistakes described and illustrated below. They're the mark of the rank beginner

Probably 90 per cent of your first failures can be chalked up to one or more of the 12 errors included here. Learn to avoid these mistakes right from the start, and you'll have made a tremendous step along the road to becoming an accomplished photographer. They are easy to avoid if you recognize the conditions that cause them and apply the remedies that correct them. A good way to do this is to go through your prints from time to time and check them off against this list to see whether you are regularly making any particular mistake. It's easy to overcome your weakness when you know where it lies.

1 CHOPPED-OFF HEADS
If you forget to correct for parallax you may chop off the top of your subject's head, left. Learn how much correction your view finder requires at different distances and allow the needed extra space at top of finder

2 SUBJECT MOTION
You may get a blurred image if you record a moving subject with a slow shutter, right. The remedy is to use a faster shutter speed. Distance, angle and timing are also important. See Chapter 14 for details on how to stop action

3 OUT-OF-FOCUS SUBJECT
Unless the camera is properly focused the subject will be blurred, bottom left. With simple camera, don't move in closer than minimum safe distance. With adjustable cameras, learn to use the focusing control quickly and well

4 CAMERA MOTION
Camera motion also will blur the picture, right. The remedy is practice in holding the camera steady and use of faster shutter speed (1/100 sec. is a safe bet). Use tripod or other support for time and bulb exposures

5 DOUBLE EXPOSURE
One plus one can equal nothing—if you put two pictures on the same frame by mistake. Make an iron-clad habit of advancing the film immediately after shooting, and you'll never be plagued by double-exposure trouble. (Some cameras are equipped with an automatic double-exposure prevention device)

6 LIGHT STREAKS
Unsightly white blobs like this are the result of letting bright light leak onto the film. To prevent such leakage, always load and unload the camera in shade or subdued light. If light streaks persist, check camera body and bellows for possible cracks or leaks

7 OBSTRUCTED LENS
Classic boners are getting your thumb into the picture and forgetting to remove the protective lens cap. Always check before shooting to see that the lens is uncovered and its field of view is clear. Remove dust with a camel's-hair brush; clean off grease by rubbing gently with a sheet of lens tissue

8 TILTED CAMERA
A minor but irritating fault is a horizon which slants like the deck of a liner in rough seas. The remedy is simply to study your view finder carefully before shooting and to keep horizontal lines in the scene parallel with the top and bottom edges

FIGURE 143. Photographer unknown, "The 12 Most Common Camera Errors," in Arthur A. Goldsmith, *How to Take Better Pictures* (New York: Arco Publishing, 1957), 18.

Source: Author's collection.

effects, especially for viewers accustomed to the unified ideal of the person established by nineteenth-century portraiture. The prohibition against these awkward, partial framings had gone unvoiced during most of photography's first century, although its edict was followed closely. Portraits were made in just a few standard sizes: full length, three-quarters, and bust. Working in a studio with a large camera mounted on a tripod rendered the accidents of casual composition all but impossible for the nineteenth-century portrait photographer.

At the turn of the century, however, the growing class of amateurs working with handheld cameras had to learn how to select a picture from an expansive visual field outside the studio and account for every element in the frame. [See also Chapter 17, "The Kodak."] At first, how-to authors chastised amateurs for failing to adequately limit their views. A Kodak handbook complained, "One of the faults most often seen in the work of the beginner is the desire to include too much within the confines of the picture. There is frequently material for two or even more complete pictures crowded into one."[6] New photographers were instructed to home in on the central elements of a picture by changing camera position to eliminate extraneous details. One miniature camera guide admitted, "You may not always be able to get just as close to the subject as you would wish, but get as close as you can."[7] Another noted, "By getting up close . . . you automatically simplify, trim off unwanted details."[8] There was a fine balance, however, between getting close and getting too close. The same manuals also placed "chopped-off heads" on their lists of "most common camera errors."[9]

Ironically, how-to guides started breaking their own rules in the 1930s, though no mention of this change was signaled in their textual descriptions. As camera sizes proliferated, instruction manuals began including photographs that demonstrated proper camera technique and position. These illustrations typically featured a model holding a camera to his or her face or body, stabilizing the instrument by propping an elbow on the hip or supporting the camera with a free hand while shooting. Often the camera was centered in the frame, and almost invariably, part of the model's head was cropped out of the image in favor of emphasis on the camera. With these pictures, the photographic establishment started to relax the long-standing rules against closely cropped portraits.

Instructional literature began officially recommending the use of tight framing in portraits in the early 1960s, following the adoption of the technique in advertising and art by Bert Stern, Richard Avedon, and others in the late 1950s. In articles such as "Shoot It Close! Crop It Tight!" and "Crop Close

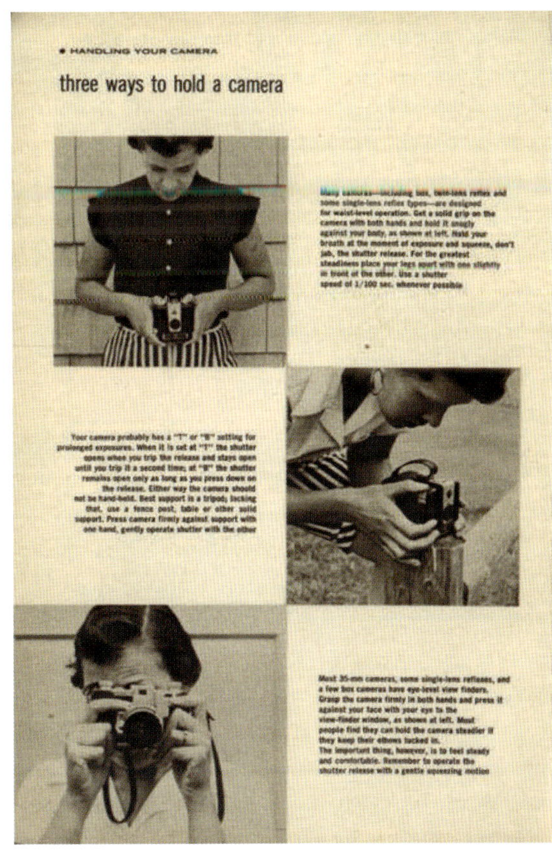

FIGURE 144. Photographer unknown. "Three Ways to Hold a Camera," in Arthur A. Goldsmith, *How to Take Better Pictures* (New York: Arco Publishing, 1957), 14.

Source: Author's collection.

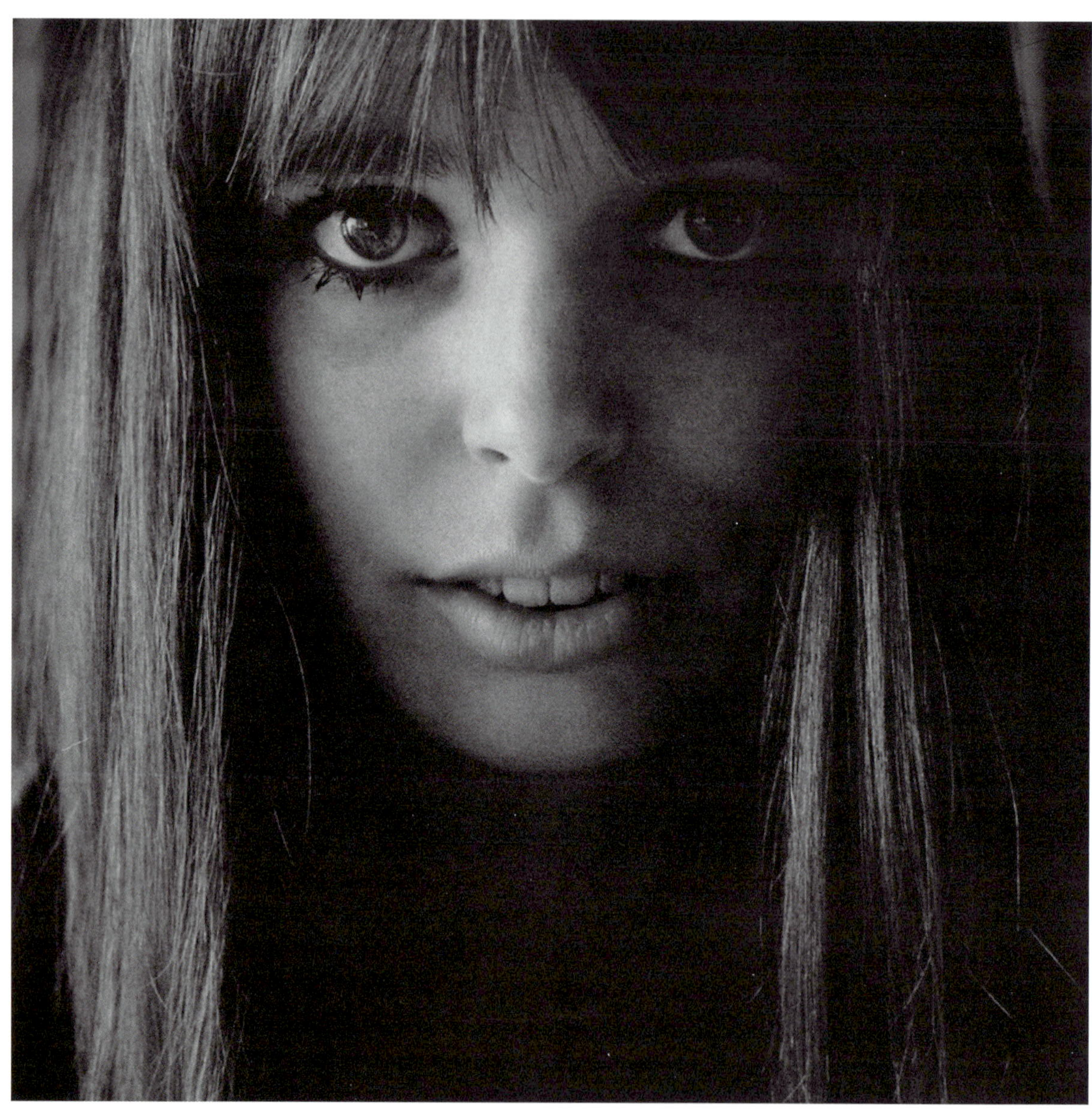

FIGURE 145. Jini Dellaccio, "Merrilee Rush, Sag Harbor," 1967. Gelatin silver print.

Source: Courtesy of the Jini Dellaccio Collection.

for Impact," authors pointed to the dramatic possibilities of breaking the old rules.[10] For many period commentators, these new, tightly cropped portraits created a sense of casual intimacy, which was visually suggestive of the social transformations of the era.

37

POLAROID MANIPULATIONS

ADVERTISING FOR THE POLAROID SWINGER, the company's best-selling and least expensive instant camera released in 1965, promised that it would make its users better photographers. One ad for the camera featured a haphazardly framed snapshot, while the copy maintained, "If you know any students of elementary photography . . . you can recommend a great teacher."[1] As the ad explained, Polaroid gave the photographer "a chance to see what he did wrong on his first picture while he's still on the spot" rather than waiting for the film to come back from the lab.[2] Polaroid promised that barring operator error, the camera could deliver a perfect print in seconds.

Polaroid's film and developing procedures were notoriously finicky, however. The cameras themselves often introduced mistakes into the final prints. Faulty or dirty rollers applied uneven pressure to prints as they were ejected, resulting in smears and streaks. The need for photographers to wait for the print to develop then remove the protective surface layers from peel-apart film introduced more room for accidents. Smudged fingerprints and striated effects, caused by pulling back the protective layer too quickly, were common. (See Figure 147.) As Polaroid's attention to the amateur market increased, the company aimed to simplify the process, leaving even less room for operator error with cameras that promised "one-step" photography. This distillation of the process had the opposite effect on some artists. After the release of the Polaroid SX-70 camera and film in 1972, which

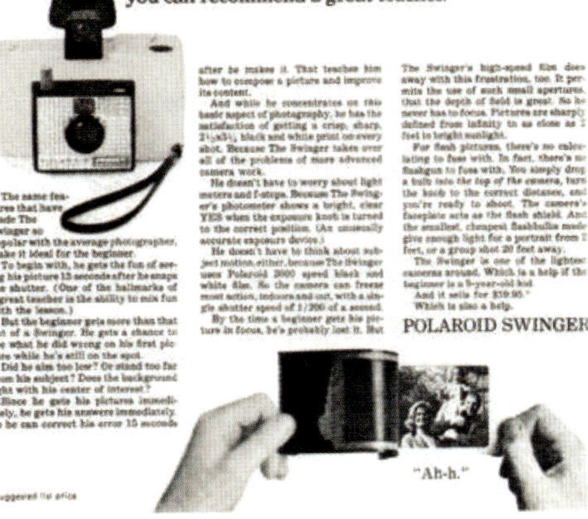

FIGURE 146. Polaroid Swinger, "If You Know Any Students of Elementary Photography . . .," *Popular Photography*, March 1967, 1.

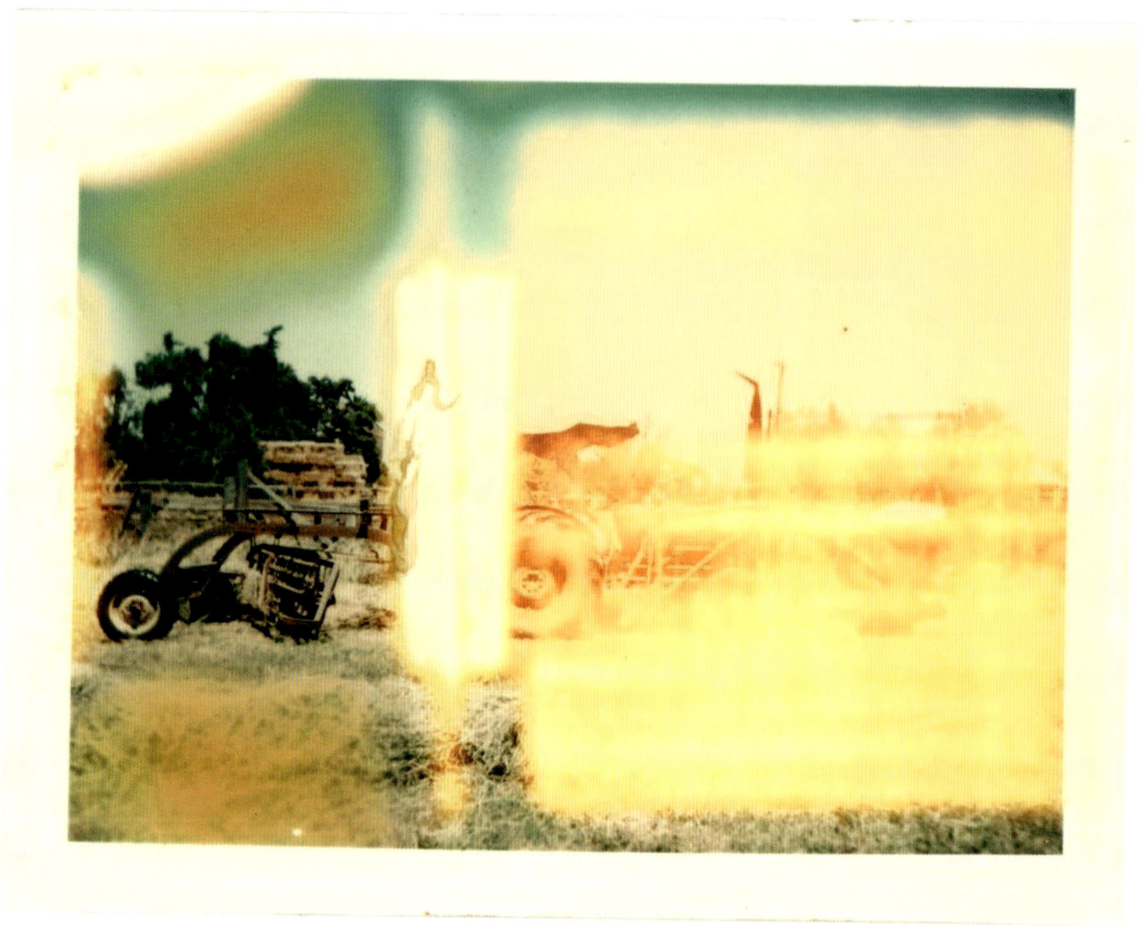

FIGURE 147. Photographer unknown, "Untitled (Tractor)," n.d. Polaroid.

Source: Collection of Barbara Levine/ Project B.

required three to five minutes of developing time and initially as long as forty-eight hours for the emulsion to harden,[3] photographers began reinserting creative agency into the increasingly hermetic process.

While some popular photography magazines criticized the extended developing time and the color rendering of SX-70 film, others emphasized the creative potential of the updated materials.[4] By taking the warnings of the instruction manual as suggestions, artists developed unique aesthetic effects that were entirely unintended by Polaroid's inventor. The photographer Ralph Gibson described a couple of popular techniques in the exhibition catalog, *SX-70 Art*: "Placing an SX-70 image in a toaster produces distortions and cracking. Freezing the film after exposure . . . results in a faint pastel image."[5] Other photographers worked the print surface, using everything from spoons to bobby pins and dental tools to layer hand-drawn effects on top of the photographic image.[6]

By the late 1980s, two new genres of Polaroid manipulations were being widely used by fashion and editorial photographers. Transferring the Polaroid image onto other surfaces had been possible since the reengineering of SX-70 film. By exposing the gooey negative prior to full development and putting it into contact with another surface, an artist could make a second print. When transferred onto rough paper, the liquid dyes of the Polaroid took on the appearance of watercolor paintings. By the early 1990s, the *Washington Post* noted that "Polaroid image transfer has become so popular that one cannot open a magazine today without seeing at least one of these photographs prominently displayed."[7] As one fashion photographer explained, editors were obsessed with Polaroid transfer images because the unique style created a "romantic, period feel," perfect for expressing the concept behind the era's style in the postdecadent 1990s.[8] [See also Chapter 20, "Painterly Photographs."]

Other photographers experimented with "emulsion lifts," which moved the entire image area to another support. The wrinkled edges of the emulsion resembled the wavy pour marks characteristic of nineteenth-century wet collodion negatives. [See also Chapter 6, "Cloudy Skies."] The photographer Ed Scully wrote, somewhat disparagingly, "If . . . you would like an image on an egg, or a cocktail glass, or whatever, have a go at peeling the now membranous image from its black backing."[9] By the 1980s, both emulsion lifts and image transfers were widely used effects.

Some photographers went to great lengths to achieve perfect transfer images, although their version of perfect was notably different from that

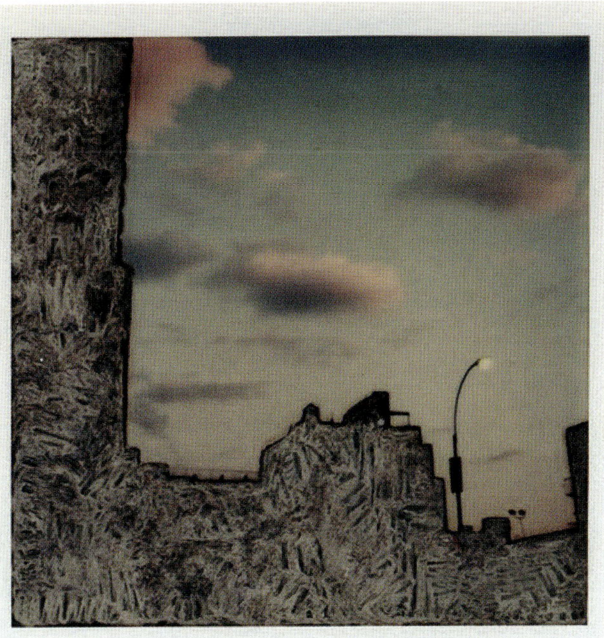

FIGURE 148. Norman Locks, "City View: New York," 1977. Manipulated Polaroid SX70.

Source: Courtesy of Norman Locks, professor emeritus, University of California, Santa Cruz.

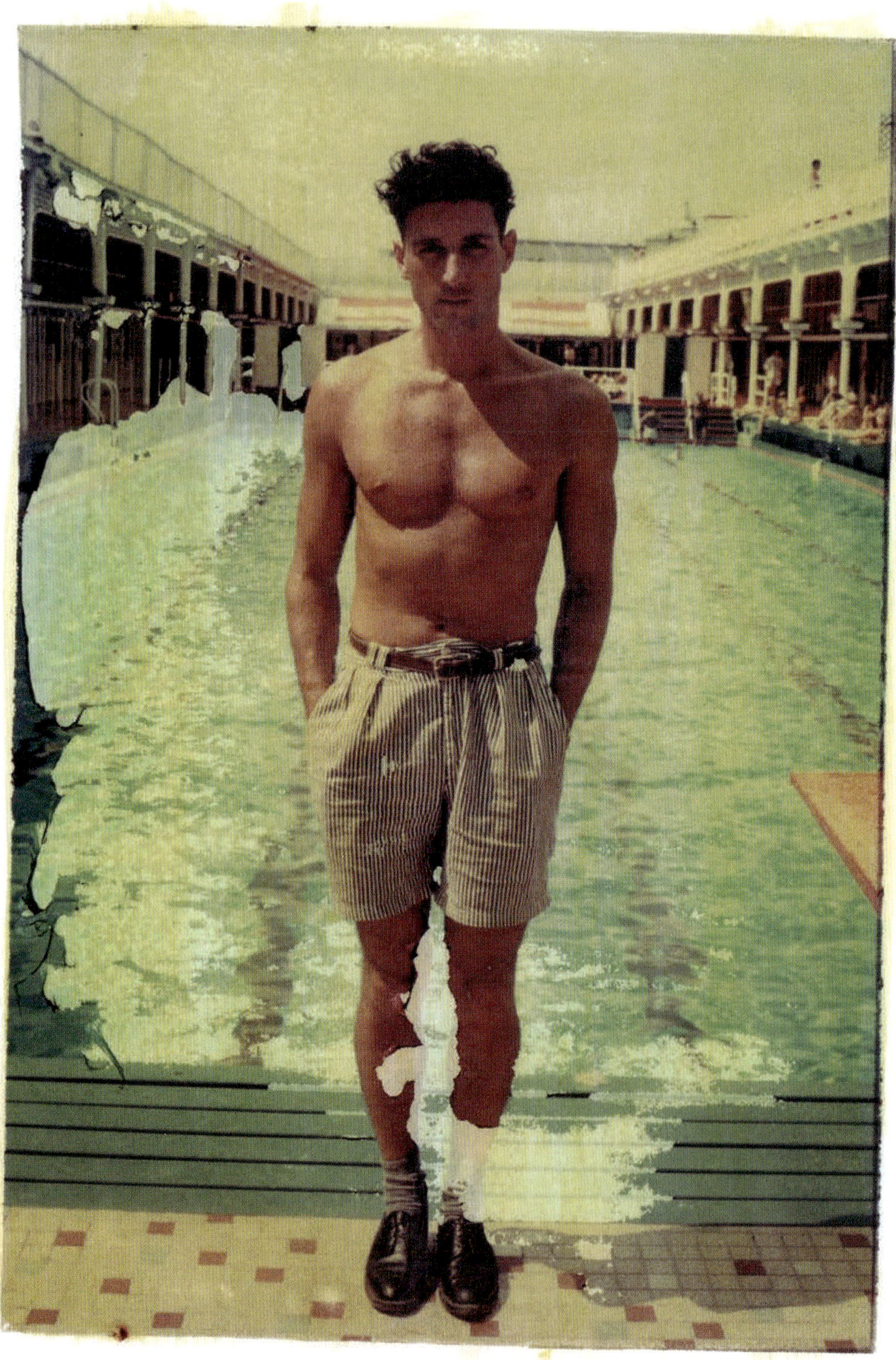

envisioned by the Polaroid Corporation. Instructional articles generally recommended exposing Polaroids in the studio, using a slide printer to project light through existing photographic transparencies. Making new images on location meant that the entire transfer process also had to be conducted in the field. The photographer Mark Bugzester joked, "If anyone really wants to frustrate a client, I can't imagine a better way than by shooting a Polaroid and then going through the hit-or-miss process of transfer while they wait around."[10] The process was uncertain at best. Bugzester estimated that he was able to maintain "about twenty percent control over the end image."[11] This uncertainty, though, was also critical to the appeal of the process. By subverting Polaroid's one-step process, photographers made unique images that suggested historical aesthetics. These fallible manual procedures reestablished the photographer's role in image making as the medium became ever more automated near the close of the millennium.

< **FIGURE 149.** Mark Bugzester, "Paris," 1992. Polaroid transfer.

Source: Courtesy of the artist and the Great Highway Gallery.

38

SEPIA

IN 1991, *Popular Photography* magazine struggled to pinpoint the difference in effect between a black-and-white print and a sepia-colored one. Illustrated with a series of photos taken at a Civil War reenactment, the article explained, "Black-and-white photographs can impart an aura of nostalgia like nothing else." But, the author continued, "they can also acquire a deeper patina of age by the simple technique of sepia or brown toning."[1] Another photography manual maintained, "People associate [sepia] tinted pictures, rather than plain black-and-white ones, with antique photos."[2] For many guidebook authors, brown-colored prints suggested a sense of history. They were frequently described as "timeless" or "classic," in contrast to what critics typically identified as the more contemporary feeling of black-and-white prints.[3]

Throughout most of the nineteenth century, photographs weren't black and white at all. They were brown and white. Nineteenth-century references to a photograph's "black-and-white" tones were often critiques of prints that were too high in contrast and lacking "middle tints," or what are now referred to as gray values.[4] This judgment was borrowed from painterly conventions, which permitted very few unmixed whites or blacks in any composition.[5] Many early photographs were toned in a gold solution to improve image permanence and increase the density of the picture's dark areas. Especially for albumen prints on paper, the gold imparted a warm, yellowish tint, transforming the weak gray-and-white photograph into a rich brown-hued one. Later, toning with less expensive sepia created a brown-hued image, plus a rotten egg smell as silver crystals were converted into more stable silver sulfides.

With the increased popularity of the gelatin silver printing process in the early twentieth century, however, gold and sepia toning passed out of favor. It was no longer necessary to amplify the image, nor was toning required to improve longevity. [See also Chapter 14, "Permanent Carbon Prints."] Eventually, however, toning was reintroduced by art photographers to mimic the look of old photographs. Turn-of-the-century pictorialist photographers emulated the heavy shadows in salted paper prints by David Octavius Hill and Robert Adamson from the 1840s and the deeply toned albumen prints that Julia Margaret Cameron made in the 1860s and 1870s. The revival of hand-toning and other obsolete printing practices was meant to distinguish the pictorialists' artistic work from the mass-produced prints churned out by Kodak at the same time. By 1913, though, Kodak joined the trend by introducing Royal Bromide, a printing paper designed especially for sepia toning.[6]

An interest in pure blacks and whites plus a long range of middle gray emerged in the late 1930s and dominated photography through the 1960s. [See also Chapter 22, "Straight Photography."] During these years, black-and-white photography was associated with advanced work in both art and journalism. In contrast to what was described as the crass commercialism of color advertising or the amateurism of snapshots, black-and-white signified serious, sober work.[7] As the viability of color photography expanded in the late 1930s, the monochrome processes were increasingly lumped together and referred to as black-and-white photographs, reversing the old stigmatization against those pure tones. In the nineteenth century, the word *photograph* had been used primarily to describe a picture made by one of the positive-negative methods on paper, while the unique processes were called by their proper names: daguerreotype, ambrotype, tintype, and

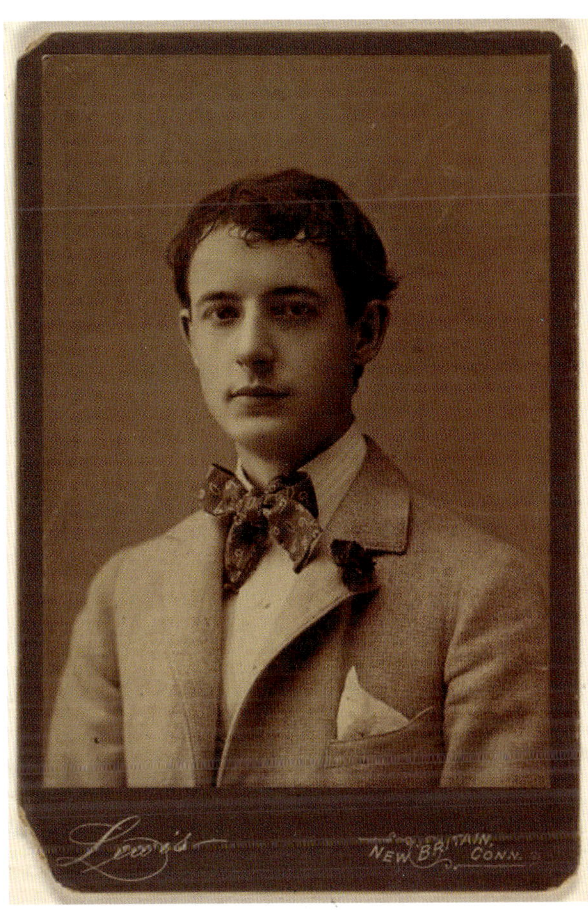

FIGURE 150. Lewis, "Walter Thomas [young man in bow tie and carnation in lapel of coat]," ca. 1910. Bromide print.

Source: J. Paul Getty Museum, Los Angeles. Digital image courtesy the Getty's Open Content Program.

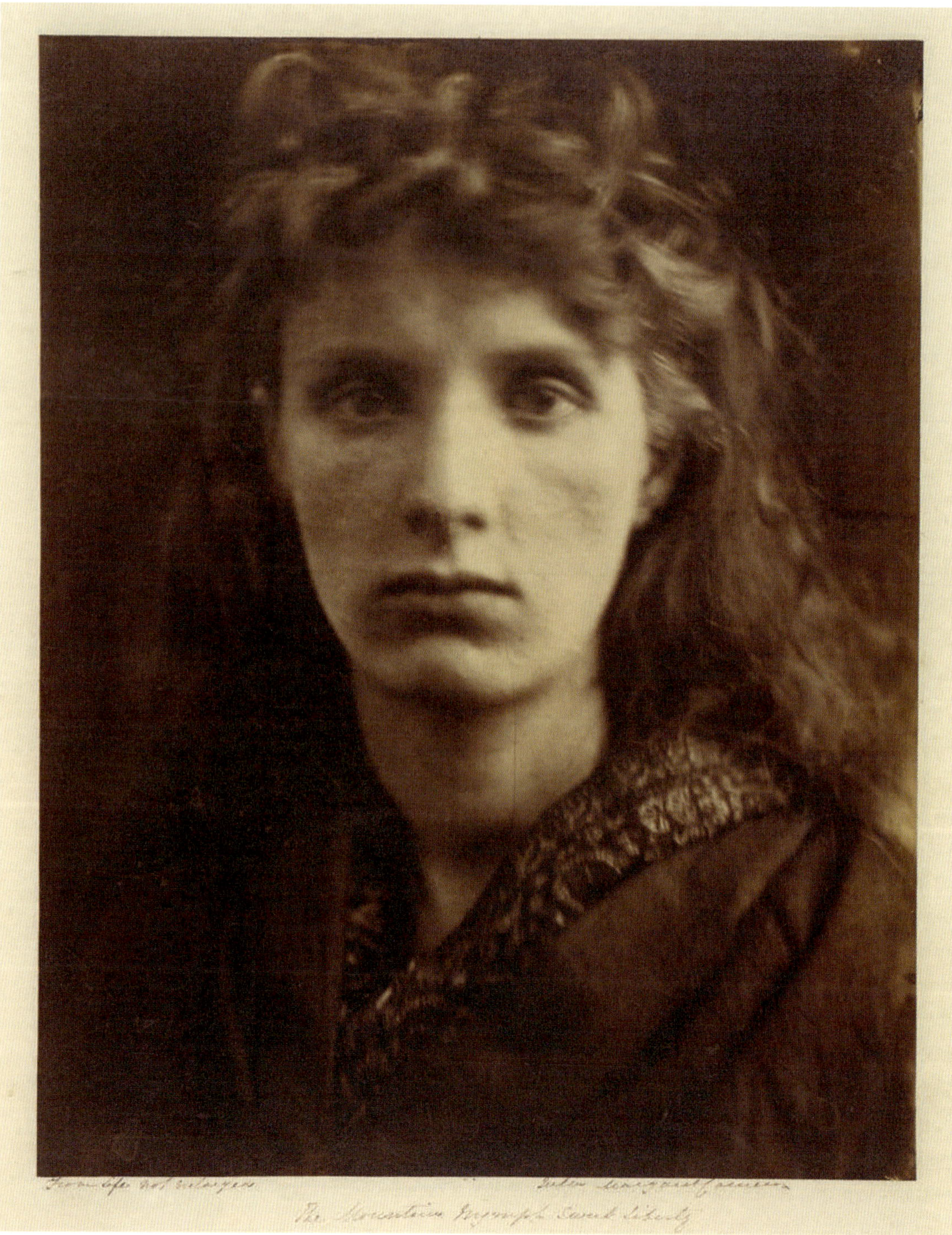

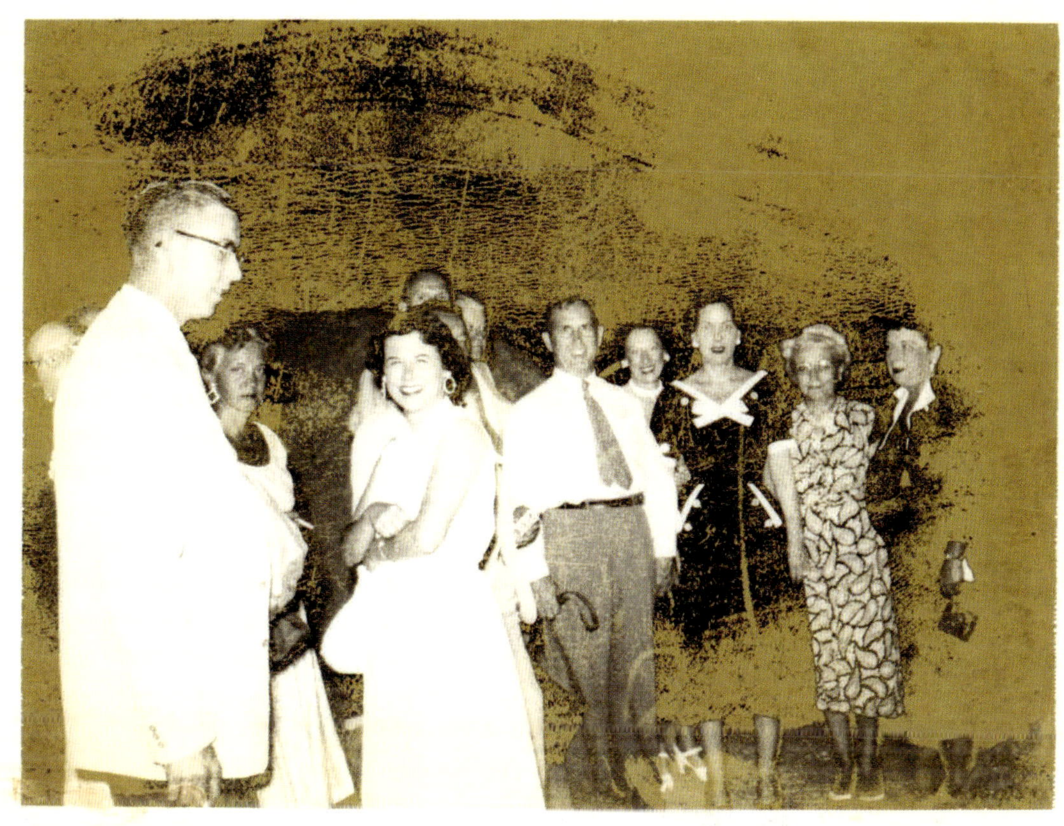

even ivorytype. The historically distinct monochrome techniques were now united in their difference from color work and called simply black-and-white photographs.

Sepia-colored pictures and the comparatively cool tones of gelatin silver prints made an uneasy pair within this catchall category of the "black and white." For many commentators, monochrome pictures conjured something less glaringly contemporary than the brilliant colors of advertising and snapshots, but it was difficult to say precisely why sepia or gold-toned images felt older than untoned black-and-white prints. While black-and-white photographs made on gelatin silver paper have been a near constant of the twentieth and twenty-first century visual landscape, sepia and brown-toned photographs have been most popular in times of prosperity. They

FIGURE 152. Photographer unknown, "Untitled," 1954. Polaroid.

Source: Collection of Barbara Levine/ Project B.

< FIGURE 151. Julia Margaret Cameron, "The Mountain Nymph Sweet Liberty," 1866. Albumen silver print, 14 ¼" × 11 ⅛".

Source: J. Paul Getty Museum, Los Angeles. Digital image courtesy the Getty's Open Content Program.

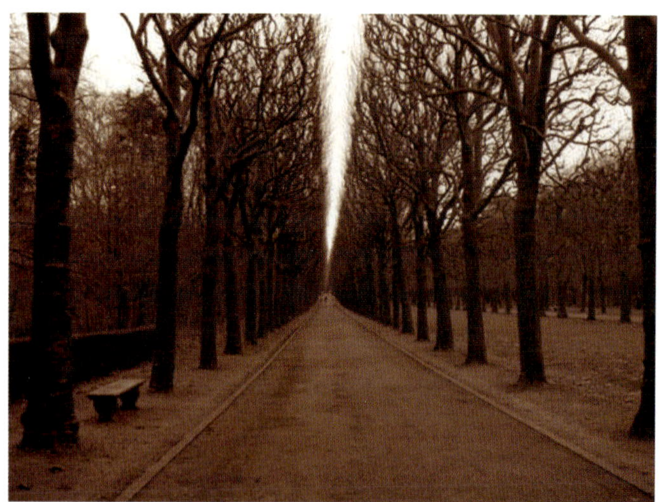

were fashionable during the postwar years, again in the 1980s through early 1990s, and returned in the 2000s.

Polaroid's first instant camera, released in 1947, initially made brown-toned prints; the company released a new sepia product in 1994.[8] (See Figure 152.) In the 1980s, sepia was used to signify history and simplicity, contrasting with the decade's economic boom. The ease of applying sepia or brown tones in Photoshop, available commercially for both Macintosh and PC after 1992, resulted in another surge of antique advertisements and editorial work. Amateurs could even order their own sepia-toned prints direct from the lab after Kodak released a class of paper designed to create brown prints from any type of negative.[9] But during the Great Depression and the energy crisis of the 1970s, sepia-toned prints were strictly historical. The austere quality of sepia may have proved threatening to Americans already suffering economic hardship, although it was a welcome nostalgic dream in times of colorful prosperity.

39

FISH-EYE

HOW-TO MANUALS since the nineteenth century have cautioned novice photographers about "violent perspective," that is, the distortion introduced by the use of a wide-angle lens at close range.[1] Early portraitists were well aware of these effects and they devised poses to keep subjects' body parts at equal distances from the lens. [See also Chapter 2, "Portrait Props and Poses."] But distortion also made for amusing trick pictures. In the early twentieth century, two popular tropes made use of these magnifying effects. Images of fishermen displaying seemingly enormous fish, dangling close to the camera, appeared in many amateur collections (Figure 155), as did foreshortened pictures of people, seated, with their giant feet outstretched.

Lenses covering wide angles of view had been used primarily for landscape photography in the nineteenth century and eventually became the preferred lens for aerial photography in the twentieth century, although the distortion at their edges remained a source of frustration.[2] [See also Chapter 8, "Foreground Interest."] These wide-angle lenses started appearing in larger numbers on the commercial market following World War II. *Life* magazine featured a wide-angle picture taken over New York City in 1947, describing its warping effect on skyscrapers as if "some new, smokeless bomb had just burst on midtown Manhattan."[3] [See also Chapter 49, "Drone Photography."] In spite of these strange effects,

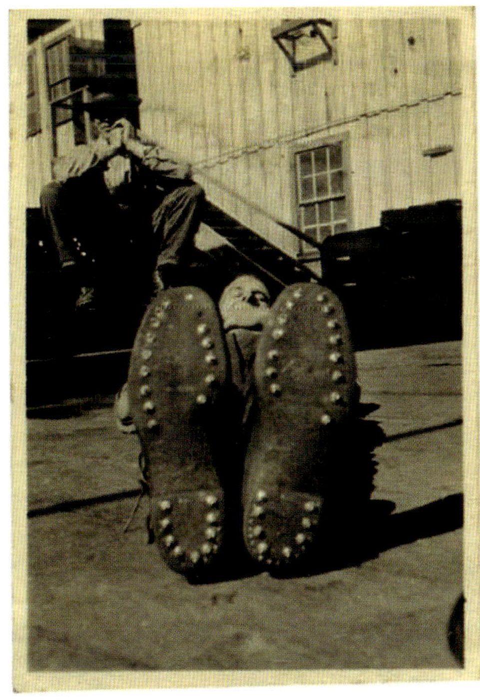

FIGURE 154. Photographer unknown, "Feet (Distortion)," n.d. Gelatin silver print.

Source: Collection of Barbara Levine/ Project B.

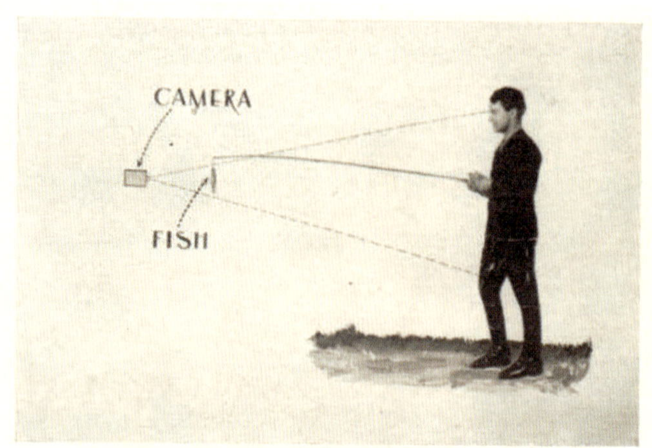

214

FIGURE 155. Sam Brown, "How the Fish Picture Is Made," from Frank Roy Fraprie and Walter Woodbury, *Photographic Amusements* (Norwood, MA: Plimpton Press, 1931), 66.

Source: Author's collection.

> **FIGURE 156.** Hiroshi Nakanishi, "Fish-Eye Camera," *Popular Photography*, September 1962, 50.

when photographers referred to "the wide-angle lens problem," they were alluding to journalistic situations that demanded a broader angle of view or greater depth of field than could be attained with a normal lens.[4]

After the release of several wide-angle lenses by prominent manufacturers, including Zeiss and Nikon, some editors began questioning the description of the standard lens as "normal." As one photographer argued, " 'Real perspective' does not exist. It is merely a combination of distance, actual size, and what we know is real. We see objects with our mind as well as with our eyes and relegate to each familiar object a specific size. Distortion or exaggeration of perspective, therefore, is really the introduction of the unusual, the angle we haven't seen, or the relationship we have never noticed."[5]

Following the popularization of extreme wide-angle pictures in the late 1950s, some writers even began to question the longstanding criticisms of the fish-eye lens with its characteristic barrel distortion and circular field of view. These lenses were originally created to record hemispherical images of cloud formations for study by weather scientists in the 1920s.[6] Initially they were custom-made, noninterchangeable lenses permanently attached to a camera body. Hasselblad and Nikon both produced fish-eye cameras, but the cost of these specialized units limited their use to photographers working for major publications, such as *National Geographic* or *Life*. Most photographers could afford to experiment with fish-eye effects only in the late 1960s, when attachments that screwed onto existing lenses were introduced by second-tier manufacturers. The fish-eye's challenge to convention was eagerly taken up in this period. Ultra-wide-angle and fish-eye lenses represented a rejection of the status quo. As a how-to article in *Popular Photography* reasoned, "Nowadays even the standard of normality is in a state of confusion."[7]

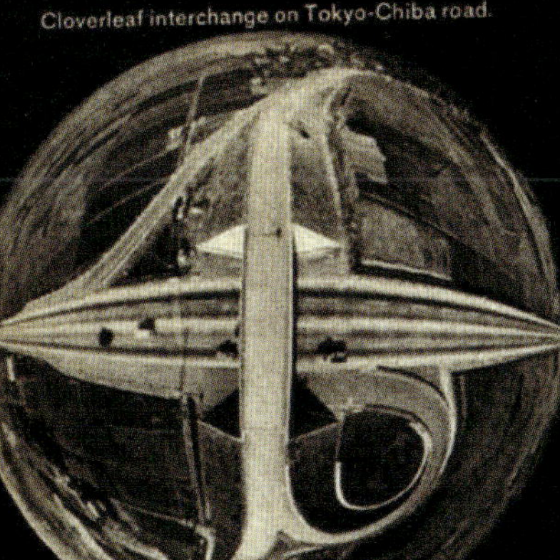

Cloverleaf interchange on Tokyo-Chiba road.

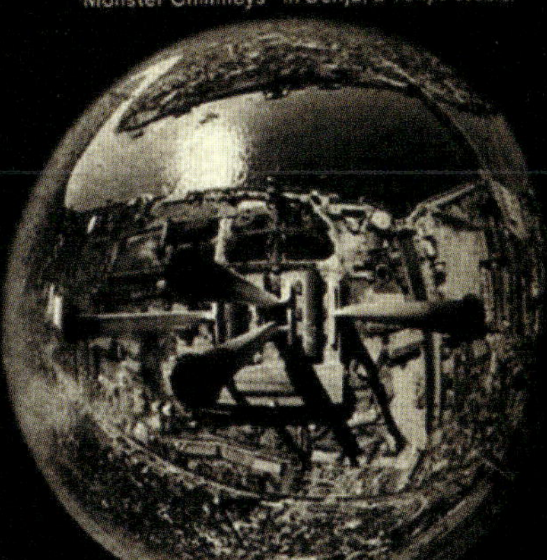

"Monster Chimneys" in Senju, a Tokyo suburb.

FISH-EYE CAMERA

Scheduled for release in this country soon is the new Nikkor Fisheye lens. It covers a total of 180 degrees, and the round picture it produces on a 35-mm frame yields dramatic images of even the most commonplace subjects, as these pictures show.

The 8-mm lens is designed to fit the Nikon F single-lens reflex camera. It has a maximum aperture of $f/8$ and a price tag of $449.50. The lens, which is supplied with a case and centering viewfinder, is used with the camera's mirror in the locked-up position.

The lens used to make the pictures on these pages is a prototype of the one which should be on the market by about the time this issue of POPULAR PHOTOGRAPHY goes on sale.

On this page appear three scenes made by photographer Hiroshi Nakanishi. Opposite, free-lance photographer Neil Leifer presents an unusual view of Yankee Stadium.

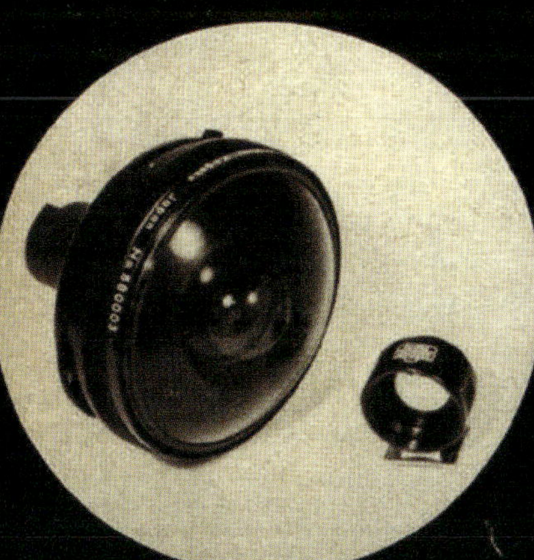

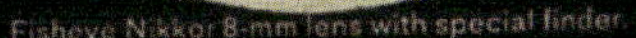

Fisheye Nikkor 8-mm lens with special finder.

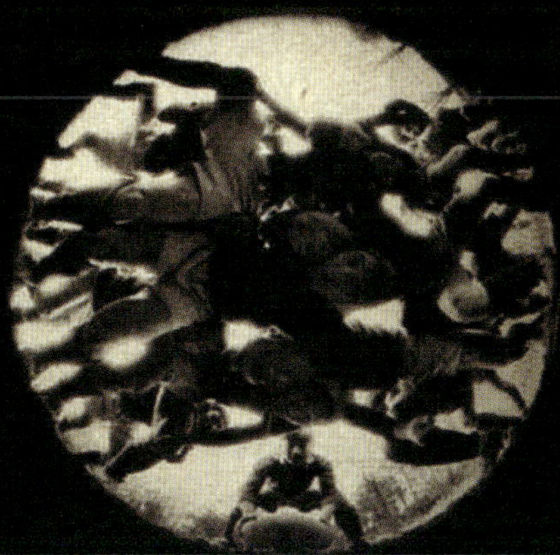

Camera on ground caught university rugby team.

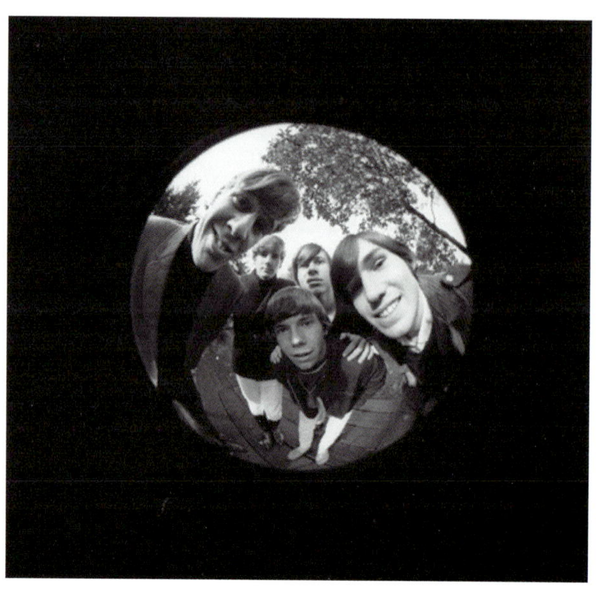

By the late 1960s, the relatively conservative publication *Modern Photography* asked, "Who could have imagined . . . that one day the fish-eye concept and resulting pictures would be as understood and acceptable as they are today? It's hard to open up a single national magazine without seeing fisheye pictures used in advertising for special effects in distortion or to cover a vast area as no other lens can do."[8] The distortion of wide-angle lenses and fish-eyes continued to gain popularity through the 1970s, appearing frequently in the new music magazine *Rolling Stone*. One how-to manual described them as "caricatures or satirical portraits" and suggested that the style was "well worth exploring as a new technique to be used when the photographer wishes to evoke surprise or shock, or to make a great impact on the viewer."[9] By the 1980s, the trend had waned. In the article, "Fisheye Lenses: You Either Love 'Em or Hate 'Em," the author pointed to the limits of the fish-eye fad, looking back on his own experiences with the lens in the mid-1960s. He recalled, "I fisheyed everything in sight. The novelty soon wore off. Round images of ordinary subject matter and situations just looked goofy, not more interesting."[10] He suggested that the subject matter should match the unusual aesthetic of the lens and recommended that the fish-eye be limited to portraits of clowns, comedians, and rock musicians.[11]

When the fish-eye reappeared briefly in the early 2000s, it aimed to impart some of this sense of fun to a more conventional subject: weddings. Wedding photography handbooks recommended the use of a fisheye lens for shots of dancing guests or chairs arranged before the altar, although the technique quickly went the way of chocolate fountains.[12] Even as the moderate distortions of wide-angle lenses have been fully accepted in everything from reportage to smartphone photos, the fish-eye lens has remained too radical for regular use.

40

GOLDEN HOUR

FOR MOST OF THE TWENTIETH CENTURY, there was no golden hour. This is not to say that the sun ceased to rise and fall, rather that amateur photographers were counseled to avoid the warm-colored, low-angle light associated with sunset and sunrise, particularly when making portraits in color. Only when this dramatic quality of light became recognized as a desirable aesthetic did the phrase *golden hour* achieve prominence in the how-to literature.

Exposure guidelines were included in every box of Kodachrome from its 1936 debut. However, these printed charts guaranteed accuracy only for pictures taken more than one hour after sunrise or one hour before sunset.[1] Independently published handbooks also toed the line: "Follow rigidly the exposure chart on the instruction sheet which is packed with every roll of color film. You will find, for instance, that outdoor pictures should be taken between the hours of 10 in the morning and 4 in the afternoon to obtain true color reproductions. Before and after these hours the light will cast a reddish or orange glow on your film."[2] [See also Chapter 29, "Distracting Color."] Some authors allowed that this color could be a beneficial feature when representing landscapes but warned that it was unsuitable for portraits. One noted, "Just before sunset the color of the light is markedly red; it is only natural that pictures made at that time sometimes appear abnormally colored. Avoid this difficulty by making your color pictures of people earlier than two hours before sunset."[3] Until the 1990s, instructional guides recommended the use of corrective filters to simulate normal daylight color balance for portraits taken in these extreme lighting conditions.[4]

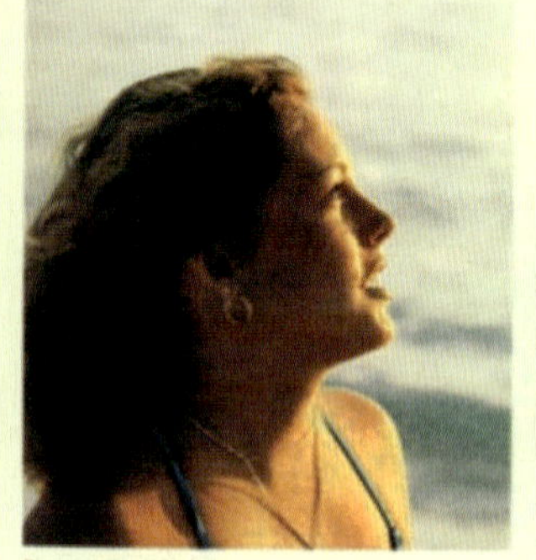
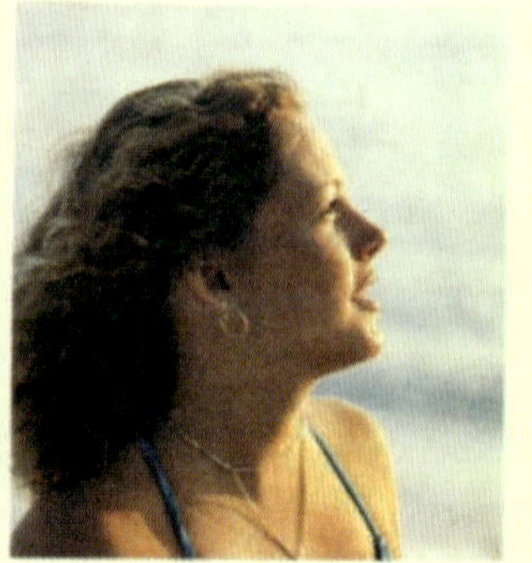

FIGURE 158. Eastman Kodak Co., *How to Take Good Pictures* (New York: Ballantine Books, 1981), 169. Source: Author's collection.

While it was easy in the early years of Kodachrome to blame this difficulty on the tendency of film to exaggerate saturated colors, the problem wasn't wholly a technical one, as a few books recognized. The popular how-to author Fred Bond wrote of photographing in color during the forbidden hours: "If flesh tones appear badly 'sun-burned' do not blame Kodachrome. It recorded what it saw."[5] The photographer Louis Stettner took this explanation even further, arguing that "film can in no way make the psychological and psycho-physical adjustments to color that human [sic] are capable of. Therefore, *we must train ourselves to see colors in terms of how the film will record them* [emphasis in the original]."[6] Not only was it difficult for photographers to anticipate these results, as Stettner suggested, but it took nearly half a century for the sun-burned effect to be read as a golden glow, when it would become an asset rather than an obstacle to making good portraits.

The prohibition on photographing people during these transitional hours did not extend equally to other subjects. In fact, the appeal of evening light was so widely accepted in amateur landscape photography that by 1974, Susan Sontag would write that even the experience of watching the setting sun felt hackneyed: "The image-surfeited are likely to find sunsets corny; they now look, alas, too much like photographs."[7] By the late 1970s, filmmakers especially were trying to rehabilitate the sunset genre, which had for so long been the province of amateurs. Terrence Malick's film *Days of Heaven* (1978) and Stanley Kubrick's *Barry Lyndon* (1975) both introduced audiences to new extremes of light, working almost exclusively during golden hour and in candlelight, respectively. In the same period, Joel Meyerowitz's photo book, *Cape Light*, took up Sontag's challenge in the world of still photography, although few of the pictures in the book applied the characteristic golden light of sunset to people. As the *New York Times* wrote, "Meyerowitz captures stunning sunset effects that recall the great days of Brown and Bigelow calendars, and that no one lacking his Museum of Modern Art credentials could get away with in respectable artistic society."[8] Mobilizing a solidly middle-brow effect as an intentional artistic technique required a pass from art world cognoscenti. Another whole decade passed before golden hour would earn an uncontested place in the repertoire of portraiture.

The pejorative language that how-to guides used to describe the effects of photographing people in warm light underlines the apparent threat that these pictures posed. For more than a century, photographic literature, as well as the camera and film industry at large, assumed their readers and consumers were white. [See also Chapter 3, "Hand Painting," and Chapter 11, "The Rembrandt Effect."] Visualizing these assumptions, most guidebooks featured images of white photographers taking pictures of white models. When authors described the effects of golden hour on skin tones, they meant pale white skin, which had been used as the benchmark for accurate exposure by camera and film manufacturers since the medium's invention.[9] Although photographs of white models taken in golden hour light occasionally appeared in fashion magazines during the 1970s and 1980s, these pictures were usually limited to summertime subjects.

In the early 1990s, however, fashion photographers, including Francesco Scavullo and Patrick Demarchelier, began liberally applying the golden glow to models in outdoor photo shoots. Even street scenes far removed from the beach received the golden hour treatment. By the mid-1990s

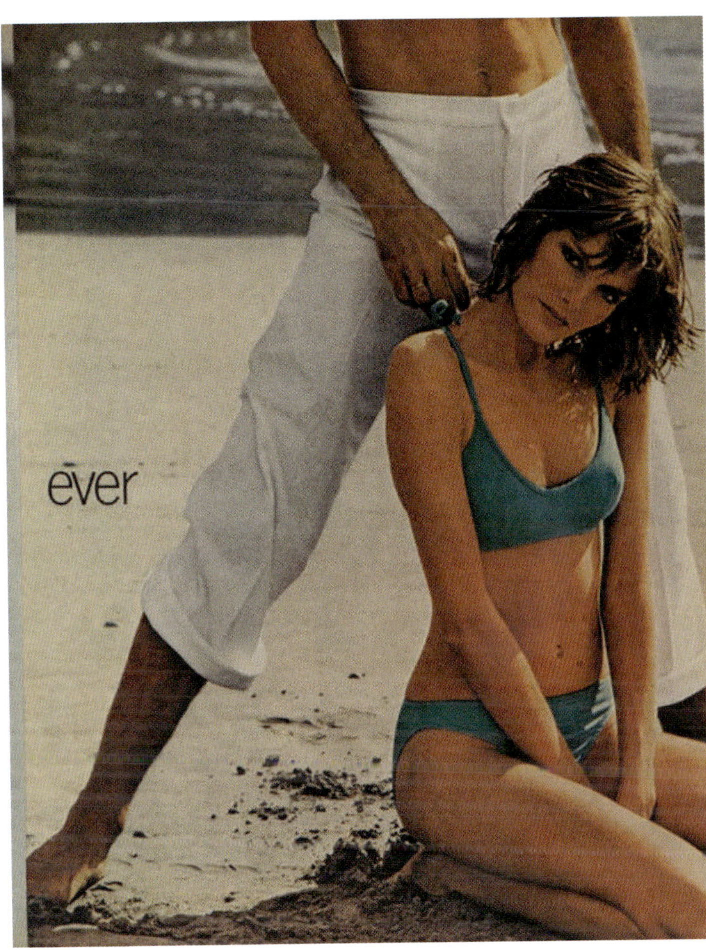

FIGURE 159. Francesco Scavullo, "Easy to Love! The Prettiest New Summer Dressing," *Vogue*, May 1976, 150–151.

Source: Francesco Scavullo, *Vogue* © Condé Nast.

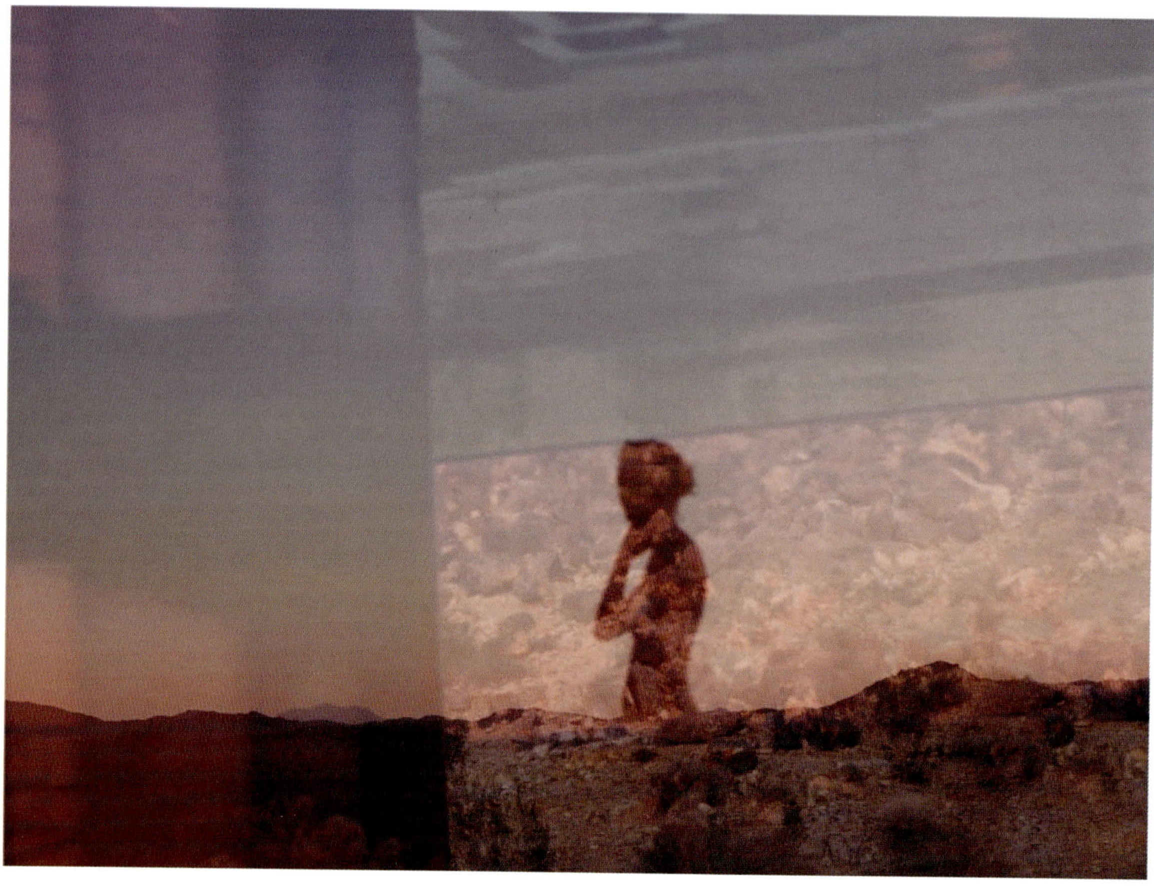

the amateur photographic literature reflected this stylistic shift. The photographer's working times were inverted; now the midday hours from 10 a.m. until 4 p.m. were useless. As *Popular Photography* advised in 1997, "The quality of light during the last hour before sunset is better than the rest of the day put together. Avoid it at your peril."[10] While the term *golden hour* appeared occasionally in photographic literature as early as the 1980s, it was not in wide circulation until the effect was celebrated.[11] By the late 1990s, the descriptive phrase was used in all manner of periodicals, from local newspaper articles on how to take the best summer snapshots to the advice columns of specialist photography publications. Most of these articles took time to point out that *golden hour* was a term borrowed from the pros, giving the technique the aura of a trade secret.[12]

Cultural as well as technological changes contributed to this revolution in photographic aesthetics. Although people of color appeared on runways and in high-fashion photography through the 1970s and 1980s, these models were rarely featured in mainstream advertising by ready-to-wear brands. Ads that included models of many skin tones in one image were not popular until the Italian clothing brand Benetton introduced its "All the Colors of the World" slogan in 1984.[13] Although Benetton's later marketing campaigns would prove highly controversial, this imagery at least visualized the need for improved film and printing technology that could accommodate all skin tones. As the communications scholar Lorna Roth has revealed, Kodak color film stocks long privileged the light end of the spectrum, sacrificing detail in dark image areas to achieve accurate rendering of lighter areas, especially white skin. The company distributed a preprinted card featuring a white woman wearing brightly colored clothing in order to help local photo labs balance skin tones in their prints, thereby privileging white subjects. These stock images came to be known as "Shirley cards," after the model who first appeared on them in the 1950s. According to Roth, it was not until commercial advertising accounts complained about the film's inadequate representation of brown tones in their products that research was undertaken to produce a more brown-sensitive film stock.[14] VeriColor III and the popular amateur film Gold Max, released in the 1980s, were both known for their improved rendition of brown tones and expanded dynamic range.

The elements of so-called good pictures are tightly bound up with cultural proscriptions. Acceptance of golden hour lighting in popular portraiture required much more than simply learning how to anticipate the objective rendering of warm light on film. Embracing golden hour also meant that white photographers, critics, and subjects had to expand their understanding of the variable nature of skin tones as represented by color film.

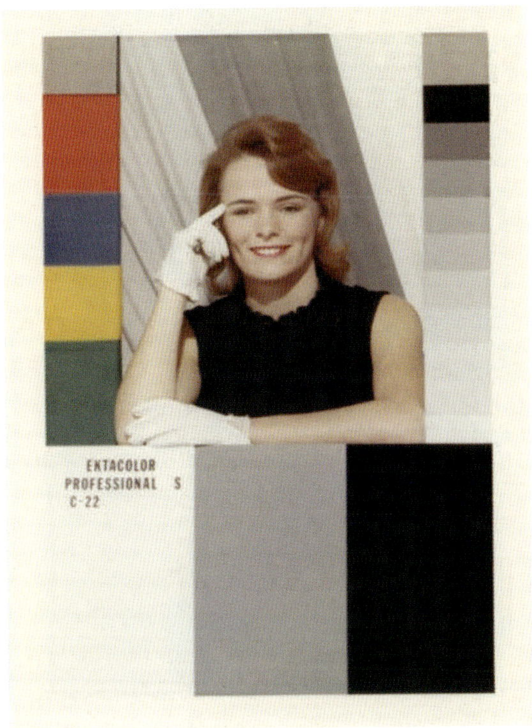

FIGURE 161. Kodak, "Ektacolor Professional, C-22," 1966.

Source: Collection of Hermann Zschiegner.

41

CROSS-PROCESSING

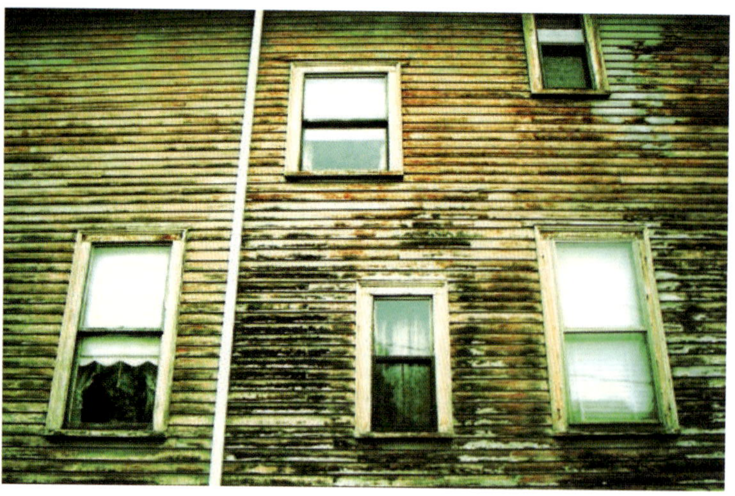

UNLIKE SOME PHOTOGRAPHIC STYLES, which look so much like normal vision that they escape explicit notice, cross-processing stands out. It appears intentional and unnatural, and that's exactly why photographers gravitated to it. The technique generates ultrasaturated colors, high contrast, and sometimes radical color shifts by developing slide film in chemicals meant for negative film. Although such accidents in the darkroom could (and presumably did) occur as soon as color negative film joined positive slide film on the market in the 1940s, cross-processing wasn't widely practiced until the early 1990s. [See also Chapter 29, "Distracting Color."]

The style was easy to identify and proliferated rapidly as photographers emulated the work of pioneering fashion photographers Nick Knight and Anton Corbijn in collaboration with the London-based printer Brian Dowling.[1] As *Popular Photography* exclaimed in 1995, "You can't scan the advertising and editorial pages of any major fashion or interior design magazine without encountering the super-saturated, somewhat unnatural color that's the tell-tale sign of cross processing. It shows up regularly on CD covers, in fine-art still lifes, and in

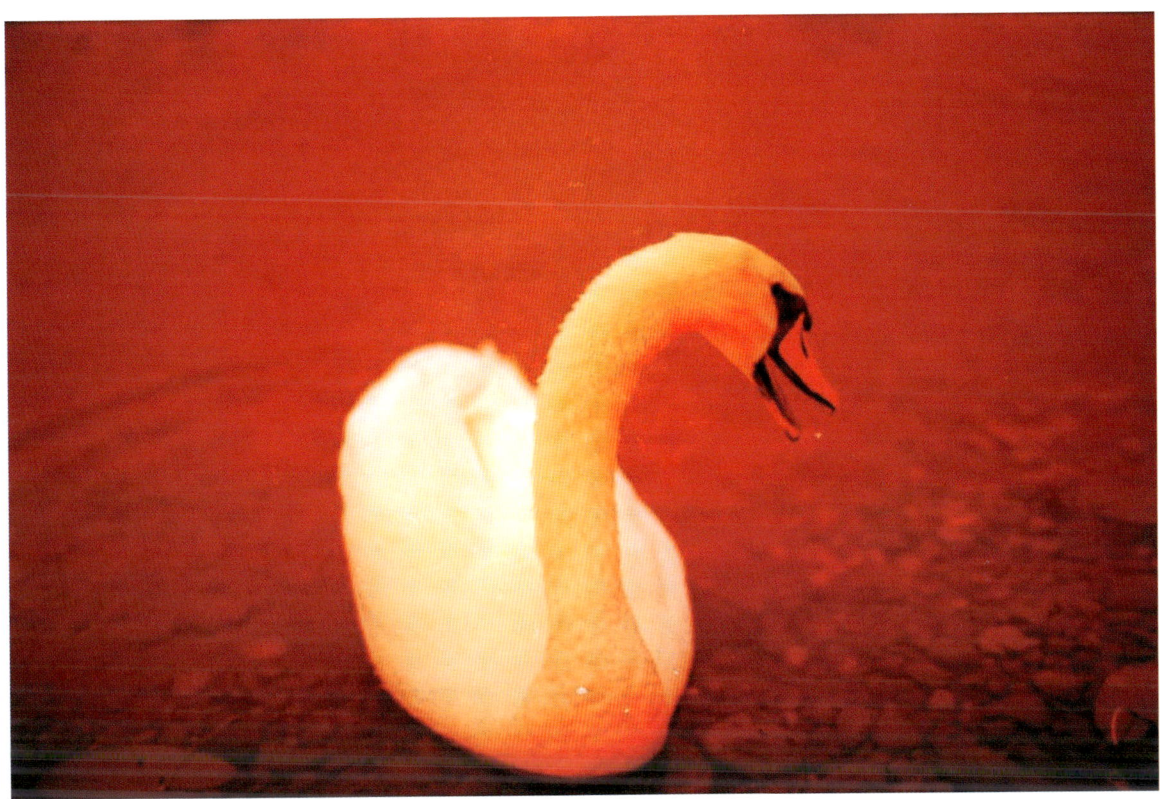

portraiture. Student portfolios from all the major art and photography schools are filled with it."[2] The rapid rise and decline of cross-processing in the 1990s anticipated the accelerated trend cycles of the digital world.

Cross-processing intentionally inserted chance into the otherwise exacting science of color photography. With the use of unintended chemicals, the manufacturer's recommendations no longer held up. It was difficult to achieve the same vibrant, unnatural colors every time, so photographers either had to leave the process entirely open to accident or create their own standards for timing, temperatures, and chemical mixtures. Coincident with the digital revolution, cross-processing became a way for photographers to realign themselves with the technical demands of film photography. A writer for the *Creative Review* reasoned, "It is as if the pressure to be computerized has made photographers all the more

FIGURE 163. hnt651, "More Pose: Fuji Sensia 100, xpro," 2011. Flickr. CC BY 2.0. https://creativecommons.org/licenses/by/2.0/.

Source: https://flic.kr/p/cGWf6d.

aware of the traditional magic in their craft, pushing the boundaries and finding new potential within the film, paper and chemicals."[3]

Photographers bemoaned the boredom of making perfect prints that were "bland and predictable."[4] Instead, they embraced the arduous process of becoming proficient in cross-processing, carefully recording their experiments with different film stocks, exposures, and developing temperatures in order to create more predictable, though still visually arresting, results. Blood reds, electric blues, and chalky whites were typical of cross-processing as a whole, although each film stock responded with slight differences. Many preferred the effects produced by cross-processing Kodak Pro Gold or Fujifilm Sensia or Velvia, although the film manufacturers were quick to warn consumers that these unauthorized uses would void any guarantees of the film's longevity.[5]

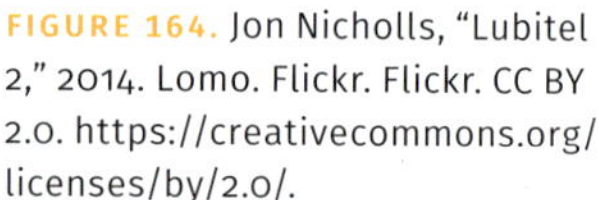

FIGURE 164. Jon Nicholls, "Lubitel 2," 2014. Lomo. Flickr. Flickr. CC BY 2.0. https://creativecommons.org/licenses/by/2.0/.

Source: https://flic.kr/p/oz9Trs.

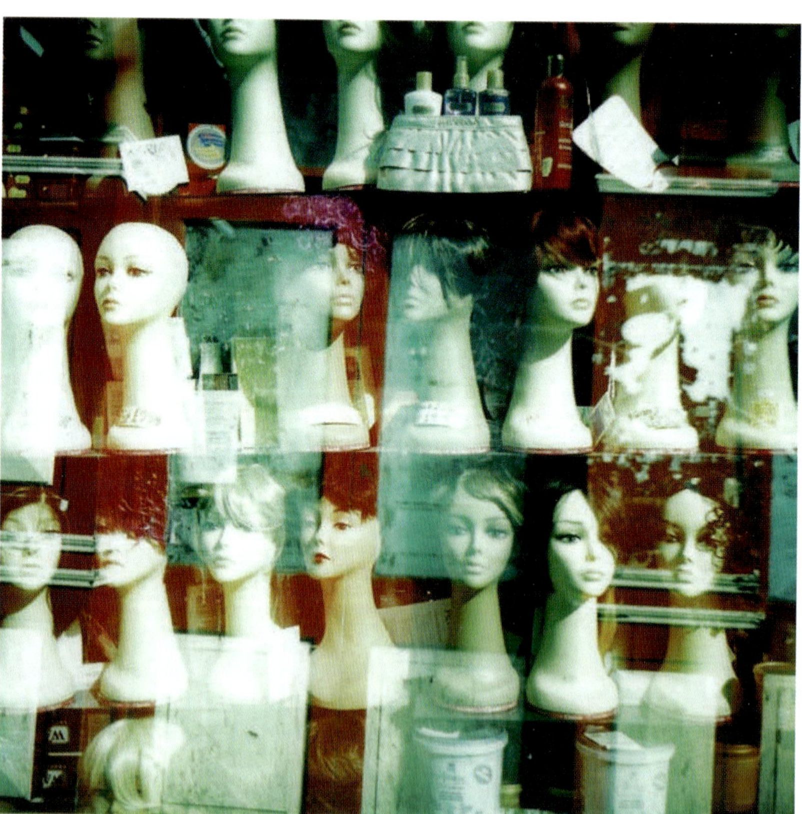

As many custom film labs were shuttered following the shift to digital in the early 2000s, tutorials describing how to create cross-processing effects in Photoshop began circulating on the Internet. Photoshop plug-ins simulating the color casts unique to each brand of film were developed, translating photographers' carefully plotted wet-processing notes to the dry digital world. In 2008, the hobbyist camera and creative photography collective, Lomography added film to its lineup of plastic cameras modeled after the Russian Lomo. Lomo's first film, called X-Pro, was designed especially to create extreme color shifts when cross-processed even by drugstore photo labs.[6] With the discontinuation of many color slide films since the turn of the millennium, Lomography's X-Pro film was one of the few viable options for analog photographers wishing to create cross-processed photographs without access to a professional lab.

The cross-processed look has shifted ever more into the digital realm since the 2010s. The popular digital image processing app, VSCO, released a set of smartphone camera presets in 2015 that mimicked the effects of cross-processing.[7] By 2016, Instagram's own cross-processing filter, X-Pro II, was among the top twelve most frequently used filters posted by commercial accounts.[8] As in its earlier phase of popularity, cross-processing effects were valued for their ability to suggest that the magic of the photographic image lies in its chemistry, even as these effects were no longer causally linked to analog processes.

42

BOKE

DEPTH OF FIELD has been a concern for photographers since the medium's earliest days. The large aperture required to let in more light for a shorter exposure time also limits depth of focus; everything that falls outside this shallow plane of focus is blurred. As one later author remarked snidely of nineteenth-century portraiture, "Increasing fuzziness back from the sharp plane of the eyes and mouth was supposed to create the illusion of depth. Usually all it accomplished was to fuzz up the ears so they looked like bits of old cloth tacked on each side of the head."[1] The twentieth-century historian Robert Taft also criticized these early pictures because of their shallow focus, including one he considered otherwise "magnificent": Alexander Gardner's 1863 portrait of Abraham Lincoln.[2] Even as intentional soft focus became desirable in pictorial photography of the late nineteenth century, softening was usually applied uniformly across the image through the use of a soft-focus lens or by separating the negative and paper slightly during printing.[3] [See also Chapter 2, "Portrait Props and Poses," and Chapter 21, "Soft Focus."]

Shallow depth of field was still considered a limiting factor for photography well into the twentieth century. Especially in the popular "instantaneous" genre, pictures that aimed to arrest rapid motion required fast shutter speeds and therefore larger apertures, which correspondingly reduced depth of field. Kodak's *How to Make Good Pictures* took this shortcoming as a given in 1928: "In high speed work, it is not possible to secure perfect definition of all objects in the field and the photographer must be content with securing perfect definition in the portion containing the greatest interest."[4] [See also Chapter 15, "Instantaneous Photographs," and Chapter 19, "Wildlife Photography."]

The century-old depth-of-field problem was nearly solved by the introduction of miniature cameras and the popularization of wide-angle lenses in the 1950s. Both technologies made it possible for photographers to work in low-light situations with smaller apertures, thus increasing depth of field. As soon as these solutions were in hand, however, instructional authors backtracked and began recommending shallow depth of field as an aesthetic effect. In particular, the guides suggested that backgrounds should be thrown out of focus to eliminate distracting

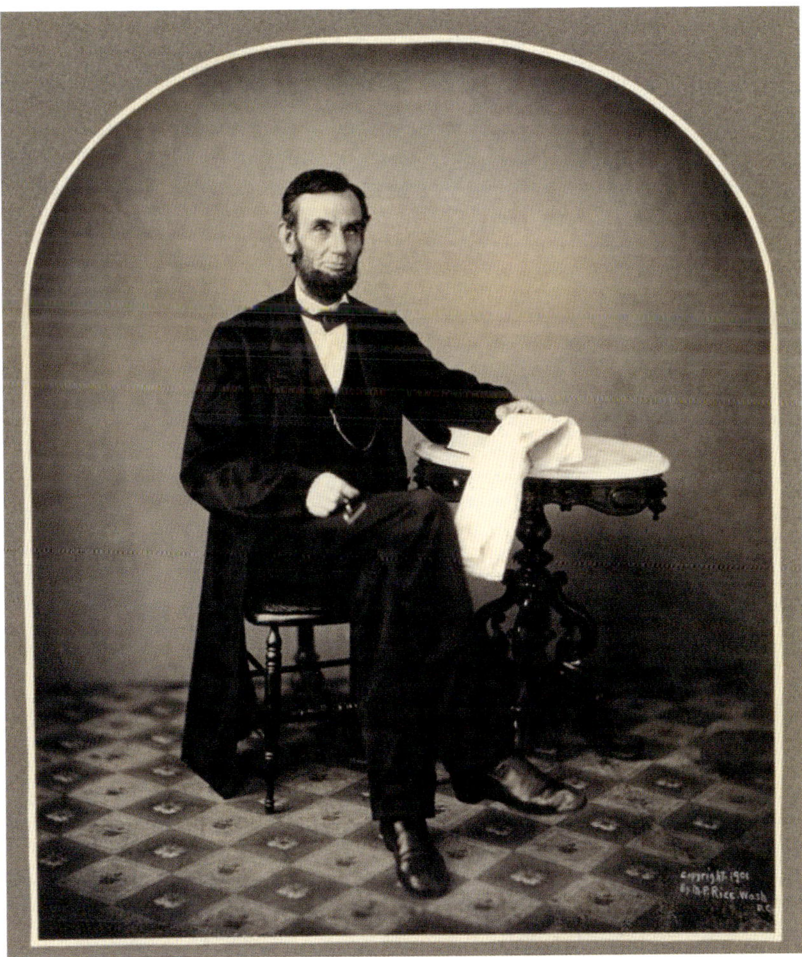

FIGURE 165. Alexander Gardner, "Abraham Lincoln": negative, 1863; print, 1901. Gelatin silver print, 15" × 18".

Source: Metropolitan Museum of Art, Warner Communications. Purchase Fund, 1976.

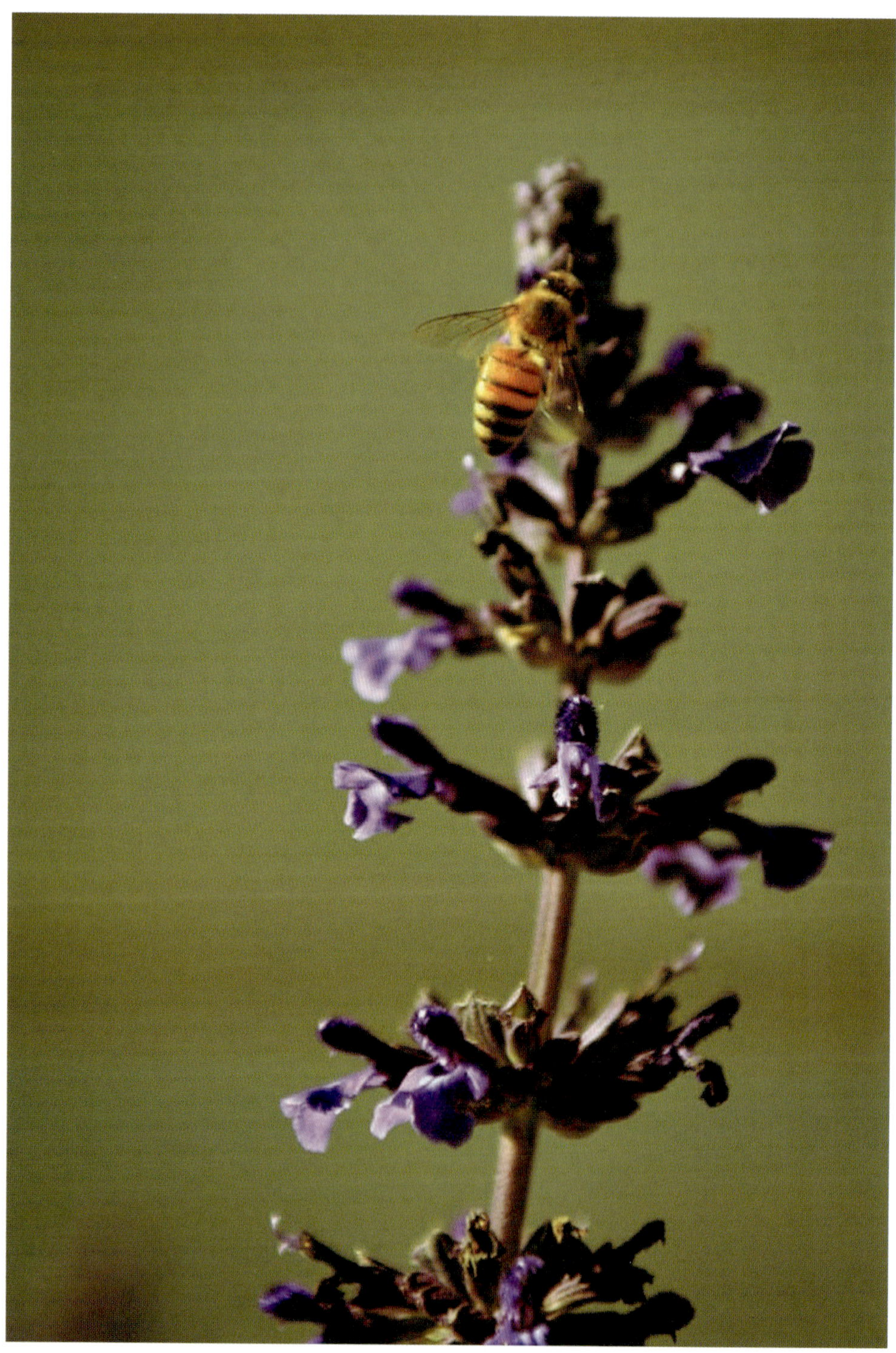

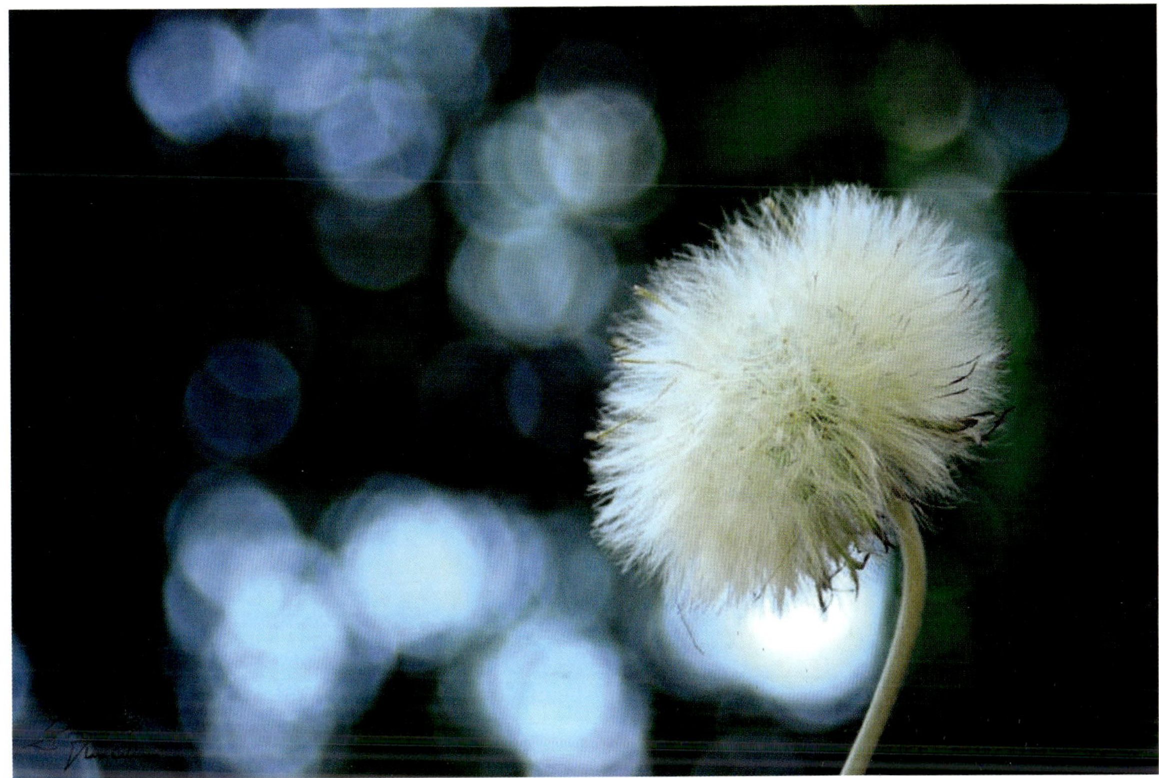

picture elements.[5] Midcentury American writers attempted to describe this effect by pointing to the "fuzzy shapes and masses" characteristic of shallow depth of field.[6] They struggled, however, to distinguish the lens-based out-of-focus effect from motion blur, which was a result of either subject or camera movement. [See also Chapter 31, "Motion Blur."]

The solution to the semantic problem posed by the two kinds of blur was borrowed from a group of Japanese photographers working in the 1960s, including Daido Moriyama and Takuma Nakahira. The aesthetic that they promoted in their short-lived journal, *Provoke*, was described as "*are, bure, boke*," often translated as "rough, blurred, out of focus."[7] [See also Chapter 33, "Graininess."] Moriyama's photographs were seen widely in the United States in a traveling retrospective organized by the San Francisco Museum of Modern Art in 1999. In the wake of this exhibition, a growing number of popular photographers began using the Japanese term, *boke*, to describe the quality of lens-based blur.[8]

FIGURE 167. Daniel Iván Lara Calderón, "Diente de León," 2014. Flickr. CC BY-SA 2.0. https://creativecommons.org/licenses/by-sa/2.0/.
Source: https://flic.kr/p/nNS9xZ.

< FIGURE 166. Cristeen Quezon, "Circle of Life," 2008. Flickr. CC BY 2.0. https://creativecommons.org/licenses/by/2.0/.
Source: https://flic.kr/p/5H3iLx.

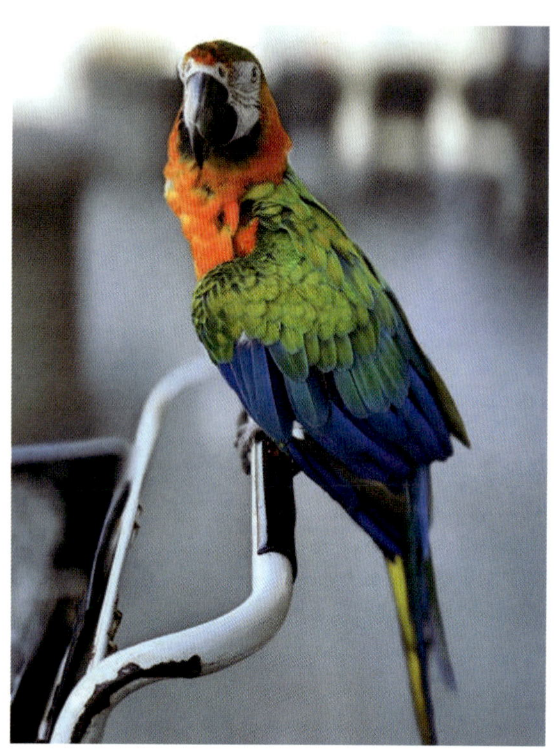

The term quickly spread through online photo-sharing platforms, especially Flickr, and lens makers began advertising lenses for the quality of their boke. Much debate centered on these qualitative judgments of boke, whether the shapes made by the aperture leaves should remain visible or whether the blur should be entirely "creamy," with no distracting edges.[9] Cheaper lenses have fewer aperture blades, resulting in pentagram shapes rather than smoothly blurred circles. Cinematographers recommended using 35 millimeter lenses on video cameras for better boke effects.[10] A Photoshop plug-in developed in 2009 could add boke in postprocessing to any image.[11]

The prevalence of boke also led instructional authors to caution against its overuse. Just days before Apple released the iPhone 7 Plus in September 2016, the first smartphone camera capable of creating simulated boke, *Popular Photography* listed "super shallow depth of field" among the "10 Photography Techniques You Might Be Overusing."[12] Still, boke's popularity among smartphone photographers soared, and Instagram joined the trend by adding a "focus" mode for portraits to its in-app camera in 2018.[13] [See also Chapter 50, "Digital Filters."]

Like many other photographic techniques, the battle over boke emerged only after the technical limitations of shallow depth of field were overcome. Reintroducing background blur in the age of smartphone cameras suggests a connection to the historically analog aspects of photography. The addition of technical limits—even those that are digitally applied—underscores the artistry of the photographer who knows how to manipulate the medium's limitations for intentional aesthetic effects.

PART VI

1996–2019

THE INTRODUCTION OF PHOTOSHOP, the growth of the Internet, and the development of consumer-grade digital cameras massively impacted photography in the late 1990s. In the wake of this digital revolution, after low-cost digital cameras and image processing software were widely available, many professional photographers advocated a return to simple analog processes and tools, from the Holga medium-format film camera to small 35 millimeter point-and-shoot cameras. Soon, however, the analog effects of these cameras were being recreated digitally, and any casual photographer with a smartphone could easily apply their aesthetic markers to any picture.

New distribution methods, particularly Instagram, enabled would-be photographers to see and emulate more photographs than ever before, leading to a decrease in the life span of trends, as well as more frequent adaptation of recently outmoded styles. The how-to publishing market also expanded online, enabling individual photographers to provide detailed advice through tutorials on personal blogs and instructional videos on YouTube, which bypassed the publishing industry entirely. Despite this circumvention of institutional gatekeepers, critics in the mid-2010s were alarmed by the overwhelming uniformity of pictures shared online. While the growth of photographic practice throughout the twentieth century had upended the traditional rules, new rules and new tastemakers were reestablished with each subsequent stylistic development.

43

ON-CAMERA FLASH

AMATEUR PHOTOGRAPHERS were still struggling to conquer the darkness at midcentury. Although single-use flash bulbs, which made dramatic action-stopping pictures, had been available since the 1930s, their high price tag limited their use to professionals. When Kodak released the affordable Brownie Starflash in 1957, the company's first camera with a built-in on-camera flash, a new style of amateur picture was born. The integrated bulb unit on the Starflash made casual snapshots in low-light situations possible, although even Kodak admitted that the technology had some limitations. The 1957 edition of *How to Make Good Pictures* conceded, "The only real shortcoming of flash-on-the-camera snapping is that, like many convenient ways of doing things, it doesn't handle the job quite as well as it can be done. Pictures of people tend to have a somewhat pasty, flat look, because everything the camera lens sees of a subject gets an equal dose of light."[1] Other manuals decried the deep shadows that loomed behind portrait subjects, suggesting that photographers avoid shooting flash-lit portraits too close to walls.[2] [See also Chapter 16, "Magnesium Flash."]

As these technical errors proliferated with increasing access to flash photography, Kodak and many other guidebooks began recommending a new technique to solve the problem of harsh lighting and hard-edged shadows. "Bounce flash," as they dubbed it, required detaching the flash unit from the camera and angling it toward a nearby wall or ceiling. The reflected light was distributed more softly and evenly over the subject. Howard Luray wrote in a midcentury guidebook dedicated to artificial lighting,

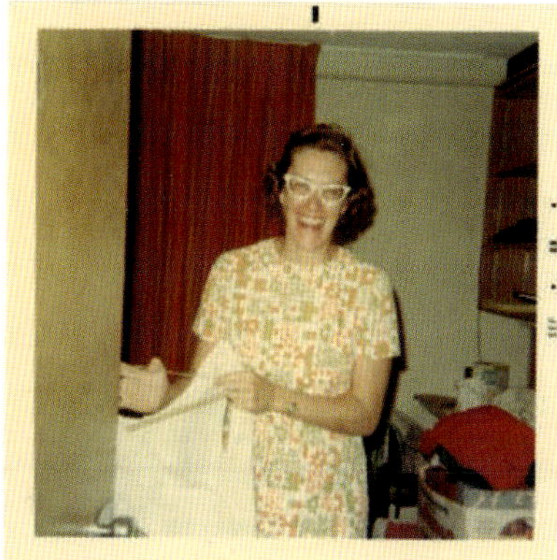

FIGURE 169. Photographer unknown, "A Gal in Glasses," 1968.
Source: Collection of Barbara Levine/ Project B.

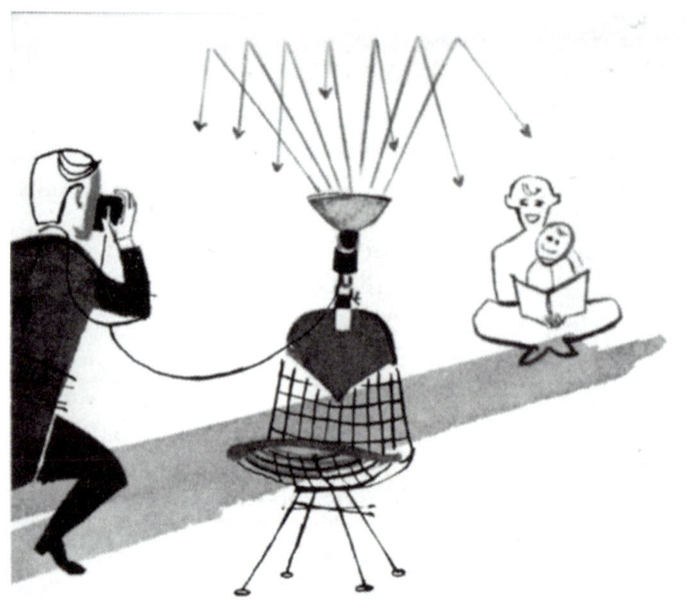

FIGURE 170. Eastman Kodak Co., *How to Make Good Pictures* (Rochester, NY: Eastman Kodak, 1957), 42.

Source: Author's collection.

"Bounce flash . . . has evolved from the fad stage to a useful, desirable technique."[3] He explained that the reflected light "eliminates that artificial look you get sometimes even from carefully used direct flash."[4] Despite this widespread celebration of the bounce-flash technique by how-to books, it was unachievable for users of the Starflash and other box-type cameras, since their flashes were built into the camera body and therefore impossible to detach. The characteristic overexposure and hard shadows of on-camera flash were thus firmly linked with amateur snapshots and point-and-shoot cameras, as advanced amateurs and professionals adopted the bounce-flash method made possible by their more sophisticated cameras.

On-camera flash reemerged as an aesthetic choice in the early 1990s, pioneered by the German photographer Juergen Teller. Searching for a style that could combat the highly produced and heavily retouched fashion photography of the 1980s, Teller embraced the effects of on-camera flash.[5] In widely published photographic campaigns for the fashion houses of Marc Jacobs and Céline, Teller photographed models with a small Contax camera with built-in flash. The powerful flash at close range washed out the models' faces and cast deep black shadows onto white backdrops. With their centered subjects and subtly tilted frames, Teller's pictures were reminiscent of snapshots taken at late-night parties. They suggested an insider's view of celebrity culture, which had been kept at a carefully produced remove since the rise of the Hollywood star system in the 1920s. [See also Chapter 28, "Hollywood Glamour."] While on-camera flash seemed "artificial" to writers in the 1950s,[6] its meaning was radically inverted when it returned in the 1990s as a guarantor of authenticity.

As Teller revealed in an interview, the aesthetic was also a response to the increasing vanity of contemporary culture. He said, "It's getting harder to take portraits because people are taking selfies, which they can retouch themselves."[7] The overexposure of Teller's flash-lit portraits washes out detail and reduces the need for retouching, while using the mark of the amateur to signify the picture's guilelessness. [See also Chapter 12, "Retouching Cabinet Cards."] In the United States, the photographer Terry Richardson (now banned from working with many publications due to sexual misconduct[8]) also adopted this aesthetic, challenging expectations for professional photographic work by showing up to assignments with just one point-and-shoot camera.[9]

Critical responses to the resurgence of the on-camera flash aesthetic were divided in the 2000s, though. The bounce-flash technique was gospel for nearly half a century, a crucial marker that distinguished professional practice from amateur snapping. Many commenters on popular photographic forums found it difficult to consider "bad" technique as an intentional aesthetic. One wrote disparagingly of Teller and Richardson, "I refer to this style of shooting as the 'look mom, they let me into the afterparty' pics."[10] Like earlier trends, which were transformed from failures into deliberate effects, on-camera flash defied the rules of good photography. [See also Chapter 4, "Crayons and Vignettes" and Chapter 31, "Motion Blur."]

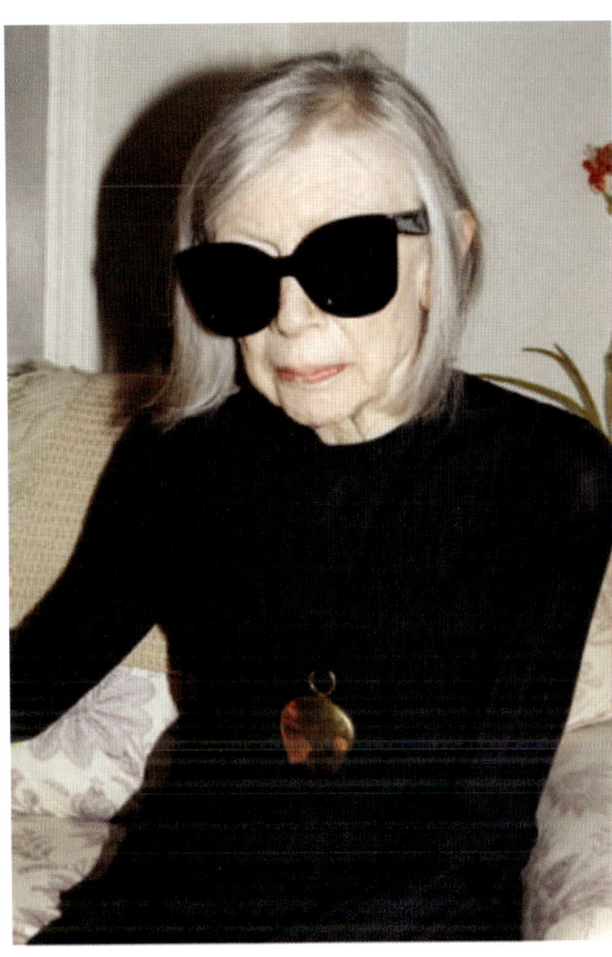

FIGURE 171. Joan Didion, Celine Campaign Spring Summer 2015, New York, 2014.

Source: © Juergen Teller, All rights reserved.

44

SQUARES

PHOTOGRAPHS WERE NEVER MEANT to be square. Although 120, or medium-format, film was used by the earliest Kodak Brownies and revived by the Rolleiflex camera in 1929, their 2 ¼″ square negatives were not intended to be the finished picture size. Rollei advised photographers, "Picture shapes are, of course, a matter of taste, but with the Rollei you shoot first and decide afterwards on the shape. It is easy enough to trim off part of the print (or enlarge only part of the negative) for horizontal or vertical formats, or just leave it as it is. But it need cause no worry when taking pictures."[1] [See also Chapter 35, Full-Frame Prints."]

This format agnosticism was partially a solution to the awkward shape of the Rolleiflex twin-lens reflex camera. The camera's ground glass focusing screen was mounted on top of its two vertically stacked lens boxes, which made it nearly impossible to rotate the camera for landscape perspective and see the focusing screen at the same time. Rollei's adoption of the square format turned this limitation into a distinctive feature.

While even the manufacturer admitted that the Rolleiflex was "a little bulky,"[2] it was still less cumbersome than the large-format 4″× 5″ Graflex camera, which had long been the choice among press photographers requiring a negative larger than 35 millimeters. Rolleiflex soon became popular with commercial photographers. Andreas Feininger, a one-time *Life* photographer, described the camera's impact in the 1930s and 1940s: "After using the Rolleiflex for a while most of *Life*'s photographers more or less stopped composing their pictures on the horizontal or vertical. Instead, they subconsciously arranged their subjects to fit the

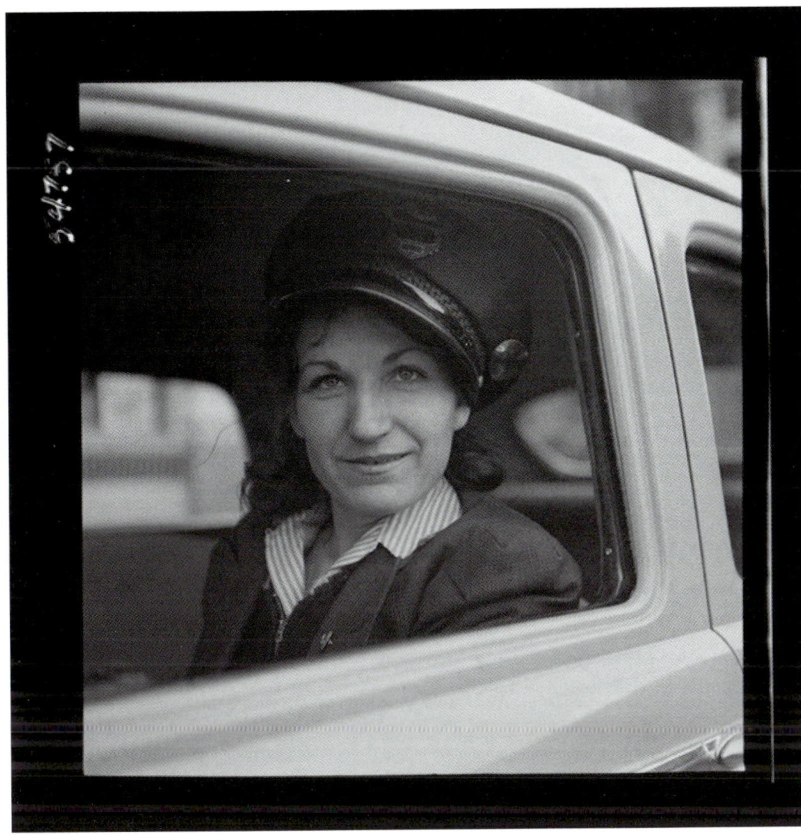

square, to the consternation of the editors who couldn't make effective use of these squares in their layouts."[3] Despite Rollei's expectation that photographers would want to crop to the more conventional rectangular format, the square proved difficult to resist.

As Feininger notes, however, squares rarely appeared in print, since the magazines were organized around the vertical format of their two facing pages. Later, the use of 120 film with an even wider horizontal frame was introduced by the Japanese company Mamiya, which dubbed their 6 × 7 centimeter size (or roughly 2 ⅓" × 2 ¾") the "ideal format." This scale came closer to filling a double-page spread, so the pictures could either be laid out vertically, or horizontally across the magazine's gutter. Seldom featured in print publications during this time, squares were limited to artistic practice through the 1950s. Richard Avedon's early Rolleiflex

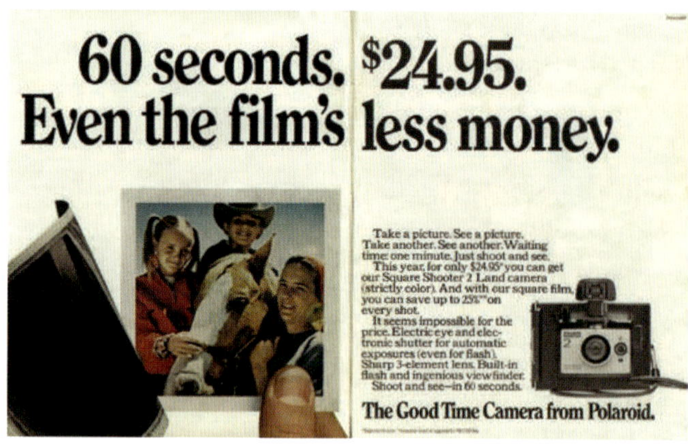

FIGURE 173. Classic Film, Flickr, "60 Seconds. $24.95. Even the Film's Less Money." Polaroid Square Shooter 2 Land Camera, 1972.

pictures from the 1950s were cropped for publication in *Harper's Bazaar*, but he included full-frame square prints in his 1962 exhibition at the Smithsonian. The square format was also linked with Hasselblad, the Swedish company, whose 120 roll film cameras attracted attention from professional photographers in the United States in the 1950s. As rock music grew in popularity, photographers such as Jini Dellaccio began using a Hasselblad to compose in camera for the square format record covers.[4]

The square was revived among amateur photographers in the early 1970s when Polaroid released the Square Shooter camera. Square-format Polaroids were advertised as a cost-saving option. The company pointed out, "The money you save on 8 [pictures] almost pays for 2 more. You save up to 25 percent with this film just because our new square pictures are a little smaller than our regular ones."[5] The square format had developed a split personality; they were either cheap Polaroids or high art.

Not until the 1980s, however, did the square surface regularly in mainstream publications. When squares were published, they were often printed full frame, including the black edges of the unexposed film, to reinforce the intentionality of the format. [See also Chapter 35, "Full-Frame Prints."] Some instructional authors remained adamantly opposed to the square, following the longstanding compositional credo: "Beware of the square!"[6] Michael Freeman argued in his 2007 guide that the square format "suffers from a lack of direction," meaning that without a "distinction between height and width," the eye cannot easily orient the view.[7] Advocates for the square, on the other hand, appreciated this equanimity; they preferred the square's balanced and symmetrical composition, which is difficult to achieve in other formats.

Instagram and an earlier smartphone photography app, Hipstamatic, both originally featured square format pictures. Instagram's cofounder, Kevin Systrom, has explained that his preference for the square was derived from his use of the Holga, a medium-format plastic camera

manufactured in China beginning in 1982. For Systrom, the poor quality of early iPhone pictures made the comparison to the Holga obvious.[8]
Holga cameras were notorious for light leaks and the distortions created
by their plastic lenses, aesthetic features that Instagram emphasized to
make up for the low resolution and limited dynamic range of the iPhone
3GS in late 2010. The square format was the only option on Instagram

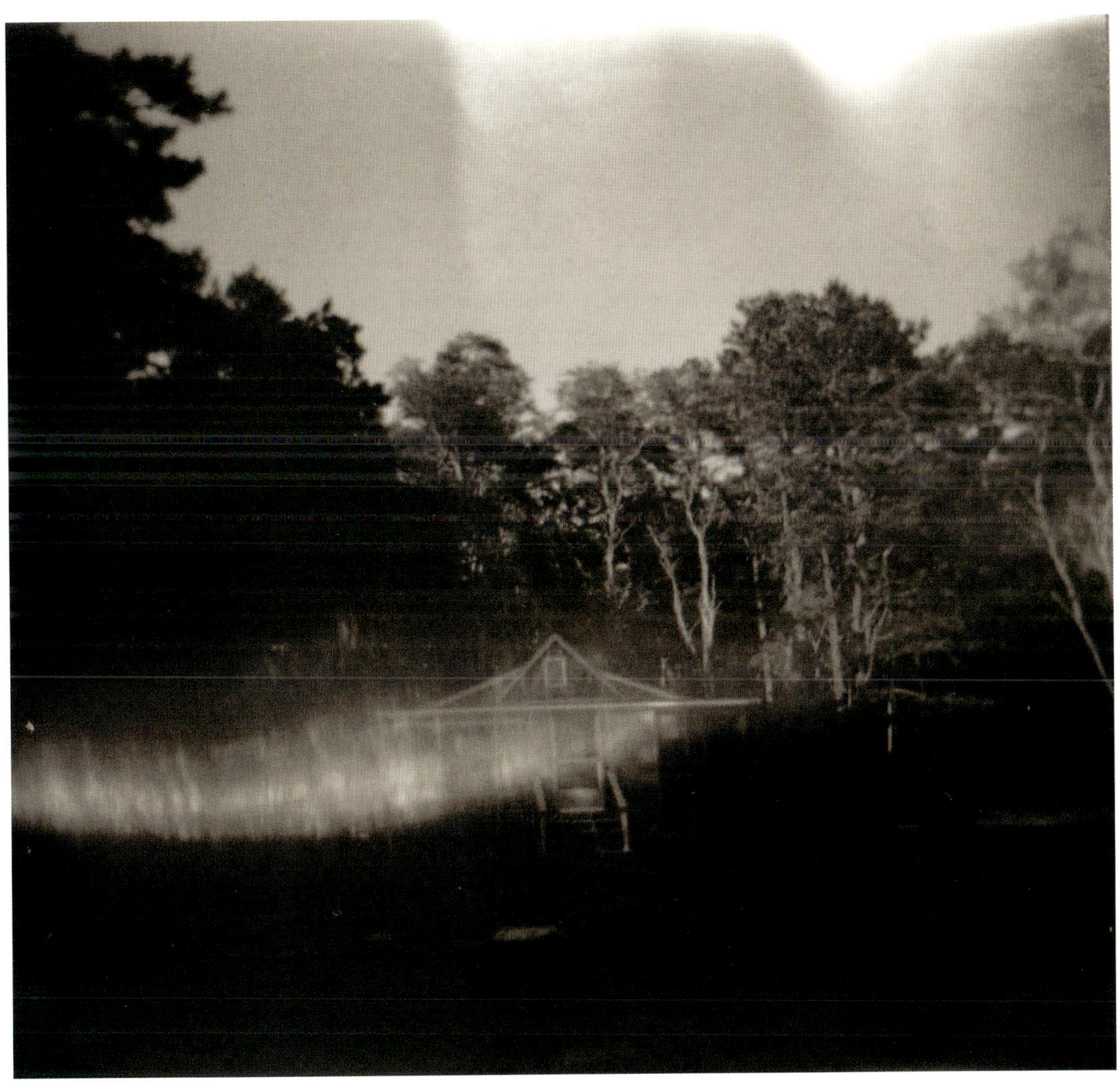

FIGURE 174. "Untitled," 2003.
Gelatin silver print (Holga),
3 ½" × 3 ½".

Source: Author's collection.

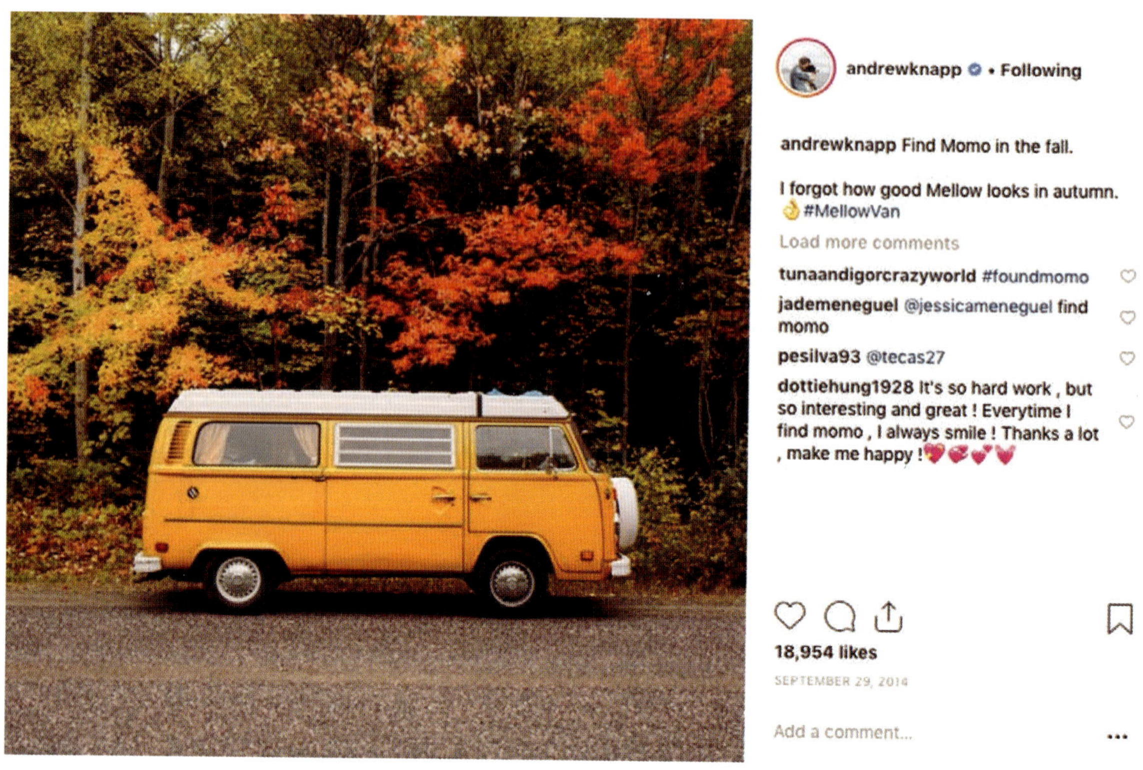

FIGURE 175. Andrew Knapp, "Find Momo in the Fall," 2014. Instagram.
Source: https://www.instagram.com/andrewknapp/. Courtesy of the artist.

until 2015, after which time the company began allowing other picture orientations. During those first few years, however, Instagram had acquired half a million active users, all of whom were quickly conditioned to the square format. The once-maligned square had become a dominant feature of millennial visual culture, carrying with it the contradictory associations of Rolleiflex and Hasselblad art photography, as well as cheap snapshots made with Polaroid's Square Shooter and the artfully flawed Holga. These cross-class associations revitalized the square; its bifurcated history lent an air of artistry to the pictures of daily life that pervaded social media in the early 2010s.

45

FOOD

IN 2008, the celebrity chef David Chang touched off a controversy by banning photography in his New York fine dining restaurant, Momofuku Ko. Inspired by the rise of foodie culture and the voracious appetite for pictures of food on social media, diners regularly toted cameras into the dining room. Some were discreet, but others spent precious minutes at the beginning of each course rearranging the table and setting off flashes to get the perfect shot. Chang, and other chefs who followed his lead, wanted diners to concentrate on eating the food.

Most unusual about this practice was that food, especially restaurant food, had rarely been a subject for amateur photographers prior to the advent of social media. In the nineteenth century, occasional still-life photographs featured food or after-the-hunt scenes, in emulation of the historical painting genres. If anything, though, these photographs were too realistic. Hanging game was difficult to idealize in a photograph, despite the genre's long popularity in trompe l'oeil painting. Set tables, including very early examples by Joseph Nicéphore Niépce and William Henry Fox Talbot, displayed empty plates or crystal rather than the bounty seen in the traditional still life paintings. [See also Chapter 27, "Modernistic Compositions."]

By the late nineteenth century, food was depicted incidentally in snapshots of picnics or special occasions. While elegant roasts and

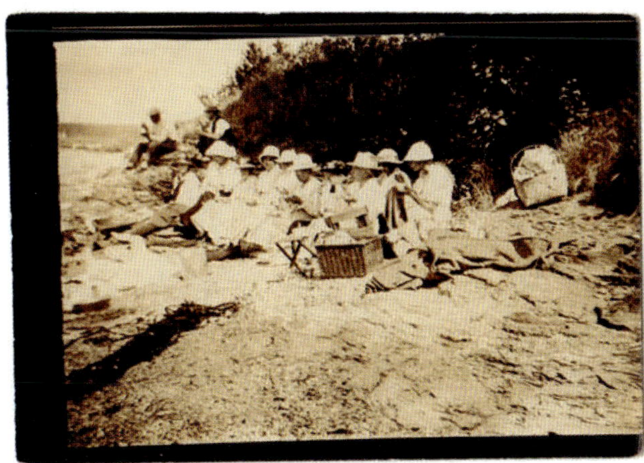

FIGURE 176. Photographer unknown, "Picnic," n.d. Albumen silver print.

Source: Author's collection.

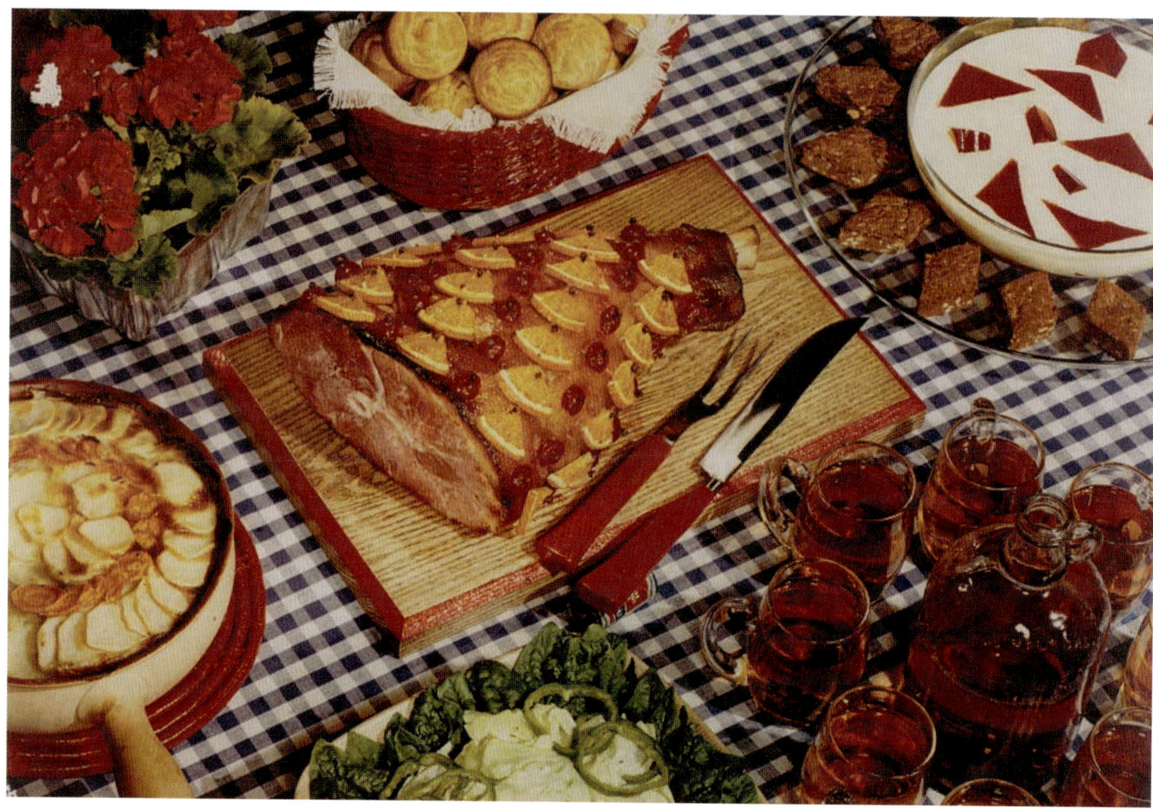

decorated cakes were sometimes recorded by amateurs, food was rarely the focus of this type of photograph. Recording the rituals of blowing out birthday candles or newlyweds cutting cake took precedence over picturing the food on the table. [See also Chapter 25, "Candids."] But with the development of social media in the early 2000s, everything from sushi to smoothies became suitable subjects.

In his 1937 handbook, Jacob Deschin allowed that the field of food photography "is not necessarily limited to the commercial photographer."[1] He offered tips for amateurs on how best to light and arrange food for artistic pictures, but he concentrated on photographs that made individual ingredients into still-life subjects rather than pictures that documented a fully prepared meal. Deschin recommended strong, angular lighting to reveal the surface textures of fruits and vegetables, recalling modernist photographs such as Edward Weston's peppers and cabbages. Commercial photographs of the time, however, featured scenes of plenty. Brightly colored foods set off by bold linens and colorful kitchenware were recorded on color film and reproduced in magazine advertising and cookbooks through midcentury.

By the 1970s, the decorators' palette was more subdued, and a preference for soft, warm lighting and differential focus was established. In the booming 1980s and early 1990s, camera angles sank low, and photographers moved in close to create tightly cropped compositions for exaggerated scale, while using soft-focus filters to "hide unseemly detail."[2] Tabletops were crowded with decorative plates and glassware, as well as flower arrangements and fresh ingredients artfully scattered around the finished food.

With the release of the first iPhone in 2007 and other small, highly light-sensitive digital cameras, a new perspective became popular. The overhead angle was quickly canonized in food photography of the 2000s. With a live LCD screen instead of a viewfinder, diners could easily position a small camera or smartphone over their plated food, autofocus, and perfect the framing later. The square format of Instagram, released in 2010, neatly contained a circular plate or latte cup. This format further reinforced the overhead shot and the arrangement that product photographers call a "flat lay." (See Figure 179.) The warm, incandescent light of 1980s food photography was replaced by the neutral and cool tones prevalent in the new millennium's restaurant design. As one guide for aspiring food photographers asked rhetorically, "You know that the very best light is natural, right?"[3]

In a best-selling book on Instagram photography, Henry Carroll began by describing, facetiously, the steps to fame on social media: "Step 1: Go to a café. Step 2: Order a salad. Better still order a salad with Kale. Step 3: Stand on your chair, take a picture and boom! You and your #kalesalad will have yourselves a million followers."[4] Carroll's aim was to

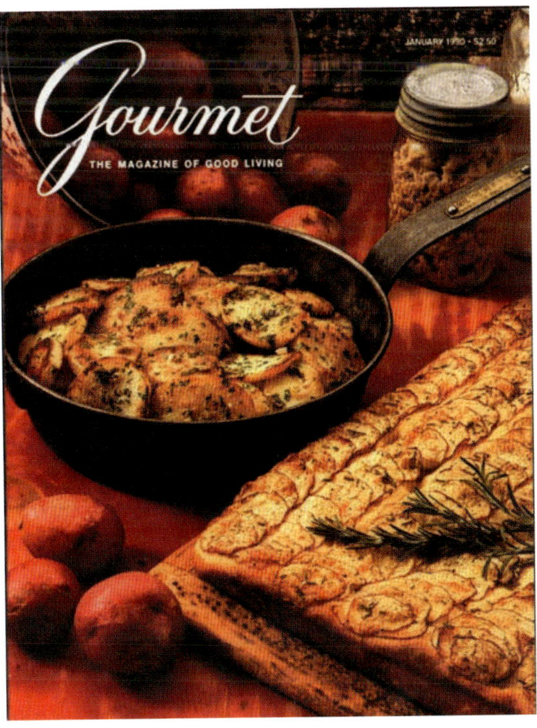

FIGURE 178. Romulo Yanes, cover of *Gourmet*, January 1990.
Source: © Condé Nast.

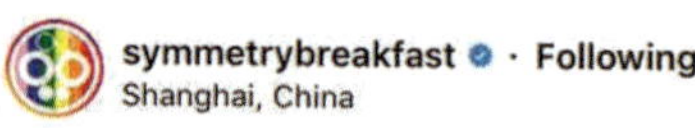

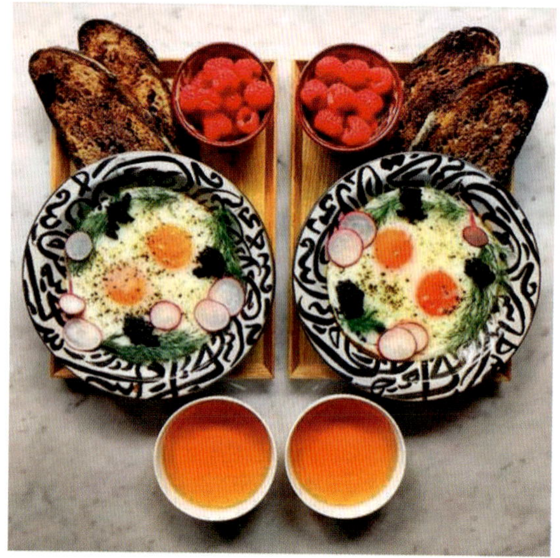

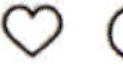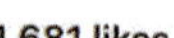

FIGURE 179. Michael Zee, "Symmetry Breakfast, Saturday: Baked eggs in crème fresh . . .," May 18, 2018. Instagram.

Source: Courtesy of the artist. https://www.instagram.com/symmetrybreakfast/.

debunk this mythical path to celebrity, but his example also underscores Instagram's impact on the stylistic elements of contemporary photography. The practice of tagging images with descriptions of their content (and sometimes even their photographic style, such as #flatlay or #nofilter) makes these trends readily identifiable and searchable. "Likes" reinforce their visibility, as do the curatorial preferences of Instagram's editors, who promote individual user accounts and hashtags. As a result, Instagram exhibits a house style, albeit one created by millions of users around the world. Popular social media photographs visually instruct their viewers in the elements of good pictures, sparking trends for what to photograph, as well as how.

46

SELFIE

LIKE ANY OTHER GENRE OF PHOTOGRAPHY, from still life to landscape, this form of self-portraiture carries with it a host of stylistic expectations. The definition of *selfie*, named the word of the year in 2013 by *Oxford Dictionaries*, emphasizes that it is not just any self-portrait, but "one taken with a smartphone or webcam and shared via social media."[1] This mode of picture taking and distribution became a touchstone for critiques of millennials, the first digital-native generation, whose production of selfies far outpaced that of any other age group.[2] A 2013 *Time* magazine cover story, titled "The Me Me Me Generation," not only addressed these charges of narcissism, but the cover image also illustrated the strict adherence to new pictorial conventions associated with the selfie, especially the high angle of view. In the photograph, a teenager holds her phone above her head, staring up into it with a coy grin.[3] The pose reads immediately as a selfie.

In the pre-selfie era of the early 2000s, the high-angle shot was considered misleading, especially for use as a profile picture on the then-new social networking sites, such as MySpace. In effect, it was too good a picture. *UrbanDictionary* called it disparagingly the "MySpace Angle," arguing that it was used deceitfully to improve one's looks.[4] But by 2010, the online dating website OKCupid ranked more than seven thousand user photos

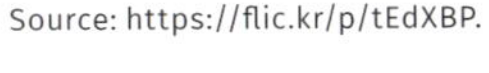

FIGURE 180. Benjamin Linh Vu, "Selfie," May 13, 2015. Flickr. CC BY-SA 2.0. https://creativecommons.org/licenses/by-sa/2.0/.

Source: https://flic.kr/p/tEdXBP.

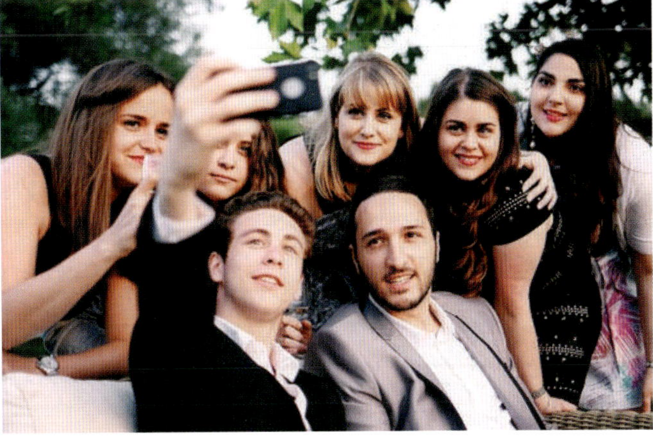

according to pose and number of messages they garnered from potential dates. Overwhelmingly, the pictures that received the most attention were photographed from high angles. OKCupid even removed cleavage-baring shots from the sample and still found that users who posted high-angle selfies received 50 percent more new monthly contacts than those who posted the second most popular pose: pictures taken in bed.[5] Contemporary viewers perhaps expect people to look better in pictures than they do in real life.

By 2013, the high-angle portrait was essentially mandatory across all social media platforms, as the use of the pose on the *Time* cover corroborates. Countless articles advised against the "up-the-nose" view or low-angle shot; most argued that this was a universal truth of photography.[6] One online how-to guide sniped, "There are about five people in the world who look good when shot from under their chin, and we haven't met any of them."[7] Social media star and author of the ultimate selfie look-book, *Selfish*, Kim Kardashian explained, "Always take your selfie from above, angling down. I think there's nothing worse than when someone wants to take a selfie and they take it from the angle down below, you know, and get some double chin action."[8] Like most universals, this too turns out to be culturally and historically specific, no matter how ubiquitous the pose was on social media in the 2010s. As recently as the 1940s, these low-angle shots were considered preferable, for the feeling of commanding presence they bestowed upon their subjects. [See also Chapter 29, "Distracting Color."]

Selfie-makers have access to a wealth of comparative material. Whereas earlier trends were sometimes inspired by professional work in the advertising, journalism, or fine art contexts, selfie photographers are inundated daily with examples made by people they know. No longer do these amateurs have to wait for a vacation slide show or a local contest to judge their work against that of their peers. As such, the technique of the

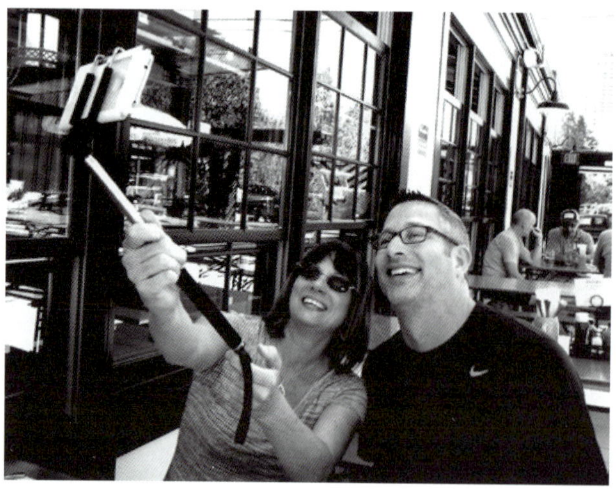

FIGURE 181. Travis Wise, "Selfie Stick," August 9, 2014. Flickr. CC BY 2.0.

Source: https://flic.kr/p/qu7K8J.

selfie is self-regulated and controlled by example or through "likes," as well as the visible practice of photographers on the street.

The tenor of how-to guides in the 2010s made the selfie appear to be one of the most difficult-to-master forms of contemporary photography. Celebrity magazines regularly checked in with social media stars for their latest tips on selfies, from microtrends in posing to advice about new filters and postprocessing apps. The popularization of selfie sticks (telescoping poles equipped with a mount for the camera and a Bluetooth trigger for its shutter), then the addition of user-facing smartphone cameras soon made the selfie project less marked by chance and more responsive to previsualization. "Duckface," a sexy-pouty face intended to enhance the lips and cheekbones, reached critical mass in 2009, then spurred a series of satirical selfie trends, including placing Pringles potato chips between the lips like a duckbill, and an anti-duckface website. Later, the invisible trend of putting the tongue to the roof of one's mouth, also in an effort to lengthen the face and make cheekbones more prominent, swept through online advice columns. [See also Chapter 28, "Hollywood Glamour."]

Trends in the location of selfies have also resulted in stylistic changes. Bathroom mirror self-portraits were considered in poor taste through the 1990s and early 2000s, associated with the preening bachelor on early online dating sites, but the bathroom or bedroom as studio experienced a resurgence of popularity on social media in the second half of the 2010s. These full-length shots don't hide the surroundings or the camera; in fact, the phone often covers the face, as many guides allow.[9] One popular style blogger described the appropriate posture:

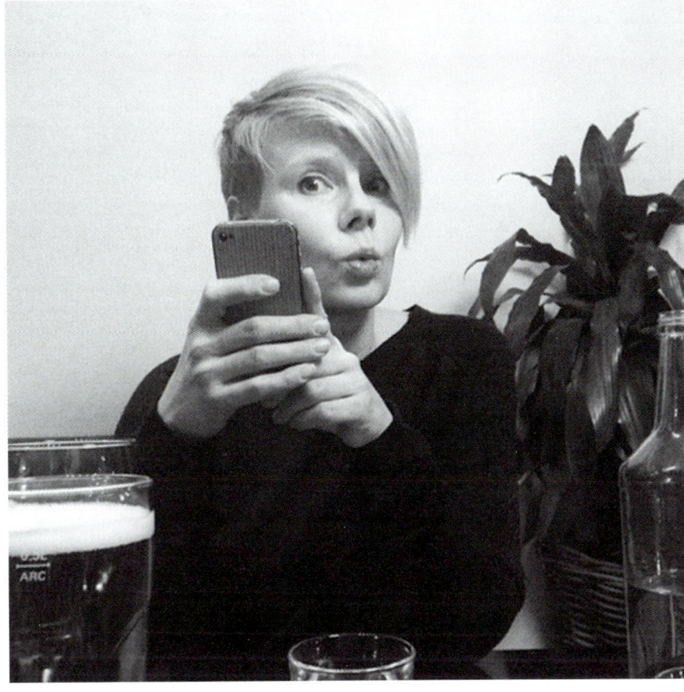

FIGURE 182. Sami Niemelä, "*duckfaces*," October 25, 2013. Flickr. CC BY 2.0. https://creativecommons.org/licenses/by/2.0/.

Source: https://flic.kr/p/gY25ro.

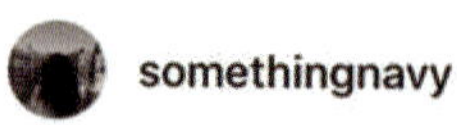

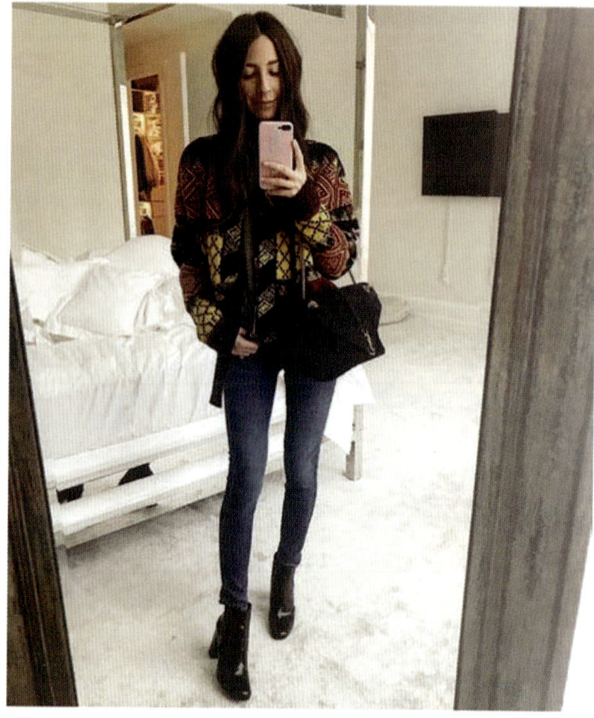

FIGURE 183. Somethingnavy, "Today's outfit. Cozy *retro* jacket sweater wrap thing that I just got and love and my Saint Laurent boots from two years ago." Instagram. November 14, 2017.

Source: Courtesy of the artist. https://instagram.com/p/BbexTyyn9IK/.

"To appear slender . . . cock your hip—on the side where you're holding the camera—and jut the other shoulder forward. Your free arm can dangle against your body—unless you are wearing a sleeveless shirt, in which case the hand should be placed on the hip."[10] This contrapposto stance was later replaced by the advice to "pop a knee" to accentuate curves[11] or to stand with one leg forward: "It'll lengthen your body while giving friends and followers a good look at your outfit. Don't forget to point that toe!"[12]

The brisk turnover in selfie trends can be attributed to the speed at which viewers access, imitate, and finally become overwhelmed by the omnipresence of similar imagery. Although the precipitous rate of change makes the rise and fall of contemporary trends easier to see, this does not suggest that previous trends were any less polarizing or less nuanced in their developments. Selfies are an instructive category because they compress the timescale of these changes, making it possible to recognize that such subtle stylistic differences—whether to "pop a knee" or "cock a hip"—must also exist in earlier portraits, despite their appearance of homogeneity for later viewers.

47

DESATURATED

IN THE SECOND DECADE of the new millennium, photographers embraced a style that looked both new and old. Photographs using a desaturated, high-contrast palette were pervasive on the emerging photo-sharing apps, as well as in high-fashion, advertising, and editorial work. Even across these varied genres, the style took on a stable, if paradoxical, meaning. The cool, restricted palette pointed toward a specific past, emulating the pastel colors of Agfacolor film stock manufactured in East Germany and used widely in Communist bloc countries in the mid-twentieth century. But the heightened contrast and sharpness of the desaturated look also signified advanced digital technologies. The style was described as moody, cinematic, gritty, and urban by online instructional guides. The application of high-contrast, high-resolution filters to the muted palette suggested a dystopian future or a faded, impoverished past, and sometimes both.

Partial desaturation was originally a technique accomplished in Photoshop by selecting an image area in which to preserve color, then desaturating its surroundings. Alternatively, Photoshop users could control hue, color balance, and saturation on individual adjustment layers, making it easy to shift particular colors throughout the image while leaving others vibrant and intact. In the early 2000s, these procedures were used to create effects that emulated the hand-painted photographs of the nineteenth century. Rendering most of the

FIGURE 184. Mike Beales, "Green Pencil," 2016. Flickr. CC BY-ND 2.0. https://creativecommons.org/licenses/by-nd/2.0/.

Source: Flickr.

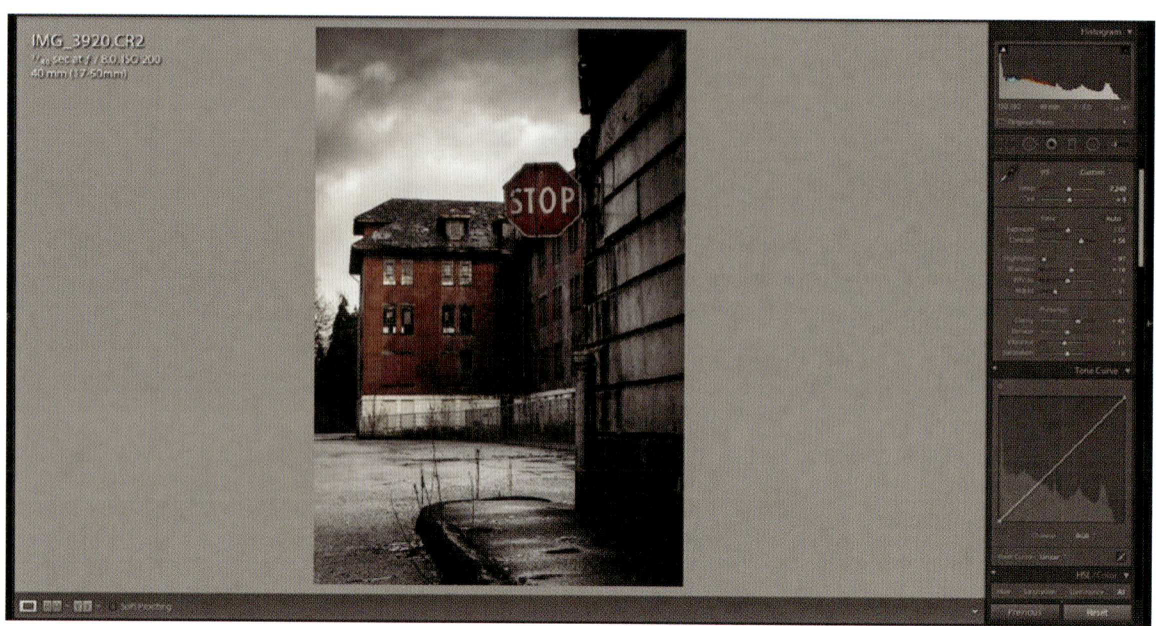

FIGURE 185. Joep Olthuis, "Riverview Ghost Hospital," 2016. Screenshot.

Source: Courtesy of the artist and www.supandshoot.com.

picture black and white, photographers could also selectively paint color back into the image by partially erasing the adjustment layers. [See also Chapter 3, "Hand Painting."]

Serge Ramelli, a photographer whose tutorials on YouTube attracted hundreds of thousands of views, posted an instructional video in 2015, noting, "A fellow photographer sent me an email telling me about a cool look that is very popular these days which is a very contrasty desaturated style."[1] Another popular YouTube tutorial by Joep Olthuis used a photograph of a decrepit alleyway, tuning down the saturation of the green, aqua, blue, and magenta channels to remove color from the sky, foliage, and crumbling macadam of the street, while isolating the red of a brick building and a stop sign.[2] He called it the "Desaturated High Contrast Grunge Look." The photography blog PetaPixel referred to the style as the "desaturated urban look," explaining that it "is incredibly popular these days, especially among rooftoppers and other city photographers who want to give their images a moody, gritty feel."[3] Like most other trends, however, PetaPixel noted, "Before we dive any deeper, it's worth noting that, for every photographer who have [sic] made a name for themselves using this 'look,' there is an equally angry photographer who thinks said look is tacky."[4] The style had already reached critical mass in

2014 when lightly desaturated presets dominated the photography app VSCO, even as the app's more extreme desaturated presets ranked least popular.[5] The trend had worn itself out.

Before lighting color and temperature could be easily manipulated in Photoshop, these techniques were crafted in-camera or in the darkroom with analog printing techniques. [See also Chapter 40, "Golden Hour" and Chapter 50, "Digital Filters."] The cinematic style in fashion photography is largely attributed to British photographer Glen Luchford's move away from the traditional studio setup, especially his acclaimed campaign for Prada's 1997 winter line. Photographing on location in Rome with a large crew of assistants, Luchford controlled the entire scene, shutting down the Tiber River and adding fog effects by burning hay bales on its banks. The mix of natural and artificial light throughout the scene is inspired by cinematography, where prodigious lighting is necessary

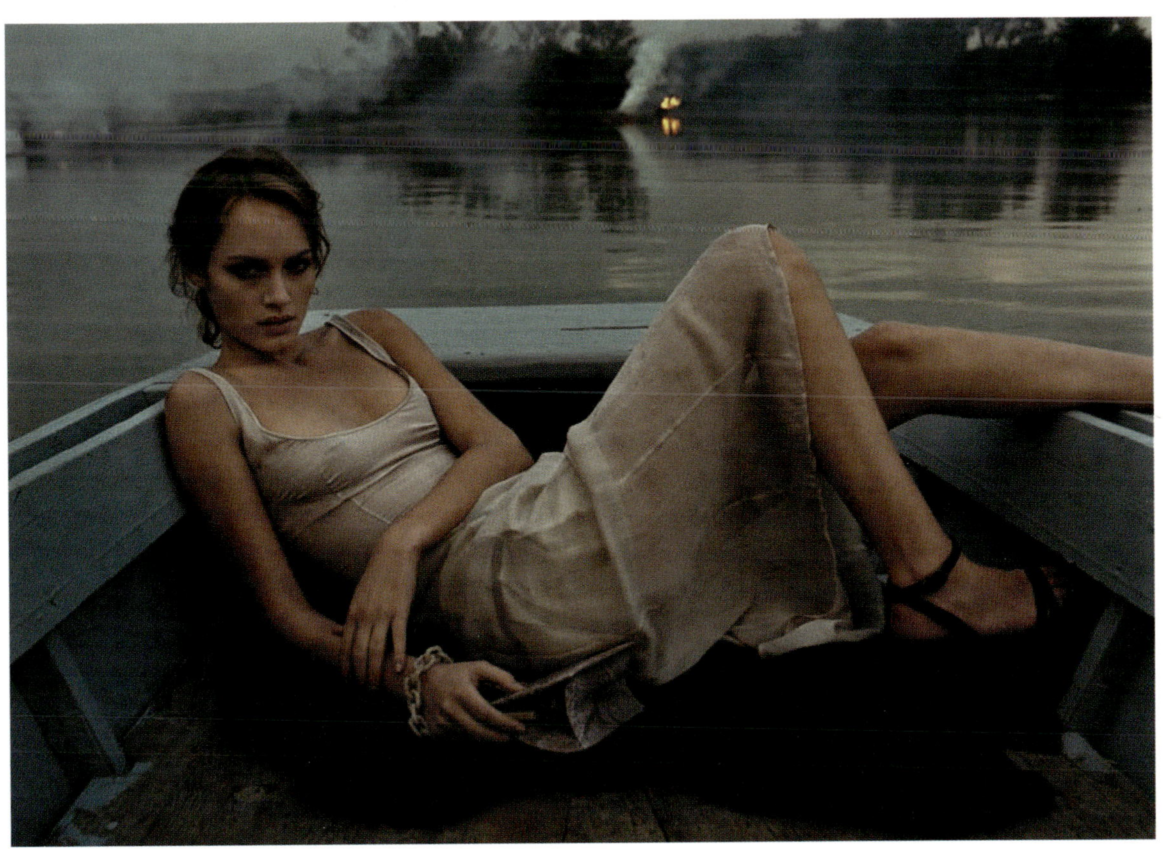

FIGURE 186. Glen Luchford, "Amber Valletta, Prada," 1997.

Source: Courtesy Glen Luchford/Art Partner.

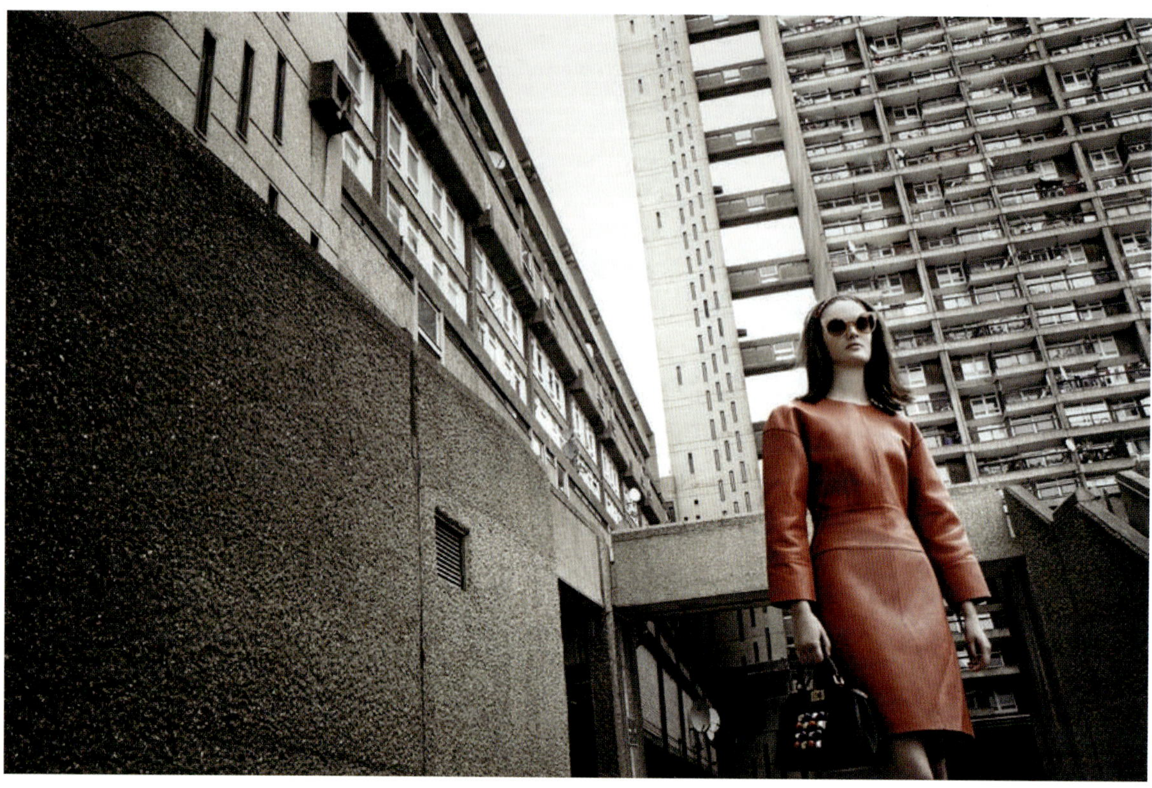

FIGURE 187. Tom Munro, "Sam Rollinson, *Vogue Italia*," 2015.
Source: Courtesy of the artist.

to draw out distinctions between foreground and background spaces, while anticipating characters' movements through the scene. Studio photography, in contrast, had traditionally relied on a simple three-point lighting system: a dominant key light, a smaller fill light to reduce deep shadows, and a third light to create separation from the backdrop. Luchford eschewed this simple setup and instead crafted dramatic scenes that looked like stills from motion pictures because they borrowed cinema's unique lighting style and elaborate locations.

At the turn of the millennium, editorial photography increasingly took on varieties of the cinematic look. Celebrity photographers including Annie Leibovitz and Tom Munro, produced desaturated, cool-toned imagery. Leibovitz's 2008 portrait of Clint Eastwood behind the wheel of a pickup truck is so dark and desaturated as to appear almost monochrome. The actor's leather jacket blends with the truck's bench seat, while the gray of the steering column and the truck's metal roof are subtly radiant. Munro's portraits are similarly subdued. Featuring women wearing vintage-style garments, often in historic locations, they summon a distinctly antique air. With nearly flat lighting, Munro washes out detail and color, leaving pale, white skin and deep black shadows. The palette and the props are reminiscent of Cold War–era film from the Eastern bloc.

A vogue for this era and these locations was also popular in film and television, kicked off by the FX spy series *The Americans* (2013) set in the 1980s. *The Americans* alternated between a normal color film palette for scenes depicting the United States and a desaturated palette when representing the Soviet Union. Later, *The Man in the High Castle* (2015), a Netflix series, also drew explicitly on the cultural associations of the desaturated palette, using it for an alternative history scenario that imagines the world divided between Nazi Germany and Hirohito's Japan after World War II. As suggested by its popular moniker, "cinematic," the desaturated style in still photography was closely linked with motion pictures.

The long lists of adjectives that often accompanied descriptions of the desaturated look in the 2010s point to the challenges of reflecting critically on a current, widespread trend. Like early twentieth-century assertions of photography's supposedly intrinsic properties (detail, contrast, and tonality), photographic styles are deliberately crafted and can be made to signify many things. [See also Chapter 22, "Straight Photography."] The desaturated aesthetic may have been read as gritty and urban or cool and moody, but these interpretations are no more a natural product of the medium than the ability to render fine detail or subtle gradations in tonality. During the development and dissemination of trends, meaning is made concrete by the words that accompany how-to articles.

48

RUIN PORN

FIGURE 188. William Henry Fox Talbot, "The Tomb of Sir Walter Scott, in Dryburgh Abbey," 1844. Salted paper print from paper negative, 6 ⅝″ × 7 ¹⁄₁₆″.

Source: Metropolitan Museum of Art, The Rubel Collection, Purchase, Lila Acheson Wallace and Jennifer and Joseph Duke

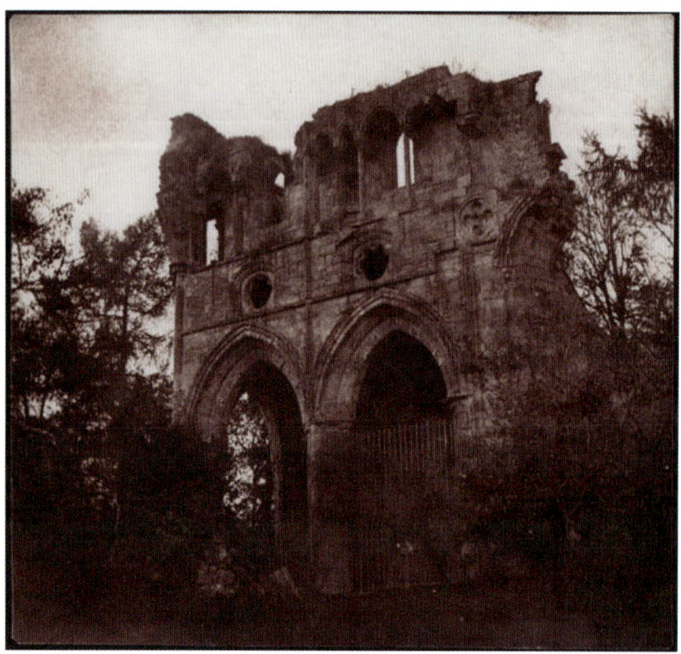

THE SECOND ENTRY in the *Oxford English Dictionary* related to *porn*, the shortened form of *pornography*, defines the word's figurative use. As an element in a compound word or phrase, "-porn" has described "written or visual material that emphasizes the sensuous or sensational aspects of a non-sexual subject, appealing to its audience in a manner likened to the titillating effect of pornography."[1] Since the 1980s, the most pervasive use of this word ending has referred to pictures of food,[2] but it was also employed to name a photographic trend in the 2000s: ruin porn. The Detroit-based blogger, James Griffioen, is regularly cited as the public originator of this phrase. In a 2009 interview with *Vice* magazine, he blasted the influx of professional photographers who had descended on Detroit seeking pictures of decaying architecture illustrative of the recent financial collapse.[3] He dubbed the pictures "ruin porn."

These photographers borrowed from a centuries-long history of artistic interest in the ruin as a metaphor of civilization in decline. While the subject may have reached its apotheosis in the eighteenth-century British tradition of the picturesque, ruins were popular both before and after that period. In the seventeenth-century, Claude

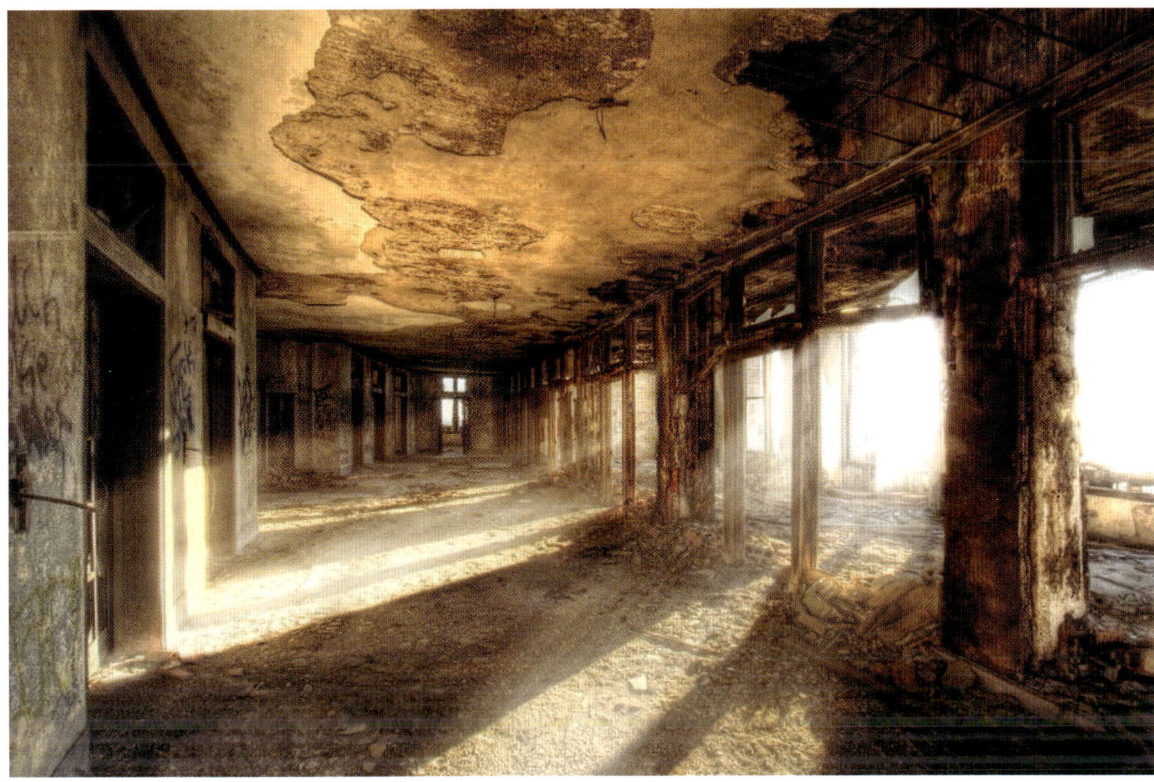

Lorrain and Nicolas Poussin included ruins from antiquity in their landscape paintings; scores of nineteenth-century photographers, including William Henry Fox Talbot and Roger Fenton, focused on Gothic ruins found in the United Kingdom. [See also Chapter 8, "Foreground Interest."]

Although similar content links these artistic productions across the centuries, several new aesthetic treatments emerged with the ruin porn fad of the early 2000s. One of the first American photographers to be recognized in the resurrection of the genre was Andrew Moore, whose book *Detroit Disassembled* was published in 2010 in conjunction with an exhibition at the Akron Art Museum.[4] Moore's large-format color photographs identified key subjects of ruin porn, focusing on sites indicative of the former riches of the region, from factories to public buildings, such as Michigan Central Station, overcome by weather or vegetation. Many of these sites have since become meccas for amateur ruin porn photographers.

FIGURE 189. Shane Gorski, "New Rising Sun: Michigan Central Station," 2000. Flickr. CC BY-ND 2.0. https://creativecommons.org/licenses/by-nd/2.0/.

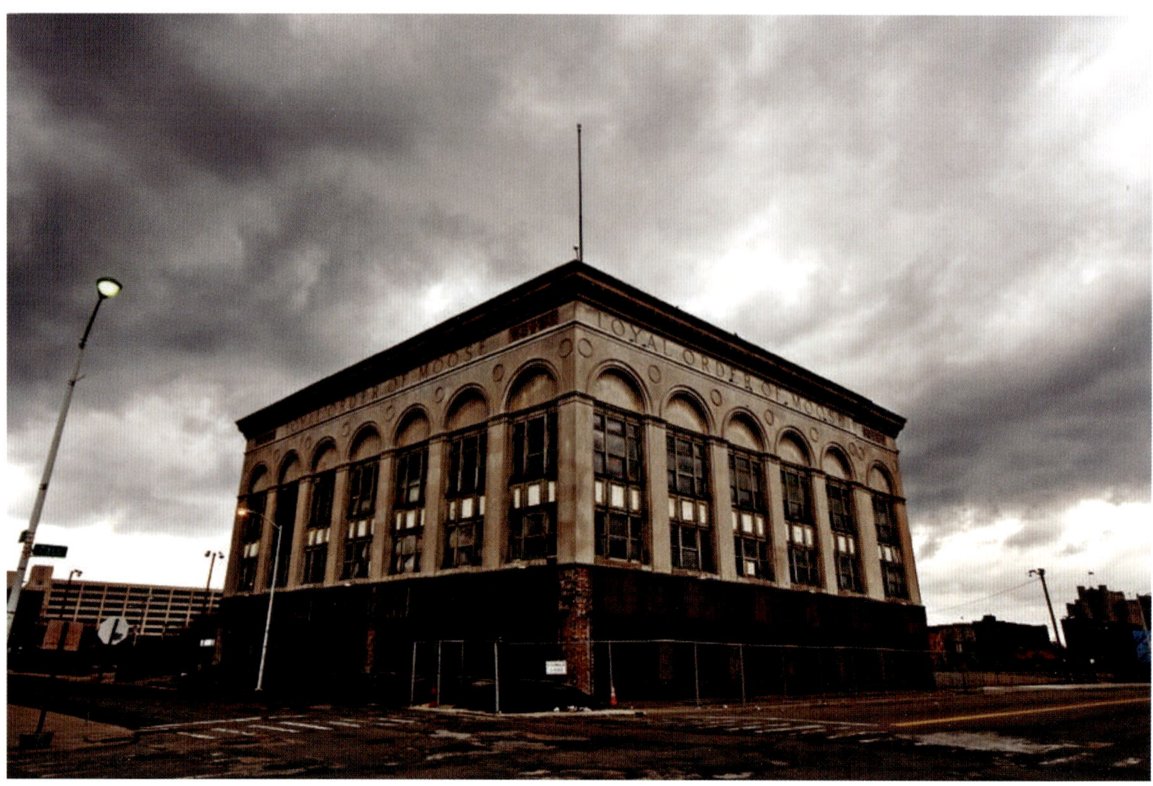

FIGURE 190. Rick Harris, "Downtown Detroit," 2010. Flickr. CC BY-SA 2.0. https://creativecommons.org/licenses/by-sa/2.0/.

Source: https://flic.kr/p/7Qzsut.

The trend coincided with the popularization of in-camera high-dynamic-range (HDR) software that expanded the allowable difference between dark and light areas in an image, which was useful for work in color. The iPhone camera operating system incorporated an HDR option in 2010 that digitally combined two different exposures of the same scene to improve dynamic range, making portable a procedure that had long been popular in Photoshop and in earlier darkroom practices. [See also Chapter 6, "Cloudy Skies."] HDR proved particularly useful to ruin porn photographers picturing crumbling interiors. While revealing the many shadowy corners of a dilapidated building, the image was also correctly exposed for light streaming through broken windows or holes in the ceiling. An entire subgenre of ruin porn pictures featured beams of light penetrating dusty, derelict interiors.

Ruin porn proliferated rapidly on social media. Style guides described how to achieve the aesthetic widely used by photographers such as Moore or Demond Meek, originator of the Instagram hashtag #slumbeautiful.[5] Meek started sharing pictures of St. Louis, his hometown, on Instagram in 2012. His account was widely hailed as an early Instagram success story: he attracted thirty thousand followers in his first year of the project. Working within the initial constraints of the app's square format, Meek's photographs were predominantly symmetrically composed shots of abandoned houses in St. Louis. Shot from street level with an iPhone, Meek also included generous green space around many former row houses to emphasize their isolation after nearby houses had been torn down. The series made liberal use of digital filters to heighten drama, adding dark vignetting at the corners and increasing contrast in highlights and shadows.[6] [See also Chapter 4, "Crayons and Vignettes."]

As the new aesthetic rocketed to popularity, it also attracted critics. Writing for *ArtNews* in 2013, Richard B. Woodward summarized the debates emerging over ruin porn, which echoed earlier discussions about photography's role in representing social crises of the twentieth century.[7] Detractors, including journalists and academics, argued that the pictures spectacularized decaying buildings with little thought given to the ongoing life of Rust Belt cities.[8] Ruin porn, critics maintained, was a titillating voyeurism, which did nothing to address the institutional causes of a city's decline or improve conditions. Like other modern debates over the social value of photography, many of these discussions focused on the aestheticization of the subject, particularly the use of filters and the genre's penchant for pictures devoid of human subjects. The style and content of these images were firmly linked, making the protest against ruin porn as much about the mode of representation as about the appropriateness of this style to depict its subject. [See also Chapter 11, "The Rembrandt Effect."]

49

DRONE PHOTOGRAPHY

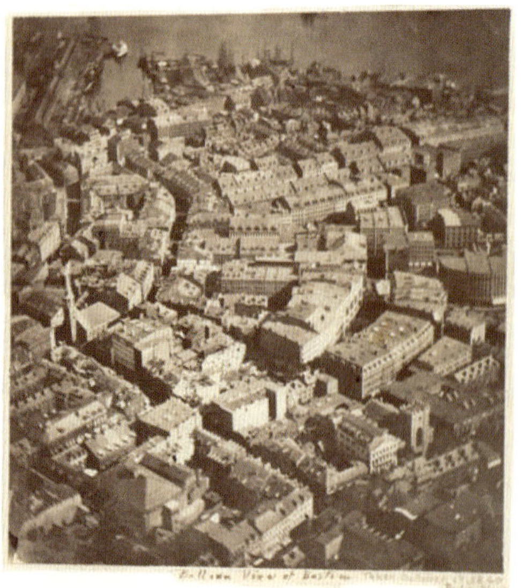

FIGURE 191. James Wallace Black, "Boston, as the Eagle and the Wild Goose See It," 1860. Albumen print, 7⁵/₁₆" × 6⁹/₁₆".

Source: Metropolitan Museum of Art, Gilman Collection, Purchase, Ann Tenenbaum and Thomas H. Lee Gift, 2005.

IN THE EARLY YEARS OF THE 2010s, the skies were teeming with a new flying machine: small remote-controlled helicopters, also called quadcopters or drones. While these consumer-grade drones were initially used by hobbyists just for the fun of flying, by spring 2015, the American company 3D Robotics had released a drone that paired with a camera to create professional-quality video from the air. Within a year, other sophisticated video-enabled drones were available on the consumer market. Just as quickly, the Federal Aviation Administration introduced a mandatory drone registry, and municipalities instituted bans on drones in the name of safety as well as privacy.[1] **[See also Chapter 25, "Candids."]** US national parks also restricted the use of drones, aiming to preserve the quiet of natural spaces and protect the wildlife within their borders.[2]

Despite the regulations, drones have continued to proliferate, making aerial photography more widely accessible than ever before. Although such pictures had been possible since the mid-nineteenth century, aerial photography was largely limited to professionals. In 1858, the French photographer Gaspard-Félix Tournachon, known as Nadar, pictured Paris from a hot-air balloon. Two years later, James Wallace Black made photographs from a balloon two thousand feet over Boston. Black's photographs took an oblique perspective, preserving the sense of three-dimensionality in the city's topography. Oliver Wendell Holmes wrote of the picture, "Boston,

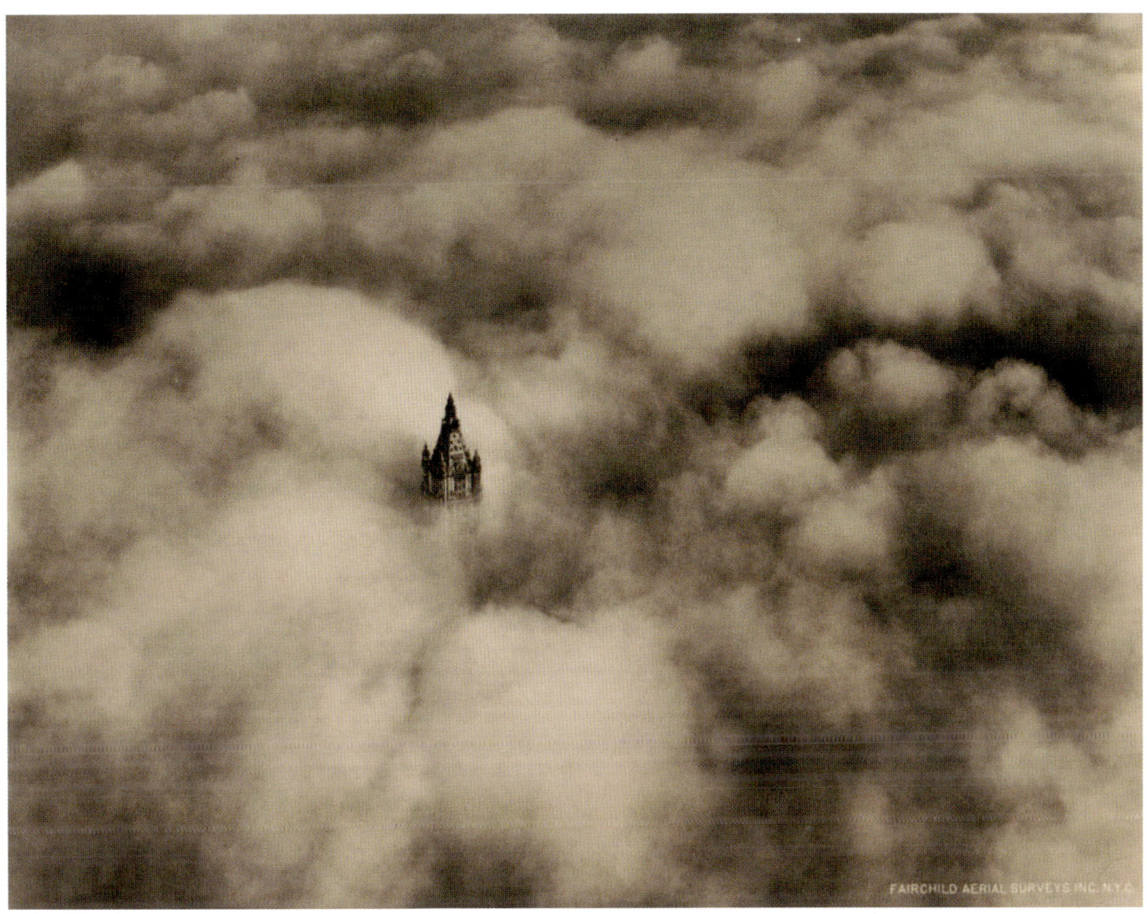

as the eagle and the wild goose see it, is a very different object from the same place as the solid citizen looks up at its eaves and chimneys."[3] Holmes's experience of wonder and disorientation would remain a recurrent trope in writing about aerial views, even as their numbers increased in the twentieth century.

Aerial photographs made from planes were widely used during World War I for reconnaissance. At the close of the war, Sherman Fairchild began producing specialized cameras for aerial photography, including models designed to capture oblique views or more cartographic images that positioned the camera directly over the ground, flattening out geographic and man-made features.[4] These two perspectival

FIGURE 192. Fairchild Aerial Surveys, Inc. "Woolworth Tower in Clouds, New York City," 1928. Gelatin silver print.

Source: Library of Congress Prints and Photographs Division.

260

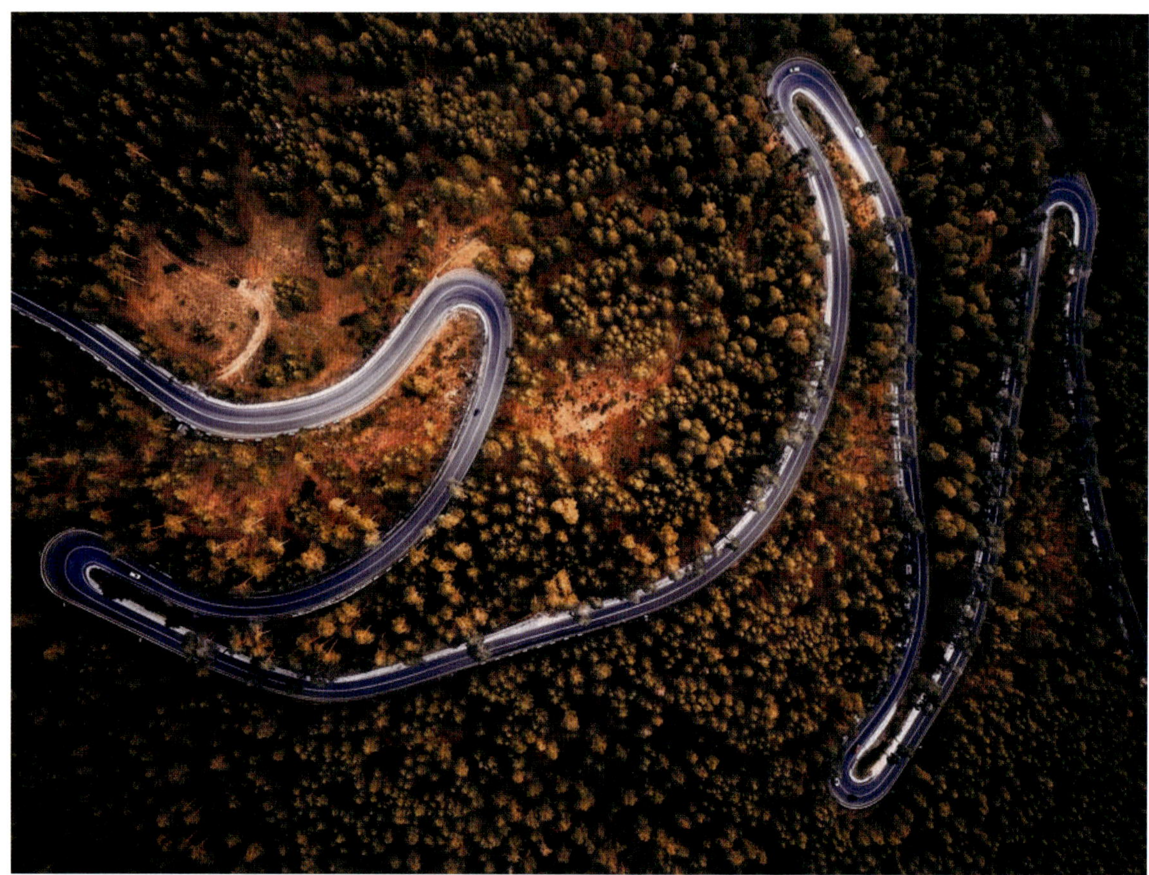

choices would dominate aerial images through the advent of the drone: the oblique view is used to emphasize a vast landscape, while the direct overhead view is more frequently applied to artful abstractions or cartographic renderings.

With the expansion of commercial air travel during the interwar years, aerial photography also grew in popularity. In June 1929, *Photo-Era Magazine* remarked on the number of aerial photographs appearing at exhibitions. The editor explained, "We believe that the increase in successful amateur pictures made from the air is due to the many new cabin planes, which afford protection to the amateur aerial photographer. During our introduction to aerial photography, we had to brave the rush of a hundred-and-twenty-mile [sic] wind, and this was not conducive to careful composition or exposure."[5] Aerial photographs of far-flung places, such as Charles and Anne Lindbergh's pictures of Chichén Itzá and Richard Byrd's of the South Pole, were all made in 1929 and reproduced in the *New York Times* and *National Geographic Magazine*, respectively.[6] The publication of these pictures likely inspired further interest in the amateur possibilities for photography from the air.

Leonard Williams, author of the guidebook *Illustrative Photography in Advertising*, linked air travel with new trends in composition also popularized in the late 1920s. He suggested that as more civilians took to the air, "things will look much different to us than they do at the present time."[7] Williams maintained that this new vantage point helped explain the "modernistic" composition, which "has not an eye level or horizon line as we have in other pictures most of the time."[8] For those as yet unable to venture into the skies, Williams recommended climbing up to the ceiling of a room and looking down at objects arranged on a table in order to hone this modern way of seeing. [See also Chapter 27, "Modernistic Compositions."] The absence of a horizon line would remain one of the most prominent recurring features of aerial photography into the twenty-first century in both oblique and direct overhead views. Instead, other lines proliferated in these abstract images. Shorelines, farmed fields, roads, and shadows created false horizons or dissected aerial views into patchwork abstractions.

These compositional moves had been standard in aerial photography since the 1930s, but they became increasingly visible on Instagram after 2015. @Insta_Repeat is an anonymous account that highlights the homogeneity of photographs popular on the social media platform. The curator of the series collages together a dozen or more examples of the most ubiquitous photographic styles, such as overhead drone shots of curvy roads in snowy conifer forests, to create a kaleidoscopic array of analogous pictures. Consumer drones made the production of these

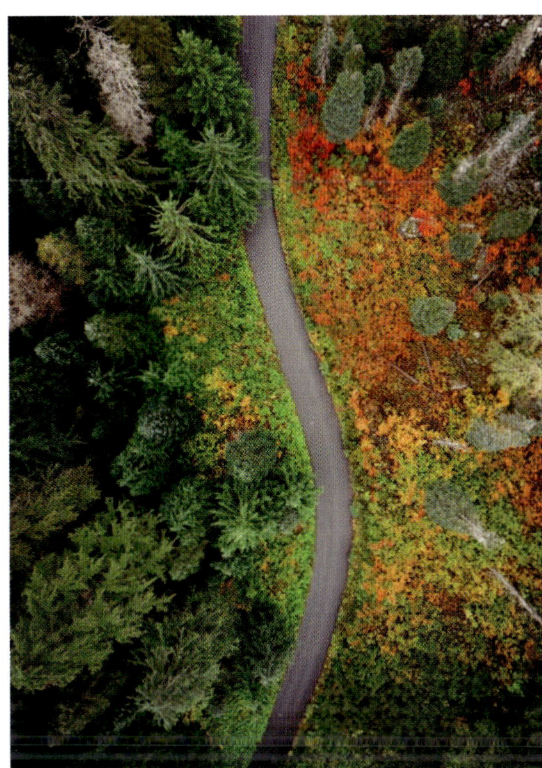

FIGURE 194. John Westrock, "Never Stop Changing," 2018. Digital photograph. Flickr. CC BY-NC 2.0. https://creativecommons.org /licenses/by-nc/2.0/.

Source: https://flic.kr/p/MCyDop.

images easy by offering a grid overlay on the camera's live feed interface, which divides the visual field into thirds. The camera retailer Adorama provided a series of tips for drone photography, recommending that operators "seek out symmetry, patterns, and lines" and always use the grid layout to ensure proper composition.[9] Despite their radical perspectives on the landscape, many drone images look remarkably similar, both in comparison to their contemporaries and their historical antecedents.

50

DIGITAL FILTERS

HIPSTAMATIC, one of the first photography apps for smartphones, was launched in 2009 as an antidote to the low resolution and limited dynamic range of the built-in camera of the iPhone 3GS. As the name implied, Hipstamatic was inspired by the look of old photos made with the Kodak Instamatic camera. Instamatic, first sold in 1963, was a point-and-shoot camera popular among amateurs because of its easy-to-load cartridge film, which didn't have to be unspooled to start or rewound at the end of the roll: users simply dropped the cartridge into the camera and began shooting. The original 126-size cartridge rendered square format color images with white borders. Hipstamatic, the app, took up the aesthetic of this format and added to it the faded colors and physically damaged surfaces typical of fifty-year-old snapshots. [See also Chapter 14, "Permanent Carbon Prints."] Improvements in dye stability eventually made Instamatic prints less prone to color shifting, although the once-white borders yellow and darken with continued exposure of the gelatin emulsion to light. The software developers of Hipstamatic repurposed these readily identifiable failures as intentional stylistic choices, which were also useful in covering up the shortcomings of early smartphone cameras. As a company representative explained, "We take a bad camera and make it worse in the most beautiful way."[1] Hipstamatic users could apply filters to their pictures, with names like "Ina's 1969" or "1982," to disguise the pixelated noise of their digital photos with blown-out highlights and vignetting typical of the Instamatic's on-camera flash or the faded and shifted colors found in old color prints. [See also Chapter 43, "On-Camera Flash."]

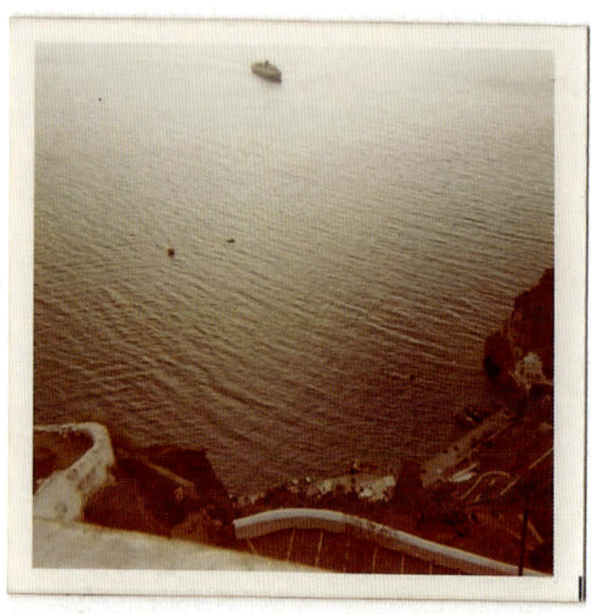

FIGURE 195. Ro Snell, "Instamatic Europe," ca. 1966–1969. Chromogenic print. 3½″ × 3 ½″.
Source: Courtesy of the artist.

> **FIGURE 196.** Pat Turner, "Untitled," Hipstamatic. 2014.
Source: Courtesy of the artist.

Hipstamatic gained widespread attention in 2010 when *New York Times* staff photographer Damon Winter won an international award for his series on American soldiers in Afghanistan made with the app. As one critic put it, "Hipstamatic generates an atmosphere, an aesthetic that ostensibly doesn't exist in reality. [. . .] Is it photojournalism when an image is deliberately changed to heighten or affect mood that we literally can't see with our eyes for the sake of aesthetics and emotion?"[2] Winter and others defended the work, explaining that soldiers found the iPhone less intrusive than a professional camera and that a Hipstamatic filter was just another technical choice. One of Winter's colleagues reasoned, "The photographer takes the picture, not the equipment. Few people care what kind of typewriter Hemingway used."[3]

The debate over filters has long been divisive and not just in photojournalism. When modernist photographers used polarizers or red filters to create higher contrast black-and-white images in-camera, allowing them to make "straight" or unaltered prints directly from the negative, others countered that such filters decreased the sharpness of the image and ran counter to the modernists' aims. [See also Chapter 22, "Straight Photography."] In color photography before the digital era, filters were necessary to adjust color temperature for daylight-balanced film used in varied lighting situations. Filters were even recommended to correct the effects of evening light on portrait subjects as late as the 1980s. [See also Chapter 40, "Golden Hour."] Through the end of the twentieth century, though, most popular journals advised "discretion" when using filters.[4] Resistance to filters, like that encountered by Winter, is not unique to the digital realm, but with increased access to these photographic tools and the social space to comment on them, attention to filters skyrocketed after Hipstamatic.

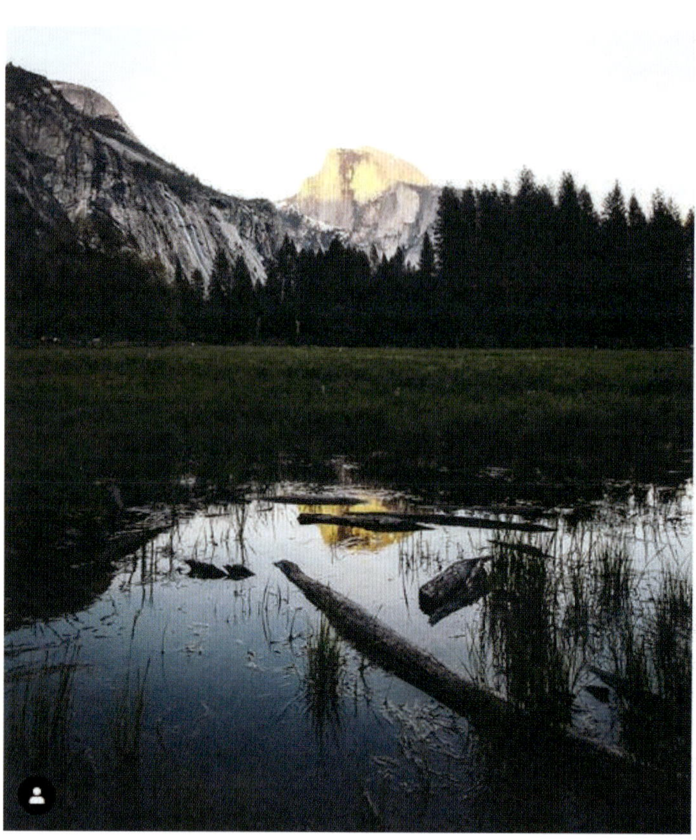

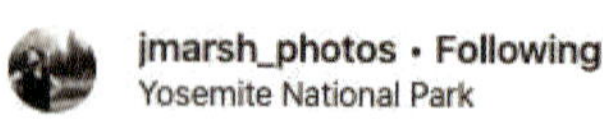

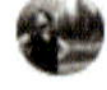

FIGURE 197. Jeff Marsh, "Springtime Reflections," Instagram, 2018.

Source: Courtesy of the artist. https://www.instagram.com/jmarsh_photos/.

Instagram, launched in late 2010, capitalized on Hipstamatic's success and turned the filter fad into a photo-sharing application and social network. Rated the iPhone app of the year in 2011, Facebook purchased Instagram the following year for $1 billion. Like Hipstamatic, Instagram offered dozens of preset digital filters to easily add warmth, contrast, or saturation to pictures taken with the app. As a 2012 *New Yorker* editorial glibly put it, Instagram is popular because it makes "everything in our lives . . . look better."[5] While the filter names didn't explicitly point to analog origins, the popularity of filters such as Gingham or Valencia, which both desaturated and color-shifted images, clearly drew on the aesthetic of old photographs.

Instagram users can caption their photos using hashtags, as on Twitter, which enables easy searching and categorization across the platform. Hashtags often refer to emotions or content—anything from #love (the most popular hashtag of 2013[6]) to #cat, #nature or #food—but they also sometimes describe the aesthetic or technique of the photo. The hashtags #iphoneonly and #nofilter, which grew in popularity in 2013, were apparent attempts to exert control over the aesthetic preferences of the community following an influx of new users. One hundred million users were active on the app by 2013; this number doubled the following year and reached 800 million, or nearly one-third of all Internet users, by 2018.[7]

The #nofilter movement began in 2013 as a response to what followers described as overuse of digital filters. In the same year, Apple added, for the first time, a suite of filters to the built-in camera app in iOS 7, which reproduced many of Instagram's effects. The distressed colors indicative of old photos became widely visible online, but also in print and even in the colors of Fujifilm's new line of instant film cameras. Following the pattern of trends throughout the history of the medium, these aesthetic choices quickly saturated the market, leading to disavowal of the filter trend by its initial proponents. The primary role of #nofilter among its originators was to attest to the photographer's talent, unadulterated by mass-produced effects. A popular blog dedicated itself in mid-2013 to unmasking "#nofilter fakers" by reading data in Instagram's application programming interface.[8] The blog boasted an automated archive of filter fakers, reposting the fraudulent photos labeled with the offender's user handle. Visitors could even submit links to suspected fakes for public shaming. By 2016, a study of the #nature category on Instagram found that while the number one most-liked photos used the Instagram filter Valencia, the natural or no-filter category ranked second in number of likes, attesting to the ongoing ambivalence of photographers to filters.[9]

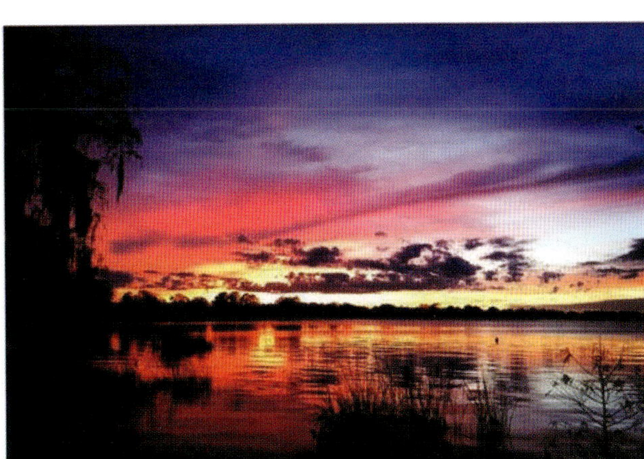

FIGURE 198. Per Stenius and Oskar Sundberg (actnormal.co), "Filter Fakers," 2016.

Source: http://filterfakers.com/post/137901396677.

Digital filters also serve as an index to contemporary photographers' enduring interest in historical styles. While analog filters are limited in their effects, digital filters can manipulate images in many ways. From simulated lens and focal effects to exposure and processing alterations, many of the trends that have cycled through photographic practice since 1839 can be recreated in seconds with the application of a digital filter. Although some of these styles, such as the #nofilter movement, are deliberately named by their makers, many other stylistic trends remain unidentified, described now only as "good pictures." These styles will likely go unnamed and unacknowledged until they are rediscovered by future generations of photographers in search of the next new (old) thing.

ACKNOWLEDGMENTS

This book has had many beginnings. In my own history with photographic history, I encounter multiple origin stories, each of which could represent the genesis of this project. One of these was in a classroom at the University of California, Santa Cruz, where one of my students identified a Stephen Shore photograph from the 1970s as a product of Instagram. Cases of mistaken identity abound in this history, as one generation's discarded trends are rediscovered and adapted by later photographers.

I am grateful to many students at Santa Cruz and at Stanford University who have shared with me their own perspectives on photography in discussion and with visual examples on Instagram. An earlier first start might have been my work on motion blur as a graduate student, a project that was generously and rigorously reviewed by Bliss Cua Lim and Sally Stein at the University of California, Irvine. From this tiny seed, one small chapter out of fifty, an entire book grew. For their continued support of this research, and indeed all of my academic work, I thank my advisors, Cécile Whiting and Lucas Hilderbrand. Lucas's candor about the writing process remains invaluable to me in my own writing and motivates much of my teaching. More recently, the sound practical advice and intellectual inspiration provided by Alexander Nemerov, Karla Oeler, and Nicholas Jenkins at Stanford University has been inimitable. *Thanks* is too small a term for what I owe to Lisa Volpe, whose insights and introductions would have made our mentor, Karen Sinsheimer, proud. Lisa worked closely with me on the early stages of this project, despite our geographic distance and her full-time responsibilities as a curator, now at the Museum of Fine Arts, Houston. Through Lisa, I also came to know two people who were critical to this project: Barbara Levine, whose knowledge of and love for amateur photography is unparalleled, and Judith Lane and the Estate of Phillip Leonian, whose books enabled much of my twentieth-century research. The Prelinger Library was also enormously influential in the early stages of this research, as was the support of a short-term fellowship at the Harry Ransom Center.

Jodi Roberts and Monica Westin provided advice and good humor along the way. Lindsey Rothfeder kindly and diligently followed the book's progress for years. Adam Katseff read the manuscript with the critical eye of an accomplished photographer and the ear of a long-time teacher. James Steichen, Hillary Miller, Ryan Tacata, and Alexander Greenhough were the best colleagues one could hope for. I am also thankful for the deep and wide-ranging expertise of numerous curators, artists, and historians, among them Micah Barrett, Frish Brandt, Monica Bravo, Clément Chéroux, Erica Deeman, Cassandra C. Jones, Corey Keller, Matthew Kluk, Danny Lyon, Dennis Reed, Vanessa Schwartz, and Eric Taubman. For designating their homes as temporary writing retreats, I thank Todd and Emily Bryan and Anne Mersmann.

In my personal history with photography, the preface was written by my parents, who gave me my first SLR camera at age thirteen: my mom, Karen, whose photographs inspired me, and my dad, Jim, who patiently sat with me through an evening course where I learned "how to make good pictures." My sister, Kirsten, was an unfailingly good-natured and beautiful subject. For sustaining me through the recent history of this project, I am eternally grateful to my husband, Pat Turner, whose belief in me and in this research has made this book—and so much more—possible.

NOTES

INTRODUCTION

1. The title of the Kodak series changed in 1981 to *How to Take Good Pictures*.

2. Ian Crouch, "Instagram's Instant Nostalgia," *New Yorker*, April 10, 2012, http://www.newyorker.com/culture/culture-desk/instagrams-instant-nostalgia; Alex Williams, "The Agony of Instagram," *New York Times*, December 13, 2013, https://www.nytimes.com/2013/12/15/fashion/instagram.html.

3. Clément Chéroux, *Avant l'avant-garde. du jeu en photographie, 1890–1940* (Textuel, 2015).

4. Walter Benjamin, "Little History of Photography," in *Selected Writings*, Vol. 2, Pt. 2: *1931–1934*, ed. Howard Eiland, Michael W. Jennings, and Gary Smith (Cambridge, MA: Harvard University Press, 1999).

5. "Vernacular Photographies," *History of Photography*, September 1, 2000, 262–71, https://doi.org/10.1080/03087298.2000.10443418; Geoffrey Batchen, "Snapshots," *Photographies* 1, no. 2 (2008): 121–42.

6. See especially Douglas Nickel's comments in "Responses to a Questionnaire," *History of Photography*, September 1, 2000, 229, https://doi.org/10.1080/03087298.2000.10443412.

7. John Szarkowski, *The Photographer's Eye* (New York: Museum of Modern Art, 1966).

8. Douglas R. Nickel, "History of Photography: The State of Research," *Art Bulletin* 83, no. 3 (2001): 556, https://doi.org/10.2307/3177242.

9. Mark Feeney, "At the MFA, a Century of Snapshots on Display," *Boston Globe*, July 21, 2015, https://www.bostonglobe.com/arts/theater-art/2015/07/20/mfa-century-snapshots-display/r4RyhoBore9KYSG9MS5e3M/story.html.

10. Helmut Gernsheim, *Creative Photography: Aesthetic Trends, 1839–1960* (New York: Bonanza Books, 1962), 12–13.

11. Pierre Bourdieu, *Photography: A Middle-Brow Art* (Stanford, CA: Stanford University Press, 1990), 7.

12. See, for example, the Instagram account begun in 2018 that aggregates images from popular travel photographers: "Insta Repeat (@insta_repeat) Instagram Photos and Videos," accessed December 3, 2018, https://www.instagram.com/insta_repeat/.

13. Susan Sontag, "Photography: The Beauty Treatment," *New York Review of Books*, November 28, 1974, http://www.nybooks.com/articles/1974/11/28/photography-the-beauty-treatment/.

14. Raymond Williams, "On High and Popular Culture," *New Republic*, November 21, 1974, https://newrepublic.com/article/79269/high-and-popular-culture.

15. Williams, "On High and Popular Culture."

16. *Popular Mechanics Photokinks* (Chicago: Popular Mechanics Press, 1948), 1.

17. Andreas Feininger, *Feininger on Photography* (Chicago: Ziff-Davis, 1949), v.

18. Henry G. Abbott, *Modern Photography in Theory and Practice: A Hand-Book for the Amateur*, 3rd ed. (Chicago: G. K. Hazlitt & Co., 1899), 2, http://hdl.handle.net/2027/gri.ark:/13960/t8qc0zc57.

19. Nancy Fraser and Michael Warner's theorization of a "counterpublic" is particularly useful here. Fraser first identified these as "parallel discursive arenas where members of subordinated social groups invent and circulate counter-discourses, which in turn permit them to formulate oppositional interpretations of their identities, interests, and needs." Although access to the publishing industry was limited, I consider the making of photographs as one such oppositional discursive arena. See Nancy Fraser, "Rethinking the Public Sphere: A Contribution to the Critique of Actually Existing Democracy," *Social Text* no. 25/26 (1990): 67, https://doi.org/10.2307/466240, and Michael Warner, "Publics and Counterpublics," *Public Culture*, January 1, 2002, 49–90.

20. "Studies in Photography: Joint Exhibition of the Work of Amateurs," *New York Times*, March 18, 1889, 8.

21. Catherine Weed Barnes, "Photography from a Woman's Standpoint," *Photographic Times and American Photographer*, December 27, 1889, 652–53.

22. Keith F. Davis, *The Origins of American Photography, 1839–1885: From Daguerreotype to Dry-Plate* (Kansas City, MO: Hall Family Foundation in association with the Nelson-Atkins Museum of Art, 2007), 18.

23. George Sullivan, *Black Artists in Photography, 1840–1940* (New York: Cobblehill Books, 1996), 25.

24. Sarah Greenhough, "'Of Charming Glens, Graceful Glades, and Frowning Cliffs': The Economic Incentives, Social Inducements, and Aesthetic Issues of American Pictorial Photography, 1880–1902," in *Photography in Nineteenth-Century America*, ed. Martha A. Sandweiss (Fort Worth, TX: Amon Carter Museum, 1991), 261.

25. "How Is Business?" *Philadelphia Photographer*, September 1, 1877, 260.

26. For a detailed time line of the Kodak Girl, see Alison Nordström, "Lovely, Smart, Modern: Women with Cameras in a Changing World," in *Kodak Girl: From the Martha Cooper Collection*, ed. John P. Jacob (Göttingen: Steidl, 2011), 66.

27. The art historian Patricia Vettel-Becker has argued that photography as described by the popular midcentury literature represented one such site for a white-collar worker to exert masculine control. See her *Shooting from the Hip: Photography, Masculinity, and Postwar America* (Minneapolis: University of Minnesota Press, 2005), 10.

28. Vettel-Becker, *Shooting from the Hip*, 7–9.

29. Bert Stern and Annie Gottlieb, *The Last Sitting* (New York: Morrow, 1982).

30. Peter Gowland, *How to Photograph Women* (New York: Crown, 1953), 33.

31. Marcus Aurelius Root, *The Camera and the Pencil* (Philadelphia: Lippincott, 1864), 67–83, http://archive.org/details/cameraandpencil00rootgoog.

32. "Plumbotypes," *National Era*, January 7, 1847.

33. Deborah Willis, "Photography, African American," in *Africana: The Encyclopedia of the African and African American Experience*, 2nd ed., ed. Kwame Anthony Appiah and Henry Louis Gates Jr. (Oxford: Oxford University Press, 2005).

34. Sullivan, *Black Artists in Photography, 1840–1940*.

CHAPTER 1

1. Beaumont Newhall, *The History of Photography: From 1839 to the Present* (New York: Museum of Modern Art, 1982), 34.

2. "The Fine Arts," *Daguerreian Journal*, November 1, 1850, 25.

3. Newhall, *History of Photography*, 33.

4. "Daguerreotypes at the Crystal Palace," *Humphrey's Journal of the Daguerreotype and Photographic Arts and the Sciences and Arts Pertaining to Heliography (1852–1862)*, August 15, 1853, 139–40.

5. "Our Foreign Correspondent: State of the Daguerreotype Art in London," *Humphrey's Journal of the Daguerreotype and Photographic Arts*, March 15, 1853, 365.

6. "Photograph Publications: Myall's [Sic] Daguerreotypes," *Humphrey's Journal of the Daguerreotype and Photographic Arts*, April 15, 1852, 8.

7. "Daguerreotypes at the Crystal Palace," 140.

8. Robert Taft, *Photography and the American Scene: A Social History, 1839–1889* (New York: Macmillan, 1942), 44.

9. Reese V. Jenkins, *Images and Enterprise: Technology and the American Photographic Industry, 1839 to 1925* (Baltimore, MD: Johns Hopkins University Press, 1987), 22.

10. Keith F. Davis, *The Origins of American Photography, 1839–1885: From Daguerreotype to Dry-Plate* (Kansas City, MO: Hall Family Foundation in association with the Nelson-Atkins Museum of Art, 2007), 20.

11. Davis, *The Origins of American Photography*, 371.

CHAPTER 2

1. The collodion process was invented in 1851 by Frederick Scott Archer. It called for dissolving gun-cotton in alcohol, applying the mixture to a glass plate, sensitizing the plate to light, loading it into the camera, and exposing it to the lens image, all while the plate was still wet. The process is also sometimes called wet-plate collodion. These negatives were then printed on albumen paper, which held silver salts suspended in an egg-white emulsion. (See also Chapter 5, "Intensifying Negatives.")

2. W. H. Hewitt, "Improvement in Photography," *Daguerreian Journal*, January 1, 1851, 122.

3. Edmund de Valicourt, "A New and Complete Photographic Manual," trans. W. Grigg, *The Photographic and Fine Art Journal*, November 1, 1854, 335.

4. Gérard de Lairesse, *A Treatise on the Art of Painting, in All Its Branches*, trans. William Marshall Craig (London: E. Orme, 1817), 6.

5. "Diffusion of Focus," *Philadelphia Photographer*, September 1, 1867, 290.

6. George W. Dewy, "Portraiture, from Levi Hill's Treatise on Heliochromy," *Daguerreian Journal*, May 1, 1851, 366.

7. Marcus Aurelius Root, "The Photographic Art: In the Great International Exposition," *Philadelphia Photographer*, December 1, 1875, 375.

8. E. K. Hough, "Expressing Character in Photographic Pictures," *American Journal of Photography*, November 1, 1858, 171.

9. Henry Peach Robinson, "Photography, Artistic and Scientific," *Humphrey's Journal of the Daguerreotype and Photographic Arts*, December 1, 1858, 233.

10. de Valicourt, "A New and Complete Photographic Manual," 347.

11. Marcus Aurelius Root, *The Camera and the Pencil* (Philadelphia: Lippincott, 1864), http://archive.org/details/cameraandpencil00rootgoog.

12. William Kurtz, "Rembrandt-Ish," *Philadelphia Photographer*, January 1, 1871, 4.

13. Robinson, "Photography, Artistic and Scientific," 233.

CHAPTER 3

1. Samuel F. B. Morse, "The Daguerrotipe," *New-York Observer*, April 20, 1839.

2. Sir John Robison, "Notes on Daguerre's Photography," *Edinburgh New Philosophical Journal* 27 (October 1839): 155.

3. Robert Taft, *Photography and the American Scene: A Social History, 1839–1889* (New York: Macmillan, 1942), 45.

4. Daniel Davis, Improvement in coloring daguerreotype-pictures, US Patent 2826A, filed September 20, 1842, and issued October 22, 1842, https://patents.google.com/patent/US2826A/en?q=(daniel+davis)&oq=(daniel+davis)&sort=old.

5. Minotto, "Methods of Coloring Photographic Pictures," *Humphrey's Journal of the Daguerreotype and Photographic Arts and the Sciences and Arts Pertaining to Heliography*, October 15, 1854. 197.

6. Henry Hunt Snelling, *The History and Practice of the Art of Photography* (New York: Putnam, 1849), 131–32, http://archive.org/details/ost-art-the_history_and_practice_of_the_art_of_p.

7. "Fair of the American Institute for 1857: Photographic Department," *Photographic and Fine Art Journal*, November 1, 1857, 346.

8. Alfred H. Wall, "Practical Instructions on Coloring Photographs," *Humphrey's Journal of the Daguerreotype and Photographic Arts and the Sciences and Arts Pertaining to Heliography*, June 1, 1859, 45.

9. "Value of a Daguerreotype," *Humphrey's Journal of the Daguerreotype and Photographic Arts*, January 15, 1854, 297.

10. Snelling, *History and Practice of the Art of Photography*, 76.

11. "Heliography," *Humphrey's Journal of the Daguerreotype and Photographic Arts*, December 1, 1852, 247.

12. Samuel Dwight Humphrey, *A System of Photography* (Albany, NY: C. Van Benthuysen, 1849), 7.

13. Edward Livingston Wilson, *Wilson's Cyclopedic Photography: A Complete Handbook of the Terms, Processes, Formulae and Appliances Available in Photography, Arranged in Cyclopedic Form for Ready Reference* (New York: E. L. Wilson, 1894), 96.

CHAPTER 4

1. John Adams Whipple, Improvement in Taking Daguerreotype-Pictures, patent 6056, Boston, issued January 23, 1849.

2. Marcus Aurelius Root, *The Camera and the Pencil* (Philadelphia: Lippincott, 1864), 108–9.

3. "The Photo-Crayon Process," *Philadelphia Photographer* 8, no. 82 (n.d.), 352.

4. G. Wharton Simpson, "Practical Notes on Photographic Subjects," *Philadelphia Photographer*, April 1, 1869, 100.

5. "Sarony's Celebrated Photo-Crayon," *Philadelphia Photographer*, March 1, 1870.

6. John Werge, *The Evolution of Photography* (London: Piper & Carter, 1890), 173, http://archive.org/details/evolutionofphotooowerguoft.

CHAPTER 5

1. "Louis Désiré Blanquart-Evrard (French, 1802–1872) (Getty Museum)," J. Paul Getty in Los Angeles, accessed July 31, 2018, http://www.getty.edu/art/collection/artists/1992/louis-dsir-blanquart-evrard-french-1802-1872/.

2. John C. Browne, "After-Intensifications of Portrait and Landscape Negatives," *Philadelphia Photographer (1864–1888)*, March 1, 1870, 72.

3. Browne, "After-Intensifications of Portrait and Landscape Negatives," 72.

4. Ibid.

5. W. J. Baker, "Negative Retouching," *Philadelphia Photographer (1864–1888)*, April 1, 1870, 126.

6. George B. Ayres, *How to Paint Photographs in Water Colors and in Oil* (New York: D. Appleton, 1878), 26.

7. Ayres, *How to Paint Photographs*, 27.

CHAPTER 6

1. Lumiere, "On Views of Buildings, Landscapes, and Instantaneous Proofs," *Humphrey's Journal of the Daguerreotype and Photographic Arts and the Sciences and Arts Pertaining to Heliography (1852–1862)*, August 15, 1852, 138.

2. Walter Woodbury, "Cloud Negatives and Their Use," *Philadelphia Photographer*, November 1, 1868, 388.

3. M. A. Gaudini, "Negatives on Glass," *Humphrey's Journal of Photography and the Heliographic Arts and Sciences*, June 1, 1853, 54.

4. William Kent, "Gleanings Arranged from an Amateur's Scrap-Book for the Aid of Beginners," *Humphrey's Journal of Photography and the Heliographic Arts and Sciences*, January 15, 1861, 273.

5. Woodbury, "Cloud Negatives and Their Use," 388.

6. An Old Amateur, "Our Amateur Class," *Philadelphia Photographer*, January 1, 1884, 27.

7. Gaudini, "Negatives on Glass," 54.

8. Andrew Pringle, "Mr. Macbeth on Legitimate Photography," *Philadelphia Photographer (1864–1888)*, April 16, 1887, 245.

9. Edward Dunmore, "The Legitimacy of Double Printing," *Philadelphia Photographer*, April 16, 1887, 243.

10. H. Vogel, "German Correspondence," *Philadelphia Photographer (1864–1888)*, September 1, 1873, 470.

11. An Old Amateur, "Our Amateur Class," 25.

CHAPTER 7

1. Robert Taft, *Photography and the American Scene: A Social History, 1839–1889* (New York: Macmillan, 1942), 131.

2. "Fine Painting," *Photographic and Fine Art Journal*, September 1855, 288.

3. "Something New: The Art Progressing," *Photographic and Fine Art Journal*, April 1855, 127.

4. F. E. Gage, "Enlarging Photographs," *Humphrey's Journal of Photography and the Allied Arts and Sciences*, March 1, 1859, 204; John Towler, *The Silver Sunbeam: A Practical and Theoretical Text-Book on Sun Drawing and Photographic Printing* (New York: J. H. Ladd, 1864), 263, http://catalog.hathitrust.org/api/volumes/oclc/4718720.html.

5. Augustin Testelin, "Negatives for the Solar Camera," *Humphrey's Journal of Photography and the Allied Arts and Sciences*, November 1, 1862, 152.

6. Towler, *The Silver Sunbeam*, 221.

CHAPTER 8

1. Reverend H. J. Morton, "Broad Lights and Shadows in Photography," October 1, 1865, 167; M. Carey Lea, "Toning Landscapes," *Philadelphia Photographer (1864–1888)*, April 1, 1868, 118, "Linn's Landscape Photography," *Philadelphia Photographer*, July 1, 1872, 268; "Wilson's Landscape Studies," *Philadelphia Photographer (1864–1888)*, May 1, 1872.

2. Frank Howard, "Some of the Defects in Landscape Photography," *Humphrey's Journal of Photography and the Allied Arts and Sciences,* April 15, 1865, 379.

3. Edward L. Wilson, *Photographic Mosaics: An Annual Record of Photographic Progress* (Philadelphia: Benerman & Wilson, 1870), 14–15.

4. Howard, "Some of the Defects in Landscape Photography," 380.

5. M. Carey Lea, *Manual of Photography* (Philadelphia: Benerman & Wilson, 1868), 165.

6. Howard, "Some of the Defects in Landscape Photography," 380.

7. Rudolf Kingslake, *A History of the Photographic Lens* (Orlando, FL: Academic Press, 1989), 60.

8. "Wilson's Landscape Studies," 137.

9. "Wilson's Landscape Studies," 137.

10. Lea, *Manual of Photography*, 174–75.

11. Lea, *Manual of Photography*, 177.

12. W. F. Carlton, *The Amateur Photographer: A Complete Guide for Beginners in the Art-Science of Photography* (Rochester, NY: H. J. Haigh, 1892), 36.

CHAPTER 9

1. Grant B. Romer, *Young America: The Daguerreotypes of Southworth & Hawes* (Rochester, NY: George Eastman House, 2005), 38–39.

2. John Hannavy, ed., *Encyclopedia of Nineteenth-Century Photography* (New York: Taylor & Francis, 2008), 1340.

3. Charles A. Seely, "Editorial Miscellany," *American Journal of Photography*, August 1, 1858, 82, http://archive.org/details/americanjournal01858newy.

4. Reese V. Jenkins, *Images and Enterprise: Technology and the American Photographic Industry, 1839 to 1925* (Baltimore, MD: Johns Hopkins University Press, 1987), 50.

5. "A Visit to Anthony's Photographic and Stereoscopic Establishment," *Spirit of the Times*, July 23, 1859, 273.

6. Hannavy, *Encyclopedia of Nineteenth-Century Photography*, 49.

7. "The Stereoscope: Its Wondrous Beauty and Power," *New York Observer*, December 22, 1859, 405.

8. Oliver Wendell Holmes, "The Stereoscope and the Stereograph," *Atlantic*, June 1, 1859, https://www.theatlantic.com/magazine/archive/1859/06/the-stereoscope-and-the-stereograph/303361/.

9. Henry Clay Price, *How to Make Pictures: Easy Lessons for the Amateur Photographer* (New York: Scovill Manufacturing Co., 1887), 63, http://hdl.handle.net/2027/uiug.30112071176538.

10. Oliver Wendell Holmes, *Soundings from the Atlantic* (Boston: Ticknor and Fields, 1864), 179.

11. "Photographers' Association of America: Milwaukee Convention," *Photographic Times and American Photographer* 13 (1883): 403.

CHAPTER 10

1. Steven Kasher, *America and the Tintype* (New York: International Center of Photography, 2008), 79.

2. "State of Business," *Humphrey's Journal of the Daguerreotype and Photographic Arts and the Sciences and Arts Pertaining to Heliography (1852–1862)*, August 1, 1861, 112.

3. "Editorial Miscellany," *Humphrey's Journal of the Daguerreotype and Photographic Arts and the Sciences and Arts Pertaining to Heliography (1852–1862)*, December 1, 1861, 240.

4. "New Year's Day," *Humphrey's Journal of the Daguerreotype and Photographic Arts*, January 1, 1862, 272.

5. "Photography in the Army," *Humphrey's Journal of the Daguerreotype and Photographic Arts*, February 15, 1862, 319.

6. "A Boston Gallery on Broadway," *Humphrey's Journal of the Daguerreotype and Photographic Arts*, July 1, 1862, 32.

7. *History of Wages in the United States from Colonial Times to 1928* (Washington, DC: US Government Printing Office, 1934), 225, 415, http://hdl.handle.net/2027/uc1.32106007458745.

8. "Correspondence," *Philadelphia Photographer (1864-1888)*, July 1, 1865, 112.

9. Kasher, *America and the Tintype*, 79–80.

10. Kasher's *America and the Tintype* boasts a wealth of examples of trick photographs and other stereotypical poses of the nineteenth century.

11. "A Story of a Tintype and the Good It Did," *Philadelphia Photographer*, April 1, 1869, 123.

12. "Manipulations Continued," *Philadelphia Photographer*, September 1, 1873, 333.

13. "How Is Business?" *Philadelphia Photographer*, September 1, 1877, ß 260.

CHAPTER 11

1. C. W. H., "The 'Lights' and Formulae: Of Kurtz; Gurney & Sons; and Bogardus, of New York," *Philadelphia Photographer (1864–1888)*, November 1, 1868, 404.

2. George B. Ayres, "Rembrandt and 'Rembrandts,'" *Philadelphia Photographer (1864–1888)*, November 1, 1870, 381.

3. Edward L. Wilson, *Photographic Mosaics: An Annual Record of Photographic Progress* (Philadelphia: Benerman & Wilson, 1870), 13.

4. Charles Wagner Hull, "A Few Facts," *Photographic Mosaics* (Philadelphia: Benerman & Wilson, 1870), 79.

5. G. Wharton Simpson, "Notes in and out of the Studio," *Philadelphia Photographer (1864–1888)*, October 1, 1870, 362.

6. Simpson, "Notes in and out of the Studio," 363.

7. William Kurtz, "Rembrandt-Ish," *Philadelphia Photographer*, January 1, 1871, 4.

8. Kurtz, "Rembrandt-Ish," 4.

CHAPTER 12

1. Robert Taft, *Photography and the American Scene: A Social History, 1839–1889* (New York: Macmillan, 1942), 323.

2. John Hannavy, ed., *Encyclopedia of Nineteenth-Century Photography* (New York: Taylor & Francis Group, 2008), 233.

3. "Our Picture," *Philadelphia Photographer*, March 1867, 111.

4. "Our Picture," 114.

5. Ibid.

6. "Cabinet Portraits," *Philadelphia Photographer*, April 1, 1867, 113.

7. "Cabinet Portraiture," *Philadelphia Photographer*, August 1, 1867, 247.

8. "Manipulations Continued," September 1, 1873, 336.

9. W. J. Baker, "Negative Retouching," *Philadelphia Photographer*, April 1, 1870, 128.

10. Baker, "Negative Retouching," 128.

11. Edward L. Wilson, *Photographic Mosaics: An Annual Record of Photographic Progress* (Philadelphia: Benerman & Wilson, 1870), 13.

12. "Manipulations Continued," 333.

13. Baker, "Negative Retouching," 126.

14. W. J. Baker, "The New Size, Etc," *Philadelphia Photographer*, February 1, 1871, 41.

15. John L. Gihon, "Views That May Not Be Well Received," *Philadelphia Photographer*, June 1, 1872, 197.

CHAPTER 13

1. "Microphotography," *Journal of the Society of Arts*, November 18, 1870, 146.

2. John Towler, *The Silver Sunbeam: A Practical and Theoretical Text-Book on Sun Drawing and Photographic Printing* (New York: J. H. Ladd, 1864), 266, http://catalog.hathitrust.org/api/volumes/oclc/4718720.html.

3. "Notes on Science: A Rare Mineral, a Monster Fish, Micro-Photography," *Chicago Tribune*, December 17, 1867, ProQuest Historical Newspapers.

4. Marcus Aurelius Root, *The Camera and the Pencil* (Philadelphia: Lippincott, 1864), 324, http://archive.org/details/cameraandpencil00rootgoog.

5. Wilson A. Bentley, "The Story of the Snow Crystals," *Harper's Monthly Magazine*, December 1901, 111.

6. T. C. Roche, *How To Make Photographs: A Manual for Amateurs* (New York: E. & H. T. Anthony, 1883), 82.

7. Alexander Black, *Photography Indoors and Out: A Book for Amateurs* (Boston: Houghton Mifflin, 1894), 212, http://archive.org/details/photographyindoo00blac_0.

CHAPTER 14

1. "American Carbon Prints," *Philadelphia Photographer*, March 1, 1867, 82.

2. "Photography at the Great Exhibition of the American Institute," *Philadelphia Photographer*, November 1, 1867, 359.

3. "The Future of Photography," *Littell's Living Age*, December 26, 1868, 821.

4. John R. Clemons, "The Fading of Albumen Prints," in *Photographic Mosaics: An Annual Record of Photographic Progress*, ed. Edward L. Wilson (Philadelphia: Edward L. Wilson, 1878), 123, https://babel.hathitrust.org/cgi/pt?id=hvd.32044096812011;view=2up;seq=8.

5. "How Is Business?" *Philadelphia Photographer*, September 1, 1877, 258.

6. "How Is Business?" 259.

CHAPTER 15

1. Samuel F. B. Morse, "The Daguerrotipe," *New-York Observer*, April 20, 1839, 62.

2. William Henry Fox Talbot, "On the Production of Instantaneous Photographic Images," *Humphrey's Journal of the Daguerreotype and Photographic Arts*, April 15, 1852, 1.

3. Oliver Wendell Holmes, *Soundings from the Atlantic* (Boston: Ticknor and Fields, 1864), 181.

4. Lumiere, "On Views of Buildings, Landscapes, and Instantaneous Proofs," *Humphrey's Journal of the Daguerreotype and Photographic Arts and the Sciences and Arts Pertaining to Heliography*, August 15, 1852, 138.

5. "A Horse's Notion Scientifically Determined," *Scientific American (1845–1908)*, October 19, 1878, 241.

6. W. F. Carlton, *The Amateur Photographer: A Complete Guide for Beginners in the Art-Science of Photography*, 2nd ed. (Rochester, NY, 1885), 35, http://hdl.handle.net/2027/coo.31924073901906.

7. Charles Maus Taylor, *Why My Photographs Are Bad* (Philadelphia: G. W. Jacobs, 1902), 164, http://archive.org/details/whymyphotographsootayl.

CHAPTER 16

1. J. J. Higgins, "On the Magnesium Light in Photography," *Philadelphia Photographer*, October 6, 1888, 577.

2. "Magnesium for Illuminating Purposes," *Humphrey's Journal of Photography and the Allied Arts and Sciences*, September 1, 1865, 143.

3. "Photographing the Pyramids by Magnesium Light," *Humphrey's Journal of Photography and the Allied Arts and Sciences*, July 1, 1865, 70.

4. "A Day or Two in Boston," *Philadelphia Photographer*, February 1, 1865, 27.

5. "A Day or Two in Boston," 27.

6. Professor Towler, "How to Take Photographs by the Magnesium Light: Lamps and Reflectors to Focus the Sitter," *Humphrey's Journal of Photography and the Allied Arts and Sciences*, December 1, 1865, 229.

7. Towler, "How to Take Photographs by the Magnesium Light."

8. "Editorial Notes," *Anthony's Photographic Bulletin*, April 14, 1888, 194.

9. Jacob August Riis, *The Making of an American* (New York: Macmillan, 1901), 267.

10. Kate Flint, *Flash! Photography, Writing, and Surprising Illumination* (London: Oxford University Press, 2017), 26.

11. Higgins, "On the Magnesium Light in Photography," 577.

CHAPTER 17

1. "Correspondence," *American Amateur Photographer*, September 1, 1889, 119–20.

2. "Busy Times for Amateurs: Photographers Awaiting the Summer Campaign," *New York Times*, May 20, 1889, 5.

3. Reese V. Jenkins, "Technology and the Market: George Eastman and the Origins of Mass Amateur Photography," *Technology and Culture* 16, no. 1 (1975): 16, https://doi.org/10.2307/3102363.

4. "The Kodak Camera," *Photographic Times and American Photographer*, October 5, 1888, 476.

5. "Historical Statistics of the United States Millennial Edition Online," accessed August 8, 2018, https://hsus-cambridge-org.stanford.idm.oclc.org /HSUSWeb/toc/tableToc.do?id=Ba4280-4282.

6. Todd Gustavson, *Camera: A History of Photography from Daguerreotype to Digital* (New York: Fall River Press, 2009), 143; Sarah Greenough, ed., *The Art of the American Snapshot, 1888–1978: From the Collection of Robert E. Jackson* (Washington, DC: National Gallery of Art, 2007), 14.

7. M. L. Carleton, "A Clear Case of Photographic Fever," *Century Illustrated Magazine*, October 1890, 13.

8. "The Astor Funeral Party," *New York Times*, May 2, 1892, 1; G. Brown Goode, "Facts and Fancies," *Wilson's Photographic Magazine*, April 4, 1891, 207; Robert E. Mensel, "'Kodakers Lying in Wait': Amateur Photography and the Right of Privacy in New York, 1885–1915," *American Quarterly*, March 1, 1991, 24–45, https://doi.org/10.2307/2712965.

9. "Snap-Shot, N.," *OED Online*, accessed August 8, 2018, http://www.oed .com/view/Entry/183040.

10. W. H. Walmsley, "The Abuse of the Hand Camera," *The American Annual of Photography and Photographic Times Almanac*, January 1, 1891, 215.

CHAPTER 18

1. Seneca Camera Manufacturing Company, *The Amateur Photographer's Manual: A Complete Compendium for the Beginner and Advanced Amateur* (Rochester, NY: Seneca Camera, 1920), 4.

2. Daniel J. Tapley, *The New Recreation: Amateur Photography* (New York: Hurst, 1884), 9–10.

3. "Busy Times for Amateurs: Photographers Awaiting the Summer Campaign," *New York Times*, May 20, 1889, 5.

4. Arthur Hope, *The Amateur Photographer's Hand Book: A Manual of Instruction for the Amateur* (New York: J. Wilkinson Company, 1891), 97.

5. Hope, *The Amateur Photographer's Hand Book*, 97.

6. W. F. Carlton, *The Amateur Photographer: A Complete Guide for Beginners in the Art-Science of Photography* (Rochester, NY: H. J. Haigh, 1892), 38–39.

7. Carlton, *The Amateur Photographer*, 39.

8. Marcus Aurelius Root, *The Camera and the Pencil* (Philadelphia: Lippincott, 1864), 438, http://archive.org/details/cameraandpencil00rootgoog.

9. Root, *The Camera and the Pencil*, 439.

10. Alexander Black, *Photography Indoors and Out: A Book for Amateurs* (Boston: Houghton Mifflin, 1894), 117, http://archive.org/details/photographyindoooblac_0.

11. J. W. Ridpath, "Pictorial Composition for Beginners in Photography," *Wilson's Photographic Magazine* 44, no. 602 (February 1907): 86.

12. *How to Make Good Pictures: A Text Book for the Every-Day Photographer*, 22nd rev. ed. (Rochester, NY: Eastman Kodak, 1936), 74.

13. Lake Price, *A Manual of Photographic Manipulation: Treating of the Practice of the Art; and Its Various Applications to Nature* (London: J. Churchill, 1858), 157.

14. *How to Make Good Pictures*, 75.

CHAPTER 19

1. Eastman Kodak Company, *The Modern Way in Picture Making: Published as an Aid to the Amateur Photographer* (Rochester, NY: Eastman Kodak, 1905), 158, http://archive.org/details/cu31924003618968.

2. Rudolf Kingslake, *A History of the Photographic Lens* (Orlando, FL: Academic Press, 1989), 133.

3. Rev. H. J. Morton, "The Trials of the Photographer," *Philadelphia Photographer*, March 1, 1865, 37.

4. Julius F. Sachse, "The Parvin Tele-Photo Lens," *American Journal of Photography*, June 1, 1893, 263.

5. George Shiras, "Photographing Wild Game with Flashlight and Camera," *National Geographic Magazine*, July 1906, 367–68.

6. William L. Finley, "Hunting Birds with a Camera: A Record of Twenty Years of Adventure in Obtaining Photographs of Feathered Wild Life in America," *National Geographic Magazine*, August 1923, 161.

7. Todd Gustavson, *Camera: A History of Photography from Daguerreotype to Digital* (New York: Fall River Press, 2009), 208.

8. Elbert Smith, *Practical Notes on Photography* (Brooklyn, NY: Brooklyn Daily Eagle, 1905), 49.

9. Frank Roy Fraprie and Franklin I Jordan, *Photographic Hints and Gadgets* (Boston: American Photographic Publishing, 1937), 266.

CHAPTER 20

1. Alfred Stieglitz, "Pictorial Photography," *Scribner's Magazine* (November 1899): 528.

2. Alex Eddington, "The Modern School of Photography," *Wilson's Photographic Magazine*, May 1, 1898, 226.

3. Watchman, "Words from the Watchtower," *American Amateur Photographer*, February 1, 1898, 68.

4. W. B. Bolton, "Pure Photography versus the New Art: Read at the Glasgow Convention by W. B. Bolton," *American Amateur Photographer*, September 1, 1898, 388.

5. James Packham, "The Gum Bichromate Process," *Wilson's Photographic Magazine (1889–1914)*; New York, January 1, 1898, 3.

6. "Object Lessons," *Camera Notes* 4, no. 1 (July 1900): 65.

7. Eddington, "The Modern School of Photography," 226.

8. Sidney Allan, "Eduard J. Steichen, Painter-Photographer," *Camera Notes* 6, no. 1 (1902): 15.

9. Eduard Steichen, "The American School," *Camera Notes* 6 (July 1902): 22.

10. Malcolm Dean Miller, "Notes on Pictorial Landscape Photography," *American Annual of Photography*, January 1, 1912, 100.

11. Stieglitz, "Pictorial Photography," 530.

CHAPTER 21

1. "Diffusion of Focus," *Philadelphia Photographer*, September 1, 1867, 290.

2. "Photographs Received," *American Amateur Photographer*, March 1, 1895, 133.

3. "Photographs Received," 133.

4. *Catalogue of the International Exhibition of Pictorial Photography* (Buffalo, NY: Buffalo Fine Arts Academy, Albright Art Gallery, 1910), 17.

5. "Diffusion," *Wilson's Photographic Magazine* 48, March 1, 1911, 127; Malcolm Dean Miller, "Notes on Pictorial Landscape Photography," *American Annual of Photography*, January 1, 1912, 96.

6. Arthur Hammond, "Pictorial Lenses in America," *Wilson's Photographic Magazine*, May 1, 1912, 226.

7. Flambeau, "Soft-Focus Lenses—Their Use and Abuse," *Photographic Journal of America*, September 1, 1920, 344.

8. Paul Strand, "Photography," *Camera Work* 49 (June 1917): 3.

9. Paul Anderson, *Pictorial Photography: Its Principles and Practice* (Philadelphia: Lippincott, 1917), 137.

CHAPTER 22

1. W. E. Bertling, "A Plea for the Commonplace," *American Annual of Photography*, January 1, 1904, 70.

2. Sadakichi Hartmann, "A Plea for Straight Photography," *American Amateur Photographer*, March 1, 1904, 102.

3. Bertling, "A Plea for the Commonplace," 73.

4. Hartmann, "A Plea for Straight Photography," 108.

5. Paul Strand, "Photography," *Camera Work* 49 (June 1917): 3.

6. Strand, "Photography," 3.

7. Dan Dunlop, "A Plea for Straight Photography," *Photo Era*, May 1, 1912, 208.

8. Amateur Photographer, "The Straight Print and Technic," *Photographic Journal of America: The Oldest Photography Magazine in America*, June 1, 1918, 285.

9. "The Straight Photograph, and Why," *Photographic Journal of America*, August 1, 1916, 340.

CHAPTER 23

1. Alfred Stieglitz, "Night Photography with the Introduction of Life," *American Annual of Photography and Photographic Times Almanac*, January 1, 1898, 204.

2. Arthur Hammond, "Notes on Night Photography," *American Annual of Photography*, January 1, 1913, 266.

3. Sadakichi Hartmann, *The Photo-Miniature: Leaves from an Amateur's Notebook*, vol. 8: *Night Photography* (New York: Tennant and Ward, 1910), 341.

4. "Night Photography," *Wilson's Photographic Magazine*, July 1, 1907, 327.

5. Stieglitz, "Night Photography with the Introduction of Life," 205.

6. Chas M. Smyth, "Night Photography," *American Annual of Photography*, January 1, 1912.

7. Smyth, "Night Photography," 147.

8. Sadakichi Hartmann, "Recent Conquests in Night Photography," *Photographic Times*, December 1, 1909, 449–50.

9. H. Powell Higgins, "Night Photography," *American Annual of Photography*, January 1, 1910, 322.

10. Hammond, "Notes on Night Photography," 254.

11. Hammond, "Notes on Night Photography," 256.

CHAPTER 24

1. Edgar Allan Poe, "The Daguerreotype," *Alexander's Weekly Messenger,* January 15, 1840, 2.

2. "Remedy for Business Depression," *Photographic Times and American Photographer,* August 21, 1885, 480–81.

3. Charles Scolik, "Orthochromatic Plates," *Photographic Times and American Photographer,* June 26, 1885, 345.

4. Edward L. Wilson, ed., *Photographic Mosaics: An Annual Record of Photographic Progress,* vol. 26 (New York: Edward L. Wilson, 1890), 13.

5. Arthur Hope, *The Amateur Photographer's Hand Book: A Manual of Instruction for the Amateur* (New York: J. Wilkinson Company, 1891), 100.

6. Scolik, "Orthochromatic Plates," 345.

7. "Orthochromatic Plates in Portraiture," *Photographic Journal of America,* July 1, 1922, 276.

8. Scolik, "Orthochromatic Plates," 345.

9. Eastman Kodak Company, *How to Make Good Pictures: A Book for the Amateur Photographer* (Rochester, NY: Eastman Kodak, 1912), 15, https://catalog.hathitrust.org/Record/008915628.

10. Jacob Deschin, *New Ways in Photography* (New York: Whittlesey House, 1936), 152.

11. Eastman Kodak Company, *How to Make Good Pictures: A Text Book for the Every-Day Photographer* (Rochester, NY: Eastman Kodak, 1938), 89.

12. Ansel Adams, *The Negative: Exposure and Development* (Hastings-on-Hudson, NY: Morgan & Morgan, 1948), 4, http://hdl.handle.net/2027/uc1.32106006023045.

13. Adams, *The Negative* , 4–5.

CHAPTER 25

1. John Hannavy, ed., *Encyclopedia of Nineteenth-Century Photography* (New York: Taylor & Francis Group, 2008), 254.

2. Todd Gustavson, *Camera: A History of Photography from Daguerreotype to Digital* (New York: Fall River Press, 2009), 101.

3. "The Distinguished Company at the Royal Academy Banquet: After-Dinner Speakers and Listeners," *Graphic,* May 11, 1929, 265.

4. "First Lady in Milwaukee," *Life,* December 7, 1936, 18.

5. "Speaking of Pictures," *Life,* March 15, 1937, 6.

6. Richard L. Simon, *Miniature Photography from One Amateur to Another* (New York: Simon and Schuster, 1937), 128.

7. Deschin, *New Ways in Photography* (New York: Whittlesey House, 1936), 22.

8. Deschin, *New Ways in Photography*, 22.

CHAPTER 26

1. Eastman Kodak Company, *How to Make Good Pictures*, 27th ed. (London: Kingsway, 1942), 34.

2. Charles Maus Taylor, *Why My Photographs Are Bad* (Philadelphia: G. W. Jacobs & Co., 1902), 123, http://archive.org/details/whymyphotographsootayl.

3. Katherine Stanberry, "Leaves from an Amateur's Notebook," in *Photo-Miniature*, vol. 8 (New York: Tennant and Ward, 1911), 257.

4. Aleksandr Rodchenko, "The Paths of Modern Photography," in *Photography in the Modern Era: European Documents and Critical Writings, 1913–1940*, ed. Christopher Phillips (New York: Metropolitan Museum of Art; Aperture, 1989), 262.

5. Eastman Kodak Company, *How to Make Good Pictures: A Text Book for the Every-Day Photographer*, 22nd rev. ed. (Rochester, NY: Eastman Kodak, 1936), 67.

6. Jacob Deschin, *New Ways in Photography* (New York: Whittlesey House, 1936), 100.

7. Eastman Kodak Company, *How to Make Good Pictures: A Text Book for the Every-Day Photographer*, 25th ed. (Rochester, NY: Eastman Kodak, 1939), 69–71.

8. Eastman Kodak Company, *How to Make Good Pictures,* 25th ed., 71.

9. Eastman Kodak Company, *How to Make Good Pictures,* 25th ed., 71.

10. Thomas H. Miller and Wyatt Brummitt, *This Is Photography: Its Means and Ends* (Garden City, NY: Garden City Books, 1952), 175, http://catalog.hathitrust.org/api/volumes/oclc/21208833.html.

11. Eastman Kodak Company, *How to Make Good Pictures*, 26th ed. (Rochester, NY: Eastman Kodak, 1941), 74–75.

12. Arthur Hammond, *Pictorial Composition in Photography* (Boston: American Photographic Publishing, 1939), 89.

CHAPTER 27

1. Ernest H. Washburn, "Our Illustrations," *Photo—Era Magazine: The American Journal of Photography (1921–1932)*, June 6, 1929, 327.

2. "Here, There and Everywhere," *Photo-Era Magazine*, June 6, 1929, 335.

3. Patricia A. Johnston, *Real Fantasies: Edward Steichen's Advertising Photography* (Berkeley: University of California Press, 2000), 32–39.

4. Paul Outerbridge, "Visualizing Design in the Commonplace," *Arts and Decoration* 17 (September 1922): 320.

5. M. F. Agha, "A Word on European Photography," *Pictorial Photography in America* 5 (1929), quoted in Johnston, *Real Fantasies*, 121.

6. Charles Clayton, "Why I Am a Pictorial Photographer: (Number Twelve)," *Photo-Era Magazine: The American Journal of Photography (1921–1932)*, April 4, 1929, 177.

7. A. H. Beardsley, "Our Illustrations," *Photo-Era Magazine: The American Journal of Photography (1921–1932)*, May 5, 1931, 280.

8. G. W. Gibbs, "Annual Members' Show of the Camera Club, 1930," *Photo-Era Magazine: The American Journal of Photography (1921–1932)*, March 3, 1931, 152–53.

9. Beardsley, "Our Illustrations," 279.

10. Frank Roy Fraprie and Walter Woodbury, *Photographic Amusements* (Norwood, MA: Plimpton Press, 1931), 242.

CHAPTER 28

1. William Lynch Vallee, "So You're Having Your Picture Taken?" *Silver Screen*, September 1939, 72.

2. Ruth Tildesley, "What's Wrong with Your Pictures," *Screenland*, February 1937; E. Harvey, "Judy Holliday Takes Her Own Glamor Picture," *Colliers*, January 26, 1952, 42–42.

3. Tildesley, "What's Wrong with Your Pictures," 54.

4. Jack Grant, "How to Be Photographed like a Star," *Movie Classic*, May 1934, 29–30.

5. Harvey, "Judy Holliday Takes Her Own Glamor Picture," 42.

6. John Reiner, "Posing for Glamor," *American Photography* 45 (November 1951): 659.

7. Vallee, "So You're Having Your Picture Taken?" 42.

8. Tildesley, "What's Wrong with Your Pictures," 55; Vallee, "So You're Having Your Picture Taken?" 42.

9. Sam Wu, "Glamor with a 35," *Popular Photography*, May 1957, 72.

CHAPTER 29

1. Tom Maloney, "Letter from the Editor," *U.S. Camera Annual*, 1940, 1.

2. Berenice Abbott, *A Guide to Better Photography* (New York: Crown, 1944), 153–55.

3. Ivan Dmitri, *Kodachrome and How to Use It* (New York: Simon and Schuster, 1940), 8.

4. Dmitri, *Kodachrome and How to Use It*, 11.

5. Dmitri, *Kodachrome and How to Use It*, 108.

6. "Speaking of Pictures . . . These Are Kodachromes," *Life*, April 1, 1940.

7. Leonard Ross, "Portrait Magic," *Popular Photography*, November 1939, 94.

8. Thomas H. Miller and Wyatt Brummitt, *This Is Photography* (Garden City, NY: Garden City Publishing, 1945), 176.

CHAPTER 30

1. "Television: The Next Great Development in Radio Is Ready Now for Its Enormous Postwar Market," *Life*, September 4, 1944, 85.

2. Lawrence Wilson Lichty, *American Broadcasting: A Source Book on the History of Radio and Television* (New York: Hastings, 1975), 521–22.

3. "Television: The Next Great Development in Radio Is Ready," 85.

4. "TV's Images Can Be Photographed," *Popular Science*, August 1950, 184.

5. Lynn Spigel, *TV by Design: Modern Art and the Rise of Network Television* (Chicago: University of Chicago Press, 2008), 85–98.

6. R. P. Stevenson, "How You Can Photograph the Fights via Television," *Popular Science*, February 1951, 214.

7. Joseph Charles Keeley, *Taking It Easy with Your Camera* (New York: Duell, Sloan and Pearce, 1957), 85, https://catalog.hathitrust.org/Record/008703789.

8. "TV's Images Can Be Photographed," 184–85.

9. "From Readers' Albums of Television Photos," *Popular Science*, December 1950, 166; "TV's Images Can Be Photographed," 187.

10. "From Readers' Albums of Television Photos," 166–67. I am grateful to Barbara Levine for her insights into this genre of photographic production, which comes from her careful study and collecting of amateur images from this period.

11. Keeley, *Taking It Easy with Your Camera*, 85.

12. Arthur Rothstein, *Creative Color in Photography* (Philadelphia: Chilton Books, 1963), 79, https://catalog.hathitrust.org/Record/006237604.

CHAPTER 31

1. Peter Gowland, "To Blur or Not to Blur," *Popular Photography*, April 1957, 87.

2. "There's More Than One Way to Interpret Motion with Your Camera," *Popular Photography*, July 1955; "Action—Frozen or Fluid, It Adds Excitement," *Popular Photography*, February 1956; "Eight Action Ideas," *Popular Photography*, April 1957.

3. "Are Photographers Going Blur Crazy?" *Popular Photography*, February 1962, 50.

4. "The Battle over Blur," *US Camera*, December 1961.

5. Bernard Alfieri, "Conveying the Illusion of Motion," *American Photography*, April 1950; Walt Seng, "How to Photograph Motion," *Petersen's Photographic*, July 1978.

6. Clément Chéroux, "Vues du train: Vision et mobilité au XIXe siècle," *Études Photographiques*, November 1, 1996, http://etudesphotographiques.revues.org/index101.html.

CHAPTER 32

1. Wilson Hicks, *Words and Pictures* (New York: Harper, 1952).

2. Kristen Lubben, *Magnum Contact Sheets* (London: Thames & Hudson, 2011), 9.

3. "JFK Picks a Picture for a Great Occasion," *Life*, January 20, 1961, 89.

4. "The Photo Essay Press Release," Museum of Modern Art, March 16, 1965, 2, https://www.moma.org/documents/moma_press-release_326378 .pdf.

5. Arthur Goldsmith, "How to Read a Contact Sheet," *Popular Photography*, August 1969; Michael Edelson, "How Pros Edit Contact Sheets," *U.S. Camera*, August 1965.

6. Edelson, "How Pros Edit Contact Sheets."

7. Sarah Greenhough, *Looking In: Robert Frank's "The Americans,"* National Gallery of Art, April 18, 2009, https://www.nga.gov/exhibitions/2009/frank. html; Neil Selkirk, "In the Darkroom," in *Diane Arbus: Revelations* (San Francisco: San Francisco Museum of Modern Art, 2003), https://www.sfmoma .org/exhibition/diane-arbus-revelations/.

CHAPTER 33

1. Jacob Deschin, "Pictures in Review: 1964 Selections Offered in Newest 'Annual,'" *New York Times*, September 8, 1963.

2. Joseph Charles Keeley, *Taking It Easy with Your Camera* (New York: Duell, Sloan, and Pearce, 1957), 183.

3. Jacob Deschin, *Making Pictures with the Miniature Camera: A Working Manual* (New York: McGraw-Hill, 1937), 110.

4. Duane Featherstonhaugh, *Press Photography with the Miniature Camera* (Boston: American Photographic Publishing, 1939), 54.

5. Jacob Deschin, "Limitations Discussed," *New York Times*, February 15, 1953, sec. 10, 12.

6. Louis Stettner, *U.S. Camera's 35mm Photography* (New York: U.S. Camera Publishing, 1956), 69, http://catalog.hathitrust.org/Record/008546381.

7. "Beachheads of Normandy," *Life*, June 19, 1944.

8. "Grain, When It Helps the Picture," *Popular Photography*, May 1964, 60.

9. "Grain, When It Helps the Picture," 60.

10. A. Francekevich, "Creative Grain," *Popular Photography*, August 1964, 14; E. Scully, "Graininess: You Can Control It," *Modern Photography*, April 1968, 60–65; James Stamp, "How to Get the Most Grain in 35-mm," *Popular Photography*, August 1965, 66.

11. Francekevich, "Creative Grain," 14.

CHAPTER 34

1. Eastman Kodak, *How to Make Good Pictures: A Text Book for the Every-Day Photographer*, 26th ed. (Rochester, NY: Eastman Kodak Company, 1941), 72.

2. Eastman Kodak, *How to Make Good Pictures* (Rochester, NY: Eastman Kodak, 1937), 79.

3. Eastman Kodak Company, *How to Make Good Pictures: A Text Book*, 26th ed., 72

4. Ibid.

5. Michael Edelson, "Wrong Exposures for the Right Reasons," *U.S. Camera*, January 1965, 58.

6. Ron Harris, "That Old Backlight Magic," *Popular Photography*, March 1962, 50.

7. Edelson, "Wrong Exposures for the Right Reasons," 59.

8. Phil Edwards, "We've Hit Peak Lens Flare. Here's How It Started," *Vox*, March 28, 2016, http://www.vox.com/2016/3/28/11306906/lens-flare-history.

9. Meredith Woerner, "J.J. Abrams Admits Star Trek Lens Flares Are 'Ridiculous,'" io9.gizmodo.com, accessed November 30, 2016, http://io9.com/5230278/jj-abrams-admits-star-trek-lens-flares-are-ridiculous; CraveOnline.com, *J.J. Abrams Apologizes for Lens Flare (Star Trek into Darkness Blu-Ray Release Party)*, accessed December 2, 2016, https://www.youtube.com/watch?v=LWNGMTtD_jY.

10. Henry Sainsbury Newcombe, *35 mm. Photo Technique*, 2nd ed. (London: Focal Press, 1946), 261; *How to Make Good Pictures* (1937), 79.

11. Herbert S. Zim, R. Will Burnett, and Wyatt Brummitt, *Photography: The Amateur's Guide to Better Pictures* (New York: Golden Press, 1964), 20.

12. Andreas Feininger, *Basic Color Photography* (New York: Amphoto, 1972), 83.

13. Feininger, *Basic Color Photography*, 83.

CHAPTER 35

1. Katherine Stanberry, "Trimming, Mounting, and Framing," *Leaves from an Amateur's Notebook*: *Photo-Miniature*, November 1909, 243.

2. R. W. B., "To Enlarge Photographs: Amateurs Select Summer Snapshots for Effect," *New York Times*, October 10, 1937.

3. Andreas Feininger, *Feininger on Photography* (Chicago: Ziff-Davis, 1949), 398.

4. Henri Cartier-Bresson and E. Tériade, *The Decisive Moment* (New York: Simon and Schuster, 1952).

5. Joseph David Cooper, *Ultraminiature Photography* (New York: Universal Photo Books, 1958), 57.

6. Louis Stettner, *U.S. Camera's 35mm Photography* (New York: U.S. Camera Publishing, 1956), 71, http://catalog.hathitrust.org/Record/008546381.

7. Stettner, *U.S. Camera's 35mm Photography*, 71.

8. Neil Selkirk, "In the Darkroom," in *Diane Arbus: Revelations*, ed. Doon Arbus and Sandra Phillips (San Francisco: San Francisco Museum of Modern Art, 2003), 271, https://www.sfmoma.org/exhibition/diane-arbus-revelations/.

9. David Vestal, "The Fine Art of Dodging and Burning-In," *Popular Photography*, February 1983, 122.

10. Hedi Levine, "Close to the Edge: Will the Real Full Frame Photo Please Stand Up," *Art Direction*, December 1986, 28–31.

11. Peter Kolonia, "In the Dark," *Popular Photography*, June 1990, 33.

12. "Imagexperts [advertisement]," *Popular Photography*, October 1999, 100.

CHAPTER 36

1. D. X. Fenten, *Better Photography for Amateurs* (New York: Verlan Books, 1960), 65.

2. Charles Maus Taylor, *Why My Photographs Are Bad* (Philadelphia: G. W. Jacobs & Co., 1902), 33, http://archive.org/details/whymyphotographsootayl.

3. *Popular Mechanics Photokinks* (Chicago: Popular Mechanics Press, 1948), 8.

4. Joseph Keeley, *How to Take Better Pictures: How to Get the Most Out of Your Camera* (New York: Dell, 1957), n.p.

5. Fenten, *Better Photography for Amateurs*, 65.

6. *How to Make Good Pictures: A Text Book for the Every-Day Photographer*, 22nd rev. ed. (Rochester, NY: Eastman Kodak Company, 1936), 70.

7. Stanley W. Bowler, *Beginner's Guide to the Miniature Camera* (New York: McBride Books, 1962), 40.

8. Arthur A. Goldsmith, *How to Take Better Pictures* (New York: Arco Publishing, 1957), 22.

9. Goldsmith, *How to Take Better Pictures*, 18.

10. "Shoot It Close! Crop It Tight!" *U.S. Camera*, December 1963; "Crop Close for Impact," *U.S. Camera*, October 1962, 46–49.

CHAPTER 37

1. "Polaroid Swinger" [advertisement], *Popular Photography*, May 1967.

2. "Polaroid Swinger."

3. Peter Buse, *The Camera Does the Rest: How Polaroid Changed Photography* (Chicago: University of Chicago Press, 2016), 47.

4. E. Scully, "Ed Scully on Color Film for the New Polaroid SX-70 Land Camera," *Modern Photography*, February 1973, 56; N. Goldberg, N. Rothschild, and D. Kirkland, "Polaroid SX-70: The Facts behind Ballyhoo," *Popular Photography*, April 1973, 80.

5. Ralph Gibson, *SX-70 Art* (New York: Lustrum, 1979), 130.

6. Peggy Sealfon, "Some Notable Trends in Instant Photography," *New York Times*, July 27, 1980.

7. Frank Van Riper, "New Purpose of Polaroid," *Washington Post*, February 12, 1993, https://www.washingtonpost.com/archive/lifestyle/1993/02/12 /new-purpose-of-polaroid/a528b60d-7620-405b-a5a7-36d696a7e46f/.

8. Peter Lester, "Romancing the Tones," *British Journal of Photography*, July 23, 1992, 1.

9. Scully, "Ed Scully on Color Film for the New Polaroid SX-70 Land Camera," *Modern Photography*, February 1973, 62.

10. Lester, "Romancing the Tones," 15.

11. Lester, "Romancing the Tones," 14.

CHAPTER 38

1. "The Case for Black and White," *Popular Photography*, January 1991, 41.

2. Michael J. Hammel, "Antiquing with Sepia Tones," in *The Artist's Guide to GIMP Effects* (San Francisco: No Starch Press, 2007).

3. Suzanne Slesin, "Two New Books Celebrate the Country Style," *New York Times*, July 3, 1980, Style sec. 8.

4. G. H. P., "The Collodion Process," *Humphrey's Journal of the Daguerreotype and Photographic Arts and the Sciences and Arts Pertaining to Heliography*, August 15, 1853, 133; Henry Peach Robinson, "Photography, Artistic and Scientific," *Humphrey's Journal of the Daguerreotype and Photographic Arts*, December 1, 1858, 232.

5. Liverpool Photographic Society, "Harmony of Shades in the Photograph, as Relating to the Background," *Humphrey's Journal of the Daguerreotype and Photographic Arts and the Sciences and Arts Pertaining to Heliography*, August 1, 1855, 116.

6. "Royal Bromide," *Kodakery*, November 1913, 19.

7. For a comprehensive history of these attitudes, see Sally Stein, "The Rhetoric of the Colorful and the Colorless: American Photography and Material Culture between the Wars" (PhD diss., Yale University, 1991).

8. Hannah Gal, "Instant Sepia in 4 × 5," *British Journal of Photography*, June 1, 1994, 16.

9. "Eastman Kodak: New Kodak Professional Portra Sepia Black & White Paper Simplifies the Production of High-Quality Sepia Tone-Type Prints; Ease of RA-4 Processing, Print Life of Color Neg Paper, Look of 'Classic' Sepia," *Presswire*, February 25, 2002.

CHAPTER 39

1. Paul Louis Hexter, *Make Your Pictures Sing!* (San Francisco: Camera Craft Publishing, 1946), 41; Frank Roy Fraprie and Walter Woodbury, *Photographic Amusements* (Norwood, MA: Plimpton Press, 1931), 64.

2. Rudolf Kingslake, *A History of the Photographic Lens* (Orlando, FL: Academic Press, 1989), 119; Milan Zahorcak, "Evolution of the Photographic Lens in the 19th Century," in *Focal Encyclopedia of Photography: Digital Imaging, Theory and Applications, History, and Science*, 4th ed., ed. Michael R. Peres (New York: Elsevier, 2007), 157–76.

3. "Speaking of Pictures: Wide-Angle Camera Explodes New York Skyscrapers," *Life*, September 1947, 15.

4. Arthur Rothstein, "Super Wide-Angle Camera," *Lens-Swinging Panon*, May 1954, 50.

5. G. D. Margolin, "How Wide a Wide Angle Lens?" *Popular Photography*, August 1960, 58.

6. David Brooks, *Lenses and Lens Accessories: A Photographer's Guide* (London: Curtin & London, 1982), 29.

7. Margolin, "How Wide a Wide Angle Lens?" 58.

8. E. Scully and Herbert Keppler, "Fisheyes: Some Are Better Than Others," *Modern Photography*, April 1969, 69.

9. Jack Manning, *The Fine 35mm Portrait* (Garden City, NY: Amphoto, 1978), n.p.

10. Norman Rothschild, "Fisheye Lenses: You Either Love 'Em or Hate 'Em," *Popular Photography*, December 1980, 128.

11. Rothschild, "Fisheye Lenses," 144.

12. Julie Oswin and Steve Walton, "Cake and Party Time," in *Contemporary Wedding Photography* (Newton Abbot, UK: David & Charles, 2006).

CHAPTER 40

1. Eastman Kodak, *How to Make Good Pictures: A Text Book for the Every-Day Photographer* (Rochester, NY: Eastman Kodak Company, 1938), 54.

2. Godfrey Frankel, *Short Cut to Photography* (New York: Sterling Publishing, 1954), 115.

3. Thomas H. Miller and Wyatt Brummitt, *This Is Photography: Its Means and Ends* (Garden City, NY: Garden City Books, 1952), 225, http://catalog.hathitrust.org/api/volumes/oclc/21208833.html.

4. Eastman Kodak, *How to Take Good Pictures: The World's Best-Selling Photography Book: A Photo Guide* (New York: Ballantine Books, 1990), 171.

5. Fred Bond, *Kodachrome and Kodacolor from All Angles* (San Fran-

cisco: Camera Craft Publishing, 1945), 63, http://hdl.handle.net/2027 /mdp.39015006379799.

6. Louis Stettner, *U.S. Camera's 35mm Photography* (New York: U.S. Camera Publishing, 1956), 95–96, https://catalog.hathitrust.org/Record/008546381.

7. Susan Sontag, "Photography: The Beauty Treatment," *New York Review of Books*, November 28, 1974, http://www.nybooks.com/articles/1974/11/28 /photography-the-beauty-treatment/.

8. Gene Thornton, "Photography View: The Masterly Style of Meyerowitz," *New York Times*, June 27, 1981, Arts sec., http://www.nytimes .com/1981/06/27/arts/photography-view-the-masterly-style-of-meyerowitz .html.

9. Lorna Roth, "Looking at Shirley, the Ultimate Norm: Colour Balance, Image Technologies, and Cognitive Equity," *Canadian Journal of Communication* 34, no. 1 (2009), https://doi.org/10.22230/cjc.2009v34n1a2196; Brian Winston, "A Whole Technology of Dyeing: A Note on Ideology and the Apparatus of the Chromatic Moving Image," *Daedalus* 114, no. 4 (1985): 105–23.

10. Lee Frost, "Sunsets: How to Get the Best from the Golden Hour," *Practical Photography*, November 1997, 69.

11. The first use of the term *golden hour* in *Popular Photography* appeared in 1983, although it wasn't used widely for another decade. Don Leavitt, "First Look: Polachrome 35-mm Color," *Popular Photography* 90 (June 1983): 81.

12. Frost, "Sunsets," 75; M. Sloan, "Wild about Wolves," *Popular Photography*, June 1995, 71.

13. "African-Americans: Representations in Advertising," *AdAge*, September 15, 2003; Serra A. Tinic, "United Colors and Untied Meanings: Benetton and the Commodification of Social Issues," *Journal of Communication* 47 (1997): 5.

14. Roth, "Looking at Shirley," 118–22.

CHAPTER 41

1. Charlotte Cotton, *Fashion Image Revolution: The Art and Technique of Brian Dowling* (Munich: Prestel Verlag, 2018).

2. "Try Cross Processing," *Popular Photography*, April 1995.

3. Tom Wyatt, "This Year's Colour," *Creative Review* 17 (February 1997): 50.

4. Steve Newman, "Cross Purpose," *British Journal of Photography* 144 (August 20, 1997): 22.

5. Newman, "Cross Purpose," 23.

6. "Lomography—History," Lomography, accessed November 8, 2018, https://www.lomography.com/about/history.

7. "VSCO Cam Alchemy Collection Filters Emulate Cross-Processed Film," *Popular Photography*, accessed November 7, 2018, https://www.pop-photo.com/how-to/2015/04/vsco-cam-alchemy-collection-filters-emulate-cross-processed-film.

8. Kara Burney, "New Instagram Research Says When in Doubt, Choose Mayfair," TrackMaven, September 22, 2016, https://trackmaven.com/blog/best-instagram-filters/.

CHAPTER 42

1. Paul Louis Hexter, *Make Your Pictures Sing!* (San Francisco: Camera Craft Publishing, 1946), 30.

2. Robert Taft, *Photography and the American Scene: A Social History, 1839–1889* (New York: Macmillan, 1942), 322.

3. Taft, *Photography and the American Scene*, 330.

4. Eastman Kodak, *How to Make Good Pictures: A Book for the Amateur Photographer* (Rochester, NY: Eastman Kodak Company, 1928), 39, https://catalog.hathitrust.org/Record/003478290.

5. Louis Stettner, *U.S. Camera's 35mm Photography* (New York: U.S. Camera Publishing, 1956), 48; Arthur Rothstein, *Creative Color in Photography* (Philadelphia: Chilton Books, 1963), 65, https://catalog.hathitrust.org/Record/006237604.

6. Stettner, *U.S. Camera's 35mm Photography*, 48.

7. "Takuma Nakahira: 'Circulation: Date, Place, Events,'" *New York Times*, July 19, 2013, https://www.nytimes.com/2013/07/19/arts/design/museum-and-gallery-listings-for-july-19-25.html.

8. The editor of *Photo Techniques* explained that although in English, this effect was often transliterated as "boke," he would prefer the spelling "bokeh," to better approximate its Japanese pronunciation. "Bokeh" and "boke" are both widely used in contemporary photographic literature in English. John Kennerdell, "What Is 'Bokeh'?" *Photo Techniques* 18, no. 3 (June 1997): 29.

9. Bob Atkins, "Bokeh Photography 101: The Basics of Creating Good Bokeh in Your Photos," *Adorama Learning Center* (blog), October 29, 2011, https://www.adorama.com/alc/0008042/article/FOCUS-ON-LENSES-Fuzzy-Logic; Nasim Mansurov, "What Is Bokeh?" *Photography Life* (blog), December 17, 2009, https://photographylife.com/what-is-bokeh.

10. Kyle Cassidy, "35mm Lens Adaptors for Video," *Videomaker* (blog), December 1, 2008, https://www.videomaker.com/article/c10/13538-35mm-lens-adaptors-for-video.

11. Diane Berkenfeld, "Give Any Photograph a Little Bokeh," *Studio Photography*, March 2009, 42.

12. Stan Horaczek, "10 Photography Techniques You Might Be Overusing," *Popular Photography*, September 1, 2016, https://www.popphoto.com/10 -photography-techniques-you-might-be-overusing.

13. "Introducing Focus," *Instagram* (blog), April 10, 2018, https://instagram -press.com/blog/2018/04/10/introducing-focus/.

CHAPTER 43

1. Eastman Kodak Company, *How to Make Good Pictures: An Entertaining Authoritative Handbook for Everyone Who Takes Pictures*, 30th ed. (New York: Random House, 1957), 140.

2. Joseph Charles Keeley, *Taking It Easy with Your Camera* (New York: Duell, Sloan and Pearce, 1957), 29, 121, https://catalog.hathitrust.org/ Record/008703789.

3. Howard Lee Luray, *Strobe: The Lively Light* (San Francisco: Camera Craft Publishing, 1954), 118.

4. Luray, *Strobe,* 118.

5. Hans Ulrich Obrist, "By Now, People Know What They're Getting Into with Me: Juergen Teller Goes Back to School," *System Magazine* (blog), accessed October 17, 2018, http://system-magazine.com/issue3/ how-does-he-do-it-juergen-teller/.

6. Luray, *Strobe,* 118.

7. Obrist, "By Now, People Know What They're Getting Into with Me."

8. Lauren Cochrane, "Why Has It Taken so Long for Magazines to Distance Themselves from Terry Richardson?" *Guardian,* October 24, 2017, https://www .theguardian.com/fashion/shortcuts/2017/oct/24/terry-richardson-sexual -harrassment-vogue-conde-nast.

9. CyanaTrend, *Terry Richardson Interview #3 on His Snapshot Technique,* 2009, https://www.youtube.com/watch?v=JKQDsGvVJ9M.

10. "Juergen Teller's Flash Technique," Photo.net Photography Forums, accessed October 17, 2018, https://www.photo.net/discuss/threads /juergen-tellers-flash-technique.164329/.

CHAPTER 44

1. L. A. Mannheim, *The Rollei Way: The Rolleiflex and Rolleicord Photographer's Companion* (London: Focal Press, 1952), 12.

2. Mannheim, *The Rollei Way,* 13.

3. Andreas Feininger, *Feininger on Photography* (Chicago: Ziff-Davis, 1949), 378.

4. Gravitas Ventures, *Her Aim Is True* (2017).

5. "Polaroid Minute Maker Kit 1963 Ad," Advertisement Gallery, accessed

October 22, 2018, http://www.magazine-advertisements.com/polaroid-minute-maker-kit.html.

6. Feininger, *Feininger on Photography*, 398.

7. Michael Freeman, "Frame Shape," in *The Photographer's Eye* (Waltham, MA: Focal Press, 2007).

8. Steve Bertoni, "Instagram's Kevin Systrom: The Stanford Billionaire Machine Strikes Again," *Forbes*, August 1, 2012, https://www.forbes.com/sites/stevenbertoni/2012/08/01/instagrams-kevin-systrom-the-stanford-million aire-machine-strikes-again/#2cb1d29f45b9.

CHAPTER 45

1. Jacob Deschin, *Making Pictures with the Miniature Camera: A Working Manual* (New York: McGraw-Hill, 1937), 52.

2. Michael Freeman, *Achieving Photographic Style* (New York: Images Press, 1992), 129.

3. Serious Eats, "Gift Guide: For the Aspiring Food Photographer," Serious Eats, accessed October 12, 2018, https://www.seriouseats.com/2012/12/gift-guide-for-the-aspiring-food-photographer-camera-accessories.html.

4. Henry Carroll, *Read This If You Want to Be Instagram Famous* (London: Laurence King, 2017), 7.

CHAPTER 46

1. "Selfie, n.," in *OED Online* (Oxford: Oxford University Press), accessed February 9, 2018, http://www.oed.com/view/Entry/390063.

2. Paul Taylor, "More Than Half of Millennials Have Shared a 'Selfie,'" *Pew Research Center* (blog), March 4, 2014, http://www.pewresearch.org/fact-tank/2014/03/04/more-than-half-of-millennials-have-shared-a-selfie/.

3. Joel Stein and Josh Sanburn, "The New Greatest Generation," *Time*, May 20, 2013, 26.

4. "Myspace Angle," *Urban Dictionary*, accessed February 8, 2018, https://www.urbandictionary.com/define.php?term=myspace%20angle.

5. OkCupid, "The 4 Big Myths of Profile Pictures," OkCupid (blog), January 20, 2010, https://theblog.okcupid.com/the-4-big-myths-of-profile-pictures-41bedf26e4d.

6. Lindsay Adler, *Creative 52: Weekly Projects to Invigorate Your Photography Portfolio* (San Francisco: Peachpit Press, 2013), 102.

7. Stephanie Saltzman and Jenna Rosenstein, "How to Take a Good Selfie: 12 Selfie Tips to Consider," *Allure*, accessed February 7, 2018, https://www.allure.com/story/how-to-take-good-selfies.

8. Victoria Jowett, "Is This Instagram Hack the Secret to the Perfect Selfie?" *Cosmopolitan*, August 18, 2016, http://www.cosmopolitan.co.uk /beauty-hair/a45410/best-instagram-filter-for-selfies/.

9. Samantha Sutton, "The Easy Way to Achieve a Blogger-Approved Feed—without a Professional Camera," *Popsugar Fashion*, August 10, 2017, http://www.popsugar.com/fashion/How-Take-Mirror-Selfie-37520749.

10. Katherine Rosman, "Style—Tricks of the Trade: Super 'Selfies': The Art of the Phone Portrait," *Wall Street Journal*, June 28, 2012.

11. Kristin Chirico, Lindsay Farber, Sheridan Watson, Jazmin Ontiveros, Ochi, Caitlin Cowie, and Jazzmyne Robbins, "A Model Taught Us How to Take Selfies and It Made a Huge Difference," *BuzzFeed*, accessed February 7, 2018, https://www.buzzfeed.com/kristinchirico/a-model-taught -us-how-to-not-suck-at-selfies-and-it-actually.

12. Sutton, "The Easy Way to Achieve a Blogger-Approved Feed."

CHAPTER 47

1. Serge Ramelli Photography, *Using Lightroom Presets to Make a Cool Urban Desaturated Look* (2015), https://www.youtube.com/watch?v=TbJugWvYVr4.

2. Shutter Up & Shoot, *How to Edit Your Photos and Give Them A Desaturated High Contrast Grunge Look* (2016), https://www.youtube.com/watch ?v=2bApYWSKEOM.

3. D. L. Cade, "A Simple Guide to the 'Desaturated Urban Look' in Light room," PetaPixel, March 6, 2017, https://petapixel.com/2017/03/06/simple -guide-desaturated-urban-look-lightroom/.

4. Cade, "A Simple Guide."

5. Doug Pardee, "The Most Popular VSCO Cam Presets in VSCO Selects: Mobile Photography Talk Forum: Digital Photography Review," accessed November 2, 2018, https://www.dpreview.com/forums/post/53922879.

CHAPTER 48

1. "Porn, n.2," *OED Online* (Oxford: Oxford University Press), accessed October 24, 2018, http://www.oed.com/view/Entry/148003.

2. "Gastro-Porn," Google Ngram Viewer, accessed October 24, 2018, https://books.google.com/ngrams/graph?content=gastro-porn&year_start =1800&year_end=2008&corpus=15&smoothing=3&share=&direct_url =t1%3B%2Cgastro%20-%20porn%3B%2Cc0.

3. Thomas Morton, "Something, Something, Something, Detroit," *Vice* (blog), August 1, 2009, https://www.vice.com/en_us/article/ppzb9z/some thing-something-something-detroit-994-v16n8.

4. Andrew Moore, *Detroit Disassembled* (Akron, OH: Akron Art Museum, 2010).

5. Laura Pullman, "City of Ghosts: Haunting Abandoned Buildings of St. Louis after the City's Population Fell by 70% in a Century," *Daily Mail*, July 6, 2012, http://www.dailymail.co.uk/news/article-2169773/Stunning -photographs-transform-St-Louis-landscape-crumbling-buildings-aban- doned-homes-slum-beautiful-art.html.

6. "Interview with Demond Meek of Slumbeautiful," Global Yodel, ac- cessed October 25, 2018, https://www.globalyodel.com/yodels/slumbeautiful/. My thanks to photographer Erica Deeman for her technical analysis of these photographs.

7. Richard B. Woodward, "Disaster Photography: When Is Documen- tary Exploitation?" *Artnews* (blog), February 6, 2013, http://www.artnews .com/2013/02/06/the-debate-over-ruin-porn/.

8. Dora Apel, *Beautiful Terrible Ruins: Detroit and the Anxiety of Decline* (New Brunswick NJ: Rutgers University Press, 2015); Siobhan Lyons, *Ruin Porn and the Obsession with Decay* (New York: Springer, 2018).

CHAPTER 49

1. Nick Wingfield, "A Field Guide to Civilian Drones," *New York Times*, November 23, 2015, https://www.nytimes.com/interactive/2015/technology /guide-to-civilian-drones.html.

2. Sujata Gupta, "The Drones Invade Yosemite," *New Yorker*, May 9, 2014, https://www.newyorker.com/tech/annals-of-technology/the-drones -invade-yosemite.

3. Oliver Wendell Holmes, *Soundings from the Atlantic* (Boston: Ticknor and Fields, 1864), 228–81.

4. Denis Cosgrove and William L. Fox, *Photography and Flight* (London: Reaktion Books, 2010), 46.

5. "Here, There and Everywhere," *Photo-Era Magazine*, June 6, 1929, 337.

6. For a comprehensive survey of aerial photography, as well as discus- sion of the Byrd and Lindbergh missions, see Cosgrove and Fox, *Photography and Flight*, 44, 87.

7. Leonard A. Williams, *Illustrative Photography in Advertising* (San Fran- cisco: Camera Craft Publishing, 1929), 78.

8. Williams, *Illustrative Photography in Advertising*," 78.

9. "12 Drone Photography Tips," *Adorama Learning Center* (blog), October 27, 2017, https://www.adorama.com/alc/12-drone-photography-tips.

CHAPTER 50

1. "Hipstamatic—behind the Lens," Pocket-lint, accessed February 2, 2015, http://www.pocket-lint.com/news/106994-hipstamatic-iphone-app-android -interview.

2. Matt Buchanan, "Hipstamatic and the Death of Photojournalism," Gizmodo, accessed February 17, 2018, https://gizmodo.com/5756703/is -hipstamatic-killing-photojournalism.

3. James Estrin, "Finding the Right Tool to Tell a War Story," Lens Blog, 1290397910, https://lens.blogs.nytimes.com/2010/11/21/finding-the-right-tool -to-tell-a-war-story/.

4. Carl Purcell, "When Used with Discretion, Filters Can Add Creative Touches to Your Travel Pictures," *Popular Photography*, November 1982, 38.

5. Ian Crouch, "Instagram's Instant Nostalgia," *New Yorker*, April 10, 2012, http://www.newyorker.com/culture/culture-desk/instagrams-instant -nostalgia.

6. Brian Honigman, "The 100 Most Popular Hashtags on Instagram," *Huffington Post* (blog), January 15, 2013, https://www.huffingtonpost.com/ brian-honigman/the-100-most-popular-hash_b_2463195.html.

7. Salman Aslam, "Instagram by the Numbers (2018): Stats, Demographics & Fun Facts," January 1, 2018, https://www.omnicoreagency.com/instagram- statistics/; "Our Story," *Instagram* (blog), November 29, 2016, https://instagram -press.com/our-story/.

8. "Filter Fakers," accessed February 16, 2018, http://filterfakers.com.

9. "Study: The Most Popular Instagram Filters from around the World," Canva, February 10, 2016, https://www.canva.com/learn/popular-instagram -filters/.

FURTHER READING

PART I: 1839–1860

Baldwin, Gordon, ed. *Gustave Le Gray, 1820–1884.* Los Angeles: Getty, 2002.

Bear, Jordan. "Dangerous Combinations: Photography, Illusion, and the Conspiracy of Labor in the 1850s." *Nineteenth-Century Contexts,* June 1, 2010, 139–52.

———. *Disillusioned: Victorian Photography and the Discerning Subject.* University Park: Pennsylvania State University Press, 2015.

Braun, Marta. *Eadweard Muybridge.* London: Reaktion Books, 2010.

Brunet, François. "Nationalities and Universalism in the Early Historiography of Photography (1843–1857)." *History of Photography,* April 26, 2011, 98–110.

Davis, Keith F. *The Origins of American Photography, 1839–1885: From Daguerreotype to Dry-Plate.* Kansas City, MO: Hall Family Foundation in association with the Nelson-Atkins Museum of Art, 2007.

Gillespie, Sarah Kate. *The Early American Daguerreotype: Cross-Currents in Art and Technology.* Cambridge, MA: MIT Press, 2016.

Grigsby, Darcy Grimaldo. "Negative-Positive Truths." *Representations* 113, no. 1 (2011): 16–38.

Hamber, Anthony. *Photography and the 1851 Great Exhibition.* New Castle, DE: Oak Knoll Press, 2018.

Howe, Daniel Walker. "American Victorianism as a Culture." *American Quarterly* 27, no. 5 (1975): 507–32.

Jenkins, Reese V. *Images and Enterprise: Technology and the American Photographic Industry, 1839 to 1925.* Baltimore, MD: Johns Hopkins University Press, 1987.

McCauley, Elizabeth Anne. *A.A.E. Disdéri and the Carte de Visite Portrait Photograph.* New Haven, CT: Yale University Press, 1985.

Pierce, Sally. *Whipple and Black: Commercial Photographers in Boston.* Boston: Boston Athenaeum, 1987.

Reynolds, Leonie L., and Arthur T. Gill. "The Mayall Story." *History of Photography,* April 1, 1985, 89–107.

Romer, Grant B. *Young America: The Daguerreotypes of Southworth & Hawes.* Rochester, NY: International Center of Photography, George Eastman House, 2005.

Sandweiss, Martha A., ed. *Photography in Nineteenth-Century America.* Fort Worth, TX: Amon Carter Museum, 1991.

Schaaf, Larry J. "Mayall's Life-Size Portrait of George Peabody." *History of Photography,* October 1, 1985, 279–88.

Sekula, Allan. "The Body and the Archive." *October* 39 (Winter 1986): 3–64.

Smith, Shawn Michelle. "Augustus Washington: Looks to Liberia." *Nka: Journal of Contemporary African Art* 41, no. 1 (2017): 6–13.

Tagg, John. *Burden of Representation: Essays on Photographies and Histories.* Minneapolis: University of Minnesota Press, 1993.

Trachtenberg, Alan. "Photography: The Emergence of a Keyword." In *Photography in Nineteenth-Century America,* edited by Martha A. Sandweiss, 17–45. Fort Worth, TX: Amon Carter Museum, 1991.

Wallace, Maurice O., and Shawn Michelle Smith, eds. *Pictures and Progress: Early Photography and the Making of African American Identity.* Durham, NC: Duke University Press, 2012.

PART II: 1861–1900

Allen, William. "Legal Tests of Photography-as-Art: Sarony and Others." *History of Photography* 10, no. 3 (1986): 221–27.

Bergstein, Mary, and Maureen C. O'Brien, eds. *Image and Enterprise: The Photographs of Adolphe Braun.* London: Thames and Hudson, 2000.

Crary, Jonathan. *Techniques of the Observer: On Vision and Modernity in the Nineteenth Century.* Cambridge, MA: MIT Press, 1990.

Doane, Mary Ann. *The Emergence of Cinematic Time: Modernity, Contingency, the Archive.* Cambridge, MA: Harvard University Press, 2002.

Elkins, James. *Six Stories from the End of Representation: Images in Painting, Photography, Astronomy, Microscopy, Particle Physics, and Quantum Mechanics, 1980–2000.* Stanford, CA: Stanford University Press, 2008.

Flint, Kate. *Flash! Photography, Writing, and Surprising Illumination.* London: Oxford University Press, 2017.

Greenough, Sarah, and Diane Waggoner. *The Art of the American Snapshot, 1888–1978: From the Collection of Robert E. Jackson.* Washington, DC: National Gallery of Art 2007.

Hales, Peter B. *Silver Cities: Photographing American Urbanization, 1839–1939*. Albuquerque: University of New Mexico Press, 2005.

Kasher, Steven. *America and the Tintype*. New York: International Center of Photography, 2008.

Krauss, Rosalind. "Photography's Discursive Spaces: Landscape/View." *Art Journal* 42, no. 4 (1982): 311.

Lindquist-Cock, Elizabeth. "Stereoscopic Photography and the Western Paintings of Albert Bierstadt." *Art Quarterly* 33 (1970): 360–78.

Moore, Kevin. *Jacques Henri Lartigue: The Invention of an Artist*. Princeton, NJ: Princeton University Press, 2004.

Natale, Simone. "Photography and Communication Media in the Nineteenth Century." *History of Photography* 36, no. 4 (2012): 451–56.

Rudd, Annie. "Victorians Living in Public: Cartes de Visite as 19th-Century Social Media." *Photography and Culture* 9, no. 3 (2016): 195–217.

Sandweiss, Martha A. *Print the Legend: Photography and the American West*. New Haven, CT: Yale University Press, 2002.

Sheehan, Tanya. "Looking Pleasant, Feeling White: The Social Politics of the Photographic Smile." In *Feeling Photography*, edited by Elspeth H. Brown and Thy Phu. Durham, NC: Duke University Press, 2014.

Siegel, Elizabeth. *Galleries of Friendship and Fame: A History of Nineteenth-Century American Photograph Albums*. New Haven, CT: Yale University Press, c. 2010.

Smith, Shawn Michelle. *At the Edge of Sight: Photography and the Unseen*. Durham, NC: Duke University Press, 2013.

Solnit, Rebecca. *River of Shadows: Eadweard Muybridge and the Technological Wild West*. New York: Viking Press, 2003.

Sternberger, Paul Spencer. *Between Amateur and Aesthete: The Legitimization of Photography as Art in America, 1880–1900*. Albuquerque: University of New Mexico Press, 2001.

Trachtenberg, Alan. "Albums of War: On Reading Civil War Photographs." *Representations* 9 (1985): 1.

——. *Reading American Photographs: Images as History, Mathew Brady to Walker Evans*. New York: Hill and Wang, 1990.

Vettel-Becker, Patricia. *Shooting from the Hip: Photography, Masculinity, and Postwar America*. Minneapolis: University of Minnesota Press, 2005.

West, Nancy Martha. *Kodak and the Lens of Nostalgia*. Charlottesville: University Press of Virginia, 2000.

Zuromskis, Catherine. "Ordinary Pictures and Accidental Masterpieces: Snapshot Photography in the Modern Art Museum." *Art Journal* 67, no. 2 (June 2008): 104–125.

PART III: 1901–1929

Alinder, Mary Street. *Group f.64: Edward Weston, Ansel Adams, Imogen Cunningham, and the Community of Artists Who Revolutionized American Photography.* New York: Bloomsbury, 2014.

Armstrong, Nancy. "Modernism's Iconophobia and What It Did to Gender." *Modernism/Modernity* 5, no. 2 (1998): 47–75.

Bochner, Jay. *An American Lens: Scenes from Alfred Stieglitz's New York Secession.* Cambridge, MA: MIT Press, 2005.

Brower, Matthew. "George Shiras and the Circulation of Wildlife Photography." *History of Photography* 32, no. 2 (2008): 169–75.

Bunnell, Peter C. "Alfred Stieglitz and Camera Work." In *Inside the Photograph: Writings on Twentieth-Century Photography.* New York: Aperture Foundation, 2006.

Dunaway, Finis. "Hunting with the Camera: Nature Photography, Manliness, and Modern Memory, 1890–1930." *Journal of American Studies* 34, no. 2 (2000): 207–30.

Francisco, Jason. *The Steerage and Alfred Stieglitz.* Berkeley: University of California Press, 2012.

Kroiz, Lauren. *Creative Composites: Modernism, Race, and the Stieglitz Circle.* Berkeley: University of California Press, 2012.

McCauley, Elizabeth Anne. *Clarence H. White and His World: The Art and Craft of Photography, 1895–1925.* Princeton, NJ: Princeton University Art Museum, 2017.

Mensel, Robert E. "'Kodakers Lying in Wait': Amateur Photography and the Right of Privacy in New York, 1885–1915." *American Quarterly* 43, no. 1 (1991): 24–45.

Nordström, Alison Devine, and J. Luca Ackerman, eds. *Truth Beauty: Pictorialism and the Photograph as Art, 1845–1945.* Vancouver: Vancouver Art Gallery, 2008.

Phillips, Christopher. "The Judgment Seat of Photography." *October* 22 (Autumn 1982): 27–63.

Pyne, Kathleen A. *Modernism and the Feminine Voice: O'Keeffe and the Women of the Stieglitz Circle.* Berkeley: University of California Press, c2007.

Riley, Caroline M. "Selling Pictorialist Photography as Craft: Alice Austin's Artistic Production and Role in the Boston Society of Arts and Crafts between 1900 and 1933." *Journal of Modern Craft* 8, no. 3 (2015): 333–58.

Rudd, Annie. "Erich Salomon's Candid Camera and the Framing of Political Authority." *Information and Culture: A Journal of History* 52, no. 4 (2017): 412–35.

Seiberling, Grace. *Amateurs, Photography, and the Mid-Victorian Imagination.* Chicago: University of Chicago Press, 1986.

Sekula, Allan. "On the Invention of Photographic Meaning." In *Photography against the Grain: Essays and Photo Works, 1973–1983.* Halifax: Press of the Nova Scotia College of Art and Design, 1984.

Stebbins, Theodore E. *Edward Weston: Photography and Modernism.* Boston: Museum of Fine Arts, Boston, in association with Bulfinch Press, 1999.

Sternberger, Paul Spencer. *Between Amateur and Aesthete: The Legitimization of Photography as Art in America, 1880–1900.* Albuquerque: University of New Mexico Press, 2001.

Stieglitz, Alfred. "Pictorial Photography." In *Classic Essays on Photography*, edited by Alan Trachtenberg. New Haven, CT: Leete's Island Books, 1980.

Warren, Beth Gates. *Margrethe Mather and Edward Weston: A Passionate Collaboration.* Santa Barbara, CA: Santa Barbara Museum of Art and New York: Norton, 2001.

Wigoder, Meir. "Paul Strand's New York Portraits." *History of Photography* 27, no. 4 (2003): 349–62.

PART IV: 1930–1965

Belden-Adams, Kris, ed. *Photography and Failure: One Medium's Entanglement with Flops, Underdogs and Disappointments.* London: Bloomsbury Academic, 2017.

Benjamin, Walter. "Little History of Photography." In *Selected Writings*, vol. 2, pt. 2: *1931–1934.* Cambridge. MA: Harvard University Press, 1999.

Bull, Clarence. *The Man Who Shot Garbo: The Hollywood Photographs of Clarence Sinclair Bull.* New York: Simon and Schuster, 1989.

Chéroux, Clément. "Vues du train: Vision et mobilité au XIXe siècle." *Études Photographiques*, November 1, 1996.

Dance, Robert, and Bruce Robertson. *Ruth Harriet Louise and Hollywood Glamour Photography.* Berkeley: University of California Press, 2002.

Duffy, Enda. *The Speed Handbook: Velocity, Pleasure, Modernism.* Durham, NC: Duke University Press, 2009.

Eisinger, Joel. *Trace and Transformation: American Criticism of Photography in the Modernist Period.* Albuquerque: University of New Mexico Press, 1995.

Fahey, David, and Linda Rich. *Masters of Starlight: Photographers in Hollywood.* New York: Ballantine Books, 1988.

Fay, Brendan. "How to Hold a Camera: Harry Callahan's Early Abstractions." *History of Photography* 39, no. 2 (2015): 160–76.

Finler, Joel W. *Hollywood Movie Stills: Art and Technique in the Golden Age of the Studios,* 2nd ed. Richmond, VA: Reynolds & Hearn, 2008.

Gervais, Thierry. *The Making of Visual News: A History of Photography in the Press.* London: Bloomsbury Academic, 2017.

Hill, Jason, and Vanessa R. Schwartz, eds. *Getting the Picture: The Visual Culture of the News.* London: Bloomsbury Academic, 2015.

Johnston, Patricia A. *Real Fantasies: Edward Steichen's Advertising Photography.* Berkeley: University of California Press, 2000.

Keller, Ulrich. "The Myth of Art Photography." *History of Photography* 9, no. 1 (1985): 249–273.

Lubben, Kristen. *Magnum Contact Sheets.* London: Thames & Hudson, 2011.

Moholy-Nagy, László. *The New Vision*, 4th rev. ed. New York: Wittenborn and Co., 1928.

———. *Vision in Motion.* Chicago: P. Theobald, 1947.

Panzer, Mary. "Shot Out of the Canon: Advertising Photography in 'Vogue' Magazine, 1930s–1950s." *Aperture*, no. 208 (2012): 62–65.

Phillips, Christopher, ed. *Photography in the Modern Era: European Documents and Critical Writings, 1913–1940.* New York: Metropolitan Museum of Art, 1989.

Powers, Alan. *Bauhaus Goes West: Modern Art and Design in Britain and America.* London: Thames & Hudson, 2019.

Raeburn, John. *A Staggering Revolution: A Cultural History of Thirties Photography.* Urbana: University of Illinois Press, 2006.

Reed, Dennis. *Making Waves: Japanese American Photography, 1920–1940.* Japanese American National Museum exhibit, February 28, 2016–June 26, 2016.

Rohrbach, John, Sylvie Pénichon, and Amon Carter Museum of American Art, eds. *Color: American Photography Transformed.* Austin: University of Texas Press, 2013.

Solomon-Godeau, Abigail. "The Armed Vision Disarmed: Radical Formalism from Weapon to Style." In *Photography at the Dock: Essays on Photographic History, Institutions, and Practices.* Minneapolis: University of Minnesota Press, c1991.

Tagg, John. "The Currency of the Photograph: New Deal Reformism and Documentary Rhetoric." In *The Burden of Representation: Essays on Photographies and Histories.* Amherst: University of Massachusetts Press, 1988.

Willis-Tropea, Liz. "Glamour Photography and the Institutionalization of Celebrity." *Photography and Culture* 4, no. 3 (2011): 261–75.

PART V: 1966–1995

Adler, Renata, Frank Henry Goodyear, and Paul Roth. *Richard Avedon: Portraits of Power.* Göttingen: Steidl, 2008.

Arbus, Doon, Sandra S. Phillips, and Elisabeth Sussman. *Diane Arbus: Revelations.* New York: Random House, 2003.

Avedon, Richard. *Evidence, 1944–1994.* New York: Random House, 1994.

Baker, Simon, ed. *Daido Moriyama.* London: Tate, 2012.

Buse, Peter. *The Camera Does the Rest: How Polaroid Changed Photography.* Chicago: University of Chicago Press, 2016.

——. "The Polaroid Image as Photo-Object." *Journal of Visual Culture* 9, no. 2 (2010): 189–207.

Cartier-Bresson, Henri. *The Mind's Eye: Writings on Photography and Photographers.* New York: Aperture, 1999.

Cartier-Bresson, Henri, and E. Tériade. *The Decisive Moment.* New York: Simon and Schuster, 1952.

Cotton, Charlotte. *Fashion Image Revolution: The Art and Technique of Brian Dowling.* Munich: Prestel Verlag, 2018.

Dahlgren, Anna. "Magazined Art." In *Travelling Images: Looking across the Borderlands of Art, Media and Visual Culture.* Manchester: Manchester University Press, 2019.

Ewing, William A. *The Polaroid Project.* New York: Thames & Hudson, 2017.

Panzer, Mary. *Things as They Are: Photojournalism in Context since 1955.* New York: Aperture Foundation, 2005.

Dufour, Diane, Matthew S. Witkovsky, Duncan Forbes, and Walter Moser. *Provoke: Between Protest and Performance.: Photography in Japan 1960–1975.* Göttingen: Steidl, 2016.

Purcell, Kerry William. *Alexey Brodovitch.* London: Phaidon Press, 2002.

Roth, Lorna. "Looking at Shirley, the Ultimate Norm: Colour Balance, Image Technologies, and Cognitive Equity." *Canadian Journal of Communication* 34, no. 1 (2009).

Ryan, Kathy. *New York Times Magazine Photographs.* New York: Aperture Foundation, 2011.

Szarkowski, John. *The Photographer's Eye.* New York: Museum of Modern Art, 1966.

Zuromskis, Catherine. *Snapshot Photography: The Lives of Images.* Cambridge MA: MIT Press, 2013.

PART VI: 1996–2019

Apel, Dora. *Beautiful Terrible Ruins: Detroit and the Anxiety of Decline.* New Brunswick NJ: Rutgers University Press, 2015.

Batchen, Geoffrey. "Snapshots." *Photographies* 1, no. 2 (2008): 121–42.

Bright, Susan. *Feast for the Eyes: The Story of Food in Photography.* New York: Aperture, 2017.

Chopra-Gant, Mike. "Pictures or It Didn't Happen: Photo-Nostalgia, IPhoneography and the Representation of Everyday Life." *Photography and Culture* 9, no. 2 (2016): 121–33.

Cosgrove, Denis, and William L. Fox. *Photography and Flight. Photography and Flight.* London: Reaktion Books, 2010.

Cotton, Charlotte. *Fashion Image Revolution: The Art and Technique of Brian Dowling.* Munich: Prestel Verlag, 2018.

Douglas, Nick. "It's Supposed to Look Like Shit: The Internet Ugly Aesthetic." *Journal of Visual Culture* 13, no. 3 (2014): 314–39.

Eckel, Julia. *Exploring the Selfie: Historical, Theoretical and Analytical Approaches to Digital Self-Photography.* New York: Springer, 2018.

Gansky, Andrew Emil. " 'Ruin Porn' and the Ambivalence of Decline: Andrew Moore's Photographs of Detroit." *Photography and Culture* 7, no. 2 (2014): 119–39.

Hand, Martin. *Ubiquitous Photography.* Oxford: Wiley, 2013.

Kane, Carolyn L. "Photo Noise." *History of Photography* 40, no. 2 (2016): 129–45.

Kismaric, Susan, Eva Respini, and Museum of Modern Art. *Fashioning Fiction in Photography since 1990.* New York: Museum of Modern Art, 2004.

Lavoie, Vincent. *Maintenant: images du temps présent.* Montréal: Vox, centre diffusion de la photographie, 2003.

Mirzoeff, Nicholas. *How to See the World: An Introduction to Images, from Self-Portraits to Selfies, Maps to Movies, and More.* New York: Basic Books, 2016.

Murray, Derek Conrad. "Notes to Self: The Visual Culture of Selfies in the Age of Social Media." *Consumption Markets and Culture* 18, no. 6 (2015): 490.

Murray, Susan. "Digital Images, Photo-Sharing, and Our Shifting Notions of Everyday Aesthetics." *Journal of Visual Culture* 7, no. 2 (2008): 147–63.

Orvell, Miles. "Photographing Disaster: Urban Ruins and the Destructive Sublime." *Amerikastudien/American Studies* 58, no. 4 (2013): 647–71.

Pasek, Anne. "The Pencil of Error: Glitch Aesthetics and Post-Liquid Intelligence." *Photography and Culture* 10, no. 1 (2017): 37–52.

Slater, Don. "Domestic Photography and Digital Culture." In *The Photographic Image in Digital Culture*, edited by Martin Lister. New York: Routledge, 1995.

Willim, Robert. "Enhancement or Distortion? From The Claude Glass to Instagram," 2013.

INDEX